SIR HUGH CHOLMLEY OF WHITBY 1600 – 1657

Ancestry, Life & Legacy

by

Jack Binns

Jack Binns

BLACKTHORN PRESS

Blackthorn Press, Blackthorn House
Middleton Rd, Pickering YO18 8AL
United Kingdom

www.blackthornpress.com

ISBN 978 1 906259 09 9

© Jack Binns 2008

Printed and bound by CPI Antony Rowe, Eastbourne

SIR HUGH CHOLMLEY OF WHITBY 1600-1657: ANCESTRY, LIFE AND LEGACY

Acknowledgements

My earliest thought was to write a family history of the Cholmleys of Whitby, spanning two centuries from 1540 to 1740. However, it soon became clear that the content and scope of such an undertaking would run to several volumes and was much beyond my capability and time. Reluctantly, therefore, I have had to settle for just one of the Cholmleys, who was neither born nor died in Whitby , yet has been often claimed as the town's greatest and most illustrious benefactor.

Sir Hugh Cholmley, the first baronet, Royalist and autobiographer, was the central subject of my unpublished PhD thesis, so that my first debt is to Mr G C F Forster of the School of History at Leeds University, my mentor and supervisor. Though the thesis was approved as long ago as 1994, the present work rests substantially on research done between 1986 and 1992.

For this research I travelled the length of the kingdom from Edinburgh to Kent and had to call upon the assistance of the staffs of many university libraries and county record offices. However, in particular, I am especially grateful to Mr M Y Ashcroft, then North Yorkshire County chief archivist, to Mr C B L Barr, formerly chief librarian at York Minster Library, and to Mr C Webb, now chief archivist at the Borthwick Institute at York University.

Percy Burnett, for many years secretary and librarian of Whitby's Literary and Philosophical Society, died in 1972, but without his remarkable skill, stamina and industry much of what follows would not have been possible. He alone rescued the holograph of Sir Hugh's memoirs from oblivion and probable destruction and his immaculate copy of it, in advance of further decay, proved indispensable. He alone preserved and transcribed meticulously a huge archive of Cholmley family and estate papers. Any subsequent study of the Whitby Cholmleys must necessarily rely heavily on Burnett's manuscripts held in the library of the Literary and Philosophical Society. And it is to the present volunteer staff of WLPS, ably led by Christiane Kroebel, that I owe another vote of thanks for their invaluable help.

Finally, for the fifth time, I am indebted to Alan Avery and Blackthorn Press for publishing my work with so much care and patience.

Maps and Illustrations

Abbreviations

Unless stated otherwise, all works cited were published in London.

APC	*Acts of the Privy Council of England,* ed. J R Dasent *et al.* NS, 46 vols (1890-1964)
Ashcroft	M Y Ashcroft (ed.), *Scarborough Records 1600-1660,* 2 vols, NYCRO, 47, 49 (Northallerton, 1991)
Atkinson, *Memorials*	J C Atkinson, *Memorials of Old Whitby* (1894)
Aveling,	N R H Aveling, *Northern Catholics* (1966)
Baker	J B Baker, *History of Scarbrough* (1882)
Bell, *Memorials*	R Bell (ed.), *Memorials of the Civil War,* 2 vols (1849)
BIHR	Borthwick Institute of Historical Research, York University
BL	British Library
Bod. Lib.	Bodleian Library, Oxford
Brooke, thesis	T H Brooke, The Memoirs of Sir Hugh Cholmeley, B. Litt., Oxford Univ. 1937
CFR	*Calendar of Fine Rolls*
CPCC	*Calendar of the Proceedings of the Committee for Compounding,* 3 vols (1888-91)
CPR	*Calendar of Patent Rolls*
CSPD	*Calendar of State Papers, Domestic*
CSPF	*Calendar of State Papers, Foreign*
CSPV	*Calendar of State Papers, Venetian*
Cartwright	J J Cartwright, *Chapters in the History of Yorkshire* (Wakefield, 1872)
Chapman	J Chapman (ed.), *Scarborough Records,* 3 vols (Scarborough, 1909)
Charlton, *History*	L Charlton, *The History of Whitby* (York, 1779)
Cholmley, *Memoirs*	*The Memoirs of Sir Hugh Cholmley* (printed privately, 1787) *The Memoirs of Sir Hugh Cholmley* (Malton, 1870)
Cholmley, Memorials (Marston Moor)	Memorials Touching the Battle of York, Bod. Lib., Clarendon Papers, MS 1764
Scarborough Memorials,	Memorials Touching Scarborough, Bod. Lib., Clarendon Papers, MS 1669
Observations,	Observations and Memorials Touching the Hothams, Bod. Lib., Clarendon Papers, MS 1809
Clarendon State Papers	R Scrope & T Monkhouse (eds), *State Papers Collected by Edward, Earl of Clarendon,* 3 vols (1767-86)
Clarendon, *Rebellion*	Edward, Earl of Clarendon, *The History of the Rebellion and Civil Wars in England,* ed. W D Macray, 6 vols (Oxford, 1888)
Cliffe, *Yorks Gentry*	J T Cliffe, *The Yorkshire Gentry from the Reformation to the Civil War* (1969)

Coates, *Journal*	W H Coates (ed.), *The Journal of Sir Simonds D'Ewes* (New Haven, 1942)
Coates, Young & Snow	W H Coates, A S Young & V F Snow (eds), *The Private Journals of the Long Parliament* (New Haven, 1982)
CJ	*Journals of the House of Commons*
CRO	County Record Office
CWT	Civil War Tracts
DC/SCB	Scarborough Borough Corporation Records
DCY	Cholmley of Howsham MSS
DNB	*Dictionary of National Biography*
EcHR	*Economic History Review*
EHR	*English Historical Review*
Fairfax, *Correspondence*	G W Johnson, *The Fairfax Correspondence,* 2 vols (1848)
Fletcher, *Outbreak*	A Fletcher, *The Outbreak of the English Civil War,*(1985)
Gardiner, *Civil War*	*S R Gardiner, History of the Great Civil War 1642-1649*, 3 vols (1886-91)
Gardiner, Docs	S R Gardiner (ed.) *Constitutional Documents of the Puritan Revolution, 1625-1660*, 3rd edn. (Oxford, 1906)
Hasler	P W Hasler (ed.), *The House of Commons 1558-1603*, 3 vols (1981)
HCA	Hull City Archives
Henning	B D Henning (ed.), *The House of Commons 1660-1690,* 3 vols (1983)
Hinderwell	T Hinderwell, *The History and Antiquities of Scarborough*, 3 editions, i (1798), ii (1811), iii (1832)
HJ	*Historical Journal*
HMC	Historical Manuscripts Commission
HUL	Hull University Library
Jones, thesis	J Jones, The War in the North: The Northern Parliamentary Army in the English Civil War 1642-45, PhD, York Univ., Ontario, Canada (1991)
Knowler	W Knowler (ed.), *The Earl of Strafford's Letters and Despatches*, 2 vols (Dublin, 1739, 1740)
L&P	*Letters and Papers of the Reign of Henry VIII*, 21 vols (1862-1932)
LJ	*Journals of the House of Lords*
Meads	D M Meads (ed.), *The Diary of Lady Margaret Hoby of Hackness* (1930)
MA	*Mercurius Aulicus (Oxford Royalist Newsbooks)* i -iv (1971)
MIC	Microfilm edition
NA	National Archives, Kew
NH	*Northern History*
Notestein, *Journal*	W Notestein (ed.), *The Journal of Sir Simonds D'Ewes,* (New Haven, 1923)
NRQSR	J C Atkinson (ed.) *North Riding Quarter Sessions Records*, NRRS, i-vii (1884-8)
NRRS	North Riding Records Series

NRS	Navy Records Society
NYCRO	North Yorkshire County Record Office, Northallerton
ODNB	*Oxford Dictionary of National Biography* (2004)
PW	Probate Wills
Reckitt	B N Reckitt, *Charles the First and Hull 1639-1645* (Howden, 1988)
Roebuck	P Roebuck, *Yorkshire Baronets 1640-1760* (Hull, 1980)
Rowntree	A Rowntree (ed.), *The History of Scarborough* (1931)
Rushworth, *Collections*	J Rushworth, *Historical Collections,* 7 vols (1659-1701)
SCL	Scarborough Central Library
Shaw Jeffrey	P Shaw Jeffrey, *Whitby Lore & Legend*, 3rd edn., (Whitby, 1952)
Slingsby, *Diary*	D Parsons (ed.), *The Diary of Sir Henry Slingsby* (1836)
Snow & Young	VF Snow & A S Young (eds), *The Private Journals of the Long Parliament* (New Haven, 1987)
SP	State Papers
StaC	Star Chamber Records
Stirling	A M W Stirling, *The Hothams*, 2 vols (1918)
TRHS	*Transactions of the Royal Historical Society*
TSAHS	*Transactions of Scarborough Archaeological and Historical Society*
TT	Thomason Tracts
Turton, *Alum Farm*	R B Turton, *The Alum Farm* (Whitby, 1938)
VCH, Yorks	*Victoria County History of Yorkshire*
Wedgwood, *King's War*	C V Wedgwood, *The King's War 1641-1647(1958)*
Wedgwood, *Wentworth*	C V Wedgwood, *Thomas Wentworth, First Earl of Strafford* (1964)
WLPS, PB	Whitby Literary and Philosophical Society, Percy Burnett papers
Wildridge, *Hull Letters*	T T Wildridge (ed.), *The Hull Letters 1625-1646* (Hull, 1887)
Woolrych, *Britain in Revolution*	A Woolrych, *Britain in Revolution 1625-1660* (Oxford, 2002)
YAJ	*Yorkshire Archaeological Journal*
YAS	Yorkshire Archaeological Society
YASRS	Yorkshire Archaeological Society Record Series
YCA	York City Archives
YML	York Minster Library
Young, *History*	G Young, *A History of Whitby,* 2 vols (Whitby, 1817)
Young, Marston *Moor*	P Young, *Marston Moor 1644. The Campaign and the Battle* (Moreton-in-Marsh, 1997)
YRCP	*Yorkshire Royalist Composition Papers,* ed. J W Clay. 3 vols, YASRS xv, xviii, xx (1893, 1895, 1896)

PREFACE

Sir Hugh Cholmley, of Whitby, in Yorkshire... was a strong
Parliamentarian. He afterwards deserted their cause, when in
command of Scarborough, which he delivered up to the
Queen at a very critical conjuncture. His history is too well
known to need further remark here.[1]

These words were printed 150 years ago, written by the editor of Sir Roger Twysden's
Journal and published by *Archaeologia Cantiana,* Kent's Archaeological Society. Sir
Roger Twysden was Sir Hugh's brother-in-law and his family home, Roydon Hall, in
East Peckham in the county of Kent, was where Sir Hugh wrote his memoirs and where
he died soon afterwards in 1657. It therefore seems somewhat surprising that Sir Hugh
Cholmley should be so well known two centuries after his death in a place 300 miles
from his own home in Yorkshire.

In fact, Sir Hugh Cholmley (1600-1657), the first baronet, is still not so well
remembered even in his native county and even less well understood in Whitby.
Historians of his time have frequently quoted his memoirs, yet his original holograph
was not re-discovered until it was 300 years old and not put into print fully until as
recently as 2000.[2] Until then commentators had to rely on the limited and imperfect
printed editions of 1787 and 1870, without knowing how accurate they were. As for
Cholmley's three essays on the Civil War, the so-called memorials, they have been
unjustly overlooked and undervalued. Only one of them, on the Hothams, was deemed
worthy of publication in the Clarendon State Papers in 1773. Of the other two,
Cholmley's paper on the battle of Marston Moor did not see the light of day until 1890,
and his 'Memorialls Tuching Scarbrough', the most valuable of all, slipped
inconspicuously into print only in 1917. Both owed their retrieval to Sir Charles Firth,
Regius Professor of Modern History at Oxford, who edited them for the *English
Historical Review.* Previously, all three had languished unread and unappreciated
amongst Lord Clarendon's manuscripts in Oxford's Bodleian Library.[3]

Even so, those few historians, local and national. who have taken the trouble to
investigate Cholmley's record have too often made the mistake of treating his memoirs
and memorials at face value, instead of regarding them as self-justifying autobiography.
Examination of more objective evidence suggests a portrait at odds with both the
received eulogies and the contemporary calumnies.

The author of Cholmley's memoirs was an unrepentant Royalist. Though he died
a year before Cromwell, he never lost hope in the restoration of the Stuart monarchy. He
had come to regret deeply his pre-war opposition to the King and his role as a
Parliamentarian colonel. He spent the rest of his life, after changing sides in the middle
of the war, trying to atone for his political errors. He was careful to complain of the
revenge Lord Strafford had taken upon him for his resistance to Ship Money, but

completely silent about his own vindictive part subsequently in the earl's trial and conviction. The execution of Charles in 1649 must have made him feel even more guilty.

Yet Sir Hugh Cholmley was much more than a Parliamentarian who turned into a Civil-War Royalist colonel: by his own estimation he has been credited with many achievements. In particular, he has been praised for rescuing his family's estate from bankruptcy and rescuing Whitby from a century of backwater poverty. It is the main purpose of this study to examine and challenge the validity of both claims.

Indeed, probably Sir Hugh's most important legacy was his youngest son of the same name, another Sir Hugh Cholmley (1632-89), the fourth and last baronet. He was a man of extraordinary but unrecognised talent and huge achievement. As surveyor-general of England's first African colony, Tangier, he designed and built the largest structure of its kind in the world - the great harbour mole; and at home in Whitby he was responsible for building one of the most ambitious new houses in the country. Nothing of Tangier's harbour mole survived and Cholmley's so-called banqueting hall lost its roof and its purpose long before English Heritage turned it into a museum "visitor centre" in 2002; but neither calamity was Sir Hugh's doing.

As for Tangier Cholmley's better-known father, his long-term legacy also takes the form of architectural ruins. As an indirect result of his change of sides from Parliament to King in 1643 and his stubborn but hopeless defence of the castle that followed in 1645, Scarborough keep has only three sides, no roof and no floors; St Mary's parish church has no chancel, a truncated tower and lacks a north transept; and the town has a street of St Thomas but no church that gave it that name. All were casualties of the Civil War.

Whitby folk might still regard the Cholmleys with mixed feelings, but Scarborians never forgave them for what had happened in 1645. For generations they had represented the borough in the House of Commons until Sir Hugh senior was disabled after changing sides. But at the Restoration of the monarchy in 1660 there was no reconciliation between the town and the family. Not even with the support of the Duke of York could young Hugh Cholmley secure one of the borough's two parliamentary seats. Thereafter, the Cholmleys represented Thirsk, Hedon, Aldborough, Boroughbridge and even Northampton, but never Scarborough again.

Finally, though the family name has survived elsewhere, the Cholmleys no longer live in and overlook Whitby. Their inability to produce fertile and legitimate male heirs has meant that Whitby's lord of the manor now goes by the name of Strickland-Constable.

CHAPTER 1

"THE GREAT BLACK KNIGHT OF THE NORTH"

The Yorkshire Cholmondeleys had abbreviated their name to Cholmeley or Cholmley soon after they crossed the Pennines from Cheshire where the main branch of the family remained and is still to be found.[1] Sir Roger Cholmley was the first of the family to settle at Roxby castle, between what is now called Thornton le-Dale and Pickering, at Thornton-on-the-hill, but he owed his Yorkshire estate to his elder brother, Sir Richard (I).

This Sir Richard, who died in 1521, had been handsomely rewarded by the first two Tudor kings for his loyal service to them. His knighthood dated from 1498 and at various times he was treasurer of war at Berwick-on-Tweed, controller of customs at Newcastle, Hull and London, and steward of a number of Yorkshire castles, such as Barnard, Cottingham and Sheriff Hutton which had once belonged to Richard III. He was also the much trusted Lord Lieutenant of the Tower of London.[2] More to the point, as constable of the royal castle of Pickering and steward, receiver and master forester of the royal honour and forest of Pickering, Sir Richard had effectively displaced the Hastings hegemony in that area. Finally, in 1519, when Francis Hastings failed to redeem the mortgages on the manors of Roxby and Kingthorpe, they were bought by Sir Richard.[3]

This Sir Richard had no legitimate children, only a bastard son, Roger (c.1485-1565), who nevertheless, after an unpromising start, eventually became Chief Justice of the King's Bench. Expelled three times as a student from Lincoln's Inn, in later years Roger advised young lawyers not to follow his bad example, otherwise they would "meet either with poverty or Tyburn in the way".[4] So it was Sir Richard's younger brother, also called Roger, who inherited his Yorkshire estate in 1521.[5]

This Sir Roger Cholmley, who died in 1538, distinguished himself in 1512 on the battlefield of Flodden and was knighted for his gallantry there. No doubt his courage was particularly pleasing to the elderly Sir Marmaduke Constable of Flamborough, who was also present at Flodden along with his son, brother, servants and kinsman, since Roger had married his granddaughter, Katherine, a year earlier.[6] Not only did Roger marry himself into "a very antient famuly" which was "one of the most eminent and potent. . . at that tyme in the Country", but he did his own family favours by marrying his children into other leading Northern houses. The second Sir Richard, born about 1516, Roger's eldest son and heir, was first the husband of Margaret, daughter of Lord Conyers of Hornby, and Roger's two daughters, Margaret and Jane, were in succession wives of the fifth earl of Westmorland. When Sir Richard's first wife died and he then married Catherine Clifford, daughter of the first earl of Cumberland and widow of John, Lord Scrope of Bolton castle, it was evidence of the great prestige the Cholmleys had gained in the North.[7]

1

Sir Richard (II) continued in the tradition founded by his father and uncle by remaining loyal to the Tudors, thereby reaping the rewards of trustworthiness. The Tudors badly needed and richly appreciated "friends in the North". Consequently, in October 1536, when the rebellion known as the Pilgrimage of Grace swept across Yorkshire, unlike their neighbours, such as the Constables and the Percys, the Cholmleys refused to lead the protestors against religious reform. As a result, "Mr Chamley's house" at Roxby was ransacked by an irate mob.[8] So that when the rising collapsed the Cholmleys were soon benefiting from King Henry's gratitude. Indeed, even before Whitby abbey was officially closed at the end of 1539, in April 1538, a few days before his father's death, young Richard was already on the look-out for government recognition and recompense. In a letter to Cromwell, the king's chief minister and architect of the Dissolution, Richard suggested pointedly that "an honest man" should be chosen to keep the courts in the Liberty of Whitby Strand, a post which was soon to fall to him.[9]

Only months after the closure of Whitby abbey in December 1539, young Richard took out a 21-year lease from the Crown on the former abbey's buildings, precinct and demesne, nearly 500 acres in all on both sides of the river Esk. The association between Whitby and the Cholmleys had begun. Most of Richard's lease was on the east bank of the river, but it also included the valuable upriver mills at Ruswarp and the manor of Staxby or Stakesby on the west side. In Whitby town itself, the lease included four of George Bushell's closes, amounting to 20 acres in all, and his windmill, "super montem juxta dem. nup' monastium de Whitby", on the hill next to the former ground of Whitby abbey. For all of this valuable acquisition Richard paid only £49 8d. annual rent, the Crown reserving only "the great trees and woods".[10]

Also in the established Cholmley custom, Richard (II) won his spurs on a Scottish battlefield. After he had taken part in the sack of Edinburgh and Leith in 1544, Richard was knighted by the earl of Hertford.[11] Fighting, beating and plundering the Scots in their homeland had become a profitable Cholmley pursuit. As his great-grandson later proudly recorded, Richard recruited and led his own armed men in the Scottish campaigns "meerely by his owne power and interest", whereas later when invading Scotland, in the absence of a professional royal army, king Charles I had to depend on the forcible impressment of militias. In other words, this Sir Richard was one of the last of the feudal Northern lords to raise, lead and provision a private army.

Soon after returning from Scotland, Sir Richard was again at war with the Scots, this time at home. From Whitby, on All Saints' Day 1544, he wrote to the earl of Shrewsbury, the Lord Lieutenant of Yorkshire, to describe recent events in his neighbourhood. The previous Thursday, though the archers of "Robynhodbay" had tried to aid them, two English crayers had been taken by two Scottish armed ships. That same night two more English vessels, bound for Newcastle, had been forced on to the rocks three miles south of Whitby by these same Scotsmen. The following day Sir Richard arrived on the scene to rescue the guns from the stricken English ships. Eight pieces of ordnance were drawn by his men up the seacliff, "by my estimacion one hundred fathoms high", out of the reach of the Scots. Without gunpowder, however, Sir Richard could not use this artillery against the enemy.[12]

The following year, from the Crown, Sir Richard bought outright first the buildings and lands of the dissolved priory at Grosmont and a few weeks later, also from the Crown, the manor of Ugglebarnby and other former Whitby monastery properties in Sleights and Aislaby. For the latter he paid £333 8s. 4d.[13]

King Henry's death early in 1547 appears only to have advanced Sir Richard's progress and prosperity. Soon afterwards he was named one of the commissioners of peace for the North Riding of Yorkshire and before the end of the year he was nominated and "pricked" for the office of high sheriff of the whole county.[14] As a mark of the trust now placed in him and "for services to the late King Henry VIII", in April 1548 Richard was granted the office of constable of the royal castle at Scarborough for life. With this important responsibility came a lifetime gift of the royal manor of Northstead, immediately north of the liberty of the borough of Scarborough, at an annual rent of £24.[15]

Though Sir Richard was to be identified later as a papist recusant who refused to conform to the Church of England, he was a willing participant in the Protestant Reformation of Edward's reign. In February 1548 he was one of the leading Yorkshire commissioners appointed to draw up a list of the county's religious chantries which were to be confiscated by the Crown under the Act of 1547.[16] Given the resistance in some parts of east Yorkshire to the closure of chantries, this commission was far from safe. For instance, one of the gentlemen commissioners, Matthew White, and three of his assistants were murdered at Seamer, just outside Scarborough, and their corpses stripped and left on the Wold for the crows to feed on.[17] Nevertheless, such violent opposition was promptly and brutally suppressed and in March 1553 Cholmley was one of the surveyors of all the "goods, plate, jewels, vestments, bells and other ornaments" of confiscated religious property in the North Riding.[18] Sir Richard was also the beneficiary of the dissolution of other monasteries beside that of Whitby. In April 1553, he put down £229 3s. 4d. in "ready money" for extensive farm lands in Ryedale, in particular at Sellybridge and the Marishes, which had once belonged to Rievaulx abbey.[19]

The succession of the Catholic Queen Mary in July 1553 was disastrous for many leading Protestant English landlords, but Sir Richard was not one of them. On the contrary, it was during Mary's brief reign that "the great black knight of the North" extended and consolidated his landed power in north-east Yorkshire. Principally, on 1 July 1555, for £5,000, he bought 22,000 acres which consisted of the Whitby lands he had tenanted since 1540 and the manors to the south of Whitby Laithes, Larpool, Stainsacre, Hawsker and Fyling. The last manor included the abbot's grange, deer park and lodge, Fyling Hall. According to the contract he made with Sir John Yorke, Sir Richard was to pay £1000 at the sealing of the indenture, another £1000 on 7 November 1555 at the baptismal stone of St Paul's in London, between eight and eleven in the morning, a further £1,250 by the Feast of St Barnabus, 11 June 1556, at the same place, £1,250 during the next 12 months, and the final £500 by 5 October 1557. The conclusion of the transaction was recorded in the Easter Term of 1557 so that the whole sum must have been handed over in advance of this final date. Additionally, in lieu of knight's service for the manors of Whitby, Whitby Laithes and Fyling, Sir Richard was required to pay £13 12s. 10d. a year into the royal treasury.[20]

Altogether this Whitby Strand estate consisted of 300 messuages, 100 cottages and several water mills, but to pay for it with ready money Sir Richard had to sell his remaining properties in Kent, much of his inheritance in Ryedale, and his second wife's portion in Wensleydale to her son by Lord Scrope. The effect of this major transaction was therefore to shift the centre of gravity of Cholmley landholding power from Roxby castle in Ryedale to Abbey House at Whitby.[21]

Queen Mary regarded Cholmley as her brother and father had done - one of those few Northern barons who could be trusted. He was again Yorkshire's high sheriff in the year 1556-7 and returned as one of the two knights of the shire in the parliament that opened on 20 January 1558.[22] In that same month Sir Richard received a letter from the Queen's Privy Council ordering him either to reside at Scarborough castle himself or to put his son in there "for the better garding of the same".[23] The explanation of this command from London was that some months earlier the royal castle at Scarborough had been seized by Thomas Stafford and his rebellious accomplices when it was without defenders or even garrison. Stafford held the castle for only three days and he and his fellow rebels were subsequently hanged and quartered for their treason, but the appointed constable of the castle was nowhere to be found. Nevertheless, instead of depriving Sir Richard of his neglected responsibility he was told only to fulfil it.[24]

Clearly, Sir Richard was a valued ally and agent in the almost perpetual wars with the Scots. At the end of 1555 he had been named as one of the Crown's commissioners to inspect and strengthen English defences along the border with Scotland;[25] and three years later he was thanked by the Privy Council for his recent military exploits there. In particular, he was complimented for burning down the Scottish town of Coldingham![26]

The succession of the Protestant Elizabeth in November 1558 seems not at first to have upset Sir Richard's authority or undermine his loyalty to the Crown. On the contrary, in 1563 he made his final purchase of the remaining former Whitby abbey properties still in royal possession. For £1,120 12s. 6d. he acquired the manors and lands of Robin Hood's Bay, Fyling Raw, Fyling Thorpe, Normanby, Thorny and Stoupe Brow. At that time there were about 50 cottagers living in Robin Hood's Bay, most of them paying an annual rent of two shillings, and about the same number in the Fyling villages, where rents had also remained unchanged since the dissolution of Whitby abbey.[27] The Cholmleys now had a compact bloc of land from Sandsend in the north to Hackness and Staintondale in the south and inland to the tops of Fylingdales moor, covering about 26,000 acres in all.[28]

However, though Sir Richard was never seduced into plotting treason against Queen Elizabeth and wisely refused to join the Rising of the Northern Earls in 1569, he would not openly conform to the Protestant Church of England established in 1559. In 1565, he was described as Scarborough's leading "papist"; in 1572, he was named in Thomas Gargrave's list of Yorkshire's principal Catholic gentlemen, though only as one of the "meane or lesse eyvell" kind; and in 1580, when he made his last appearance in such official documents, he was recorded as the head of a family of "recusants" living at Thornton.[29] As such, therefore, he came under government suspicion as a potential rebel, not least because his second wife, Lady Catherine, was known to be a staunch Catholic and their eldest son, Henry Cholmley, was married to Margaret Babthorpe of Osgodby, a member of one of Yorkshire's most stubbornly-committed recusant families.[30] As early as 1565, the archbishop of York, Thomas Young, had described Sir Richard to the Queen as "obstinant in religion" and therefore not to be trusted with the safe keeping of Scarborough castle. As a result, Sir Henry Gate of Seamer, who had unquestioned Protestant credentials, was in effect given responsibility for the castle when the Northern earls rose four years later.[31]

4

In 1562, Sir Richard had been summoned before the Council of the North at York to answer charges against him of misdeeds in the royal forest of Pickering. He was accused of poaching deer there and stealing 120 oaks from the Queen's woods in Goathland. Even more seriously, it was alleged that he had plundered the royal castle at Pickering to improve his own house at Roxby. It was said that two of his servants had robbed stones from the King's hall at the castle and to build his new gallery at Roxby his tenants had carried away 13 cartloads of stones and two loads of slates. Nevertheless, though the evidence against him seemed clear and weighty, Sir Richard was treated with respect and leniency and escaped unharmed.[32]

However, three years later, new charges brought against Sir Richard were far more serious and potentially lethal. It was now alleged that he was one of a Northern faction that secretly supported the claims to Elizabeth's title of the Countess of Lennox and her son, Lord Darnley, and that he knew and approved of the intended marriage of the latter to Mary, Queen of the Scots. Such a marriage would pose a direct threat to the legitimacy of Elizabeth. Sir Richard was called up to London to appear before the lords of the Privy Council. Yet here he was both defiant and aggressive. He contended that the Northern councillors at York had done many injuries and wrongs to him and that they were guilty of dishonesty and corruption; they had appropriated fines due to the Crown amounting to a thousand marks; and that they ought to be dismissed. Such effrontery was not well received: the Privy Council would not listen to his rash calumnies and sent him back to York in the custody of the sergeant-at-arms to be tried before the men he had denounced. The outcome was pre-determined: Sir Richard was imprisoned indefinitely in York castle.[33]

How long Sir Richard was confined is not known. By the end of 1565 he had written to the Privy Council complaining of "imprisonment and usage" and it seems that archbishop Young, who was President of the Northern Council, then ordered his release.[34] Nevertheless, Sir Richard from now on lived under a blanket of official suspicion. In January 1567 it was alleged that he had offered to hand over Scarborough castle to Lord Darnley, even though no evidence could be found to substantiate such a charge.[35] However, even without proof of disloyalty, Sir Richard was still dispossessed of the castle and the manor of Northstead that went with it.[36]

Yet it would be a mistake to assume that the great black knight of the North was no longer great. When the Northern earls rose against Elizabeth in support of the claims of Mary, Queen of Scots, in 1569, Sir Richard nursed his grievances in silence and inaction. No doubt his wife, Lady Catherine, had much influence in this matter: her eldest son, the ninth Lord Scrope, was an active supporter of Queen Elizabeth and had Mary locked up in his castle at Bolton in Wensleydale. As a consequence of Sir Richard's refusal to side with the rebels, the whole of Ryedale and Whitby Strand, where his authority was still paramount, followed his example. So when the Rising failed, unlike the rebel earls, Sir Richard kept his head and his lands intact.

Sir Richard might have forfeited his castle at Scarborough because of his religious "obstinancy", but he continued to sit on the North Riding bench as a justice of the peace,[37] and the properties he had bought from Elizabeth, namely Robin Hood's Bay, Fyling, Normanby and Stoupe, were confirmed as his and his heirs in a royal patent of 1574.[38] Later, he was named as a feodary, or trustee representing the Crown and its interests, when local landowners died. For instance, in 1575, 1576 and 1578, he was one of the feodaries following the deaths of John, Lord Lumley, Robert Percy and Arthur

Dakins.[39] In short, though no longer implicitly trusted, Sir Richard was still too powerful and experienced a knight to be ignored or alienated in a part of the kingdom which the London government regarded as potentially disloyal.

Sir Richard represented what was to be a dying breed: the last generation of Northern feudal lords. In his heyday, he could raise a hundred or more armed retainers and lead them into battle against the Scots, the old enemy. According to his great-grandson, at his fortified manor house at Roxby, "where he lived in great Port", Sir Richard maintained a permanent household of "at least 50 or 60 men servants". And these were not merely domestic staff: they included "iddle serveing men" who at breakfast time "would go into the kitching and strikeing their daggers in to the pot take out the beefe". Sometimes, when as many as "24 peices of beefe" had been cooked in the morning, not one was left for their master's own midday dinner. When he travelled abroad, even on his own, "with out his lady", Sir Richard was attended with never fewer than 30 or even 40 armed retainers. Between him and his brother-in-law, the earl of Westmorland, there was much rivalry and hostility, so that when they encountered each other in London's streets or elsewhere, their servants fought mock battles with short sword and shield in ritual combat.[40]

Yet however powerful and feared amongst men, Sir Richard did not always have his own way with the women in his family. In the words of his great-grandson: "He was a wise man, and a great improver of his estate", but he "might have prospered better with his posterety had he not bene exstraordinarely given to the love of women".[41] His second wife, Catherine Clifford, was a most eminent, widowed lady and very proud of her illustrious ancestry. She therefore took the strongest exception to Richard's philandery and in retaliation, for several years, refused to sleep with him. Only when the couple were forced by lack of lodging to share the same bedchamber were conjugal relations resumed. The result was their eldest son, Henry, and the two lived together "kindly" from then on.[42]

Even their youngest daughter, Katherine, defied her father successfully. Though Sir Richard had already arranged her marriage to Lord Lumley and even paid £1,000 in advance as her dowry, Katherine told him bluntly to his face that she would rather die than have him as her husband. She loved her penniless, music teacher, Richard Dutton, and would marry no one else. Rather than make his daughter marry against her will, Sir Richard cooled his anger, swallowed his pride and forfeited his money. Katherine married Dutton in a Catholic ceremony held at Ripley castle, home of the recusant Inglebys, and her father left her a generous allowance in his will of £500 or £600 a year. As the black knight's great-grandson concluded: "this daughter was his dareling".[43]

Sir Richard Cholmley (II) died on 17 May 1583 at Ellerburn and was buried nearby in the chancel of the parish church of Thornton. Four years earlier he had made a final will leaving his estate to his eldest son, Francis, by his first wife Margaret. There were annuities of £700 or £800 each for his two younger sons, Richard and Henry. However, if Francis died without a male heir, the Cholmley inheritance was to pass not to Richard but to Henry, Catherine's son. It seems that Sir Richard had doubts about Richard's legitimacy and no doubt Lady Clifford had some say in his decision. No provision was made in the will for the descendants of Roger, Margaret's second son, who had died in 1577. Consequently, when Francis's life ended prematurely and without issue in 1586, young Henry inherited the Cholmley lands and Marmaduke, Roger's son, had to make do with his mother's Brandsby estate. Though Marmaduke failed to win his lawsuit against Henry's claim, the Brandsby Cholmleys continued in vain to contest the consequences of Sir Richard's will for many years to come.[44]

Francis was the first male Cholmley to make Abbey House on Whitby's windswept, inhospitable East Cliff, his family home. After his death, his widowed step-mother, Catherine Clifford, who preferred to call herself Lady Scrope, her son Henry and Margaret, his wife, moved out of Roxby castle and took up residence at Whitby. The fortified house that Sir Richard had "improved" with stones and slates stolen from Pickering castle was allowed to decay slowly until eventually it was abandoned altogether; and the enormous landed estate which he had accumulated from former monastic property was gradually eroded by price inflation, extravagance and incompetent management. The Whitby Cholmleys were destined to stay on the East Cliff in the ruins of Whitby abbey for another 150 years, but none of his successors was ever able to equal the local authority, wealth and substance of the great black knight of the North.

CHAPTER 2

FRANCIS, HENRY AND RICHARD (III)

1 "A receptackle to the symenary preists"

Even before the death of Sir Richard (II) in 1583, the Cholmley estate in North Yorkshire which he had amassed was beginning to fragment. As early as April 1578, the capital messuage at Bridgeholmgreen, also known as Nether Hall, in Egton Bridge, was sold to a local yeoman, Thomas Smythe, for £316. Altogether three messuages, two cottages and 17 closes of pasture covered nearly 80 acres of ground. The Smythes were well-to-do recusants "who never quite made the armigerous class".[1]

However, with this exception, Francis inherited his father's Yorkshire estate intact, though with the proviso that he had power to dispose of land worth no more than £500 a year. Two reasons for this limitation were later given by Sir Hugh Cholmley in his memoirs: one that Francis "was a proper man and bred a souldiour" and therefore might be taken prisoner and held for ransom; and secondly that Sir Richard so disliked and distrusted his daughter-in-law that he feared she might ruin his heir and his inheritance. In fact, neither danger occurred: Francis died within three years and his widow, Joan Bulmer, had only the £500 a year settled on her out of the estate.[2]

Seventy years after the death of Francis, the Cholmleys still carried a grudge against Joan Bulmer. Her father-in-law had thought that she would have better served his eldest son as a mistress than as a wife. He clearly disapproved of the marriage because though she came of a good family she "had no gud fame or humour". To confirm his worst predictions, soon after the death of Francis, she married a young man "of mean quality" to whom she gave all of her land.[3] It was said that she had been nothing but a bad influence on Francis, who though a valiant man was bewitched by her. She had persuaded him to build the first hall on Whitby's East Cliff out of wattle, daub and wood, even though there was plenty of good stone on the site; and over the doorway to it she insisted that her initial J should precede his F. Worst of all, after his death, she ordered that Francis should be buried not "in his owne parish church with in his owne Manner [manor]" at Whitby, but in St Mary's, Beverley, a place that had no Cholmley associations.[4]

On the other hand, the early death of Francis and Joan Bulmer's failure to bear children were providential blessings: though bitterly challenged in and out of the law courts by the Brandsby branch of the family, Henry inherited the Cholmley estate as his father and mother intended. To his nephew Marmaduke, Henry granted an annuity of £50 for three lives and a lump sum of a thousand marks (£666 13s. 4d.) in the hope that this would settle the disputed succession.[5] He was mistaken: until as late as the 1620s and probably beyond, the Brandsby Cholmleys persisted with their prior claim to the Whitby estate. Not least of the reasons why the Whitby Cholmleys held on and the

Brandsby Cholmleys never made good their case was that the former turned Protestant whereas the latter remained stubbornly Catholic.[6]

On the other hand, Sir Henry Cholmley (c.1556-1616) proved to be one of the most worthless and improvident of all the male line. During the time he was head of the family the estate went downhill with alarming speed. As raging inflation in the 1590s destroyed the real value of long-term fixed rents, Henry still continued to live extravagantly and well beyond his shrinking income. He wasted much of his adult life hunting and hawking and spent his money on horses, hounds and gambling. Too vain to live frugally, Henry foolishly attempted to emulate the style of his very rich and even more profligate cousin, George, third earl of Cumberland. Even his own grandson could find nothing to write in his favour except that just when he was about to be disgraced and bankrupted by recusancy he and his wife Margaret had the good sense to declare themselves Protestants.[7]

Not that Henry was either unintelligent or uneducated. At the age of 17 he had been sent from his mother's house at Bolton to Jesus College, Cambridge and from there a few months later he transferred to Caius College. Though there is no evidence that he took a degree or even studied hard for one, as a fellow-commoner gentleman he was not expected to behave like a scholar.[8] Four years later, now 21, Henry was admitted to Lincoln's Inn. Again, we have no knowledge of how he behaved there, but at least he had the opportunity to acquire what his grandson, in similar circumstances, called "a smakering [smattering] of the law".[9] However, what does seem certain is that young Henry was brought up in the Catholic faith. His early transfer from Jesus to Caius College was highly significant. Dr Edwin Sandys, who was archbishop of York from 1577 until 1588, complained angrily about the religious indoctrination received by Yorkshiremen at Gonville Hall, as it was then called: "the popish gentlemen in this country [Yorkshire] send their sons to him [Dr Caius] … and at their return … few of them will repair to the church", he wrote. In particular, Sandys identified Richard Swale, a Yorkshireman by birth, who was a fellow of Caius from 1576 to 1589, as an arch "corruptor" of Yorkshire's young gentlemen.[10]

During the 1590s the Cholmley household at Whitby seems to have been dominated by ladies. At the head was the formidable widow, Lady Catherine Scrope, who was "a Roman Catholicke" recusant, her daughter-in-law, Margaret Cholmley, Henry's wife, and her daughter, Sir Richard's favourite, Katherine Dutton. In the words of Sir Hugh, writing more than 60 years later, Whitby was then "a receptackle to the symenary preists comeing from beyond seaes and landing frequently at that port". Sometimes there were as many as three or four such priests taken in at Abbey House, where they were hidden, fed, clothed and then provided with horses. Henry attended the adjacent parish church, but, according to his grandson, "being a little then in his heart inclyneing that way", connived at these flagrant breaches of the criminal law.[11] Yet given Henry's upbringing in the presence of such powerful Catholic parents, his experience of "a refuge of papists" at Cambridge, and his marriage into the Catholic Babthorpe family, it seems that his attachment to the old faith was probably much stronger than his grandson liked to believe.

Perhaps on account of her great age, Lady Scrope was not imprisoned for her defiant recusancy, but her daughter and daughter-in-law were both put in York castle gaol in 1592. When confronted and questioned, Margaret confessed that "she had never been to church in all her life - saving the day of her marriage - neither was she willing to

9

conform" to the Protestant faith. But conform she did after spending several months, along with her sister-in-law Katherine, in the discomforts of Clifford's Tower. Nevertheless, in 1595 and again in 1596, Henry Cholmley and all three ladies in his household were registered as recusants or non-communicants. It seems that it would take something more threatening to force the Cholmleys to abandon their non-conformity for good.[12]

However, when the grand Lady Scrope finally died in 1598, "the menage at Whitby fell asunder". According to her great-grandson, "in her harte [she]dyed a Protestant for one of the last words she spoke [to] her sonnes wife: daughter let the Preists might bee put out of the house." Whatever her final thoughts and words might have been, she was buried in the chancel of Whitby parish church "under the great blew stone" there.[13] Henry and Margaret moved back to Roxby and the Duttons wandered from place to place to escape persecution. However, there now followed a determined and sustained attack by the Council at York to root out recusancy on the Cholmley estates in Whitby Strand and Ryedale. A Protestant pincer-movement spear-headed by Sir Thomas Posthumous Hoby, who had settled at Hackness in 1596, and Lord Sheffield, who lived at Mulgrave castle, was directed by the second Lord Burghley, who was President of the Council of the North from 1599 until 1603. When Burghley arrived in York in September 1599 he carried Privy Council instructions to take severe measures against "gentlemen" who were "notoriously infected with Popery".[14] And there was no doubt who these "gentlemen" were and where they lived in Yorkshire. In the words of one informant writing at this time: "Blackamore [North York Moors] I terme to be a Bushoppricke of Papists, and Growman [Grosmont] Abbey the Headhowse, wherein the Busshop lyeth. . ."[15] Grosmont belonged to the Cholmleys and their tenants there, the Hodgsons, as well as their tenants at Fyling Hall, the Aislaby family, now felt the full weight of the law.

Consequently, in November 1599, as Catholic priests were being arrested and executed, recusants indicted before the Council at York, and Catholics compelled to listen to Protestant sermons, Henry and Margaret Cholmley received Anglican communion in York minster.[16] Henry's "conversion" was only just in time: Hoby had already told the Council at York that he had not been known to have attended church once during the past three years and had never previously taken the Anglican sacrament. Even more damning was later evidence submitted by Whitby's vicar, John Urpeth, before Star Chamber that Henry had encouraged his servants to disrupt his Sunday church services. They had even run horse races outside the church during divine service "to the disturbance of the worshippers."[17]

Such sudden, convenient conversions naturally arouse suspicion of insincerity, but neither Henry nor even Margaret was ever again accused of Catholic recusancy. Henry was one of the many Yorkshiremen knighted by the new king James when he passed through the county on his way south in 1603 and, according to their grandson, both he and Margaret "ever after . . . lived and dyed very zealous Protestants".[18] Indeed, the poacher seems to have become a gamekeeper, almost overnight. As justice of the peace in the North Riding, in 1604 Sir Henry was personally responsible for presenting 23 recusants, a "retainer" of recusants, three cases of illegal, secret marriage, and a private baptism, all within the neighbourhood of Whitby. Henry might have been idle and spendthrift, yet in the nick of time he had seen the urgent necessity of at least outward conformity. His grandson's observation was probably more wishful than factual: self-preservation rather than soul-searching had forced Henry's decision and self-preservation kept him to it.[19]

Meanwhile, as Sir Henry hunted with his fleet hounds and raced his fast horses, his inherited estate was being rapidly eaten away, mainly by runaway inflation. In June 1596, for the sum of £355, he had sold the manor house at Stakesby, with its two great barns, 15 closes and common grazing rights on the waste of Eskdaleside and Sleights to George Cockerill, a yeoman of Goathland. Two days later, Francis Huntrods and Leonard Marley, both yeomen tenants, each bought a quarter of the manor lands of Stakesby for £125.[20] Two years later, Henry also sold a burgage tenement, 12 houses and 32 cottages in Pickering.[21]

From then on Henry turned more and more of his land and rents into lump sums of ready cash. Lease Head farm in Iburnside went to Roger Beverley, a gentleman of Kirkby Misperton, for £200 in 1602.[22] Five years later, a succession of smaller sales culminated in the largest of 1607 when effectively Sir Henry divested himself of most of the remaining Cholmley properties in Ryedale and Pickering Lythe, at Kingthorpe, Roxby, Thornton, Farmanby, Ellerburn, Pickering town, Lund and Kirkby Overcarr. Altogether these lands yielded well over £2,000. The Cholmleys now retained little more than the castle at Roxby, which was occupied by Henry, one of Sir Henry's younger sons.[23] Finally, before he retired to the city of York, where he lived until his death in 1616, Sir Henry raised £320 on the sale of Carley or Cayley House in Eskdaleside.[24]

Sir Henry's addiction to hawking, hunting and horse racing was by no means the only or even the main cause of his financial problems. By Margaret, his only wife, he had "a numerous issue", all of whom had to be provided with life annuities in the case of younger sons and marriage portions in the case of daughters. In addition to Richard, their eldest son, Henry and John were also "very tall handsome proper men". And all their daughters married well: Barbara, to Thomas, Lord Fauconberg of Newburgh Priory; Dorothy, to Nicholas Bushell of Bagdale Hall; Hilda, to Toby Wright; Margaret, to Timothy Comyn; Mary, to Henry Fairfax, second son of Lord Fairfax of Denton; Susanna, to Richard Theakston; and Annabella, to Henry Wickham, son of Bishop Wickham, chaplain to Charles I. All these seven daughters had to be found dowries, which varied in value depending on the prestige of the bridegroom and his family. Barbara's dowry was the most expensive: she cost Sir Henry several thousand pounds.[25]

II "A troblesome vexatious neighbour"

Almost as costly to Sir Henry as his seven daughters was his eldest son and heir, Richard. Though handsome and intelligent, Richard was wayward, violent and headstrong. In some ways he was no better than his father when it came to estate management and public affairs. After his premature marriage in 1596 at the age of 16, he refused to return to his studies at Trinity College, Cambridge. As a result he was "noe great schollar" and lacked his father's literary skills and legal knowledge. The wedding was arranged by Sir Henry mainly to secure a dowry of "£2000 in redy mony, a faire portion at that tyme"; but Richard and his family would have been better served by a longer university experience followed by law tuition at one of the London Inns of Court. In the event, Richard was already a father before the age of 20 and by then already in trouble because of his bad temper and recklessness.[26]

11

In August 1600, young Richard was one of a wild, hunting party with five other local gentlemen: two Eures, Sir William, brother of Ralph, the third Lord Eure, and Ralph's son and heir, also called William; William Dawnay, son-in-law of Ralph; William Hilyard, the younger; and Stephen Hutchinson of Wykeham Abbey, who made a surprise visit to Hackness Hall. Apart from Sir William, all were youthful in years and highly spirited; and all were already hostile to the new master of Hackness, Sir Thomas Posthumous Hoby. Since becoming Lady Margaret's third husband in 1596, Sir Thomas had succeeded in making many enemies and arousing much local ill-feeling. His neighbours regarded him as a government spy and Southern carpet-bagger, sent North to keep a watchful eye on Yorkshiremen who were suspected of Catholic sympathies and potential treason. In 1597, Hoby had been returned to the House of Commons as one of Scarborough's two Members; soon he was collecting taxes, mustering the local militia, and busying himself in every kind of local administration. Worst of all, Hoby was detested as a Puritan "of the worst sort", who was unable and unwilling to keep his extreme Protestant views to himself. As one unfriendly witness described him: he was "the busyest, sawcie little Jacke in all the contrie, and wold have an ore in eny bodies bote". That he was very small in stature, who "useth to draw up his Breeches with a shooing-horn", and after four years of marriage, had failed to make Lady Margaret pregnant, provoked much scurrilous innuendo. It was said that he had been cuckolded by his wife's private chaplain, Richard Rhodes.[27]

However, Hoby's knowledge of the law and his powerful political connections in London made him a formidable opponent. The six gentlemen who abused his hospitality and insulted both him and his wife came to regret their foolishness, not least Richard and his father, Sir Henry. Knowing full well that Hackness Hall was a strictly pious and proper household, the notorious six did everything possible to outrage its master and mistress. They played cards and dice; they used foul language and got themselves drunk; they spoke only of horses, hounds and hawks; and during the family's evening prayers they laughed out loud, stamped their feet, and sang bawdy songs. Not even Lady Margaret was safe from them. The following morning, having long outstayed their welcome, they forced their way into her bedchamber, assaulted her servants who tried to stop them, and shouted abuse at her husband in her presence.[28]

The Cholmleys were already at the head of Hoby's black list. As early as September 1598, 80 of Henry's servants and tenants had been summoned to the North Riding court charged with being "obstinant popish recusants".[29] The following year, when all official attempts to seize men and goods on Cholmley's Whitby lands had failed, Sir Thomas wrote directly to his cousin, Lord Cecil, complaining of the Cholmleys who welcomed missionary priests into their "sundry creeks" such as Robin Hood's Bay, gave shelter and succour to them at Abbey House and in the homes of their tenants at Grosmont and Fyling Hall.[30] Richard Cholmley was particularly targeted by Hoby since soon afterwards he was accused of aiding and abetting the Essex rebellion against Queen Elizabeth. Richard was guilty of foolishness not treason, but in 1601 he was briefly imprisoned and fined £200.[31]

Sir Thomas and Lady Margaret could find no impartial justice from the council at York. In the absence of President Lord Burghley, the Vice-President, Lord Eure, was brother, father and father-in-law to three of the accused, and Hoby was a "stranger" to the country.[32] So the Hobys referred their complaint to the Court of the Star Chamber in London where they could be certain of a supportive hearing. The case was so scandalous and damaging to the defendants that the Hobys were offered out-of-court settlement, but they insisted on a trial "to the death". In October 1600 Sir Thomas and Lady Margaret took the long road to London in their private coach, itself an object of local envy and ridicule, since it was the first to be owned in the neighbourhood. They stayed in the capital until March 1601 throughout the Star Chamber hearings of their case.[33] Eventually, in 1602, the court ruled entirely in their favour. The Eures of Malton were obliged to pay £100 a year in perpetuity and their accomplices smaller fines on the same terms. For how long these penalties were in fact paid and how much the Cholmleys were fined is not known, but 400 years later the Dawnays still pay £60 a year to Hackness for what in their accounts is called the "Wykeham shame".[34] For the Hobys, the Star Chamber ruling was much more than a judicial vindication: it was divine retribution! As Lady Margaret triumphantly recorded in her diary, the justice and mercy of God had been manifested to the world "that He will bringe downe their enemies unto them".[35]

However, Sir Thomas was far from satisfied: he had not yet done with the Cholmleys. Even though Sir Henry's last-minute public conversion had saved his skin, both he and his young heir were still in Hoby's sights. Given Hoby's hatred of the Cholmleys it is unlikely that he believed in the sincerity of Henry's conformity. The Cholmleys still had many Catholic connections. For instance, in February 1601, Barbara Cholmley married Thomas Bellasis of Newburgh Priory in a secret ceremony probably conducted by a Catholic missionary priest. Soon afterwards, Thomas became a Catholic and eventually died in that faith.[37]

Moreover, the Brandsby Cholmleys, despite the financial costs and physical perils of recusancy, never made the slightest gesture in the direction of Protestantism. Indeed, between 1614 and 1642, the official recusancy count at Brandsby rose from 12 to 38. Richard Cholmley of Brandsby, whose memorandum book for the years 1602 to 1623 has survived, was frequently in trouble with the authorities. He paid regular recusancy fines and escaped a capital felony charge for harbouring two priests in 1609 only by paying a heavy bribe.[37] Ursula Cholmley, also a relative who lived in Eskdaleside, a locality much favoured by Catholics, was often presented for recusancy, but like Richard at Brandsby probably enjoyed some degree of protection from her Whitby cousins.[38] Finally, throughout Hoby's time and in spite of his persecution of them, there remained strong Catholic communities on the fringe of Cholmley territory at Egton and Egton Bridge. In 1600, 57 residents there were registered as recusants; by 1614, their number had grown to 175; and even as late as 1641, they still numbered 138.[39]

Given Richard's youth and notoriety for headstrong and sometimes violent recklessness, he, rather than his ageing father, Sir Henry, became Hoby's principal target. Even Richard's son, Hugh, later had to admit that his father was "of a haughty sperit", that he was "naturally chollericke" and sometimes "imperious over" his servants and tenants. Evidence of Richard's ill-temper is not abundant but probably sufficient to justify his son's stricture. On one occasion, when the Court of Star Chamber was in session, Richard struck a gentleman. Such a crime would normally have incurred the loss of the offending hand, "but that good friends and mony brought him of".[40] In another incident, which occurred in 1603, Richard took exception to "a young Gallant" who took his stool during an interval of a play at Blackfriars theatre. Like a good Yorkshireman, Richard invited him to a meeting outside where they might settle their differences. When the "Gallant" showed no inclination to fight with either sword or fists, Richard gave him "two or 3 gud blowes" which determined the matter.[41]

Three years later, John Boyes, a merchant of Whitby, was brought before the North Riding court at the Thirsk quarter sessions for unspecified "abuses and misbehaviour . . . towards Sir Rich. Cholmley, knt., JP". The court ruled that such contempt "by inferior persons against men of his [Richard's] authoritie and place" should not go unpunished, "least others should be thereby encouraged to perpetuate the like". As a result, John Boyes was put in the public stocks at Whitby for the whole of market day.[42] Again, in 1608, another leading Whitby merchant, Richard Wiggoner, was presented at Malton quarter sessions for accusing Sir Richard, in abusive and uncivil terms, of injustice and partiality. He was sentenced to Whitby stocks for an hour and ordered to beg for Sir Richard's forgiveness on his knees. His failure to comply would lead to a spell in York castle prison.[43] The similarity between these two unusual court cases suggests that Sir Richard had a talent for making enemies in Whitby as well as Hackness.

Soon after young Richard's disgraceful conduct at Hackness Hall in August 1600, the following February his name appeared on a Privy Council list, headed by the earl of Essex, of gentlemen who had been arrested and charged with treason.[44] Two days later, scenting his quarry, Hoby wrote to his cousin Robert Cecil, the Queen's principal Secretary of State. Though he had scant knowledge of the facts of the matter, Sir Thomas had no hesitation in pronouncing his young neighbour "guilty" and explaining why he had been "moved" to "assist the rebellious earl". The Cholmley estate, Hoby continued, was "desperate", encumbered with unsupportable debt; Richard suffered from "backwardness in religion" and a natural inability to obey "her majesty's laws"; and, as though in itself this was treasonable, he was a friend of the earl of Rutland. In case Cecil should assume that Richard was "a man of no power", Sir Thomas told him that he was the heir of Henry Cholmley, the hereditary bailiff of Whitby Strand, who could "raise 500 men". Hoby then went on to describe the wapentake of Whitby Strand as "the most dangerous part of Yorkshire for hollow hearts, for popery". There on the coast was "the chief house" of the Cholmleys, which was "very apt to entertain bad intelligenced strangers". Though much indebted to creditors, Henry still had an annual income of a thousand marks from his extensive lands and these were entailed to Richard who in turn had "issue". Hoby was well informed though prone to exaggeration. His last reference was to the seven-month-old Hugh, Richard's eldest son, and perhaps it suggests that Sir Thomas was envious of his chief rival who had a son and a grandson to succeed to his estate.[45]

Hoby's allegations were less than honest and loaded with venom. He failed to mention that Henry and Margaret Cholmley had recently conformed in public to the Anglican church or that they had removed themselves from Whitby to Roxby where Hugh had been born. As the historian of Yorkshire's post-Reformation Catholics has pointed out, Sir Thomas charged all his opponents with popish sympathies whatever their true religious beliefs and practices.[46] Moreover, there was no evidence that Richard, a "crypto-papist", had taken any part in the Essex conspiracy against Elizabeth: otherwise he would not have been soon released from prison on bail of £200 and in May 1601 fined by the same amount.[47] The earl was certainly guilty of treason and executed for it.

In the context of the outrageous events at Hackness in August 1600 and the Star Chamber case arising from it, Hoby was clearly keen to drive home his advantage. Richard's arrest and imprisonment had come as a providential opportunity to inflict mortal injury on Cholmley authority in north-east Yorkshire, but Sir Thomas would have to find other means and weapons to undermine it.

The death of Queen Elizabeth in March 1603 gave the Cholmleys a temporary respite: they welcomed the accession of James of Scotland. On his journey southwards the new king stayed at King's Manor, York, and there knighted many Yorkshire gentlemen, including Henry Cholmley, on 17 April. A few weeks later, at Grafton in Northamptonshire, Richard also received his knighthood from James.[48]

The next round in the long-running war between Hoby and the Cholmleys again took place in the Court of Star Chamber in 1609. This time the complaint was brought by Sir Richard who alleged that Sir Thomas had deliberately obstructed him and Sir Richard Etherington in carrying out their duties as North Riding justices. On three different occasions - an inquiry into recusancy, the mustering of local militia, and the conservation and distribution of food after the harvest failure of 1608 - he alleged that Hoby had refused to cooperate with his fellow magistrates and had ordered his own officials in Hackness parish to follow his example.[49]

Hoby counter-attacked by claiming that Cholmley's motives in bringing the suit were merely vindictive: he was seeking revenge for the judicial defeats he had rightly suffered. Indeed, Sir Richard had questioned his authority to issue warrants and twice had tried, unsuccessfully, to provoke a duel when they had met at musters. On the question of recusancy, Hoby raised the matter of Sir Richard's close association with the so-called Egton players. According to Hoby's testimony, these performers were operating outside their native Egton without the necessary licence and all of them were in fact "obstinant popish recusants ... who played popish plays" under Sir Richard's protection. Cholmley, he said, had allowed them to perform at Sneaton, only four miles from Whitby, and even at his own house at Roxby.[50]

Sir Richard's response to these serious accusations was weak, brief and unconvincing. He could not recall using insulting words about Hoby or challenging him to a public duel. He denied that he had ever questioned Hoby's right to issue warrants. Rather feebly, he suggested that there must have been some confusion and misunderstanding about the instructions issued to and by magistrates.[51]

As for the Egton players, led by Robert and Christopher Simpson, both convicted recusants, Sir Richard's defence was even thinner. He said that he did not know that the Egton players were Catholics; he had not permitted them to travel or perform in his neighbourhood; and he had not obstructed legitimate attempts to have them arrested.[52]

Since it was common knowledge that Egton and Egton Bridge were refuges for and nurseries of recusants and Catholic priests, Sir Richard was lying through his teeth and everyone present in the court must have known it. Though it could not be proved judicially that the Cholmleys had actually entertained the players in their homes at either Roxby or Whitby, the Simpsons were notorious and all their troupe had been presented for recusancy at some time at the North Riding quarter sessions.[53]

Sir Richard's counter-attacks had blown up in his face. Though the official verdict of the court is lost, on the evidence offered by both sides, Hoby had won heavily on points. Cholmley's bad temper and infamous lack of self-control, as well as his many known contacts with recusants, had made him vulnerable to Hoby's well-directed, withering bombardment.

Subsequent events also indicate that Hoby had scored another moral and judicial victory. Sir Richard had made his first appearance on the North Riding justices bench at

Thirsk in April 1605. For the next five years his attendance was regular whereas though Hoby was frequently referred to as a quarter sessions magistrate he did not take his place there until January 1609 at Helmsley. This was the only occasion when these two bitter antagonists sat together on the bench. Hoby made a second appearance the following April at Thirsk but Cholmley was absent. Then, in October 1609 at Malton and again in April 1610 at Thirsk, Sir Richard was present but not Sir Thomas. After April 1610, however, with one exception in January 1614, until 1622, Sir Richard did not attend any North Riding sessions, whereas from July 1610 onwards with only one exception, in January 1614 at Helmsley, Hoby did not miss one. Clearly, the two were deliberately avoiding each other and from 1610 Sir Thomas had emerged the stronger and more confident. During the time his case in Star Chamber was proceeding in 1609 and the first six months of 1610, Sir Richard, but not Hoby, attended the North Riding sessions. After the "verdict" went against him, Cholmley effectively withdrew himself from the bench. Even at the special sessions for Pickering Lythe and Whitby Strand where the Cholmleys should have dominated, in Sir Richard's absence, Hoby ruled the roost.[54]

By 1609 Hoby was so confident of gaining and retaining the upper hand over the Cholmleys that he made a serious bid for the control of the wapentake of Whitby Strand. In April he wrote to his cousin, Robert Cecil, now the first earl of Salisbury and still principal Secretary of State, to ask for a grant of the bailiwick of the Liberty. Eight years earlier he had told him that Henry Cholmley was the "hereditary bailiff" of that wapentake.[55] Nevertheless, Cecil was now Lord Treasurer as well as Secretary and next to the king the most powerful man in the land and by the end of May 1609 Hoby's request had been granted: he was made bailiff for life.[56]

Not surprisingly, the Cholmleys could not tolerate such an impertinent invasion of their territory. Before the end of 1609, the two Cholmley knights, Henry and Richard, were engaged in another legal contest, this time in the Court of Exchequer. The case dragged on for the next four years. As bailiff of Whitby Strand, Hoby would gain the exclusive right to collect for the Crown its dues from manorial courts and its residual rights to waifs and strays, the chattels of felons and wreck of the sea. For these services he would receive an annual fee of £3 6s. 8d., but what was at stake was not a small matter of money. Hoby's intrusion was only an opening manoeuvre in his ultimate attempt to supplant the Cholmleys as masters of the Liberty of Whitby Strand.[57]

While the Exchequer case was still being fought out, at the end of 1611 Hoby received from the Crown by letters patent a 21 year lease for 40 shillings a year of the stewardship of the Liberty of Whitby and Whitby Strand. He now had the sole right to hold courts throughout the Liberty, including the valuable right of returna brevium, the authority to serve, execute and return all writs and warrants within its boundaries.[58]

By Easter 1613 the Cholmleys had drawn up their final depositions for the Exchequer court. They contended that ever since 1557, when Sir Richard (II) had finally completed his purchase of Whitby, Whitby Laithes, Stainsacre, Hawsker and Fyling, the family had held the sole hereditary right to hold the manor and leet courts in these manors. As successors of the abbots of Whitby, who had been lords of the manors of Whitby and Whitby Strand, the Cholmleys were also lords of the whole Liberty of the wapentake of Whitby Strand. Moreover, they also pointed out that Sir Henry's father had compounded for the patent of steward of the Liberty at an annual fee to the Crown of £6 3s. 4d. and that his heirs still had exclusive rights to the stewardship.[59]

Hoby's claim was baseless, and he must have known it. At best, his jurisdictional rights were confined to the manor of Hackness, which Queen Elizabeth had granted to Robert Dudley, earl of Leicester, in 1563 and which in 1588 had been bought for Margaret Dakins and her first husband Walter Devereux. Hackness had never been anything more than "parcel" of the lands of Whitby abbey so that the Cholmleys had a stronger claim to jurisdiction in Hoby's territory than he had in theirs. Indeed, ever since 1557 the people of Hackness, Suffield, Silpho, Everley, Harwood Dale and Broxa had sent their constables and four men each year to the leet and manor courts of the Liberty as they had done before the Dissolution. Hoby was therefore strongly advised to withdraw his bill, but in his customary way he persisted with it stubbornly. To Lord Salisbury he appealed directly for support. The Lord Treasurer and Secretary of State was assured that Sir Thomas's purpose was not to secure Whitby Strand for himself but to recover it for the Crown![60]

Lord Salisbury died in April 1612, but even had he lived longer in office it is doubtful that he could have rescued Hoby. The barons of the Exchequer finally ruled in Cholmley's favour in November 1613. The Cholmleys were confirmed in their hereditary stewardship of the Liberty of Whitby Strand and awarded their exclusive, perpetual right to returna brevium throughout the Liberty, including the manor of Hackness. Sir Thomas was commanded to drop all his claims beyond the boundaries of Hackness. On the other hand, in compensation for the loss of the patent which the Crown should never have awarded him in 1611, Hoby received "a competent sum of lawful English money" from John Legard and Henry Trotter, acting for the Cholmley family. Finally, the two contending parties were told to be "loveing freinds and with all good respect each of them use and entrust each other at all tymes hereafter".[61]

If the barons of the Exchequer really believed that Hoby and the Cholmleys had settled their differences once and for all, they were soon disappointed and enlightened. The resentment on both sides was now too deep and sore for anything better than a temporary truce. As soon as one perceived an advantageous opportunity, he could not resist the urge to exploit it against the other.

In 1619 the pendulum swung decisively in Cholmley favour when the eleventh Lord Scrope, great-grandson of Catherine Clifford, Sir Henry Cholmley's mother, was appointed president of the Council of the North. Since the death of Lord Salisbury in 1612, Hoby had lacked a powerful government patron and protector; now a Cholmley relative, Sir Richard's "cosen jermyn half removed", was established in the seat of Northern authority at York. Sir Richard was so delighted and excited by the appointment that he rode 60 miles to Doncaster with a retinue of 20 of his own liveried servants to welcome Lord Scrope into Yorkshire. Having lived in private retirement for the past five years, he was keen to re-enter public affairs. Since the death of his father in 1616 he had become head of the Cholmley family.[62]

Sir Richard's optimism seemed well-founded: almost immediately he was raised to a place in the Council at York and made a deputy-lieutenant of the North Riding. Once again he resumed his role as justice of the peace, "the country finding a very great want of him", in the words of his son.[63] In January 1621, thanks to the lord president's "friendshippe and kindness", Sir Richard was returned as one of Scarborough's two Members of Parliament and took his family with him to live in London. Finally, three years later, after his eldest son, Hugh, had taken his Scarborough seat in the House of Commons, Sir Richard was appointed high sheriff of Yorkshire.[64]

Hoby's reaction to the new regime at York was predictably hostile. The previous president of the council there, Lord Sheffield, had suited Sir Thomas because he had taken a hard line against recusants, whereas Scrope was a notorious rake and a suspected papist. Hoby's antagonism was so outspoken that in July 1620 King James himself found it necessary to ask his Secretary to write to him that he should "behave becomingly towards the President". Nevertheless, Hoby was not to be silenced on a question that mattered more to him than any other. Three years later, he was still declaring in the Commons that Scrope's neglect of his duty had encouraged a great increase in the number of Yorkshire's recusants.[65]

Now rearmed with enlarged authority and influential allies, Sir Richard resumed the offensive against Hoby: in 1623 he brought new charges against him in Star Chamber. There was a back-log of old scores and festering grievances to be satisfied that dated from 1613 when Sir Thomas had briefly exercised his authority as bailiff of the Liberty of Whitby Strand. Sir Richard accused his neighbour of a variety of offences which had been at the expense of Cholmley officers and tenants. Least credibly, Sir Thomas was alleged to have taken deer from the royal forest of Pickering. Since it was well and widely known that Hoby condemned hunting of all kinds and took only fish from the river Derwent and that for generations the Cholmleys had been plundering the royal forest of game and timber, this particular accusation was abundantly false and hypocritical.[66]

As before, in 1609, Hoby defended himself with counter-attacks and as always previously there was mischief and malice on both sides of the argument. All the testimonies were corrupted by bias and special pleading. However, there was one charge brought by Sir Richard in this case that can be tested against the surviving evidence: that Hoby rarely attended North Riding sessions held at Malton, Thirsk, Richmond or Helmsley, but instead presided over special or "privy" sessions near to his home at Hutton Buscel or even in Hackness Hall. At these sessions, it was alleged, Hoby dispensed partial justice, in league with a fellow magistrate, Stephen Norcliffe, who was under his thumb.

In support of Sir Richard's contention, the North Riding court records show that throughout 1622 Hoby had not once sat on the bench at main quarter sessions, but had presided over "petty" sessions at Hutton Buscel and Hackness in April and October.[67] Though Sir Thomas gave ill-health and pressing personal business as excuses for his absence from the main court sessions, the true reason was probably that Sir Richard had returned to the bench after a prolonged absence. Not that Sir Richard's accusation in this matter was proof of Hoby's magisterial misbehaviour, but this episode does suggest that like many other justices at the time he used his office to suit his convenience and his interest. Not until 1630, by which time Sir Richard had retired, did Hoby return to his place as senior magistrate at North Riding quarter sessions.[68]

The outcome of this third Cholmley versus Hoby duel fought out in Star Chamber is not known. However, whatever the judicial ruling, as before, Hoby had the better of the argument. Far from being the innocent victim of "4 severall bills in the Starre chamber", as his son later wrote, Sir Richard himself had twice brought bundles of charges against his neighbour, most of them lacking convincing evidence.[69] Indeed, in his memoirs, Sir Richard's son, Hugh, betrayed the same prejudices against Hoby that had become a Cholmley addiction. No doubt aware that his father had been one of the group of outrageously guilty defendants in the Hackness scandal and the Star Chamber case that resulted from it, Hugh wrote not a word about either. Nor could he resist the temptation of implying that Hoby was incapable of producing an heir. In his first memoir reference to Sir Thomas he described him maliciously as "haveing a full purse noe children, and as it was thought not able to get one..." when he must have known that his wife was "barren". Though the memoirs were originally intended to remain within the privacy of the Cholmley family, their subsequent publication has established an uncomplimentary and largely unchallenged view of Sir Thomas as "a troblesome vexatious neighbour" who "delighted to spend his mony and tyme in sutes".[70]

Writing to a friend from his Whitby home in 1902, the distinguished local solicitor, George Buchannan, described Hoby as "one of those people. . . who are a curse to the countryside. He was a most determined litigant, and constantly at the game." These words read very much like an echo of Sir Hugh's "[he] delighted to spend his mony and tyme in sutes", written 250 years earlier.[71] Even today, more than a century after Buchannan's received verdict and the most thorough, scholarly investigation of his lifetime, Sir Thomas still suffers from historical misunderstanding and neglect. Though Lady Margaret has at last an entry in the *Oxford Dictionary of National Biography* (2004), her third husband was not considered important enough to be included; and to add injury to omission, the date of his death is wrongly given there as 1644 instead of 1640.[72]

Hoby was not an attractive person. It has been suggested that he was a real-life model for Shakespeare's Malvolio, though *Twelfth Night* was written just before the Hackness scandal became known in London. By nature, Sir Thomas was pompous, conceited, dictatorial, intolerant and abrasive. Even his own mother found him perverse. However, on the other hand, there is no evidence that Hoby was corrupt, lazy or incompetent. On the contrary, for 40 years, he took upon himself every kind of duty and responsibility. He was an immensely industrious and efficient public servant. Sir William Brereton, a contemporary puritan Member of Parliament for Cheshire, wrote in his Journal that Hoby was the most able justice of the peace in the kingdom.[73] Sir Thomas Wentworth, the future earl of Strafford, a fair judge of character and competence, thought that he "had good abilities and great experience", but tried to do too much by himself.[74] The truth is that Hoby's neighbourhood enemies, especially the Cholmleys, regarded his ceaseless activity as ambitious busybodying when much of it was no more than conscientious service. After all, Sir Thomas was a quintessential puritan who regarded idleness as sinful, a principle foreign and even insulting to his contemporary Cholmleys.

III "brought into debt"

Out of natural filial loyalty, Sir Hugh Cholmley was unwilling to criticise his dead father, Sir Richard (III) (1580-1631) too harshly: his only concession to the truth was that Richard had a violent temper, an "amerous humer" inherited from his grandfather, and that he entertained a middle-aged delusion that pewter could be transformed into gold.

Of Sir Richard's "hauty sperret and chollericke", Hugh gave only two examples in his memoirs which have both been quoted above: he nearly lost the offending hand after he had struck a gentleman in the court of Star Chamber and outside a London theatre he gave someone who had offended him "two or 3 gud blowes" when he would not fight a duel.[75]

As for Sir Richard's "amerous humer", we are not provided with details or examples except that like his father and his grandfather he sired far too many children for the well-being of his purse. Susannah Legard of Ganton, Richard's first wife, died in 1611, having borne four surviving children, Hugh, Margaret, Ursula and Henry. Two of her boys, Richard and John, died before their mother. Eighteen months after he lost Susannah, Richard married Margaret Cob. By his second wife, Richard had four sons, but only one, his namesake, reached manhood.[76] As for Sir Richard's extra-marital affairs, when challenged by his eldest son, he denied that they were "costly" in money terms. Hugh's own comment was that even if his father's philanderings were not financially burdensome, "wee may beleive that [they] diverted god Allmighty's blessings".[77]

Margaret Cholmley, Sir Richard's eldest daughter, "a very personable and beautifull woeman", was married to William Strickland of Boynton and cost her father a dowry of £2,000. Ursula, however, was probably a cheaper bride: she was married to a lesser husband, George Trotter of Skelton, a union that reinforced the blood ties between the Cholmleys and the Trotters.[78]

Susannah's premature death, when Hugh her first born was still only eleven years old, was just one of the many "crosse accydents" that happened to Sir Richard. According to Hugh, she was such "a very prudent discrett woeman" that her sudden departure threw all her husband's "domesticke affayres in to disorder" and forced him to break up his young family. Susannah had been not only a beautiful, religious and loving wife, Sir Richard had come to rely on her wisdom in "the mannageing of her husbands affayres booth domesticke and with out doores in his absence". Indeed, Hugh then went on to claim that if she had lived she would have prevented the sale of all those lands that occurred later and concluded, "soe that wee may see a virtuous wise woeman is a great support to a famuly". Though such a claim seems more sentimental than rational, it does imply that Sir Richard lacked the necessary skills and knowledge of an estate manager.[79]

After Sir Thomas Hoby, the worst of the "crosse accydents" that blighted Sir Richard's career was the succession to the presidency of the Council at York of Lord Scrope in 1619. Sir Richard came out of "his frugality and private liveing" into public display and extravagance which he could not afford. All of the offices secured for him by Scrope: member of the York Council, justice of the peace, deputy-lieutenancy, Member of Parliament for Scarborough and finally, in 1624, high sheriff of the county, proved expensive and unrewarding.[80] Sir Richard could not be rescued by political favouritism. Emanuel Scrope was just as bad an influence on him and his purse as George Clifford had once been on his father, Sir Henry. Though Sir Richard was seriously ill throughout most of 1621 and attended the Commons for only six days, he took his wife and family with him to London at ruinous expence. Only in January 1622, when ordered by the king to return home, did he take his household back to Whitby. Later, in 1624-5, being an unpaid high sheriff of Yorkshire proved a greater drain on his depleted resources and credit: according to his eldest son, the office cost him a thousand pounds.[81]

Also according to his son, Sir Richard's abrupt retirement from all his posts and public life altogether in 1626 was caused by his "great debt"; but the truth was darker. After the county election of 1625 for the first Parliament of Charles I, as returning officer sheriff Cholmley was accused of gross misconduct. More than one thousand of Yorkshire's freeholders entitled to a vote signed a petition which was presented to the

House of Commons when it first met in June. The petitioners complained about the manner in which Sir Thomas Wentworth and Sir Thomas Fairfax had been returned as knights of the shire. Sir Richard Cholmley was denounced as "wholly Wentworth's". He had closed the poll and locked the gates of York castle, the polling station, when he saw that the vote was going in favour of the Saviles, Sir John and his son, Sir Thomas. The allegations were so strong and so well supported that the Commons agreed to hold a full inquiry. Cholmley was given a fortnight to appear at Westminster to answer the charges against him.

Sir Richard came out of the affair very badly. He arrived in London two days late, failed to bring a single witness to speak on his behalf, and failed to convince the Commons that he had acted properly and impartially. His feeble excuse that he had closed the poll because the Saviles were trying to bring in unqualified apprentices was not accepted. Leader of the House, Sir John Eliot, said that little truth could be gathered from the sheriff's words and even less satisfaction from his person. Yorkshire's county election was therefore declared void and a new writ issued for August. Though Sir Richard was hardly vindicated by the result, this time Wentworth and Fairfax were returned with little opposition. This time Wentworth had taken the wise precaution of laying on "two hogsheads of wine and half a score of beer... within the castle [at York] for the freeholders". He explained that the voters would be "forced to stay long, to refresh themselves with this hot season"![82]

Sir Hugh's later version of these events was again coloured by filial loyalty. His explanation was that the first election had been invalidated not because the high sheriff had conducted it in such a one-sided way but because Sir John Savile was "an antient Parliament man and soe had many friends and acquaintance in the house". Sir Richard had not made a fool of himself at the Bar of the Commons: he "did soe well plead and answeare for himselfe and his deportment" that he "was quit, which is very raire in the like caise". Why it was thought necessary to have a re-election, Sir Hugh neglected to explain. Needless to say, he made no reference to the alcoholic treating which seems to have influenced the result of the second poll.[83]

Yet Sir Hugh was certainly right about one thing: by 1625 the Cholmley estate was virtually bankrupt. His father had continued to live imprudently beyond his shrinking means. The dowry of £2,000 he had received on behalf of his second wife was soon spent. In a vain effort to keep up with Lord Scrope, he had taken to breeding and racing horses, a very expensive investment. He had kept two or three horses "at Kiplincoates" and at other places for training and racing. His debts had grown to a staggering £12,000 and he was paying interest to money lenders at a rate of up to eleven per cent. He was borrowing even to finance his ordinary living costs.[84]

Moreover, though he was old enough to know better, Sir Richard was still "addicted to studdy the phylossopher stone". During his time in London he had taken into his home there a certain "cosen" called Mr Gascoine, who coined money out of him, claiming falsely that he could turn pewter into gold. Much later, Hugh found "a cancelled bond" whereby his father was to pay "one of that profession £200 for a secret". In retrospect, Hugh marvelled that his father, "one of the ablest and wisest gentlemen of his Country" could even at the age of 47, "when commonly men's judgements are ripest and grown more saige by exsperience", could "bee iugled by such a fopery and delusion". Fortunately, Hugh was not taken in by such fantasies, but excused his father because he was so desperate to restore his solvency.[85]

By 1625 Sir Richard's debts had become so heavy that income from his estate rents of only eight or nine hundred pounds a year was insufficient to pay even the interest he owed to scriveners.[86] Out of necessity to raise ready money, like his father had done before, Richard continued to sell parts of his entailed estate on long leases. In 1621, for instance, Normanby Hall, a capital messuage with 15 attached closes, was sold to Christopher Newton, the Whitby merchant, for £560. A few weeks later, five messuages with cottages and garths in Hawsker went to their yeomen tenants for £845. These sums had helped to keep the creditors at bay, but it was only a matter of time before Sir Richard was faced with foreclosure on properties that were heavily mortgaged.[87] His year in office as Yorkshire's high sheriff seems to have loaded the last straw onto an overburdened account.

When he had been about 56 years old, in 1611, Sir Henry had retired with his wife Margaret to the city of York. He left his eldest son to take on the estate, carry its debts and raise portions or dowries for his daughters; but it was not until Sir Henry's death five years later as a result of a fall from his horse "at the leape of a hedge", that Richard inherited the whole family estate.[88] Ten years later still, in 1626, Sir Richard followed his father's precedent, though instead of York he chose the house at Whitby as his retirement home. He kept an income of £400 a year for himself and his family and his eldest son acquired responsibility for a hugely encumbered inheritance.[89]

CHAPTER 3

HUGH (I)

I "gods great providence"

Hugh Cholmley, the eldest son of Richard and Susannah Legard of Ganton, was born in the Cholmley family home, Roxby castle, on 22 July 1600. He was baptised five days later in the nearby parish church of Thornton, now known as Thornton-le-Dale. Hugh was fortunate to have survived at all: his hired wet-nurse could not feed him and he was first suckled by his grandmother, Dame Margaret, who then had a six-month-old baby of her own.[1]

Later in life Hugh was able to convince himself that this difficult start had rendered him a weak and sickly child and robbed him of the tall and sturdy stature of his male Cholmley ancestors. If properly nourished as a newly-born he would have been "as able a man of body as most in the Nation". Not that he attached any blame to his own mother: it was not the usual custom of Cholmley mothers to breast-feed their babies; the fault lay with the dishonest and incapable wet-nurse who was pregnant and did not confess it.[2]

Lady Margaret's prompt, life-saving intervention proved to be only the first of many timely acts of "providence", an explanation which Sir Hugh offered for all his lucky escapes from premature death or mutilation. If we are to believe his later recollections, his infancy was a succession of miraculous escapes, so that in retrospect he came to believe that God had chosen him to serve some vital purpose.

At the age of three, Hugh was saved "by gods providence" from falling out of the great chamber casement on the upper floor of Roxby castle by a quick-acting servant who was waiting on his grandfather at dinner. Perhaps Hugh had been left in the care of a young and inexperienced maid servant, since Thornton's parish register records the burial on 6 March 1603 of "the old nurse of Roxbye".[3]

When Hugh was seven years old he fell off his horse under the galloping hooves of another, yet thanks to "gods protection" only his hat was crushed.[4] On his eighth birthday he was again rescued by "gods great providence", this time in the form of his father's butler. On this occasion young Hugh was staying with Sir Richard at his Whitby home on East Cliff when "out of folly and waggery" he playfully kicked one of a litter of sleeping piglets outside the kitchen door. Hearing the commotion, their mother, "a great fearce sow", advanced on Hugh, seized him by the leg, dragged him ten yards across the courtyard, and bit him in the groin. Fortunately, the family butler was then passing through the hall with a glass of beer for Sir Richard, heard the boy's cries, and came to his deliverance as the sow was about to pass from Hugh's groin to his throat.[5]

By the age of ten Hugh had survived measles and three attacks of smallpox. He was also subject to "agues and sicknes" which he thought were caused by "the bad nourishment" of his nurse's milk when she was with child. Then, when he was still only eleven and now boarding at Beverley free grammar school, Hugh was struck down by "a feaver then rife in the country". He was so dangerously ill that he was taken into her home by Lady Jane Hotham, a distant relative, who lived at nearby Scorborough, and his mother came down from Whitby to nurse him there. However, though Hugh made a full recovery, his mother did not: she caught the fever and soon died of it.[6]

This narrative of accident and illness illustrates that even the wealthy and privileged such as young Hugh Cholmley, eldest son and heir, were then vulnerable to both, though perhaps not as much as their less fortunate contemporaries. In their study of eight parishes during the years 1550 to 1649, the demographic historians Wrigley and Schofield, calculated that as many as a quarter of all children there died before they reached the age of ten.[7] Hugh's own catalogue of injury, disease and close encounters with mortality also explains why he should have come to regard himself as someone blessed with divine protection. Even when it included the tragic death of his "very fond and indulgent mother" whom he "loved dearly", Hugh never questioned that "providence" had singled him out for special favour.[8] And in this matter Hugh's assumption was far from unique or even unusual at that time. Many of his contemporaries convinced themselves that their recovery from fatal illnesses or survival on the battlefield were divinely ordained.[9]

II "youthful follies"

Many of the sons of Yorkshire's Jacobean gentry went to "free" grammar schools, day or boarding. They were "free" of fees to local boys, but not to out of town "foreigners", like Hugh. North and east Yorkshire were particularly well-served at this time by a number of such schools, notably at Giggleswick, Coxwold, Pocklington, Ripon and St Peter's, York. The nearest of them to Whitby or Thornton was at Scarborough, but that town's High School would have been ruled out by the Cholmleys because it suffered from the puritanical dominance of Sir Thomas Hoby of Hackness, who insisted on appointing its teachers.[10] Beverley free grammar school was the Cholmley choice because it had a good reputation, close connections with Cambridge university and was not far from Scorborough, the home of the Hothams.

There was a well-established link between Hugh's mother's family, the Legards of Ganton, and the Hothams of Scorborough. Susannah's cousin, Jane Legard, had become John Hotham's third and last wife in 1584, and she long outlasted her husband, living on as a wealthy widow at Scarborough until 1620. Hugh's own parents had been married in 1596 at "Mr Hothams house at Scorborough".[11] Some evidence of the regard for the Ganton Legards is to be found in Jane's will of 1620. To Susannah's brother, John, Hugh's uncle, she left a ruby ring and to his son and her godson of the same name, she bequeathed "a King Edward's 20 shilling piece".[12]

Hugh's arrival at Beverley had been well-timed. The new schoolhouse there had just been built. At a cost of £155 4s. 2d. to the town, it had taken four years to finish a fine brick building with tiled roof and freestone surrounds to its casement windows. Moreover, Hugh was also fortunate to be a pupil at Beverley when "Mr Pettie", as he wrote of him, was its grammar school headmaster. William Petty was a distinguished classical scholar, teacher and Cambridge graduate. With a stipend of £10 a year, plus free board and lodging, Petty's appointment dated from Lady day, 1608.[13]

It seems that the headmaster developed a particular liking for young Hugh and regarded him as a most promising student "apt to learn", so that when he was awarded a fellowship at Jesus College, Cambridge, he took the boy with him. However, when he went up to Cambridge at Michaelmas 1613, Hugh was then only 13 years and three months old and, in his own later words, not then "well fitt ether for learneing or yeares".[14]

Jesus College at Cambridge owed its original foundation to Bishop John Alcock, who had been a schoolboy at Beverley Minster in the middle of the fifteenth century. After its incorporation by Elizabethan charter in 1573, the town of Beverley had regularly endowed scholarships, exhibitions or sizarships at Jesus and at other Cambridge colleges for its grammar school boys. Several of these boys were studying at Cambridge when Hugh went up there. However, Hugh was not a scholarship student: at the age of 13 he was too young and also as the son of a "foreign" gentleman he would not have qualified for one of Beverley's bursaries worth 40 shillings a year. Hugh was a fee-paying Fellow-Commoner whose presence as a student at Jesus College was the result of William Petty's favour and his own social status and his father's money.

Though rather young for university matriculation, Hugh would not have been out of place at Cambridge. His grandfather Henry had spent four years there and his father Richard had been at Trinity until the age of sixteen.[15] In Hugh's own time it was the custom for Yorkshire's gentlemen to send their young sons to Cambridge: of the 172 of them in 1642 who had received some university education, as many as 134 had spent some of their youth at a Cambridge college.[16] So even without Petty's influence, Hugh might well have gone up to Cambridge, though probably to a different college and at a later time. It seems most unlikely that Sir Richard would have allowed his eldest son to enter one of Cambridge's "Puritan" colleges that did so much to form the religious outlook of so many of Hugh's contemporary relatives and gentry neighbours. Hugh's brother-in-law, William Strickland of Boynton, Hugh Bethell of Alne, Philip Stapleton of Warter and Henry Slingsby of Red House were all Queens' men; and Christopher Yelverton of Easton Mauduit in Northamptonshire, who was destined, like Hugh, to marry one of the daughters of William Twysden of Kent, was also at Queens'. Another "Puritan" college, Emmanuel, admitted Sir William's eldest son, Roger, and his younger brother, Thomas, at the same time in November 1614; but Hugh was to find his kind of puritanism from other sources.[17]

In fact, young Hugh's experiences at Cambridge were far from religious or uplifting: on the contrary. He spent four years at Jesus, but the College registers date only from 1618 after he had gone down, so that we have little official record of his presence there. There are only three references to him in the bursar's book: in 1613 he paid his caution money and in 1614 and 1615 he settled his bills for his commons of bread and beer.[18] As usual, the only source of personal detail is to be found in Hugh's own memoirs written down more than forty years later. Here he recorded that at Jesus he was placed in the care of another Beverley boy, three years his senior. At that time it was customary to put a pair of Fellow-Commoners, one elder and one junior, together in the same rooms, particularly if they were related like the Twysden brothers. In Hugh's case, however, the senior "guardian", though "a gud scholler and witty man", was also "given to drinkeing and debaushed us all". In his manuscript, Sir Hugh named the College corrupter as "Thomson", but neither of the editors of the publications of 1787 or 1870 chose to print the name.

During Hugh's years at Jesus there are at least two candidates for the title of College tippler. Marmaduke Thompson was a Beverley boy who eventually became a Fellow of Jesus, but he matriculated only one year, not three, before Hugh. He was born near Beverley, took a Master of Arts degree in 1618 and became a Bachelor of Divinity in 1627. After ten years as a Fellow of Jesus he became rector of Harlton, a village near Cambridge. The other possible culprit was Peter Tomson. He fits Hugh's chronology better because he matriculated at Jesus in 1609. Like Marmaduke, Peter was a Yorkshireman who went into the church: he was ordained deacon at York in 1614 and priest in 1617.[19]

According to Hugh's own account, Mr Petty failed in his duty to protect his young pupil from "deboshery". Though he continued to hold his College Fellowship until as late as 1624, long before then he had abandoned his Cambridge students for a far more lucrative and exciting post: Petty became the private tutor and travelling ward to the eldest son of the earl of Arundel.[20] In Greece, Italy and Turkey, Petty collected antiquities for the earl's own private collection and for several years he was professor of Greek letters in Athens. Perhaps out of a sense of guilt for neglecting and deserting his Beverley boys, when he died in 1639 Petty left £200 to his old College. Unfortunately, the dishonesty of his executors ensured that the money never found its way to Jesus.[21]

Still, Arundel's gain was also young Hugh Cholmley's gain. When Petty departed from Cambridge he left his pupils in the care of Thomas Slater, Fellow of Jesus from 1613 until his death in 1628.[22] Slater seems to have been a better guardian than his predecessor. Even though his new tutor could be expected only "to reade" to him, Sir Richard told his son that, in the absence of Petty, Hugh would have to act more responsibly in future. He gave Hugh £30 in gold and told him to look after it and improve his behaviour. Consequently, though Hugh still preferred "all sports and recreations" to books, at least he quit his drinking companions. So, in this roundabout way, Petty's new appointment might have been "prejudetiall" to Hugh's "schollershippe and learneing", initially and indirectly it rescued him from moral disaster. Since he was protected by "gods providence", all Hugh's black clouds had silver linings.[23]

Though he would not have been pleased with the comparison, Hugh Cholmley's experience of Cambridge had several points in common with that of his more famous contemporary, Oliver Cromwell. Oliver was 15 months older than Hugh when he went up to Sidney Sussex College two days short of his seventeenth birthday and was there for little more than a year. Like Hugh, however, he was a gentleman's eldest son and a Fellow-Commoner who seems to have preferred physical to intellectual exercise. It was probably after one of these boisterous sports, to which Oliver was also addicted at Cambridge, that Hugh nearly died of pleurisy, "contracted by a surfett in takeing cold and drinkeing when [he] was hott."[24] Both Hugh and Oliver left their adjacent colleges in 1617 without taking a degree and as a direct result of a death in the family. Immediately after the death of his father, Cromwell went back to Huntingdon, whereas Cholmley returned to Yorkshire on the death of his grandfather. Sir Henry, who was "much given to the pleasure of hunting and esspetially with fleet hounds", had taken a heavy fall from his horse "at the leape of a hedge". By this time Hugh's grandfather was a "corpulent" man in his late fifties and was so "bruised" by the accident that it caused his death. So Hugh went home to his father who was now head of the family and spent his eighteenth year under his supervision.[25]

Not that Sir Richard was any better influence on his son than "Thomson" had once been. The year was spent "in hunting, hawkeing and horses rases", which later an older and wiser Hugh decried as "vaine chargeable sports". Looking back 40 years later on his "wasted" youth, Sir Hugh advised parents not to allow their sons "to game" but instead train them "in such courses as is [sic] fitt for them to practise when they comes to be a man".[26]

Yet in fairness to Sir Richard, his eldest son was given every opportunity to improve himself and to prepare for future responsibilities. To complete his education, just before Christmas 1618, Hugh was sent up to Gray's Inn in London. Here again he was following a well-trodden route taken by young Yorkshire gentlemen of his generation. Membership of one of the London Inns of Court was then considered the normal conclusion of a gentleman's training for adult duties and public affairs. Though he might have been the first of the Cholmleys at Gray's, the Yelverton and the Twysden men were all there;[27] and of the 160 or so Yorkshiremen who served as magistrates in the three Ridings between 1625 and 1640, more than 90 of them had some legal tuition at one of the London Inns.[28] Usually there was no intention that such gentlemen would make a career of the law: it was assumed that basic knowledge of legal procedures would be relevant to the management of an estate and the performance of offices such as deputy-lieutenants and justices of the peace.

Nevertheless, Hugh threw away this last chance to redeem himself: London's "bowleing grounds and gameing houses" saw much more of him than Gray's library or lecture hall. Looking back on these three "totally misspent" years of his life, Sir Hugh deeply regretted his failure to acquire "but a smackereing [smattering] of the law", knowing how such knowledge would have served him advantageously when he came to be a Member of Parliament and a magistrate. In this matter he was probably mindful of the brilliance of his brother-in-law, Sir Roger Twysden, whose outstanding legal career was founded firmly on his studies at Cambridge and Gray's; and perhaps also of the humiliations he might have avoided when first he encountered Sir Thomas Posthumous Hoby on the North Riding Bench.[29]

While still at Gray's, Hugh again came perilously close to death. For a very sore throat caused by infected tonsils, his physician recommended "mercury water". As other doctors later told him, such "medicine" was much more likely to kill than to cure, and it took ten weeks for him to recover "by gods blessing". Hugh "quit" Gray's after three years there and took lodgings in Fleet Street. Now there seemed no point even pretending to be a law student. He "lived at large all the winter [of 1621-2] about the towne", continuing to misspend his time and money bowling and gambling, "though for other exstraviganses [he] was temperate". What form these "other exstraviganses" might have taken, Sir Hugh did not say.[30]

III Marriage

Just before he left Gray's, Hugh was introduced by a Kentish friend to a young lady from his county whom they met by chance in Hyde Park. At the time he remembered only that he "liked her well", unaware that "the suppreame wisdome who orders all things and disposeth all things" had determined that soon she would become his wife.[31] In this particular case, "the suppreame wisdome" was that of Sir Richard

Cholmley and Sir William Twysden, father of bridegroom and bride, who arranged the marriage settlement.

Sir William gave Sir Richard a dowry for Elizabeth, his eldest daughter, of £2,500 "in redy mony paid in one day before marridge" and security for another £500 at the end of six months. In return, Elizabeth received from her father-in-law as jointure "lands vallewed to £500 per annum but worth above six". On Hugh himself, his father settled his estate, valued at £2,700 a year, but probably worth more according to his son's later assessment. Both parties seemed satisfied with this arrangement and subsequently fulfilled all its terms.[32]

On the face of it, initially the marriage appeared too "arranged" and merely financial. The couple seemed ill-suited. Hugh was a dissolute play-boy Northerner with little to commend him. His father and grandfather had dissipated their inherited, landed estate, which was still extensive but now encumbered with crippling debt. The Twysdens were by no means rich, but they were in a league above the Cholmleys in learning, manners and culture.

A few points of comparison between the two families in 1622 describe the gulf between them. Set in the garden of Kent, amongst its orchards and hop fields, the Twysden home at Roydon Hall at East Peckham was a long way and a far cry from Abbey House on Whitby's bleak, windswept East Cliff. Roydon Hall was badly damaged by a fire in the 1870s and largely rebuilt afterwards, yet enough of the original Tudor mansion still survives to indicate what a fine house it must have been when Hugh knew it. The first date of 1535 can be seen above the entrance doorway on the north side. Even from that time Roydon Hall was built entirely of brick and stone with mullioned windows and crow-stepped gables. About 1600 Sir William had added an entrance porch with flanking Tuscan columns. To the south and west of the Hall were spacious, terraced gardens. When Roydon was assessed for the hearth tax in 1662 it was said to have had 30 chimneys.[33]

After living with his new wife's family at their home in Kent, Hugh must have been aware of and embarrassed by the inferiority of the Cholmley home at Whitby. Even as late as the 1620s, when he first brought Elizabeth and their two young sons to live there, Abbey House was then little more than an assortment of adjacent, former monastic out-buildings, grouped around a primitive timber and thatched house built by Francis Cholmley in the 1580s. Not until the 1630s did Hugh have the means to put up a stone house on the site with surroundings to match the domestic standards the Twysdens had taken for granted during the past century. For several years Hugh and Elizabeth had to make do with the monastery gatehouse. Roxby castle, where he had been born and his great grandfather had resided in such pompous power, had become too expensive to maintain and was allowed to decay.[34] A further contrast between the two families was that whereas the Twysden house in London's Redcross Street was, in Hugh's words, "soe gud a house as few gentlemen in the towne had the like, and bravely furnished", Sir Richard could not afford a house in the capital when he attended the House of Commons.[35]

Socially, also, the Cholmleys and the Twysdens were worlds apart. Sir William was more than a notch or two above Sir Richard. He was a Cambridge graduate and had studied law at Gray's Inn. In 1591 he had married Anne, daughter of Sir Moyle Finch of Eastwell and his wife Elizabeth, who was subsequently the viscountess of Maidstone and first countess of Winchilsea. Lady Anne Twysden, Hugh's mother-in-law, had been brought up in the royal court of Queen Elizabeth and in his eyes she appeared a very grand lady. Sir William had been knighted in 1603 by James I and in 1611 he was one of only eight Kent baronets who paid £1,000 for the newly-created title. By that time he was already a veteran Member of Parliament, sat on the Kent county commission of peace, and served as captain of light horse in the local militia. But it was probably Sir William's scholarship rather than his public status that impressed his son-in-law the most. At Roydon Hall, Sir William had collected an extraordinary private library of books and manuscripts bought during the past 40 years. According to his eldest son, Roger, "his learning lay much in the Hebrew text, in which he had few his equal of any condition what so ever'. And he was not only a Hebrew scholar of rare distinction: Sir William was also said to be especially well informed in palmistry, physiogmony and astronomy. To quote his eldest daughter's husband, he was "a very great scholler".[36]

In his later years, Sir William became a Puritan. Sir Roger later recorded that his father "took more pleasure in reading the Bible" than he himself found reading well-written history.[37] To what extent Sir William's religiosity derived from his wife's influence cannot be said, but Lady Anne certainly exercised a powerful affect on her son-in-law. Given Hugh's family background and his experience of the bitter feud with the Hobys, puritanism would have had only distasteful associations for him. Childless, plain, austere and vindictive, Lady Margaret Hoby was hardly an attractive advertisement for her Puritan outlook and way of life. In the greatest contrast, however, Lady Anne was beautiful in looks and manners, courtly, aristocratic and good natured, yet also extremely pious and extraordinarily prudish. Hugh described her as "that thrise noble lady". Her own son wrote that she was "wonderfully religious, pious, virtuous" and added that "she was so chast[e] as she was by many held too curious". According to her own rule, no woman should allow herself to be alone with a man in the same room, unless he was her husband or the doors were open. Hugh was in awe of her: he had never encountered a high-born lady with so much beauty, virtue and meticulous, exquisite manners. As he later wrote, "I must professe I never did know any woeman her parell in all points".[38]

Sir Roger Twysden was another good influence on Hugh in other ways. Though three years older than Hugh, he was still educating himself in 1622. After several years at St Paul's school in London, he had gone up to Emmanuel College at Cambridge in November 1614, along with his younger brother, Thomas, who was then only twelve. Though he did not take a degree, unlike Hugh he was a sober, hard-working, conscientious student, who inherited his father's love of learning and books.[39]

Less than two months after his sister's wedding, at the beginning of February 1623, Sir Roger (he had been knighted in 1620) was admitted to the Honourable Society of Gray's Inn. Again, unlike Hugh, Roger made the utmost of his legal training and was soon to put it to good use when his father's death made him solely responsible for the Tywsden family and its estate in January 1629. Roger's example of prudent living and careful, detailed management of his inheritance were eventually to rub off on to Hugh Cholmley.[40]

However, there can be little doubt that the best and strongest influence on Hugh came from his bride, Elizabeth Twysden. Their marriage had been pre-arranged when they had seen each other only once before and their backgrounds and values were much more than 300 miles apart. Yet it seems that they fell in love with each other after the ceremony at a church in Milk Street, London on 10 December 1622. From then on they were rarely parted except by circumstances beyond their control. They enjoyed each other's company. Unlike his male forebears, Hugh had no need for extra-marital relations. The couple were to suffer many disappointments and painful tragedies, yet none of them weakened the bedrock of their happiness together. When Elizabeth died at the age of 55 having borne six of Sir Hugh's children, he lost interest in his own future. His one remaining wish was to dedicate a memoir to her memory. For these reasons, therefore, 10 December 1622 was the most decisive day in Hugh Cholmley's adult life.

IV "burgess for Scarbrough"

For the first few years of their marriage, Hugh and Elizabeth lived on her dowry and the generous hospitality of her father, Sir William. During the winters they usually lived in the Twysden town house in Redcross Street and in the summer they moved down to Roydon Hall. Nevertheless, their first child, Richard, was born at Redcross Street in June 1624 and their second, William, at Roydon Hall in December 1625.[41] Both births were difficult and dangerous to their mother. Elizabeth was so weak after Richard was born that "for neare 6 monthes together she could not move from her bed to the pallett" [toilet?] and Hugh had to carry her there in his arms. Richard was taken to the village of Wateringbury near East Peckham, but his wet-nurse "was neare forty and her milk was almost two yeares old". For William's birth, Elizabeth's labour came suddenly and unexpectedly and the midwife "could scarse get [to] her in tyme."[42]

If such growing family responsibilities were not enough for such a young man, in February 1624 Hugh was elected to sit in the House of Commons as one of the burgess representatives for Scarborough. As Hugh described the event with more precision: "my father haveing procured mee to bee chosen Burgess for Scarbrough".[43]

As so often elsewhere in his memoirs, Hugh's selective memory flattered his father. Though Sir Richard had previously occupied one of Scarborough's seats in the Parliament of 1621-2, that borough's patronage then belonged to Lord Scrope, not to him. It was Scrope's authority, as president of the Council at York, that had secured the borough place for Sir Richard and then for his son. As his father had done before him, Hugh shared the representation of Scarborough in the Commons with Mr William Conyers, one of a local family with mercantile and legal connections in the city of London. There was no suggestion that young Hugh would derive any financial or political profit from a Commons place, though since he then lived in the capital at least he would be spared the extra expense incurred by his father when he had been a Member. In the event, this Parliament was the last of the reign of king James: within a little more than a month he was dead and the Parliament dissolved.

Hugh's election in 1624 might have been the beginning of a long parliamentary career. His seat at Scarborough was safe, at least as long as Lord Scrope was Lord President. Charles the First's new Parliament was as brief as the last of his father's: opening on 18 June 1625 it was dissolved exactly two months later, after plague in London had forced its removal to Oxford.[44] Hugh had again been chosen by Scarborough's corporate ruling body of 44, only this time his partner was William Thompson, godfather of the town's most powerful family. The Thompsons were then at loggerheads with Hoby, so Cholmley would have been happy to have an ally as the other Member; and when Charles called his second Parliament early in 1626, Hugh was joined by another of Hoby's antagonists, Stephen Hutchinson of Wykeham Abbey. This was the same Stephen Hutchinson who had been one of the perpetrators of the Hackness scandal in 1600 and was still paying for his rashness like all the others. So again Hugh would have been pleased with his new partner.

There is no evidence, either officially in the records of the House of Commons or personally in Hugh's own later recollections, that he played any significant part in the parliamentary politics of the years 1624 to 1626. However, his early experience of Westminster and its ways must have been a useful apprenticeship for when he returned to the House, though in very different circumstances, in 1640.

Hugh's parliamentary narrative came to an abrupt halt in 1626 when in June Charles ended his second attempt to raise taxation. When the king called a third parliament two years later, Hugh did not offer himself for re-election at Scarborough; he now had other, more pressing matters to attend. Following the closure of the Oxford parliament in the summer of 1625, Hugh had made a special journey north to see his father in Yorkshire. Sir Richard was now overwhelmed by rising debts and oppressed by increasingly impatient creditors. Father and son agreed that they would have to sell part of the estate and Hugh offered to "goe for a while beyond sea" if this would persuade their creditors "to forbeare sewing their bond". Accordingly, Hugh returned south to be present at the birth of his second son in December 1625.[45]

At this critical point in Hugh's lifetime, the chronology of his memoirs is somewhat confused. However, it seems that in the spring of 1626, after his re-election at Scarborough, he had secured a permit to travel to France, presumably to escape from his creditors. Then, as he was about to leave Roydon Hall, he received what he later described as "a passionate letter" from Sir Richard imploring him to come to Whitby. Subsequently, Hugh regarded this "just in time" intervention as yet another example of "gods great providence": if he had left the country and gone abroad, leaving his father to carry on alone, this "would have occationed great disorder if not ruine to the esstate". About May 1626 Hugh rode north to Whitby to undertake the "business" of his father's debts and save the Cholmley inheritance from imminent extinction.[46]

CHAPTER 4

"DEBTS, VAST & INSUPPORTABLE"

In May 1626, at Whitby, Hugh came to an arrangement with his father, Sir Richard: he would take over control of the Cholmley estate; his father would remain in Abbey House with his second wife, Margaret, and their children, and live on an allowance of £400 a year; and Hugh, Elizabeth and their two boys would move into the adjacent Abbey Gatehouse.[1]

Still only 25 years old, Hugh had suddenly succeeded to his family inheritance, but the prospect held little promise. Up to this moment, his personal achievement was negligible: as yet he had done nothing to show that he could manage his own life and family let alone an estate of more than 20,000 acres burdened with colossal debt. As yet he seemed no more responsible than his father and grandfather had been. His educational opportunities had been privileged and prolonged, yet he had wasted them in idleness and dissipation. His knowledge of the law was superficial. Not even marriage, parenthood and a seat in the House of Commons seem to have converted him to a life in keeping with his income and assets. He was still gambling, and even more recklessly than ever. His own personal debts amounted to six or seven hundred pounds. During the past three years he had been living at the expense of his Twysden in-laws, but now even Elizabeth's considerable dowry had been exhausted. Only his father's desperate summons had diverted him from running away to France.[2]

Nevertheless, faced with this urgent and crucial responsibility, Hugh responded with positive determination. From now on he allowed himself few pleasures or diversions; he gave up gambling and withdrew from public life. After carrying out his duties as Scarborough's representative in the second parliament of Charles I, he did not offer himself as a candidate for the third in 1628.[3] He kept out of local politics and gave Hoby a wide berth. The recovery of Cholmley solvency and the rescue from foreclosure of his burdened estate were now Hugh's overriding priorities.

Of course this was the version of events that Hugh Cholmley's later autobiography would have his readers believe: that on suddenly succeeding to his inheritance, like Prince Hall in Shakespeare's *Henry IV,* he was transformed almost overnight into Shakespeare's *Henry V,* and that every improvement thereafter was his doing. And since Cholmley's memoirs were the principal and often the only source of evidence for what followed after he took over the family estate, his self-approving gloss has never been seriously doubted or even questioned. On the contrary, in account after account, Sir Hugh Cholmley has been celebrated as Whitby's greatest benefactor, who not only saved his estate but gave prosperity and security to his home town after a century of decay.

Stretching from Sandsend in the north to Ravenscar and Hackness in the south and inland to the tops of the North York Moors, the Cholmley estate in Whitby Strand was still largely intact in 1626. In Hugh's own later words, only "2 oxgangs that antiently belonged to [the] Allatsons and the higher Normanby before my marridge sold to Newton" had been lost from "the great extent of land ... from Stoope brow to Whitby Abbey".[4] Though here Hugh forgot to include his father's sale of Hawsker properties in 1621, his generalisation was broadly true. However, most of this Cholmley land was moor, fit only for sheep grazing and of poor quality and low value. Also, most of the farmland yielded much less than its real income because it was out on lease for 14 or 15 years at low, fixed rent. In practice, therefore, though Sir Richard believed that his estate was really worth £2,700 a year, he was the only one who did. In fact, the Cholmley lands brought in no more than £1,500 a year and of that £700 or £800 was raised directly from demesne revenues.[5] Living on fixed income in a time of price inflation was a certain recipe for ruin even for thrifty spenders.

The obvious solution was to sell. Yet here again there were formidable obstacles. Most of the Cholmley lands in the manors of Whitby and Fyling were charged with the jointures of Hugh's wife, step-mother and grandmother and were therefore "not soe vendable". Moreover, looking back from the vantage point of 30 years later, Hugh contended that "the fall of the prisces of all guds at the tyme" meant that purchasers with ready money could not be easily found during the depression of the 1620s.[6]

Sir William Twysden had his own financial difficulties and would not or could not help his son in-law any more: he gave him up "for ruined". Even Hugh's close friend and uncle, John Legard of Ganton, could not be persuaded that the Cholmley lands were worth more than their current income. So for deliverance Hugh had "to rely meerely on gods providence and direction" and his "owne witts".[7] Meanwhile the pressure from creditors was steadily increasing and they were threatening to sue him and his father for their outstanding bonds.

Hugh's first move, in his own words, was "to bye in two statues of £500 a peece the greatest in cumberance on the land, and put them in friends hands I could commaund".[8] In fact, here his memory was faulty with the figures: these two "statues" were debts of a thousand pounds each owed to two London scriveners or money-lenders, Robert Harrison and John Betts. Harrison accepted £564 in settlement of his bond and Betts £568 for his. The former was bought by Hugh's uncle, Henry Wickham, archdeacon of York, who had married Annabella Cholmley, the youngest of Sir Richard's sisters; and the latter was purchased by John Legard, his mother's brother.[9] Though Hugh expressed gratitude to his uncle John, he made no reference in his memoirs to Henry Wickham's contribution.

At about the same time, John Legard and "that unfortunate but noble gentleman, Sir John Hotham" of Scorborough, together stood surety for "some of the most importunate debts to the vallew of £2,500", while Hugh himself tried to maximise the financial yield of his estate by letting out demesne to rent-paying tenants or selling it on long-term leases to sitting tenants. So that, "in the very nicke of tyme" when he was "in the greatest plounge for monyes", a necessary amount of ready cash was raised to save the estate from foreclosure. By September 1631 when his father died, Hugh was left with a manageable debt of about £4,000, about a third of what he had inherited five years previously.[10]

The documentary evidence that has survived for these five busy years shows that Hugh raised nearly £3,500 in cash by land sales. As early as June 1626, the Cholmleys sold 240 acres in Robin Hood's Bay and Fyling Bottoms for £1,020 to John Halsey, fishmonger and citizen of London. Clearly, there was money to be made selling fish, if not catching it. The following October, George Conyers, John Farside and Jacob Boyes paid the Cholmleys £120 for houses, shops and land in Fyling and Whitby town. In February 1627, George Conyers, a well-to-do gentleman farmer of Fyling Hall, bought two farms in Fyling, Cockerill's and Belt's, for £337. Next month, eight farms, covering 316 acres in Hawsker were released for £915 and the following August, for £600, the Cholmleys sold a messuage and four oxgangs of arable in Fyling to Henry Fairfax. The purchaser was rector of Ashton under Lyne, a younger son of Sir Thomas Fairfax of Denton in Wharfedale, and the husband of Mary Cholmley, one of the seven daughters of the late Sir Henry Cholmley.[11]

Further sales of houses, land and closes in Hawsker, Fylingthorpe and Fyling Raw, the largest for £270, took place in the summers of 1628 and 1629. Such transactions were of various kinds, but usually they were valid for a thousand or even two thousand years and included a peppercorn annual rent such as twopence, a penny at the Feast of St Martin the bishop and another at "Pentecoste called Whit Sunday". Often the purchaser was a Cholmley tenant; but sometimes they were outsiders such as Richard Dutchman, a weaver of Hackness, who bought a house and closes in Hawsker. In all cases, however, they required a downpayment in money to the Cholmleys who retained the freehold and lordship rights.[12]

The large sums of money handed over in some transactions, such as the £270 paid by John Harton, a yeoman of Wykeham, for Poskitt's farm in Fyling Raw, indicate that some farming land in the locality was profitable. For instance, Peter Dale, described first as a farmer and then as a yeoman of Robin Hood's Bay, made a cash payment of £96 to the Cholmleys and later £100 in five yearly instalments of £20 to John Halsey, the London fishmonger. Later, Dale moved to Wapping in Middlesex to become a "victualler" there.[13] So there was money to be made from farming as well as fishing in Robin Hood's Bay.

During these critical five years while Hugh "rescued" the Cholmley estate, he at first lived with his wife Elizabeth and the two boys in the Abbey Gatehouse. It was there that their eldest daughter, Elizabeth or "Bette", was born and baptised in the nearby parish church on 29 October 1626.[14] Though Hugh was able to make some internal improvements to the Gatehouse, it was clearly too small for his growing family. Then, in August 1628, Hugh's sister Ursula died in childbirth, an event which upset him deeply and determined him to move out of Whitby for the time being. During the following year, Hugh made preparations to transfer his family to Fyling Hall, formerly the abbot of Whitby's hunting lodge set in his deer park. Here, on a seven-year lease, lived Hugh's tenant, George Conyers. Moving to Fyling Hall therefore proved an expensive financial burden: Hugh lost the £160 a year Conyers had paid in rent and he had to spend up to £800 repairing, extending and modernising the old house.[15]

The removal from gatehouse to lodge proved even costlier than Hugh could ever have imagined. The family lived in the "new built house" before the walls and plastering work were thoroughly dried out and, in retrospect, Hugh believed that these damp conditions had caused the death of his eldest son Richard as well as Bette's French nurse. The six-year-old boy developed "a defluction of Rume" during the winter of 1629-30 and when "a great filme" had blinded one of his eyes he was taken to an occulist at Nottingham. However, on the way there, at Ferrybridge, Richard "fell in to convoultions fitts and dyed". His body was brought back to York and buried in St John's, Micklegate, alongside his great grandfather, Sir Henry, and his great grandmother, Margaret, who had died in 1628.[16]

Richard's premature death was to be the first of a succession of blows. Hugh took his wife and two remaining children, William and Elizabeth, to winter in London (1630-1) and returned the following summer to Fyling Hall, leaving William behind with his grandmother, Lady Ann Twysden. At Whitby Hugh found his fifty-year-old father, Sir Richard, in poor health. Having eaten a "surfett of oysters" he had violent "looseness" which after several painful weeks "turned in to the bluddy flux". Richard died at Abbey House "in the chamber over the seller" and was buried, as he desired, in the chancel of Whitby church under a great blue stone where his grandmother had been placed about thirty years previously. Sir Richard's burial is recorded in the parish register for 23 September 1631.[17]

The next "great griefe" for Hugh and his wife was the death of their darling daughter Bette, which occurred early in 1632. Whether the damp, unhealthy living conditions of Fyling Hall were again to blame, her father did not say; but Bette's death was a hurtful blow to her parents. She was only four and a half years old, yet "as witty a child I thinke as was in the world of her age", according to her father. Though the parish register does not record the event, Bette was buried in the chancel of St Mary's near to the wall and next to her grandfather's monument there.[18]

The death of Elizabeth soon after that of her eldest brother Richard meant that the Cholmleys now had only one surviving son. However, "the lord who after the saddest and blackest stormes causeth the sunne beames to breake out" gave them joyful compensation: on 21 July 1632 their third son, Hugh, was born at Fyling Hall.[19] By this date Fyling Hall was much more spacious and comfortable than when George Conyers had lived in it. Describing his new son's baptism there, Hugh referred to "the great chamber" and the following year Lady Ann Twysden and her daughter-in-law, Isabella Sanders, wife of Sir Roger, spent several winter months as the Cholmleys' guests at the Hall.[20] Nevertheless, the departure of Sir Richard from Abbey House meant that sooner or later his heir would return to live in Whitby.

In fact, Sir Hugh's pressing need to raise money to pay off outstanding debts, purchase new properties and renovate Abbey House and its grounds obliged him to sell Fyling Hall and its adjacent park. In 1634 Sir John Hotham paid him £4,400 for the house and deer park that went with it. Fyling Hall itself was valued at £800 and the purchase price of its demesne land was fixed at 15 years for £240 annual rental. In 1622 the hunting lodge, its eight neighbouring farms and extensive, walled deer park were included in Elizabeth Twysden's marriage portion and then valued at £200 a year. Since Sir Hugh subsequently claimed to have invested at least £800 since 1629 renovating and extending the lodge, it seems that Hotham got a bargain.[21] Cholmley needed the cash and Sir John was never without a surplus of it.

The new properties which Sir Hugh tried to acquire in 1633 were the manors of Aislaby in Eskdale and Daletown in upper Ryedale. Neither had previously belonged to the Cholmleys, but he appreciated their potential value. Aislaby was his, however, for only six months before he was "outed" by the Howards who claimed it by marriage. He had to wait another 20 years before he could buy it. With Daletown he had better luck: he had to pay a high price for it but it proved a rewarding, long-term investment. Both Aislaby and Daletown were to feature prominently in Sir Hugh's last will.[22]

In the summer of 1634 the Cholmleys had moved out of Fyling Hall back to the Abbey Gatehouse at Whitby. It was there that Ann, their second daughter, was born. She was baptised in the parish church by the vicar, Mr Remington, 7 December 1634.[23] By the time that Abbey House had been made "fitt to receyve" the family in the spring of 1636 it had been wholly transformed.[24]

As Sir Hugh proudly explained in his later memoirs, the Abbey House he had inherited from his father "was very ruinous and unhandsome"; its walls were made "only of tymber and plaster"; its courtyard perimeter wall was low and incomplete; the grounds were sloping and without trees; and its only water supply came from an old well in Almshouse Close nearby.[25] So where there had been wood, thatch and wattle and daub, he converted to stone and mortar; the walls around the courtyard were doubled in height; trees were planted to give shelter and stability to the newly-terraced grounds; the abbot's barn was repaired; and water was piped into all the buildings, including brewhouse and washhouse, from a new well dug in the centre of the courtyard.[26]

How much of all this was true cannot now be judged with certainty: we have only Sir Hugh's own selective and fallible memory as evidence. His description has been often quoted without question and accepted at face value, even though his retrospective account of other matters where it can be checked against known facts is sometimes inaccurate, incomplete and even suspiciously misleading. So was Abbey House where Sir Hugh's father, grandfather and great grandmother had lived really "only of tymber and plaster"? Was it likely that the abbots of Whitby had occupied a hall of wood and thatch when even their hunting lodge was of stone and tile? Given the abundance of excellent ashlar masonry on the monastery site nearby, it seems inconceivable that the Cholmleys would have been satisfied with little more than a peasant's cottage as late as the 1630s. Even in his own references to Abbey House in his grandfather's and father's time, Sir Hugh mentioned a chamber, a kitchen, a larder and a cellar. In the absence of other descriptive evidence, therefore, it seems more than likely that Cholmley exaggerated the improvements he made to the house itself, though his references to courtyard, out-buildings and water supply were probably justified. Curiously, he wrote nothing about his stables, which were almost certainly added by him at this time in the north-west corner of the outer courtyard.[27]

Also missing from Sir Hugh's memoirs was reference to further land sales: he would have his reader believe that he had "masterd" all his debts by 1636 and from then on lived handsomely and free of financial troubles. Other records show that this was not so. Between the sale of Fyling Hall in 1634 and 1641, Cholmley raised at least £2,249 12s. 6d. from the sale of long-term leases on entailed property. Middlewood Hall, a substantial mansion in Fylingthorpe, had already gone to George Conyers for £420 in 1633 and about the time that Fyling Hall became Hotham's in June 1634, Wragby farm and adjacent lands were bought by Ralph Postgate, a Staintondale yeoman, for £305. Another casualty of Sir Hugh's need for ready money was Park Gate in Fyling which was sold for £50 in 1635 to farmers, Robert and William Monkman.[28]

Yet these were relatively minor losses compared with the sales avalanches of 1638 and 1639. In Whitby town alone, Sir Hugh sold at least 32 properties in less than three years, nearly all to sitting tenants, for sums that ranged from £95 to £12. Altogether these sales yielded £1,183 10s. At the same time, 21 sales in Robin Hood's Bay, Fylingthorpe, Raw and Dales, brought in another £821 5s. 6d.[29] Against these sales, the only purchase recorded was the £38 Sir Hugh paid to George Conyers in 1638 for 24 acres of Fyling Ness which he had sold a decade earlier.[30]

In short, far from solvent, Sir Hugh was still having to raise money to pay for his living expenses by selling parts of his landed inheritance, a policy that could lead in the end only to bankruptcy. Piece by piece he was eating into his capital. He was living beyond his means when his means appear to have been almost entirely from rents and manorial dues. That he had been able, unlike his father and grandfather, to convert more and more of the Cholmley estate into lump sums of cash was mainly the result of the growing prosperity of Whitby as an alum port and, to a lesser degree, of the hinterland's butter trade. He had become a principal beneficiary of Whitby's economic success.[31]

CHAPTER 5

MAGISTRATE, DEPUTY-LIEUTENANT AND COLONEL

After recovering the family estate from threatened ruin, Sir Hugh Cholmley wasted no time before returning to public affairs. No parliament sat between 1629 and 1640 so that he was denied renewal of his seat in the Commons, yet as early as January 1632 he took his place for the first time on the justices bench of the North Riding at Helmsley. Other magistrates then present that day included Henry Bellasis and Sir John Hotham. Henry was the son and heir of Lord Fauconberg of Newburgh Priory and Barbara Cholmley, one of Sir Hugh's many aunts; and Sir John was the eldest son of Lady Jane, who had taken young Hugh into her Scorborough home when he was taken ill at Beverley school. Clearly, at Helmsley Hugh was amongst friends. Fortunately, though perhaps by design, the most senior and formidable magistrate in the North Riding, Sir Thomas Posthumous Hoby, was not there.[1]

Sir Hugh's own recollection of this event makes revealing reading: he wrote: "The country suffering much for want of a Justice of Peace there not beeing any with in 12 miles of Whitby (I put my selfe in to commission) I condiscended to bee put in to commission..." Perhaps "condiscended" was his second choice of verb because he then remembered his reluctance to come face to face with Hoby. Sitting at the North Riding quarter sessions he was certain to meet his "father's old enemy ... who had cost my father many a 100 [pounds] in sutes". In other words, Sir Hugh's sense of public duty was mixed with private misgivings if it also meant having to confront "a troblesome neighbour".[2]

However, on this occasion, Hugh was spared a meeting with Sir Thomas, who was again absent from the second sessions of the year at Thirsk in April. Then, when the court met for the midsummer meeting at Malton in July, Hoby was there but not Cholmley. Were the two of them playing hide and seek as Sir Richard and Sir Thomas had done earlier? There is no way of knowing. All that can be said is that Hugh was preoccupied in the summer of 1632 with his wife's advanced pregnancy and the imminent birth of his third son; and only three weeks before young Hugh's birth on 21 July, his mother had taken a heavy fall from her horse.[3]

The inevitable occurred finally at Thirsk on 3 October 1632. According to Cholmley's own later account, the only one known, he was anxious to avoid any demonstration of ill-feeling. Sharply aware of his lack of years and experience compared with Hoby, he " resolved to avoide all differences and give all the compliance that might bee". Yet Hoby "was of such a nature unlesse a man became his slave there was noe keepeing freindshippe for he loved to carry all things after his owne way and humour how unjust or injurious soever..." Consequently, "with in a yeare being at the sessions", when Hugh dared to challenge Hoby's judgement and then carried all the other justices with him, Sir Thomas was enraged. He turned to the magistrate sitting next to him and said loudly: "his Grandfather once crossed mee thus on the bench but I made him repent it and soe will I this man..." Soon afterwards, Hoby commenced a suit against Sir Hugh in Star Chamber to which he replied with a complaint against Hoby in the council at York.[4]

As usual, Cholmley's selective memory for anecdote was better than his chronology. In fact, Hoby did not bring a bill against Sir Hugh in Star Chamber until as late as the winter of 1636, more than four years after their first face-to-face encounter at Thirsk. It is much more likely that the incident described by Cholmley took place at the Malton sessions in July 1635, the only other occasion when they sat on the North Riding bench together. In 1632 Hugh had been far too "green" and lacking in self-confidence to challenge Sir Thomas where he ruled the roost, whereas three years later both their circumstances had changed: Cholmley's star was rising rapidly; Hoby's world had crashed down upon his head.[5]

On 6 September 1633 the Hackness parish register recorded the burial of "the honble vertuous and Religious Lady, the Lady Margarett Hoby, wife of the Right Worll. Sr. Thomas Posthumous Hoby, knt." Hoby took Margaret's death very badly: as he had inscribed on her funeral monument, they had been married for "seven and thirty yeares and one month ... in mutuall entire affection to both ther extraordinary comfortes".[6] If Margaret's long illness and death made Hackness' new widower melancholic and miserable, this would explain Hoby's absence from the North Riding bench through the whole of 1633 and from three of the four sessions of 1634. Also, Sir Thomas spent much of his time after her death fulfilling Margaret's last wish to have a new chapel built at Harwood Dale.[7]

The loss of his wife was not the only setback Hoby had suffered since 1632. For several years he had been openly at war with Scarborough corporation and in particular with the leaders of its oligarchy, the Thompson family. The quarrel with the town's Common Hall concerned control over Scarborough's militia or trained band. Hoby's insistence that the armed townsmen should muster for his inspection at Hutton Buscel, several miles inland but close to Hackness, and that they should number 36 instead of the customary 30, was resented and resisted by Scarborough's ruling body. Not for the first time, an appeal was made to Sir Thomas Wentworth, lord president of the Council of the North at York, who came down firmly on the side of the townsmen and against Hoby. Moreover, Hoby's suit in Star Chamber against the Thompsons collapsed when he was confronted with an exemplification of the borough's charter of Edward III which disapproved his case against them. Both these crushing defeats had been inflicted on Hoby in the summer of 1632.[8]

Whereas Hoby was forfeiting the admiration and respect of Wentworth, Cholmley was winning them. There was already a favourable connection between the lord president and the Cholmleys which dated back at least to 1624-5, when as high sheriff of Yorkshire Sir Richard was described as "wholly Wentworth's". And as Wentworth rose in power and influence, a close friendship with him was clearly worth nurturing. Sir Hugh was also conscious and proud of their family relationship. As he noted in his memoirs, Wentworth's "first ladye [was] daughter to the Earl of Cumberland ... my father's cosen-iermyn once removed". Wentworth's first wife was Lady Margaret Clifford and Hugh's great grandmother, Catherine Clifford, was one of the same family. His Clifford ancestry was particularly pleasing to Sir Hugh.[9]

As early as 1626, when he was Member of Parliament for Scarborough, Sir Hugh had failed to persuade his constituents to support his petition "for some releife towerds the repaireing the Peer" at Whitby.[10] Ever since 1614, after a great storm had washed away Scarborough's own essential harbour pier, Parliament had granted the town the right to a levy on every shipment of coal out of Newcastle and Sunderland to maintain its port of refuge for coastal traffic.[11] But there was no hope that Scarborians would promote the commerce of their principal rivals and Cholmley's quest failed to secure their backing. Six years later, during Easter term 1632, Sir Hugh tried again. This time he carried a petition from the townsmen of Whitby addressed to the Privy Council in London, and this time he had the support of Viscount Wentworth. The result was a permit for "a general contribution through out England" which eventually raised, according to Cholmley, "neare £500" and funded "part of the peere to the west of the Harbour".[12]

Since his appointment by the Crown as lord president and lord lieutenant in 1628, Wentworth had made many more enemies to add to the Saviles. His elevation to the peerage, return to court favour, and rise to power with a place in the Privy Council were regarded by many of his fellow Yorkshiremen as the rewards of dishonest apostasy and his authoritarian, haughty manner aroused anger as well as envy. Opposition to Wentworth in Yorkshire was led by Lord Fauconberg of Newburgh Priory. In March 1631 Fauconberg had been imprisoned in the Fleet for making false allegations against Wentworth. The following month, his son, Henry Bellasis, was also committed after he had refused to doff his hat to the lord president and would not apologise for his deliberate insult.[13]

At the outset it seemed that Cholmley would side with his relatives at Newburgh Priory rather than with Wentworth. The turning point might well have occurred in September 1631 when a dangerous confrontation took place. Sir Hugh was one of a party of about 20 North Riding gentlemen, who included his cousins Henry Bellasis and Marmaduke Cholmley of Brandsby, which accidentally or by design, met another party of gentlemen riders led by Wentworth's closest friend, Christopher Wandesford. Bellasis was in a characteristic belligerent mood: he accused Wandesford of fomenting the quarrel between his family and Wentworth, and tried to provoke a duel. Fortunately, Wandesford was too tolerant, well-mannered and sensible to rise to the challenge. Only harsh words, not blows, were exchanged between the two parties. This incident could have contributed to Cholmley's conviction that some of his fellow North Riding gentlemen had behaved badly, unreasonably and unfairly.[14] It was also evident that whatever Sir Hugh might think of Wentworth personally, he was now too mighty a man to challenge.

Though Wentworth sailed off to Ireland in July 1633 to become the king's lord deputy there, he retained his office as lord president and delegated its authority to his vice-president, Sir Edward Osborne, brother-in-law of Christopher Wandesford. During Wentworth's absence in Ireland, Cholmley kept up a continuous correspondence with him which revealed his concern for the lord deputy's health as well as the progress of Whitby's new west pier. For example, in May 1635, Sir Hugh sent his servant with a letter, a gift of two horses, and some medicines to his "ever honoured Lord". What he described in the covering letter as "a few balls of Gascoynes powder" were meant to relieve Wentworth from one or more of his many afflictions of rheumatism, gout, migraine, insomnia and fainting fits, all of which had grown worse in Ireland's damp weather. As for the new pier at Whitby, it was evident from Sir Hugh's letter that not all was running smoothly. Only about half of the country had been covered for contributions and much of the money collected was "in fartheings at the tyme not current". Only about half of the pier had been built and more money was needed to finish it.[15]

By the time that Cholmley wrote this letter and sent these gifts to his patron, he had gained sufficient status and self-confidence to challenge Hoby openly, even at the quarter sessions where the latter had been so dominant. Whatever the exact nature and outcome of their face-to-face encounter at Malton in July 1635, it was never repeated. Though he remained senior magistrate, or custos rotulorum, on the North Riding bench until his death at the end of 1640, Hoby never again appeared at the sessions, whereas Sir Hugh was more often present than absent in 1636, 1637 and 1638. In 1639 and 1640, Cholmley sat only twice, at Helmsley in January 1639 and, for the last time, at New Malton in July 1640, but during these final two years he was much preoccupied with duties arising from his offices as deputy lieutenant and colonel of the local militia.[16] In his memoirs, Sir Hugh gave himself far too much credit for Hoby's decline and his disappearance from the North Riding bench in the late 1630s, but he was factually correct when he wrote that "after this checke I gave him in the sessions he never appeared there more".[17]

Indeed, by 1636, Cholmley had effectively taken Hoby's place as the most active and influential gentleman in their neighbourhood. Hoby's last bill in Star Chamber was soon quietly dropped after Lord Coventry, the Lord Keeper, persuaded Cholmley to withdraw his complaint against Sir Thomas to the Council of the North at York.[18] Hoby even made a conciliatory gesture to Scarborough in 1636 when he presented the Common Hall there with a magnificent silver mace which is still today carried before the borough mayor.[19]

Nevertheless, resentment remained with Cholmley long after Hoby was dead and buried. For instance, in his subsequent memoirs, he failed to record that he had made peace with Sir Thomas in the presence of Lord Coventry who reported the event to Wentworth: "before me they joined hands professed friendships and fair respects to each other".[20] Even 20 years after this final meeting, Sir Hugh could still not bring himself round to write a favourable word about Hoby. In his memoirs he alleged that Sir Thomas had "bought" lord keeper Coventry's support in Star Chamber by settling Hackness on his granddaughter's husband, John Sydenham, thereby depriving the true heirs of the estate, the Dakins family, of their rightful inheritance.[21]

In fact, not only did Hoby's alleged bribe fail, but the boy Sydenham was a relative of Sir Thomas and in effect had been adopted by the childless Lady Margaret before her death. During the last years of her life she had given the boy "affectionate care" both for "his well doing" and "for his education". Sir Thomas himself was so fond of young John that in his will he bequeathed to him his most precious personal belongings - "a chain bracelet of gold with a picture of my late most dear and only wife deceased" and another picture of Lady Margaret "set in a box of ivory or elephants tooth with a piece of crystal to keep it from the duste".[22] A poisonous mixture of ignorance and malicious prejudice blinded Sir Hugh to the true facts of the Sydenham inheritance of Hackness and long after Hoby had gone the Cholmleys continued their vendetta against his innocent successors.

Sir Hugh's reputation in his own county and even as far away as London was greatly enhanced by an event which took place at Whitby in December 1635. According to Cholmley's own memory, the only detailed source that survives, he had taken prompt, brave and decisive action against a Dutch captain who had pursued a Dunkirker which had taken refuge in the upper harbour. Similar invasions of sovereign English territory had occurred at Scarborough the previous July, but there the Dutchmen had done as they pleased without resistance.[23] At Whitby, however, the outcome was very different. When Cholmley heard a commotion on the near riverside he came down there from his home, with only "a caine" in his hand and accompanied by only one servant. The Dutch captain refused to recall his men back to their warship, so Sir Hugh took hold of him, dispossessed him of his pistol, and used his body to shield himself from one who "leveled a musket" at him. The Hollanders retreated to their ship leaving Sir Hugh with his prisoner hostage. After he had intercepted a letter from his crew to the Dutch captain promising that 200 men would soon secure his release, Sir Hugh summoned Sir John Hotham, then the high sheriff, from Fyling Hall, who called out all the local trained bands. Two Dutch warships "hovered" outside the harbour mouth for a few days and then sailed away. Sir Hugh sent his prisoner, Captain Alexander Adrianson Van Croning, under close guard to York, and from there he was taken to London, where he was locked up for the next two years.[24] The Privy Council was delighted with Cholmley: for several years all efforts to seize Dutch men-of-war had failed. Sir Hugh had done something personally and heroically to restore national honour and punish violations by foreigners of the King's peace.[25]

In 1627 Hugh had lost all his "household stuffe and plate to the vallew of 4 or £500 " as well as his wife's clothing when the ship that was carrying them from London to Whitby was captured by a Dunkirk privateer and lost. Since this was a time "when mony was scarse" the loss to the Cholmleys was serious. Elizabeth joined her husband at Whitby with only the clothes she "had on her backe" and those in a "small cloke bag". If Hugh had not previously brought with him "a sute of Hangeings and bed" for their own chamber, the family would have lacked even these basic essentials for their home in the Gatehouse.[26]

Five years later, in July 1632, Sir Hugh wrote to Wentworth, who was then still at York, to report the presence of a French "pirate" ship lurking outside Whitby harbour mouth. A Yarmouth captain had told him that the Frenchmen were indeed pirates who had already robbed his vessel.[27] Nothing more of this incident is known, but it was yet another of many indications that the North Sea English coasts were dangerous waters, particularly when a full-scale continental war was taking place. Wentworth passed Cholmley's letter on to Sir John Coke, the king's secretary of state, who authorised the lord president to seize any such pirate ship found in English waters.[28] Yet such instructions were far easier to write than to carry out: the question was diplomatically difficult since many of the so-called "sea-rovers" carried legitimate letters of marque which permitted them to attack the enemy's merchant shipping. Above all, the royal navy was too small and weak to protect English vessels and English ports from Dutchmen, Dunkirkers or French warships.

In these circumstances, a royal writ for the collection of Ship Money addressed to the country's maritime communities in October 1634 seemed not only legitimate but urgently necessary. One such writ for a ship of 800 tons was directed to the mayors, bailiffs and burgesses of all the coastal towns between Berwick and Bridlington, naming also "Hartlepool, Newcastle, Durham, Escardlieigh, otherwise Scardburgh, Sunderland, Stockton, Cockeram (?), Blyth, Whitby and Gisborough".[29]

To this royal command there was not a hint of objection. Even the newly-chosen high sheriff of Yorkshire, Sir John Hotham, who had been imprisoned in 1627 for refusing to pay a forced loan to the king, reported in May 1635 that he had diligently collected all the money due from his county.[30] Amongst the conscientious collectors was Sir Hugh Cholmley.

Even when a second royal writ was issued in August 1635, extending the tax to cover the whole of England, inland as well as coastal, there was still no resistance to it, at least in Yorkshire. After the outrages that had recently taken place at Scarborough the previous July, which had gone unpunished, Yorkshiremen could see clearly the need for a stronger royal fleet to guard their shores and shipping. This second writ to pay for a warship of 700 tons with 240 men was addressed in particular to the city of York with the Ainsty, Hull, Leeds, Beverley, Doncaster, Ripon, Pontefract, Richmond, Scarborough and Hedon, which were assessed collectively for £1,217 of the total county liability of £12,000.[31]

Again, the necessity and fairness of this Ship Money levy on the community seemed to justify it. For example, Scarborough town, which had been assessed at £100 in 1634, was allowed a reduction to £30 the following year and every effort was made to distribute the financial burden evenly amongst its householders: the poorest property owners paid a shilling and the richest one or two pounds each.[32]

One notable Buckinghamshire squire who refused to pay his Ship Money assessment of one pound as a matter of principle not poverty was John Hampden; but his sensational case which culminated in a trial in 1637 seems not to have had much influence in Yorkshire where in that year most of the county's tax of £12,000 was soon paid in full. What did John Hampden, living in landlocked Buckinghamshire, know of Dunkirkers and Dutchmen? What could he appreciate of the vital importance of the North Sea coastal trade in coal and alum? And by 1636-7 Ship Money was beginning to make a difference. Though by then it had become an annual, rather than an exceptional tax, it was being spent by the Admiralty entirely on the navy. From then on there were regular patrols of English warships off the Yorkshire coast and there were no more unwelcome visits to Whitby and Scarborough of Dunkirkers and Dutchmen.[33]

Sir Hugh's own private doubts about the legality of Ship Money took a long time to mature into resistance to it. Until 1639 he remained an obedient, loyal magistrate and deputy-lieutenant. No doubt, in this matter, he was influenced to some extent by the views of his brother-in-law, Sir Roger Twysden, whose knowledge of the law was far better than his own. Even as early as the first Ship Money writ of October 1634, Roger had advised his widowed mother, Lady Anne, not to pay the £20 demanded from her for her house in Redcross Street. There was no precedent, he argued, for levying the tax in the city of London. In 1635, when Ship Money was broadened to cover the whole country, Sir Roger paid £7 for his property in Kent, yet in later years he seems to have avoided or evaded any further payments. How he managed to escape is not known, but Sir Hugh must have been aware of his objections to it.[34]

Cholmley and Twysden were much more to each other than distant brothers-in-law. Though their two families lived nearly 300 miles apart they were frequently host to each other. Hugh had spent most of his first four years of marriage in the Twysden home in London. His eldest son was born there and his second son first saw the light of day in Roydon Hall. After she was widowed, Hugh's mother-in-law, Lady Anne, had stayed six months with the Cholmleys at Fyling Hall. To Yorkshire she had brought with her

Isabella Saunders who, two years later, married Sir Roger. After the death of Lady Anne in 1638, the close association of the Cholmleys and the Twysdens deepened. All four of Elizabeth's younger brothers, Thomas (1602-83), William (1605-41), John (1607-88) and Francis (1610-75) were frequent guests at Whitby. Thomas and John were witnesses to William Cholmley's baptism in the chapel at "Peckham house'; William Twysden spent the winter of 1627-8 at the Abbey gatehouse; and Francis was witness to many of Sir Hugh's land leases made in 1628-9. It has been suggested, without evidence, that Hugh went abroad with John in 1634.[35]

Until 1640 the careers of Sir Hugh and Sir Roger followed similar routes. Both were eldest sons and heirs of self-impoverished fathers and stretched estates. For instance, Roger had to sell the outlying Romney marsh estate to raise his sister Anne's dowry of £2,000 in 1630. When he took over the Twysden properties the previous year he found that his debts were so heavy that interest on them absorbed a quarter of his total income.[36] Nevertheless, like his brother-in-law he had rescued the family fortune from imminent ruin, served as a Member of the House of Commons in the 1620s and as justice of the peace in Kent during the 1630s.[37] One conspicuous difference between them, however, was that whereas Hugh had acquired merely a "smackering" of legal knowledge during his wasted years at Gray's Inn,[38] Roger was soon well known for his historical learning and scholarship in jurisprudence. Among Sir Roger's personal friends and correspondents were such distinguished authorities as Sir Simonds D'Ewes, the diarist, who was convinced of the illegality of Ship Money, John Seldon, an outspoken opponent of royal absolutism and clerical power, and the historians, William Dugdale and Sir John Spelman. On the strength of his later published works, Sir Roger has been named as one of the "three really big figures" of seventeenth-century historical scholarship.[39] How much of Roger's puritanism may have rubbed off on to Hugh will be discussed later; at this point it is relevant to recognise his brother-in-law's learning and experience.

Another of Hugh's relatives by marriage, who became an intimate friend and might well have influenced his political and religious outlook, was Sir Christopher Yelverton of Easton Mauduit in Northamptonshire. Christopher had married Anne Twysden, the younger daughter of Sir William in 1630, so that he became Elizabeth Cholmley's brother-in-law. The male Yelvertons were a very distinguished family. Christopher's grandfather had been Speaker of the House of Commons and later a justice of the King's Bench. Sir Henry Yelverton, Christopher's father, was Attorney-General under James I and made judge of the Common Pleas by Charles I. Christopher succeeded his father in 1629 when he was 27 years old but already a knight and a Member of the Commons in the parliaments of 1626 and 1628-9. Though he had the notoriety of a puritan nonconformist who had refused the forced loan in 1627 and was brought before Star Chamber in 1633 for eating meat on Fridays, as a mark of great royal favour in 1636 he was host at Easton Mauduit to King Charles and Queen Henrietta Maria.[40]

By then Easton Mauduit was already well known to the Cholmleys. During the 1630s the Yelvertons and the Cholmleys spent long periods in each other's homes. From Michaelmas 1630, Hugh, Elizabeth and their two children, William and Elizabeth, lived in London for the winter with the newly-married Yelvertons. At Whitsuntide 1632 Hugh brought Lady Yelverton from London up to Fyling Hall, where she attended the birth and baptism of her nephew Hugh. Sir Christopher was another witness at Hugh's baptism. From the age of five Hugh stayed three years at Easton Mauduit with his uncle, aunt and their son, "dear cousin Henry", and for ten weeks, during the summer of 1638, the Yelvertons were guests at Abbey House. Finally, in 1639, when Sir Christopher was high sheriff of Northamptonshire, Sir Hugh came to stay at Easton Mauduit and brought eight of his men "in livery" to attend Christopher at the county assizes.[41]

The choice of Sir Christopher Yelverton as Northamptonshire's high sheriff in November 1639 was not intended as an act of royal reward: on the contrary, his consistently wayward behaviour made him an obvious candidate for what was generally regarded as an expensive and irksome post. In 1635 he was named as a musters defaulter; the following year, he had refused to contribute to the relief of victims of the plague; and in 1637 he was reprimanded for spending Christmas in the capital.[42] Since high sheriffs were personally responsible for the full collection of Ship Money assessments within their counties, reluctant gentlemen were selected for that office precisely for that reason. In Yorkshire, for example, the county's most notorious enemy of Ship Money, Sir Marmaduke Langdale, on Wentworth's advice was "pricked" for the post of high sheriff also in November 1639.[43]

Yelverton's task in Northamptonshire was unenviable. Sir John Hanbury, his predecessor, had failed to meet his Ship Money obligations, even after he had been obliged to destrain the goods of nearly 200 non-payers. By 1639, when Sir Christopher took over, the county was in open rebellion against what had become a permanent, annual tax. There were arrears dating back to 1636. From church pulpits vicars urged their parishioners not to pay; collectors were often assaulted; and bailiffs were refusing to carry out their orders. Yelverton paid his own Ship Money, but he protested to the Privy Council that his county was openly defiant and obstructive. In May 1640 he was accused of "great and supine negligence" and threatened with action in Star Chamber.[44]

Since Sir Hugh was actually in Northamptonshire and staying with Sir Christopher at Easton Mauduit when these events were taking place, he could not have been unaffected by them. Nevertheless, circumstances in Yorkshire were not the same as those in the Midlands and besides Cholmley's attachment to Wentworth remained strong.

Even though the county's rate had been reduced from £12,000 to £4,250 in 1638, after the Hampden law case, there were now many more Yorkshiremen prepared to resist Ship Money; but Sir Hugh was not one of them, yet. On the contrary, during 1638 as the king's war with the Scottish Covenanters became more certain, Cholmley proved himself to be one of the county's most active and cooperative deputy-lieutenants, raising, training, arming and leading the trained bands or home guards within his neighbourhood. Without a professional, standing army, King Charles had to rely entirely on these amateur, part-time soldiers and on local gentlemen, like Sir Hugh, to command them.

It was the mounting costs of arming, clothing and feeding the trained bands rather than the Ship Money levy which did most to provoke the opposition of some of Yorkshire's leading gentry. When in July 1638, Sir Edward Osborne, Wentworth's deputy at York, summoned the county's deputy-lieutenants to King's Manor to discuss the fulfilment of the king's mobilisation plans, Cholmley was the only one present from the North Riding.

Osborne was indeed desperate to find gentlemen who would muster and lead the North Riding militias. To Wentworth, he wrote: "There is now a want of deputy-lieutenants and colonels in the North Riding as I know not how the service can be performed there for the present: the Lord Emley dead, Sir Thomas Hoby out, Sir John Gibson not able to stir, my brother Wandesford absent, Sir Thomas Danby sheriff hath his hands full of business, Mr James Pennyman very old, so as all the burden must lie on Mr William Pennyman and Sir Hugh Cholmeley."[45]

Even more serious was the lack of cooperation from the West and East Ridings. Sir William Savile of Thornhill refused to bring his cavalry to York and Sir John Hotham, now showing the first signs of public defiance, told Osborne in his characteristic blunt manner that there could be no musters in his neighbourhood until the harvest had been gathered in. Osborne was so annoyed and frustrated by these Yorkshiremen that he asked London for eight or ten professional officers to be sent north to take command of trained band regiments.[46] In the event of a war with the Scots, the Yorkshire militias, which at full strength numbered 13,000, half the royal army, would be in the front line.

Alarmed by Osborne's difficulties, in September 1638, Wentworth wrote to Cholmley from Cosha in Ireland. First he assured Sir Hugh that he could continue to depend on his favour regarding "the Peere of Whitby" and "to doe the Country [Cholmley's locality] therin the best service". Then he went on to the chief purpose of his letter: "Wee have been all blamed for that the musters and Traynings in Yorkshire proceed soe slowly, therefore to prevent any further Reprehention, let me intreat you to give them the best assistance and speed you can." The Lord Deputy concluded with the warmest words that showed he still regarded Cholmley as a personal friend and a reliable ally: "And soe with my faithfull good wishes unto yourself I rest your very sure affectionate freind and servant."[47]

Wentworth's trust in Cholmley was not misplaced. As deputy-lieutenant in the North Riding, Sir Hugh was commissioned colonel of the regiment which consisted of the militias of the wapentakes of Whitby Strand, Pickering Lythe and Ryedale and the town of Scarborough and during the winter of 1638-9 he fulfilled his duties with conscientious zeal. Previously, Scarborough had been required to equip and mobilise a select band of only 30 armed men, but in January 1639 Sir Hugh inspected an unprecedented number. From Falsgrave, 23 men turned out, at least a dozen of them with muskets. From Scarborough's four quarters the muster roll came to 90. This was by far the largest force raised by the town since a previous Scottish war in 1542.[48]

Hoby had failed to bring Scarborough's trained band even six miles inland to Hutton Buscel, yet Cholmley had them assembled on "Scallowmore", north of Pickering, a full 15 miles away from their homes.[49] According to Sir Hugh's own later account, he trained and inspected his "whole Regement together on Pexton Morre neare Thornton".[50] By his "whole Regement" presumably he meant the combined militias drawn from Whitby, Ryedale and Pickering Lythe as well as Scarborough, a force perhaps as many as 500 armed men. Scalla and Pexton moors are close to each other on the southern escarpment of the North York Moors.

On this occasion, Cholmley's achievement was remarkable. He had succeeded where all of his predecessors, including the formidable Hoby, had failed. Not since the heyday of the great black knight of the North had a Cholmley wielded so much power and won so much prestige in his "country".

In his memoirs, written nearly 20 years later, Sir Hugh recalled an incident on Pexton Moor which had remained clear in his mind and still weighed on his conscience:

… one Halldure, a stubborne fellow of Pickering, not obeyeing his captaine and giveing mee some unhandsome languidge I strucke him with my caine and felled him to the ground the caine was tipped with silver and hitting just under the eare had greater operation than I intended; but ether the man was ill or else counterfeted soe to bee freed from servise, which I willingly granted and glad when he was well, but it was a gud monetion not to bee too hasty on the like or any other provocation, for passion doth not only blinde the iudgement but produceth ill effects.[51]

As in the case of his encounter with the Dutch sea captain at Whitby, Cholmley had acted instinctively, immediately and decisively, though on this occasion he regretted his own violence. On the other hand, he had asserted his authority in a dramatic way that was likely to be remembered by all who witnessed it and reported far and wide. By making an example of "Halldure", Sir Hugh probably saved himself and his captains from other demonstrations of disobedience. He might have lacked the height, physical strength and presence of his forebears, but like them he was a man of fierce pride, short temper and, when provoked, bold, fearless action. He would not tolerate disrespect. Nevertheless, he did not inherit his father's rashness and vindictiveness; though it did not operate all the time, Sir Hugh had an active conscience. He was capable of behaving violently, but he took no pleasure in it or satisfaction from it.

Another, even more important event that took place on Pexton Moor in February 1639 was that Sir Hugh "caught cold and a dangerous sickness" while reviewing his troops there.[52] Whether this "dangerous sickness" started as or became a convenient alibi or whether it was an entirely genuine excuse it is impossible to say, but the result was that Cholmley's place as regimental colonel was taken by Captain Launcelot Alured at Scarborough.[53] In the event, however, though all ready to go, Cholmley's regiment of Bluecoats was not required to march north to meet the Scots: king Charles abandoned his campaign and signed a truce with the Covenanters at Berwick on 18 June 1639.

If loyalty to Wentworth pulled Cholmley in one direction, by 1639 kinship and friendship ties with Sir John Hotham seemed to be pulling him in the opposite. In Clarendon's words, Sir Hugh was "a fast friend to Sir John".[54] Wentworth was his powerful patron, but Hotham was closer and dearer. The key link between Cholmley and Hotham was the Legard family: both were sons of Legard daughters and their maternal grandfathers were brothers. As his third wife Sir John had married Cholmley's first cousin, Frances Legard. Sir John's own mother, Lady Jane, became surrogate to young Hugh after his mother's untimely death and Scorborough Hall, principal Hotham residence, was the boy's second home.[55] Later, when Hugh had been engaged in a desperate struggle to save the Cholmley estate, his uncle, John Legard, and his cousin, John Hotham, had come to his rescue just in time, when others would not help him. They had pacified his voracious money-lenders and paid off his most urgent debts. Sir John's purchase of Fyling Hall in 1634 had been a decisive turning-point in Cholmley's financial history. Now some of the Hothams lived at Fyling Hall and were Cholmley neighbours. Finally, in 1635, at Whitby, when Sir Hugh was faced with the menace of armed Dutch seamen, Sir John had come to his rescue again, this time at the head of a trained band.[56]

Hotham had once been an ally of Wentworth: in 1628 he had been made governor of Hull by the newly-appointed lord president of the Council at York. Seven years later, on Wentworth's recommendation, he was chosen as Yorkshire's high sheriff. In this office he had collected the county's first levy of Ship Money with efficient fairness.[57] When he clashed with Hoby over the assessment of Ship Money, Wentworth gave him his full support.[58] As far as Wentworth was concerned, at this time, Hotham was "as considerable a person as any other gentleman in the north of England".[59]

Hotham was indeed "considerable a person" in several senses. In the words of the royalist historian, Clarendon, Sir John was "master of a noble fortune in land, and rich in money". This was no exaggeration: in 1643, his personal estate was reckoned to be £10,000, which included at least £4,800 in ready cash. Also, at a time when King Charles needed officers to raise and lead the militias and most of Yorkshire's deputy-lieutenants, including Cholmley, were ignorant of military matters, Hotham was an experienced soldier. For two years he had served with distinction on the Continent under General Mansfeld in the army of the Elector of the Palatinate. Moreover, the Hothams were one of the oldest of Yorkshire's families with a long history of loyal, public service. They had campaigned with all of the first three Edwards in the French and Scottish wars; they had fought in France with Henry V. Hothams had been present at Crecy, Calais and Agincourt. They had died on the battlefield of Towton and shared the victory at Flodden. Since the reign of Henry I, for 500 years, son had succeeded father or grandfather in unbroken line, a genealogical record almost without parallel.[60] If Cholmley was proud of his ancestry, Hotham had reason to be even prouder.

Early in 1639, when Sir John seemed to be wavering on the issue of Ship Money and a complimentary gesture from the Crown in his direction might have tipped the balance, he was replaced as governor of Hull by Captain William Legge, a professional soldier. Hotham had been appointed to this key post in 1628 as one of Wentworth's first acts as lord president, since he was all too aware of Hotham's powerful authority in the locality. Hull was a port of great strategical and military importance with formidable defences and an enormous arms magazine, so that its governor had to be a man of experience and trustworthiness, particularly when a war with the Scots was imminent. To dismiss Hotham without warning or a word of explanation and replace him with an outsider of much lower social standing was generally regarded as a huge, gratuitous insult. Because he had shown diminishing enthusiasm for Ship Money and preparations for war, it seemed that Hotham was no longer regarded by the king as reliable.

Nearly everyone, including Hotham, assumed that Wentworth was responsible for his rejection. In fact, they were quite wrong: in several letters from Ireland the lord deputy had counselled Charles against it. Wentworth understood how badly Sir John would take the injury to his pride and how severe the damage would be to royal authority in Yorkshire. As late as March 1639, Wentworth was still writing to Hotham as an ally against the opponents of Ship Money: "for love of Christ counsel them out of this madness"; but it was now too late.[61] When the king visited his town upon the river Hull on 1 April 1639 Sir John Hotham was a conspicuous absentee from the welcoming party.[62] From now on Hotham was irreconcilable: he regarded Wentworth as a deadly enemy intent on ruining him and it was his misunderstanding that ultimately proved fatal to both of them.

Cholmley did not follow Hotham at once: as in previous years, he paid his Ship Money. Nevertheless, he was one of many of Yorkshire's deputy-lieutenants who, led by Sir William Savile and Sir John Hotham, petitioned Charles in March 1639 to complain of the burden placed upon them to raise and train the county's militias. They claimed that these extra charges had already cost them £20,000, and if the king insisted on a general muster of all Yorkshire so that he could review it at York, this would cost an additional £10,000. On this occasion, a general muster was abandoned when Charles came to Yorkshire at the end of March, though three regiments of the county's trained bands were ordered to assemble at Berwick. In the event, Yorkshire's entire militia was not called upon to leave the county, though here was a preliminary warning that "coat and conduct" money might become a greater source of grievance than Ship Money.[63] Nevertheless, anticipating further resistance to the payment of yet another Ship Money charge of £12,000, acting on Wentworth's advice, Charles chose Sir Marmaduke Langdale as Yorkshire's new high sheriff in November 1639. Once he had to pay for any deficits out of his own purse, it was thought that Langdale's personal objections to the annual tax would collapse.[64] However, by December 1639, when the fifth all-county writ was received by sheriff Langdale, financial necessity had already forced Charles to call a new parliament after an interval of more than a decade.

CHAPTER 6

PARLIAMENT AND PETITIONS

It was customary for the lord president of the council at York and the lord high admiral each to nominate one of the two Members of Parliament for the borough of Scarborough. In December 1639, however, Scarborough's electorate, the 44 burgesses of the Common Hall, rejected both their nominees. At first, Wentworth had nominated Sir Edward Osborne, his vice-president. Then, when Osborne showed a preference for one of the city of York's seats, the lord president proposed that his place should go to George Butler of Ellerton, one of his deputy-lieutenants. At the same time, Algernon Percy, earl of Northumberland and lord high admiral, gave his support to Sir John Melton, another Yorkshireman without Scarborough connections, but as secretary to the council at York clearly one of Osborne's party.

None the less, Scarborough's ruling 44 councillors showed a remarkable degree of bold independence by ignoring the nominations of both great lords: instead, in March 1640, they returned Sir Hugh Cholmley and John Hotham, Sir John's eldest son, as their representatives at Westminster. Both had been recommended by Sir John who secured one of Beverley's seats for himself. That Wentworth had dismissed Cholmley's strong claim on his former place was a clear warning that he had lost the lord president's favour.[1]

In the light of these significant events it seems most unlikely that Sir Hugh's description of the public rebuff he received from Wentworth took place "at the beginning of this Short Parlament" in April 1640. Both of them had spent the winter of 1639-40 in London: Cholmley was there with his wife and family and Wentworth stayed in the capital from 21 September 1639 until 5 March 1640. Since the two had not seen each other for several years, yet during that time had been in amicable correspondence, it is inconceivable that Sir Hugh would not have tried to pay his respects to the great man in person. In January 1640, King Charles had made him the earl of Strafford. One explanation for the public snub could be that Strafford believed that Cholmley's illness the previous winter had been a dishonest device to evade his duties as deputy-lieutenant and militia colonel and that his removal to London, when he should have been in Yorkshire, was an act of cowardly disloyalty. As already indicated, Strafford's refusal to endorse Cholmley's candidature for Scarborough as early as December 1639 indicated his disapproval of Sir Hugh long before the Short Parliament opened. As for the matter of Ship Money, though Langdale had received the royal writ commanding him to collect £12,000 from Yorkshire in December 1639, he did not attempt to serve it to the head constables until the following March. In other words, during the winter months of 1639-40 Ship Money was not the most pressing issue that might have aroused Strafford's hostility to Cholmley.[2]

Cholmley's own later account of the public affront he suffered is worth quoting in full:

> At the begining of this Parlament the Earl of St[r]afford, then Deputy of Ireland, retorned to London, and I comeing to his lodgeings to doe my service to him, was not only barred the freedome of goeing in to his chamber I had used but when he came out saluteing divers other gentlemen he passed by mee as if he knew mee not and with some scorne which my nature could ill disieast...[3]

If Strafford believed that he had cause to slight Cholmley before proceedings in the Short Parliament, he could have been in no doubt after hearing of Sir Hugh's recent behaviour in the Commons. The Short Parliament had opened on 13 April 1640 and after a brief visit to Ireland, Strafford returned to London on the evening of 18 April. Crippled by gout and weakened by dysentery, the earl did not leave his lodgings and take up his seat in the Lords until 23 April. By that date Sir Hugh had drawn attention to himself in Commons debates.[4]

Charles had called Parliament to grant him the money to pay for a new military campaign against his rebellious Scottish subjects; but several Yorkshiremen were amongst those Commons members who insisted that their grievances should be settled before the king received a penny in subsidy. One of the most outspoken critics of Ship Money was Sir Hugh. Twice in debate on 18 and 20 April he raised the question of the legality of Ship Money. On the first occasion, when he said the Commons should "laye a brand upon shippmoney", he was rebuked by Mr Solicitor, Edward Herbert, for his "boldness". On the second occasion, he moved that sheriffs should not be allowed to distrain the goods of those who refused to pay the tax until its legality had been "adjudged". Finally, on 4 May, at a critical moment in proceedings, Cholmley infuriated the king's ministers by again questioning the lawfulness of Ship Money: impertinently, he asked whether the Crown was making any concession at all by offering to drop it.[5]

If there had been any possibility of a reconciliation between Strafford and Cholmley, after these words spoken in the Commons, there was none. An unbridgeable chasm now separate them. Both men were too proud and too stubborn to bury their differences. For Cholmley the fall-out with Strafford marked another decisive turning-point in his life.

The *Commons Journal* offers only a passing glimpse of Cholmley's prominent role in the crucial proceedings of the Short Parliament. On 16 April, along with his brother-in-law, Sir Roger Twysden, Sir John Hotham and the two Bellasis brothers, Henry and John, Sir Hugh was chosen to be a member of the committee of privileges. On 24 April, he was one of a powerful committee, led by John Pym, Hampden, Hyde and St John, appointed to draw up a report on all the breaches of privilege which had occurred since 1629, including "the grievance of pressing trained bands to serve outside their own country". Finally, on 2 May, Cholmley sat on a committee of the House to hear petitions concerning disputed elections. However, three days later, Charles dissolved his parliament.[6]

In fact, Sir Hugh's part in the Short Parliament was far more important than the bare, official summary of the *Commons Journal* suggests. Though he had not been a member in the last parliament of 1629, when the king had ordered the Speaker to leave the chair and two MPs had forced him to remain there, Cholmley still took a lead in the debate about this controversial event. Was the Speaker a servant of the king or the Commons? Sir Hugh moved that three questions should be put to the House: whether the Speaker might leave the chair; whether the Commons had the right to recall him to his place once he had left it; and whether the Speaker had the authority to dissolve parliament. Compared with most rambling contributions to the discussion that followed, Cholmley's was notably clear and logical. In the end no votes were taken: only a sub-committee, which did not include Sir Hugh, was asked to consider the rights and duties of the Speaker.[7]

Cholmley was also outspoken on the sore question of "military charges", as well as Ship Money. By Monday, 4 May, the king was willing to discontinue Ship Money after the writ of 1639 had been executed on condition the Commons granted him 12 subsidies during the next three years. However, rather than gratefully accepting this royal concession, John Pym, leader of the opposition, pressed for more. One of Pym's group was Cholmley. First he argued that if Ship Money was illegal then for the Crown to forego it was no concession; and, secondly, if Charles wanted subsidies he would have to reimburse all the extra militia costs of the past two years. Similar demands for "coat and conduct money" were made by Sir John Hotham and Henry Bellasis.[8]

All three Yorkshiremen had gone too far and said too much. When Charles dissolved his parliament the following day and blamed "the malicious cunning of some few seditiously affected men", no doubt he had these three in mind.[9] Three days later, on Friday, 8 May, Hotham, Bellasis and Cholmley were summoned to appear before the Privy Council. All were accused of having made improper and offensive speeches during the Commons debate of 4 May. Hotham and Bellasis were so unrepentant and belligerent before the Council that they were immediately committed to the Fleet prison. Cholmley was more diplomatic and denied the accusations made against him which lacked witness corroboration. Nevertheless, he was ordered by the Privy Council to stay in London until permitted to leave.[10] Sir Hugh's own later recollection adds a little to the official record:

> And the Parla[men]t being broake caused mee to bee cauled beefore the Counsell and indeed charged with wurds I nether spoke in the house nor could bee proved against mee, yet for further vexation I was commaunded for 3 weeks or a Month to attend the Counsell table *de die in diem;* my lord had alsoe put Sir John Hotham out of all commissions for refuseing shipmony, and him and my cosen Mr Henry Bellassis [eldest sonne to the lord Faulconbridge] in to the fleet for some wurds they had spoke in this Short Parlament.[11]

Here again there is more than a hint that Cholmley felt that he had been falsely accused and unjustly maligned, in particular by "my lord", the earl of Strafford, his erstwhile patron. Yet, if the words he spoke in the Commons on 18 and 20 April, as well as on 4 May, were accurately reported by witnesses, then he was fortunate not to join Hotham and Bellasis in the Fleet: the Privy Council lacked proof against him, not grounds for complaint.[12]

Hotham and Bellasis were soon released and Sir Hugh was soon allowed to return to his home in Whitby, but the irreparable damage had been done. Hotham and Cholmley were deprived of all their commissions, as justices of the peace, deputy-lieutenants and colonels of their local trained band regiments. When Sir Marmaduke Langdale was finally cajoled into sending out the Ship Money writs, Hotham and

Cholmley not only refused to pay their own assessments but encouraged their tenants to follow suit. Later Sir Hugh claimed that he had "carried the whole liberty of Whitby Strand" after his example.[13]

On 11 June 1640 at Abbey House, Sir Hugh named his younger brother Henry and his Twysden brothers-in-law as trustees for his son and heir William and his three younger children, Hugh, Ann and Elizabeth. For himself, he retained only the manor of Fyling. Subsequently, in his memoirs, Cholmley described these "fortunate" deeds as "upon foresight of these trobles", by which he meant the civil war that began more than two years later.[14] However, these words were written sixteen years later, whereas in June 1640 neither he nor anyone else could then have had "foresight" of such a national calamity. The truth was that after his recent experiences in London and his continued defiance of the government Sir Hugh was bound to feel nervous and apprehensive: he knew that Strafford was hot-tempered and notoriously vindictive. He might be able to carry "the whole of Whitby Strand", but resistance to Ship Money would have to be far stronger and wider before Charles and Strafford would drop it. No one yet knew how a second campaign against the Scots would fall out. Like Hotham and Bellasis, Sir Hugh hoped that the king would be persuaded to recall parliament and that Strafford might be discredited and driven out of office. So the deed he signed in June 1640 was no more than a conventional and sensible insurance policy to protect his family if the worst should happen to him.

Five days after Sir Hugh had put his estate into trust, on 16 June 1640, Yorkshire's high sheriff at last consented to gather in the county's Ship Money assessment of £12,000. Examined by the attorney-general, threatened by the king with severe penalties, badgered by the Privy Council and menaced by prosecution in Star Chamber, Sir Marmaduke Langdale had given in. By mid-August, vice-president Osborne reported that he had received £8,000 from Yorkshire and by the beginning of 1641 the remainder had been paid into the treasury.[15] So much for Cholmley's boast that he had "carried the whole liberty of Whitby Strand after my example".

None of this remarkable turn of events was recorded by Cholmley in his memoirs: he would have his reader believe that his leadership of resistance to Ship Money was entirely successful in Yorkshire; and at least one historian was misled into accepting his version.[16] In fact, as early as July 1640, the Privy Council had ordered that in future the Ship Money levy of 1639, raised in the counties of Northumberland, Cumberland, Westmorland and Yorkshire, should be used, not to build and equip warships, but to pay the expenses of the royal army gathering in the North.[17] The purpose and relevance of the Ship Money tax had changed: whereas previously it had financed a royal war fleet to provide much-needed protection to Yorkshire's coastal communities and the county's sea trade in coal and alum, from now on it would go to protect the county from an unruly English army and a threatened Scottish invasion.

Indeed, by July 1640 it was the presence of this unpaid, ill-disciplined royal army that now constituted the main source of Yorkshire's grievances. In Cholmley's own words: "the King's Army was quarterd to the great burthen of the Country and the much discontent of the greatest part of the gentry."[18] Sir Jacob Astley, the king's commanding general in Yorkshire, found his troops assembled at Selby to be no better than "undisciplined wastrels".[19] Similarly, from York, Osborne had to warn Whitehall that the royal army would prove to be "more ravenous on the county than the Scots..." Moreover, since many Yorkshiremen had expressed their sympathy for the Scottish Covenanters and their religious cause, the vice-president feared that they would be most reluctant to mobilise their militias and unwilling to move them out of the county unless paid coat and conduct money in advance.[20]

Osborne judged correctly the mood of many of Yorkshire's gentry. On 28 July, during the York assizes, nearly 50 of the county's gentlemen, many of them justices and deputy-lieutenants, met in sheriff Langdale's house to sign a petition. This was to be the first of many drawn up by Hotham and Cholmley. After claiming that Yorkshire had spent at least £100,000 the previous year on militia costs, "far abve the proportion of other Countyes", the petitioners alleged that now "unruly soldiers" were forcibly billeted on their communities, contrary to the terms of the Petition of Right of 1628, threatening their property, wives and children. Addressed directly to the king and not to his representative in the county, the lord lieutenant, this petition was no doubt meant to be a deliberate insult to the earl of Strafford.[21]

Some privy councillors were outraged by this bold petition from Yorkshire. Strafford declared it to be "mutinous". The council replied to it with a letter reprimanding its authors and signatories for exaggerating their financial burdens and asserting that billeting of troops in Yorkshire was both lawful and necessary. In future, any grievances should be addressed respectfully, not directly to the king, but through the proper channel of the county's lord lieutenant.[22]

In his unreliable memoirs Cholmley later claimed that "above a 100 of the princypall nobillety and gentry of the county" signed this petition of 28 July, which he and Sir John had "penned" and had "redy" in their pockets. However, Sir Hugh's claim seems as exaggerated as the petition's language and assertions. According to the official list of names presented to the privy council, there were only 47 signatories, not "above a 100".[23] Another slightly different version of the petition, later printed in London more than two years later, was followed by the names of only 30 Yorkshiremen, 20 of whom had signed the original.[24] So even when the two lists are added together the total number of signatories still comes to only 57. Also, at this point, it is well to emphasize that many of these 57, at least 22 such as George Wentworth, Francis Wortley, James Ramsden, Thomas Gower, Robert Strickland, Henry Bellasis and William Savile, as well as Cholmley himself, were to become active royalist combatants in the civil war. Along with that of his brother Henry, Sir Hugh's signature appeared below both versions of the petition.

It is also well to point out that Strafford himself thought that Yorkshire was being unfairly burdened compared with other counties. In April 1640, only days before the Short Parliament first assembled, at York Sir Edward Osborne had received instructions from London to send six of Yorkshire's 12 militia regiments northwards to Newcastle. The remaining six were to follow them at a day's notice.[25] Strafford thought that these orders broke previous promises and were an unwarranted demand on Yorkshire's resources. To the king he wrote: "the charge of this second year's war... is thus likely to fall on that county to their very great Impoverishment, whilst the rest of the Kingdom at Home keep their Fingers warm in their Pockets."[26] Though these privy council orders were rescinded a week later, by that time the first Yorkshire regiment had already arrived in Durham and the damage had been done.[27]

Never reluctant to overvalue himself, Sir Hugh also claimed in his memoirs that the petition of 28 July not only "did something startle the counsel", it also encouraged the Scots to take the military offensive and "gave incourridgement to the Earls of

Bedford, Hartford, Essex, Warwick, Southampton, Bristol [and] Claire and divers other Lords" to petition Charles for a new parliament.[28] So we are meant to believe that the two most important events of the second half of 1640, the resumption of the Scottish war and the summoning of the Long Parliament, owed something to this "baire face complaine of the king's prerogative".[29] Cholmley's suggestion that the Scots had been deterred from invading England by their fear of Yorkshire's "trayned bands" until they heard of his petition beggars belief. Secondly, what Cholmley could not have known then and still not appreciate 16 years later was that a majority of the 12 lords, notably Warwick, Bedford, Essex, Mandeville, Saye, Brooke and the two Yorkshiremen, Howard and Wharton, were in active and secret collusion with the Scottish Covenanters to force Charles to call a new parliament.[30] Finally, the petition of the 12 lords was not presented until as late as 28 August, a week after the Scots had already crossed the border into England, thereby altering the situation.

Not that we should be too critical of Cholmley's recall of incidents that had taken place more than 16 years previously. For example, like many subsequent students of the period, Sir Hugh confused the two Bishops' Wars of 1639 and 1640.[31] However, there can be no doubt that his narrative was heavily biased against Strafford, and his partiality in this matter needs to be distinguished from excusable lapses of memory.

That the grievances of Yorkshiremen were directed mainly against Strafford rather than his royal master is illustrated by the events that followed the petition of 28 July and Cholmley's part in them. The day after he arrived in York, on 24 August, Charles was presented with another petition from about 40 of Yorkshire's county elite. Again he was asked to give them direct access to his presence and again warned that the county could not support its trained bands without 14 days advanced payment of their expenses, and even then they would not go beyond the Tees. Nevertheless, when next day the colonels were ordered to muster their men and rendezvous at certain locations in readiness to march north to confront the Scots, there were no refusals. It seems that the presence of the king in person and his offer to lead the militias himself was sufficient to win their officers' support. Once more the conciliatory response of Charles was in the sharpest contrast to the uncompromising reaction of Strafford. On 26 August the lord lieutenant had reached York and the following day he addressed an assembly of county gentry. He told them in the strongest terms that any who would not accompany the king were "no better than beasts" and to refuse service to Charles was "little less than High-Treason". Strafford's only concession was that if now Yorkshiremen gave their full support in future the county's militia liabilities would be reduced.[32]

Whether Cholmley was at York to hear these harsh words is not known, but it must have been at this time that the king asked him to resume his regimental commission which Strafford had taken from him. In a private interview with Charles Sir Hugh explained that though he was happy to serve under him he would not serve under Strafford "being now Genrall of the Army and lyeing under his displeasure".[33] Instead, Sir Hugh recommended his brother, Sir Henry, his "Lieutenant Corronell", as his replacement and offered to bring his former regiment "to the place of Rendevouz" himself. Consequently, on the night of 28 August 1640, when the Scottish troops crossed over the river Tyne "and had foiled the king's army", Cholmley's Bluecoats stood guard over the king at Northallerton.[34]

The rout of the royal troops at Newburn and the fall of Newcastle that inevitably followed opened the way of the Scots all the way to the Tees. Charles retreated to York and Cholmley's Bluecoats dispersed to their homes in the North Riding. On 10 September Charles made yet another appeal to the Yorkshire gentry: he asked them to raise sufficient money to pay for their trained bands for the next two months.[35]

According to Sir Hugh's less than perfect memory, the king asked him and the others present at York to have "the trayned bands to march at their owne charge" and to meet the earl of Strafford the next day "at the towne Hall to consult of this". However, that evening the county's leaders, Philip, Lord Wharton, Ferdinando, Lord Fairfax, Sir John Hotham and himself, drew up a petition in which they offered only a month's subsistence for the militias backdated from the end of August. This petition of 12 September, the third of its kind, listed a familiar lengthy catalogue of misery lately endured by their county: "shippmony ... levyed for divers yeres past. The vast expenses of the county the last yere in military affaires. The biliting and insolencies of the souldiers this summer...The great decay of trade. The stopp of markets [so that] your Gentry by the failing of their rents are very much impoverished". The petition ended with a new sting in its tail: the petitioners "desired his Majestie to call a Parliament".[36]

In Cholmley's later words, this petition was "signed by the Nobillety and greatest part of the gentlemen to the number of 140, and the Lord Fairfax chosen to deliver it". Perhaps on this occasion Sir Hugh was not exaggerating the support given to this complaint by his fellow Yorkshiremen. Indeed, apart from the usual suspects such as Hotham and himself, there were many surprising signatories. Lord Ferdinando Fairfax had previously led his trained band as far as the Scottish border and paid for them out of his own purse; Sir Thomas Danby was Strafford's cousin and his close ally; Sir Edward Rodes was his brother-in-law; Sir William Pennyman had hitherto given unqualified backing to the earl. And there were many other gentlemen who had not endorsed the previous two petitions.[37]

However, from this point on, Cholmley's testimony, both at Strafford's trial and in his own memoirs, is at variance with other accounts. Clearly, Sir Hugh was concerned to blame Strafford for blocking this petition which Lord Fairfax was not allowed to present personally to the king. Only the following day, 13 September, after most of the petitioners had left York and accompanied by "some few gentlemen his creatures", did Strafford "deliver to the king the sence of the country quite contrary to what they intended and had expressed in the great pet[it]ion". As a result of Strafford's dishonest attempt to misinform Charles and misrepresent the petitioners, "16 of the princypall and most active gentlemen met together with intent to petetion his majestie against the answear given by Lord Strafford". The sixteen included Lord Wharton, Sir John Savile, Henry Bellasis, Hotham and Cholmley.

After one of the sixteen, Sir William Savile, had betrayed the meeting to the king, he summoned four of them, Wharton, Bellasis, Hotham and Cholmley; rebuked them for unlawful conduct; and threatened them in future with Star Chamber. However, on this occasion, Charles pardoned their gross misbehaviour "because he loved us all well ... and after many gud words dismissed us".[38]

The next morning, as Hotham and Cholmley were "redy to put foot in to stirrappe", the king's messenger arrived to tell them that Charles wished to see them both at once. Clearly, the king's mood had changed since the previous day. Now he "reprehended" them "in very sharpe woords", telling them that they had been "the cheife cause and promoters of all the petetions from the Country (which indeed was truth)". Then he warned them both "in plane tearmes" that if they had a hand in any more petitions he would have them hanged! Whether the king's attempt to frighten the two of them was advised by Strafford, Cholmley did not say, but he probably suspected it.[39]

Sir Hugh's version of what happened at these critical encounters in York is not entirely credible. Several other accounts of the meeting that took place on 13 September between Strafford and about 200 Yorkshiremen agree that a majority of them consented to maintain the county's trained bands for at least another fortnight and drop the demand for a new parliament if, in return, Yorkshire's future militia requirement was halved from 12,000 to 6,000. These accommodating Yorkshiremen were certainly not all Strafford's "creatures" who later, at Strafford's trial, Cholmley alleged were all papists and convicted recusants. On the contrary, adopting an uncharacteristic tactic, on this occasion Strafford had outmanoeuvred the hostile faction led by Hotham and Cholmley, and won over a majority of fellow Yorkshiremen.[40]

Throughout this episode Cholmley emphasized that his quarrel was with Strafford and not with the king. At their final meeting at York, once again Sir Hugh had protested against the denial of direct access to the sovereign by "our Lord President", implying that Strafford was unable or unwilling to accept the justice of the grievances of "Country gentlemen ... with out acquaintance in Court". And the king's farewell response could hardly have been more encouraging and sympathetic: to Sir Hugh, he said: "...when soever you have any cause of complaynt come to mee and I will heare it".[41]

During this time of petition-drafting and head-on conflict with Strafford, it would be wrong to assume that Cholmley was in league with the other English conspirators who were secretly colluding with the Scots. It is doubtful whether Sir Hugh was even aware of the treasonable correspondence that passed between the puritan peers such as Warwick, Bedford, Saye, Brooke, Essex and Mandeville and the Scottish Covenanters, or even of the pro-Scottish intrigues of his neighbour, Henry Darley of Buttercrambe and his brother-in-law, John Alured of Sculcoates. As the most recent, thorough investigator of this collusion had to concede: "How closely, if at all, Hotham and Cholmeley were involved with the London-based Petitioners remains obscure..."[42]

If Sir Hugh had been aware that Thomas, Lord Savile, Strafford's long-time enemy, or Philip, Lord Wharton, had encouraged the Scots to invade England, then he would have strongly disapproved of their treason.[43] Several of Cholmley's illustrious forebears had literally won their spurs on the battlefield fighting the Scots and there is no evidence that he had any fellow-feeling with the Covenanter rebels. Though Sir Hugh's self-justifying memoirs must be read with cautious scepticism, no evidence elsewhere has come to light to link him with the faction of noble conspirators in London or collusionists in Yorkshire.[44] On the other hand, if Cholmley had known that in May 1640 Strafford had negotiated a secret treaty with Catholic Spain against Protestant Holland that would finance the war with the Scots and that he planned to bring 3,000 Irish troops to fight them, he would have had even greater cause to fear and hate "our Lord President". Only the failure of the Spanish to deliver a promised loan of £300,000 forced Strafford and Charles to seek the financial aid of another parliament.[45]

Strafford's presence in York in the late summer of 1640 gave Charles new heart, but it also stiffened the resistance of Yorkshiremen like Sir Hugh to a war with the Scots. There was a significant contrast between how so many of Yorkshire's elite responded positively to Charles's perceived concessions and how they reacted robustly to Strafford's brusque insults. When Charles conferred on his Lord Lieutenant, Lord President and Lord Deputy the blue ribbon of the Knight of the Garter, it was intended as a gesture of royal faith and favour; it did nothing to reconcile the earl's enemies to serve under him. Sir Hugh was not the only Yorkshireman who was loyal to the king, yet would not take orders from his commanding general.[46]

The king's decision to call a new parliament before the end of the year was not forced upon him by Cholmley and his fellow petitioners as he liked to believe. In fact, by 12 September, Charles was under the greatest pressure from several directions to make a truce with the Scots and resume a campaign against them after a new parliament had filled his empty treasury. And the terms of the agreement made at Ripon in mid-October only exacerbated the king's financial dilemma: the Scots were to receive £850 a day for at least the next two months while they continued to occupy Northumberland and Durham.[47] The crown's dependence on parliamentary subsidy had become urgent and desperate.

CHAPTER 7

LONG PARLIAMENT

The October elections for the new parliament that opened on 3 November 1640 were a disaster for Strafford's cause in Yorkshire. Of the county's 30 seats in the Commons, only five were won by his committed supporters. For the shire, Yorkshire's freeholders chose Ferdinando, Lord Fairfax and Henry Bellasis, two of Strafford's "thorns", in preference to Sir William Savile and Sir Richard Hutton, despite the high sheriff's efforts to frustrate them by transferring the poll from York to Pontefract, a Wentworth pocket-borough. The burgesses of Beverley again elected Sir John Hotham and put one of Strafford's "papist creatures", Sir Thomas Metham of North Cave, bottom of the poll. The citizens of the city of York spurned both of the earl's nominees, Sir Edward Osborne, who had sat in the Short Parliament, and Sir Thomas Widdrington, the recorder, and selected two puritan aldermen instead. At Scarborough, the 44 electors rejected Strafford's cousin, Sir George Wentworth of Woolley, and William Sheffield of Mulgrave, who recommended himself, and remained loyal to their two former representatives, Sir Hugh Cholmley and John Hotham.[1] When they were newly-enfranchised, Northallerton and New Malton chose Henry Darley, who had been imprisoned by Strafford for "treason", and Sir Henry Cholmley, Hugh's younger brother.[2] The result was a landslide victory for Yorkshire's anti-Straffordians.

There are many inexplicable gaps in Cholmley's retrospective memoirs: the most conspicuous and, from an historical viewpoint, the most serious and disabling is the hiatus between November 1640 and August 1642. During most of these 20 months Sir Hugh was a very active leading member of the Long Parliament, yet though these times were vital in the history of the nation and in his own career, he allowed them little more than a single folio out of 155.[3]

Sir Hugh's subsequent neglect of parliamentary affairs and his own part in them was not accidental or the result of a curious lapse of memory. As a latter-day royalist, who had changed sides during the first civil war, he was embarrassed by and perhaps even ashamed of his earlier parliamentary loyalties and activities. Secondly, though he continued to believe that personally he had been ill-treated by Strafford, he could not bring himself to describe, even less excuse, his role in the denunciation and death of that man. Of Strafford's trial and execution there is not one word in Cholmley's memoirs.

Not much of Sir Hugh's conduct in the proceedings of the Long Parliament is revealed in the *Commons Journal,* yet even according to that bald, brief summary he attended Westminster almost daily, apart from the summer recess of 9 September to 20 October 1641 and his six-week absence in York as a parliamentary commissioner during May and June 1642.[4]

There is no mention of Cholmley in the *Commons Journal* between 27 February and 2 April 1641 because during that time he brought Elizabeth and their children from Whitby to London. The presence of a Scottish army in Durham "did not a little disquiet [his] mynde": he was afraid that it might cross the Tees into north Yorkshire. However, that winter the snow was so heavy that it was not until the end of February that "the wayes were passeable" and they were able to come south to London. The Cholmleys lived first at "Thisselworth" (Isleworth) and then, from the beginning of 1642, in a house in Chiswick rented from Lord Paulet. In both these places they were very comfortable. "I prayse god," Sir Hugh afterwards wrote, "I lived in great plenty and in a handsome condetion haveing neare 30 in famuly, 4 coachhorses and 1 saddle horse." During most of the week he was at Westminster, returning home every Saturday.[5]

Sir Hugh sat on more than 30 parliamentary committees: some afternoons he had a choice of several. They ranged in importance from the fairly trivial, which sat to determine the length of the Michaelmas term or the organisation of inland posts, to the crucial, which drew up charges against the earl of Strafford and archbishop Laud, examined complaints against the assessment and collection of Ship Money, monopolies, breaches of House of Commons privileges, and the conduct of the royal army garrisoned in Yorkshire. Cholmley was a member of the Commons committees that drafted bills on annual parliaments, "the securing of true religion in the Kingdom", compensation for forced billeting, and trained bands. He was one of the members who investigated the records of the Court of High Commission, of Star Chamber, and of the Council of the North at York. Frequently, he acted as messenger between the two Houses and often reported back to the Commons from committee. He proposed motions, made speeches in major debates, and acted as teller in divisions. Though never chairman of any important committee, and therefore not quite of the parliamentary rank of Fairfax or Hotham, for nearly two years he was one of the most busy and influential 20 or 30 members of the Commons.[6]

During the first few months of the Long Parliament, one of Sir Hugh's less honourable purposes was to seek out and bring down those he regarded as his enemies in Yorkshire. Starting with smaller fry, Sir William Pennyman and Francis Nevile of Chevet, he later moved on to Sir William Savile and finally to "that great engine", the earl of Strafford. These were actions of calculated and unscrupulous revenge which in much later years Sir Hugh probably came to regret. Predictably, there is no reference to them in his memoirs.

On 4 December 1640, Sir Henry Anderson of Long Cowton, one of Sir John Hotham's many relatives, raised the subject in the Commons of what he called "the insolencies of the Kings armie". These "insolencies", he argued, had inflicted more injury on innocent Yorkshire folk than the Scots had done in Durham. Among these outrages Anderson identified the forcible collection of money by a certain Captain Yoward in Langbaurgh (Cleveland) wapentake in the North Riding. Cholmley then intervened by saying that all the irregularities in Langbaurgh sprang from the warrant of the local deputy-lieutenant, Sir William Pennyman. This warrant, dated 19 October 1640, had authorised constables to collect money or conscript defaulters. On 15 December, Sir William, member for Richmond and a most active officer in the royal army, confessed to the Commons that his warrant "might perhapps bee illegal". However, in self-defence, he pleaded "the law of necessitie": the Scots were then "advanced to the verie skirts of Yorkshire" and he preferred to "fall under the mercie of this House then under the contribution of the Scotts".[7]

Cholmley brushed aside Pennyman's excuses: like a later Nuremberg prosecutor he dismissed the plea of necessity. Before the warrant was even issued "all things were settled" and therefore there was no necessity to issue or execute it. If by "settled" Cholmley meant the conclusion of the treaty of Ripon with the Scots, then he was wrong: it was not signed until two days after the date of Pennyman's warrant. Nevertheless, Sir Hugh's argument went unchallenged and the matter was referred to the committee set up to examine the misconduct of lords lieutenants during the late war with the Scots. Cholmley was also a member of that committee and everyone knew that the greatest of these lords lieutenants was Strafford.[8]

Clearly, Cholmley had a sharpened knife out for Pennyman. Sir William's close attachment to Strafford was enough to place him on Sir Hugh's short black list, but there were other related reasons. Pennyman was from Marske, further up the coast from Whitby, and therefore a fairly adjacent neighbour. As such, he owned the land where alum was mined and manufactured at Slapewath and Selby Hagg. For these he received £600 a year in rent from the leaseholder of the alum monopoly, the earl of Strafford. Cholmley already knew that there were alum shales on his land at Saltwick, yet Strafford had denied him a permit to exploit them. This explains some of the sources of Sir Hugh's hostility to Strafford and his envy of Pennyman. Certainly Pennyman and Strafford were hand in glove. When Sir William later spoke in the earl's favour at his trial and was then threatened by one of the prosecution lawyers, Strafford told the court: "This gentleman is my noble friend and I would give him my life on any occasion."[9] Pennyman was one of only two Commons-men who asked for leave to visit Strafford in the Tower just prior to his execution in May 1641.[10]

Another North Riding gentleman in the Commons, Sir Thomas Danby, who owed his knighthood to Strafford, and whose regiment along with Pennyman's held the south bank of the Tees against the Scots, was also reprimanded by the House for his alleged misdeeds as a deputy-lieutenant.[11]

From the previous Short Parliament there were also scores to settle with Francis Nevile and Sir William Savile. These two had revealed to the Privy Council what Hotham and Bellasis had said in the Commons about the burden on Yorkshire of militia coat and conduct money. Nevile had also informed against Cholmley. However, when Nevile had consulted his "table-bookes" to check what had been said but was unable to substantiate his allegation against Sir Hugh, he was sent to the Tower during the pleasure of the Commons. Savile was also treated as a "delinquent" for ratting on his former friends: to escape further punishment he pleaded guilty and asked for pardon which was granted.[12]

Finally, there was "the great incendiary" himself, Lord Strafford. Cholmley's own part in the lengthy, squalid, vindictive and ultimately successful pursuit of the Lord President to the scaffold was relatively insignificant. As with many of his fellow Yorkshiremen who nursed grudges against him and feared his revenge, for Sir Hugh it was not safe enough to put him in prison and remove him from all his positions of power: he had to die. Cholmley would have endorsed Lord Essex's blunt conclusion that "stone dead hath no fellow."[13]

As early as 30 November 1640, Sir Hugh was named as one of the 30 Commons-men who were to form a joint committee with the Lords to draw up articles of impeachment against Strafford, who had already been arrested and imprisoned in the Tower. As for the trial itself, which began on 22 March 1641, Cholmley does not appear to have attended Westminster Hall until its twelfth day, 2 April. Five days later, he was called as a prosecution witness to support Article 27 which read:

> That in or about the month of August last, he was made Lieutenant-General of all his Majesty's forces in the North, prepared against the Scots; and being at York, did then in the month of September by his own authority and without any lawful warrant, impose a tax on his Majesty's subjects in the county of York of 8 pence per diem for maintenance of every soldier of the trained bands of the county: which sums of money he caused to be levied by force... [14]

Though Cholmley had nothing relevant to offer in direct endorsement of Article 27, he still launched into his own attack on Strafford. The Lord Lieutenant had intercepted and rejected the petition of the Yorkshire gentry of 12 September addressed to the king; he had mischievously misreported the intent of this petition to the king; and when some of the petitioners had protested at his misconduct he had failed to convey their dissatisfaction to the king. Charles was blameless; Strafford alone was culpable. [15]

Cholmley's next contention that the county's gentry had not agreed to finance their militia for another month drew no backing from the prosecution and was strongly denied by Strafford himself and his witnesses, Osborne, Savile, Rodes and Danby. In his defence, Strafford said that only three or four out of 200 gentlemen present at York had opposed an extension of the county's contribution to militia costs. [16]

When cross-examined about his accusation that all Strafford's friends at York were Catholic recusants, Sir Hugh's reply was vague, evasive and unconvincing. As far as he could recall, about 24 or 26 of the earl's "creatures" were suspected of being clandestine papists, but he could not say whether any of them were convicted recusants. Cholmley's performance was weak: not until a year later did he actually identify some of Yorkshire's Straffordians by name. Finally, since Sir Hugh had himself been deprived of his colonel's militia commission in the early summer of 1640, it was left to his brother Henry, who had succeeded to it, to provide relevant evidence in support of Article 27. [17]

At first, Henry could say only that Strafford in person had told him that he intended to impose a levy on the goods of anyone who refused to fund Yorkshire's militias. When questioned closely, however, he then had to admit that to his knowledge the Lord Lieutenant had never carried out this threat. Later, Henry produced the warrant issued by Osborne, dated 31 August 1640, requiring him to raise 20 shillings and eight pence, 31 days allowance for each of his common soldiers; but again he could not cite evidence to endorse the charge alleged in Article 27 that force had been used to collect the money. Strafford denied point blank that he had issued a warrant to Pennyman for the Cleveland trained band and no proof could be found that he had done so. Whatever the so-called "insolencies" committed by the infamous Captain Yoward or Yaworth, the general could not be blamed for them. [18]

The failure of the Yorkshire anti-Straffordians to pin the charge in Article 27 on Strafford at his trial was characteristic of the general ineffectiveness of the prosecution. Nevertheless, since "Black Tom" could not be proved guilty of a capital crime according to the judicial rules of evidence put before his peers in the House of Lords, some speedier and certain way had to be found to exterminate him. [19] So John Pym, leader of the dissident Commons-men, came up with a Bill of Attainder. Accordingly, within eleven days, the Bill had been introduced and passed its third reading in the Commons by 204 votes to 59. Only six Yorkshire MPs voted against Strafford's death: Sir Thomas Danby and Sir William Pennyman (Richmond); Sir Henry Slingsby (Knaresborough); Richard Aldeburgh (Aldborough); one of the Mallorys (Ripon) and one of the Wentworths (Pontefract). Needless to say, both Hothams and both Cholmleys voted with the majority. The names of the 59 who had tried to save Strafford were advertised in the streets of Westminster and London with the words: "These are the Straffordians, enemies of justice, betrayers of their country."[20]

On most issues at this time Cholmley was at one with Pym and his reformist party. Sir Hugh welcomed the abolition of the unpopular royal prerogative courts - Star Chamber, High Commission and the Council of the North. The Council at York, through which Strafford had exercised so much power even from Ireland, was of special concern to Yorkshiremen like Cholmley. As Lord Clarendon later observed, Yorkshire's MPs "were marvellously solicitous to dispatch the commitment of the court at York" because to them it was "illegal ... and very prejudiciall to the liberty and property of his majesty's subjects..."[21] Furthermore, Cholmley had long since questioned the legality of the annual Ship Money tax and was glad to see the Long Parliament declare it illegal in August 1641; and as a champion of "the liberty of the subject", he also welcomed attacks on commercial monopolies, forced loans and free billeting. However, it was on this same principle of individual freedom that he first came into conflict with Pym when in February 1641 he proposed that the city of London should be compelled to make a loan to the Commons. In the words of Peyton's contemporary journal:

> Sir Hugh Cholmeley disliked the motion exceedingly as contrary to the fundamental liberty of the subject and said, that every poore man and every riche man had equall power and right in the Lawes of the Land...

On this occasion, Cholmley carried the House and Pym's motion was rejected. Instead, the Commons voted two subsidies to maintain the royal army in Yorkshire.[22]

This was not the first time that Sir Hugh had stood up in the Commons chamber for the rights of the poor. In a disputed case arising from an election in October 1640 when propertyless voters had been denied the franchise, "Sir Hugh Cholmeley mooved that they should have voices". And even more surprisingly, Sir John Hotham, a notorious conservative, supported Cholmley's motion.[23]

In what might seem a directly contradictory viewpoint, Sir Hugh also displayed an unusual and unfashionable respect for King Charles and his Catholic queen. In February 1641 he expressed a surprising degree of graciousness towards Henrietta Maria. The House had accused her of collecting money to help recusants, of consorting with the Pope and his envoys, and of encouraging English Catholics to attend her private chapel. In reply, the Queen defended herself against these charges and, as a gesture of goodwill, promised to dismiss the Pope's representative from the royal court. After her response had been read out to the Commons, "there was a general silence", followed by calls to proceed with the business of the day. At this point, Cholmley intervened and moved that the House might thank the Queen for her conciliatory message; "but none said well moved or gave anie great approbation of it". Given Sir Hugh's well-known hostility to Catholics, his lone defence of Henrietta Maria suggests either guileless political innocence, a strong personal attraction to her, or both. Two years later, when he changed sides in the civil war after a private audience with the Queen at York, his earlier words in the Commons were remembered by his enemies.[24]

At the beginning of 1642, Sir Hugh again made public his protective and respectful attitude to the royal family. After the king's foolhardy failure to arrest his leading parliamentary adversaries, the Five Members, he retreated from the palace of Whitehall with his wife and children first to Hampden Court and then to Windsor Castle on 12 January. Hearing the news, Sir Hugh moved that the Commons "might send to his majesty to express our grief for his absenting himself from us and to desire him to return and to conceive that we are his best and surest guard". In reply, Denzil Holles, one of the famous Five, protested that until Charles had withdrawn his allegations and apologised for violating the privileges of the House of Commons, he did not deserve such expressions of loyalty.[25]

Despite the hostility of the majority of the House, the following day, 14 January, Cholmley tried again. He said that he understood that the king and queen entertained many fears and "jealousies" [misunderstandings?] and that Charles believed that Parliament intended to erode his authority and impeach his wife for "high crimes". He moved therefore that the House might "think of some speedy way of removing these jealousies between King and Parliament". As on the previous day, Sir Hugh's conciliatory words were not well received by some Members. Indeed, so distrustful were they of the Stuarts that it was seriously suggested that the heir to the throne, the young Prince Charles of Wales, should be removed from his parents and placed in the custody of the Commons. Cholmley promptly parried this new insult by a moderate motion that the king should not "permit the prince to be carried out of the realm with[out] the humble advice and consent of parliament", a motion that was carried.[26] Another version of this episode to be found in the private journal of John Moore records that it was Sir Hugh himself who proposed that Prince Charles should be brought back from Windsor to Whitehall;[27] but this seems inconsistent with what we know of his favourable and forgiving attitude to the royal family.

Sir Hugh's genuine concern for the welfare of the heir to the throne had been already demonstrated in the Commons six months earlier. In June 1641, after the earl of Newcastle, a close friend of Strafford, was suspected of plotting against Parliament, Sir Hugh moved that he should be dismissed from his post of governor and guardian of the Prince and replaced by Thomas Howard, the reliable and "innocuous" earl of Berkshire. However, Sir Henry Mildmay and others regarded this motion as an unwarranted trespass on the king's right to choose his own son's governor. In the event, Newcastle soon resigned from the position and Charles appointed the marquess of Hertford instead of Berkshire.[28] Though it is not entirely clear what Cholmley's motives were in this matter, given his record on royalty, they were probably protective, not sinister. Any former friend and past ally of Strafford was no friend of Cholmley.

As for Sir Hugh's religious views at this time, they are the hardest to discover and define, though doubtless they coloured his outlook on many controversial issues. His attitude to Catholicism in general was somewhere in the contemporary English Protestant spectrum between the extremes of grudging tolerance and hysterical hatred. Reference has already been made to his scornful description of Strafford's "creatures" as papists and recusants. Time and again he returned to this theme, not just before and during Strafford's trial, but long after the earl was safely beheaded. For instance, on 22

April 1642, in the name of the whole county, about 20 Yorkshire gentlemen asked the king to leave the arms and ammunition at Hull where they were stored. They knew that Parliament was anxious to transport the contents of the Hull magazine to London so that they and not the king could use it. Among the Yorkshire petitioners were Sir Francis Wortley, Sir Richard Hutton, Sir William Wentworth, Sir John Gibson, Sir Thomas Metham and Sir Bryan Palmes. Three days later, the Commons reacted indignantly to news of this petition. Sir Philip Stapleton of Warter denounced it as an attack on Parliament. Cholmley's response was to deride the petitioners as the same men who had colluded with Strafford at York in September 1640. In fact, of these Yorkshire "Royalists" none was a Catholic and only Metham had Catholic family relations. Nevertheless, in Sir Hugh's irredeemably partisan mind, "papist" and "Straffordian" had become the same.[29]

Cholmley seems to have been constantly on his guard in fear of Catholics. When in January 1642, Ralph Killingham asked for a military post, Cholmley said: "there were many of that name who were papist" and recommended that he should first be "examined" before his fate was determined.[30] But the papists who troubled Sir Hugh the most were fellow countymen. At the beginning of February 1642, when the House was discussing the security situation in Yorkshire, the name of Henry Constable, first Viscount Dunbar of Burton Constable in the East Riding, came up. Then "Henry Bellasis, Sir Hugh Cholmley and others ... moved that the Lord Dunbar in Yorkshire was a powerful papist and had lately provided great store of arms and had great resort to him."[31] In this there was certainly some truth: Henry Constable was one of the most influential landowners in the East Riding who had compounded for his recusancy in 1630 and had collected money from other Catholics in 1639 for the royal army. Also, Burton Constable in Holderness was dangerously close to the port and magazine at Hull.[32] Consequently, the House ordered Dunbar to appear before it to answer the charges against him.

Sir Hugh was especially sensitive about the threat of home-grown Catholics because of his own family associations, past and present, with them and their continued strength in his locality. In 1641 there were said to be as many as 138 recusants living at Egton, 39 at Whitby and 38 at Brandsby, where his Cholmley cousins remained steadfastly loyal to the old faith.[33]

Though Whitby is as distant from Ireland as any place in England, events there preyed on his mind. In March 1641, for instance, when Strafford was locked up in the Tower and the Irish Catholic rebellion still in the future, Sir Hugh was worried by the thought of papists in arms, Irish or English. In an irrelevant interruption, for which he was rebuked by the Speaker, he moved that "wee might take into consideration the disbanding of the new popish armie in Ireland and the disarming of the papists at home".[34]

After the Irish Catholic revolt in October 1641 confirmed his worst fears, like most English Protestants, Cholmley suffered from nightmares about invasion, rapine and slaughter. Anti-Catholic prejudice was already deeply ingrained in English Protestant society, but events in Ireland raised endemic fears into hysteria. The facts were bad enough: perhaps as many as 4,000 Protestant men, women and children had been murdered, some after terrible torture and mutilation, and double that number had died of starvation and exposure. Many more thousands had fled to England and Scotland bringing with them terrifying tales of their sufferings. Yet soon the true figures were totally distorted and the atrocities multiplied. By April 1642, 154,000 Protestant murders were reported and generally believed when there had been fewer than 100,000 Protestants living in the whole of Ireland. By then the Irish rising had come to be regarded as part of a devilish papist plot to wipe out Protestantism there as a prelude to a Catholic invasion of England.[35]

Normally level-headed and moderate, Sir Hugh seems to have caught some of the epidemic of paranoia which swept England after the alarming news from Ireland. In January 1642, for example, he reported to the Commons that he had received a letter from Yorkshire "which concerned the public". The letter had been sent from Whitby by his "cousin" James Cholmley and referred to the activities of a notorious papist, Sir Basil Brooke, who had "come lately out of Ireland". Though Brooke was said to be "at a castle called Desborough" which was in West Wycombe, Buckinghamshire, according to the *Commons Journal,* Cholmley's letter concerned "the great Fears of the people of the East Riding of Yorkshire are in, by reason of the Papists thereabouts". What Brooke had to do with the East Riding was not explained, though Cholmley's letter was just one more illustration of the widespread fear of a Catholic uprising in England.[36]

To say that Sir Hugh was hostile to and fearful of Catholics is to say no more than that he was a typical Protestant of his time and place. A far more difficult question is to ask where in the wide Protestant range between the extremes of Laudian and Calvinist were his views to be found. For a matter which had such great contemporary significance there are surprisingly few clues in the records and therefore any conclusion reached is necessarily tentative.

One of the historians of the church in England, Thomas Fuller, identified two different kinds of Protestant Puritans at this time: "some mild and moderate, contented only to enjoy their own conscience; others fierce and fiery, to the disturbance of church and state".[37] Of Sir Hugh Cholmley it can be safely written that his religious inclination was closer to the former than the latter kind.

There is little evidence in the parliamentary proceedings of 1640 to 1642 of Cholmley's religious views, but what there is suggests strongly that his puritanism was reformist and temperate. During the 1630s attempts made by archbishops Laud at Canterbury and Neile at York to restore altars to the eastern end of Anglican churches and rail them off from the laity were deeply resented and resisted by Puritans who regarded such changes as "papist". Railed stone altars set at the chancel end of churches, rather than plain wooden communion tables in the body of the congregation, were associated with the Catholic mass and the separation of clergy from the people. In October 1640, a London mob had invaded St Paul's cathedral and attacked its restored altar and during the following year there were many similar acts of violent iconoclasm.[38]

On Wednesday, 19 April 1640, during an assembly of the Short Parliament, the Commons debated the controversial question of the proper location of church altars. After many Members had spoken condemning Laudian innovations as "popish", according to one eyewitness, "Sir Hugh Chamley" then stood up to say that he did not care where the altar was placed; for him the offence was to bow to it. "Hee cares not which way it stands but to the matter of bowing to it, offence."[39] This was the opinion of a man whose family had built their private pew across the chancel arch so that they sat with their backs to the altar facing the preacher's pulpit below them.

Condemnation of Laudian reforms in the Short Parliament of 1640 was merely the opening salvo of a bombardment directed against the established Anglican church in the

Long Parliament which culminated in the debate on the Grand Remonstrance in November 1641. Up to this point Cholmley had gone along with the radical reformers led by Pym and Hampden. More or less in harmony with them, he had joined in the attack on and the expulsion of royal ministers, the abolition of unpopular taxes and prerogative courts, and even given his assent to the Triennial Bill in February 1641, which effectively made Parliament a permanent and indispensable part of the government of the kingdom. However, by the autumn recess of 1641, the question of the Church of England Book of Common Prayer, its Thirty-Nine Articles of doctrine and the status and role of its bishops had become issues that opened up growing divisions between Commons-men.

The direct, radical assault on the Anglican episcopacy came to a climax in the final stages of the heated debate on the Grand Remonstrance, a lengthy catalogue of grievances against the Crown dating back to 1627 and drawn up by Pym and his accomplices. It was at this moment that Cholmley was identified with what came to be called "the episcopall partie" by Simmonds D'Ewes, who kept a record of the debate. When the Commons reached clause 189, which accused the bishops of introducing "idolatrous and Popish ceremonies",[40] Sir Edward Dering spoke strongly against it and Cholmley supported him. D'Ewes took the opposite side. The House was fairly evenly and passionately divided. The Speaker therefore put it to the vote. Dering and Cholmley were appointed as tellers for the Noes "who were 99", but the vote in favour was 124. With undisguised satisfaction, D'Ewes wrote in his diary that "the episcopall partie failed of ther expectation".[41] Nevertheless, whatever his misgivings about some of its clauses, Sir Hugh was one of the 159 members who subsequently supported the Grand Remonstrance and not one of the 148 who voted against it. Perhaps like others of the "episcopall partie" he was mollified by Pym's concession not to include a clause condemning the "errors and superstitions" of the Book of Common Prayer.[42]

If Cholmley belonged to a moderate Anglican persuasion he still had some Puritan tendencies. He wanted to keep bishops but agreed that they exercised too much power; he wanted to keep the Anglican Prayer Book with only minor revisions; he certainly wanted a more severe and sustained campaign against Catholics; and he probably preferred a greater emphasis on preaching in the ministry. These are thinly-informed suppositions, rather than established facts, derived mostly from hints and clues and not based firmly on direct documentary evidence.

Some of these "clues" have been mentioned earlier. In his adult years, Sir Hugh reacted against his misspent youth for practical rather than moral reasons. Though coloured by filial devotion, his account of Sir Richard could not have been that of a stern, unforgiving Puritan of the Hoby kind. Without any trace of disapproval, he recorded in his memoirs that his father had fought several duels and at length, with obvious pleasure and pride, he described how Sir Richard got the better of an impertinent Southerner who had tried to make a fool of him in public. For Sir Hugh, as for his father, personal honour had to be upheld even if it meant employing physical violence. He did not regret that he had floored "the stubborne fellow of Pickering" who had given him "some unha[n]dsome langwidge": the fault had been to lose his temper and hit the man too hard. Personal and family honour were clearly the highest considerations to Cholmley.[43]

Cholmley deplored the sexual licence of his male ancestors; yet again, not for moral reasons: producing too many bastard children as well as legitimate ones was an unnecessary impoverishing drain on a gentleman's estate. He would have to find portions for his daughters and legacies for his sons. As for his own sexual history, there are no frank revelations in Sir Hugh's memoirs, only references to unspecified debaucheries and youthful extravagances. In later life he condemned swearing, loss of self-control, time-wasting and expensive, vain outdoor pursuits such as hunting, hawking and horse-racing, as well as indoor gambling, card-playing, dicing and bowling. On the other hand, whereas most Puritans disapproved heartily of stage-plays, there is no evidence that Sir Hugh shared this prejudice. On the contrary, he took pride in the fact that his father had been an amateur actor during his time at Trinity College, Cambridge and was a devotee of the London theatre. As for self-indulgence at the dining table, the death of Sir Richard after "a surfett of oysters" as described by his son was intended as a medical rather than a moral warning.[44]

If Sir Hugh encountered no examples of puritan behaviour at home, as an adult he came under the influence of puritan relatives. He had married upwards into a strictly puritan family. Reference has been made already to the cultural chasm that separated the Cholmleys of Whitby from the Twysdens of Kent when Hugh married Elizabeth in 1622; and to the entirely beneficial affect of Elizabeth herself, her learned father, her pious, prudish, aristocratic mother and her distinguished brothers on young Hugh. With the Twysdens he had his first close encounter with puritan religiosity, high seriousness, frugality and scholarly learning.

Then there were the Yelvertons, who were at least as "godly" as the Twysdens. Sir Christopher has been called "a third-generation Puritan". The London preacher, Richard Stock, dedicated his puritan sermons to Sir Christopher's wife, the lady Anne, who was Hugh's sister-in-law.[45] The close contact between Hugh and Christopher during the 1630s has been noted and their friendship was to last until the former turned royalist in 1643.[46]

Of all the men who exercised influence on Cholmley, Sir John Hotham was the one who whose outlook, though not temperament, came closest to his own. The two had much in common. Lord Clarendon did not like Hotham, yet he had to admit that he was "as well affected to the government of the church of England ... as any man that had concurred" with the Roundhead party and the historian of the Yorkshire gentry thought that much the same could be said of Cholmley.[47] When Sir Hugh later wrote his essay on the Hothams for Clarendon's history, at some points he might have been describing himself. Of Sir John he wrote: " ... he was a man that loved libertie, which was an occation to make him ioyne att first with the puritan partie, to whome after hee became neerer lincked meerely for his owne interest and security, for in more than concerned the civill libertie he did not approve of their wayes". And of Hotham's relations with whom Cholmley called "the Presiser cleargie" who found sanctuary in Hull, he wrote: "they neither loved Sir John not hee them; of whome though hee made use out of politicke ends he did as much disrellish their humours and wayes as anie man livinge ..."[48]

The only direct contemporary reference to Cholmley and puritanism is to be found in the Morrice manuscripts quoted by Dr Cliffe. According to the antiquarian, though not himself a Puritan in religion, Sir Hugh was "kind and friendly to the Puritans or Professors of Religion".[49] Much depends on the timing of this observation, since Cholmley's attitude to radical religious reformers probably changed a great deal between the 1630s before the civil war and the late 1640s after it when he wrote his paper on the Hothams.

68

One such "professor of religion" who might have been in Morrice's mind was Robert Remmington, vicar of Whitby from 1624 until 1638. Sir Hugh had first met Remmington at Gray's Inn when they were both admitted there in 1618. However, at that time Hugh was more interested in games than in God and Robert had not yet experienced his own religious conversion. When Remmington took up his curacy at Whitby his predecessor there, Daniel Toes, had already established a puritan ministry. Toes had a local reputation as a fiery preacher with a passionate hatred of Catholicism. In his will he left a copy of Foxe's *Acts and Monuments* to the parish church with instructions to his executors to chain the volumes to the pew so that "well affected parishioners" might read them when they were free "from the preaching of the word and divine service". Since it described in graphic detail the Marian persecution of Protestant martyrs, Foxe's book was second only to the Bible as the favourite reading of Puritans. Finally, on condition that none of them married "a papist convicted", Toes left all his personal property to his widow and two daughters.[50]

After his arrival in Whitby, Remmington was troubled by the Court of High Commission. In 1627 he confessed that "he had bene divers tymes at Conventicles and unlawlull meetings contrarie to the Laws and Canons of the Church of England". For these transgressions he said he was "verie heartelie sorie" and promised "never to doe the like". This honest admission seems to have satisfied the commissioners: the following year, Remmington's preaching licence was restored to him. Perhaps he kept his promise: there is no further record of the High Commission having business with him.[51]

Alternatively, Remmington might have been shielded from the High Commission by his patron, Sir Hugh. Presumably the vicar owed his position to Hugh's father, Sir Richard, who had bought the lease of the rectory for £1,500.[52] Effectively, Whitby's parish church belonged to the Cholmleys who as rectors received the church tithes and appointed its priests to serve it.

Whatever Richard Remmington's religious views were by the 1630s, he and Cholmley had by then become much more than vicar and rector: they were good and trusted friends. Remmington's name appears three times in Sir Hugh's later memoirs, first as "Mr Reming(sic) the Minister then preacher", then, simply as "Minister of Whitby", and finally as "a grave Minister one Mr Remington". In 1632 the vicar travelled all the way from Whitby to Fyling Hall to baptise young Hugh Cholmley there. Six years later, he moved from Whitby to become rector of Lockington, one of Hotham's parishes in the East Riding; and during the civil war he and his family were in Scarborough with the Cholmleys. In August 1644 when Cholmley, the Royalist, asked in his terms of surrender for the re-instatement of all local clergymen then with him in the town, Parliament rejected this request, except in the case of "Mr Remmington". Nevertheless, the Remmingtons were not tempted by this concession to desert the Cholmleys. On the contrary, when the Scottish army began to close in on Scarborough in February 1645, Sir Hugh and Lady Elizabeth sent their two daughters to the safety of Holland in the care of Mr and Mrs Remmington. Robert was deprived of his living at Lockington in 1647, but unusually for an expelled minister he was provided with another place at Guisborough in 1650. After the Restoration, in 1661 he went back to Lockington.[53]

Sir Hugh's only explicit revelation of his religious views is to be found at the end of his memoirs where he described the death of his wife. After fulsome and lengthy praise of Elizabeth's many talents and virtues, he identified her as a "trew daughter of the Church of England dyeing in profession of [that] fayth booth in doctrine & discipline here established and practiced since the Reforma[tion] in the tyme of Ed[ward] the 6th till the beginning of these trobles". When Lady Elizabeth had known that she was dying she rejected the Presbyterian minister and asked instead for archbishop James Ussher of Armagh, a learned and godly divine. Though Ussher had faithfully attended Strafford at his execution, it seems that Sir Hugh shared his wife's approval of him by the time of her death.[54]

No doubt Cholmley's account of these events, written at the end of his life during Cromwell's Protectorate, was coloured and qualified by all that had happened during and since "these trobles" of civil wars and their aftermath. By 1655 he was much less of a Puritan and more of a remorseful conservative than he had been as a member of the Long Parliament. Nevertheless, the respected historical authority on that body was surely right when she wrote of Sir Hugh: "He seems to have been loyal to the Anglican church, with no leaning towards Presbyterianism"; whereas the nineteenth century's greatest historian of the civil wars was surely wrong to declare that Cholmley "had nothing of the Puritan in him".[55]

1. Sir Hugh Cholmley

2. Lady Elizabeth Cholmley

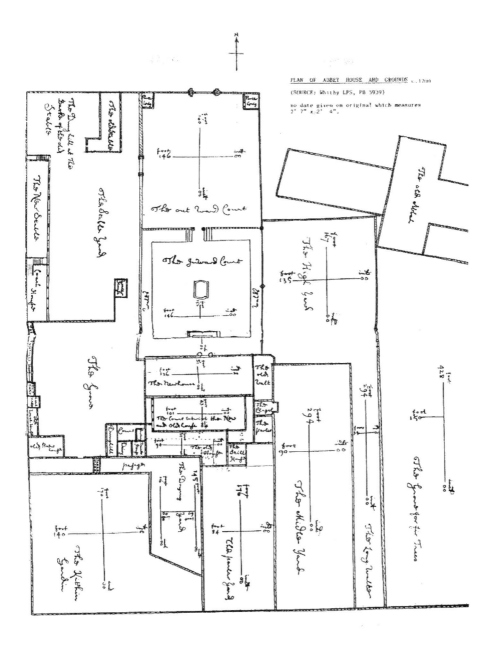

PLAN OF ABBEY HOUSE AND GROUNDS c.1700

(SOURCE: Whitby LPS, PB 5939)

no date given on original which measures
2' 7" x 2' 4".

3. Plan of Abbey House c.1700

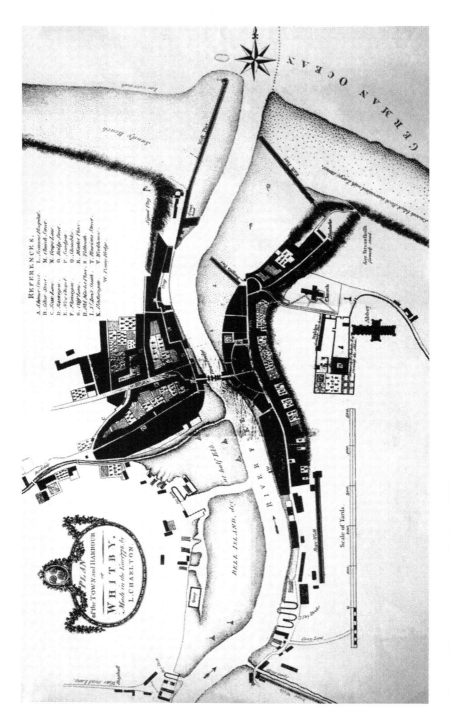

4 Lionel Charlton's map of Whitby 1778

5 Whitby and Harbour

6 Cholmley Pew in Whitby Parish Church

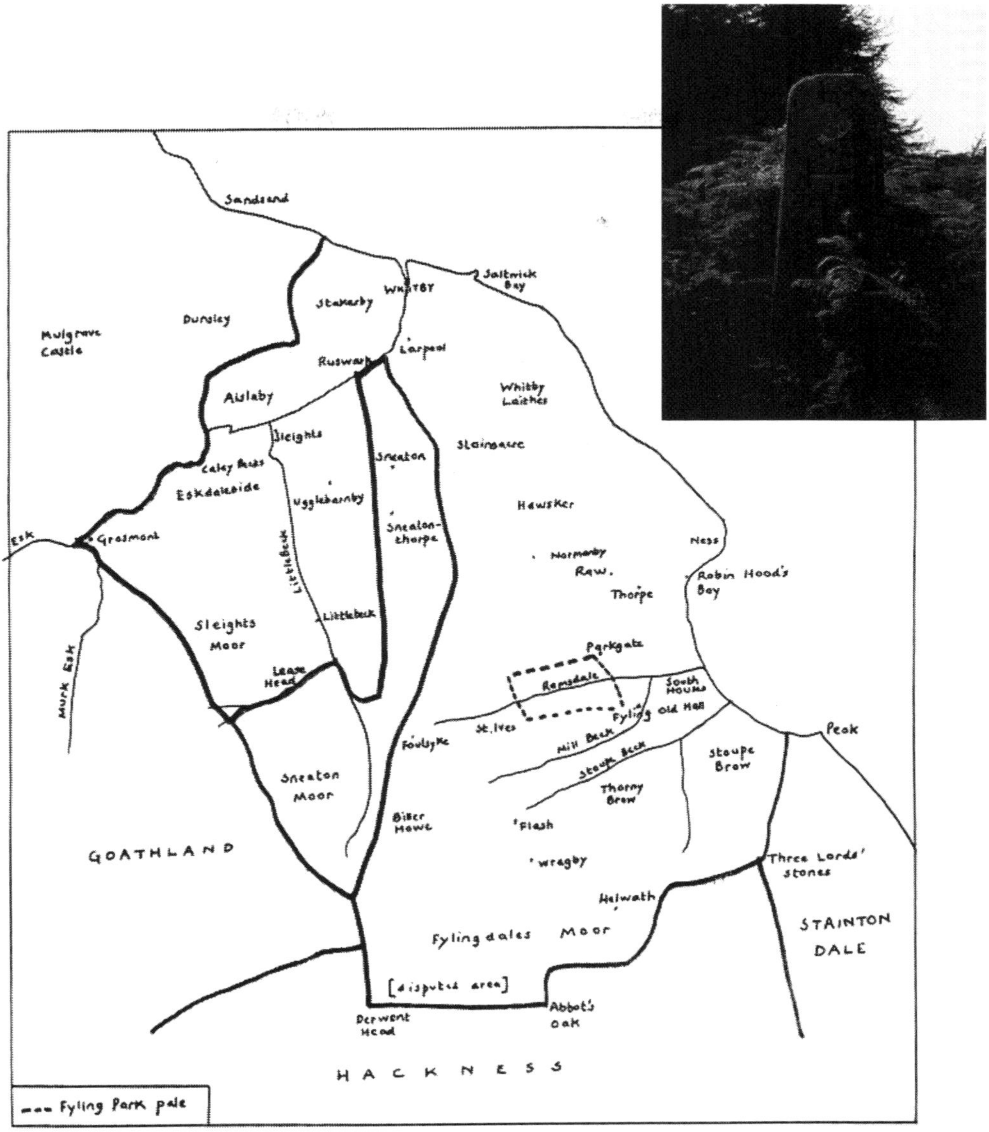
Sandsend
Saltwick Bay
WHITBY
Stakesby
Dunsley
Mulgrave Castle
Ruswarp
Larpool
Whitby Laithes
Aislaby
Sleights
Stainsacre
Sneaton
Eskdaleside
Ugglebarnby
Hawsker
Esk
Grosmont
Sneaton-thorpe
Ness
Normanby
Raw.
Robin Hood's Bay
Thorpe
Littlebeck
Littlebeck
Sleights Moor
Parkgate
Murk Esk
Lease Head
Ramsdale
South House
Fyling Old Hall
St. Ives
Foulsyke
Mill Beck
Stoupe Beck
Peak
Stoupe Brow
Sneaton Moor
Thorny Brow
Biller Howe
Flash
GOATHLAND
Wragby
Three Lords' stones
Helwath
STAINTON DALE
Fylingdales Moor
[disputed area]
Derwent Head
Abbot's oak
HACKNESS
Fyling Park pale

7 The Cholmley Estate in Whitby Strand with a Cholmley boundary stone inset

8 *Charles I and Henrietta Maria* by Daniel Mytens, 1630 -2

9 Fyling Old Hall

10 Thornton Parish Church where Sir Hugh was baptised and the "great blacke Knight of the North", his great-grandfather, Sir Richard (II), is buried

11 Jesus College, Cambridge

12 Roydon Hall, East Peckham, Kent

13 The keep of Scarborough Castle, ruined during the siege of 1645

14 Capt Browne Bushell 1609-51
[reproduced by kind permission of Pannett Park Museum, Whitby]

CHAPTER 8

"I AM FOR PEACE ... THEY ARE FOR WARRE"

Forty years ago the historian of the Yorkshire gentry believed that it could "no longer" be seriously entertained that "the Civil War was pre-eminently a conflict over religion".[1] Since then the historiographical wheel has turned full circle. In 1981, Professor Fletcher thought that it seemed "probable that religious commitment was a decisive factor for many who fought in the first campaign".[2] A few years later, John Morrill adventured even further in this direction: he asserted boldly that "the English Civil War ... was the last of the Wars of Religion".[3] This strong view seemed to endorse, at least on one side, Gardiner's late nineteenth century conclusion that the main driving force behind active resistance to Charles I was puritanism.[4] Yet the most recent scholarly and thorough investigation of the causes of the civil war that began in 1642 concluded that "the conflict could never have been exclusively, or perhaps even primarily, a "war of religion"; for ... the future state of the Church would ultimately be determined by the preferences of those who commanded the structures of secular power ..."[5] So the Civil War was about who ruled Charles's three kingdoms, a conflict for constitutional and political power with profoundly religious consequences.

Nevertheless, as Dr Cliffe had to concede, in Yorkshire at least there was a significantly close correlation between a gentleman's religious persuasion and his civil-war loyalties, particularly for Puritans and Catholics. According to his classification, of 132 Puritan gentry families in the county, 64 became actively Parliamentarian and only 24 fought on the king's side; and of 157 Catholic families, 86 were Royalist and no more than ten Parliamentarian. Not one Catholic gentleman in the North Riding took Parliament's side: the only exception, that of William Salvin of Newbiggin, was, it seems, a doubtful case. As for their opponents, the more Calvinist a gentleman the more likely he was to take up arms for Parliament. For intensely religious Puritan knights, such as Matthew Boynton, Edward Rodes, Philip Stapleton, William Strickland, John Bourchier, William Constable and Richard Darley, there were no nagging doubts about which cause they should aid.[6]

So if Hugh Cholmley was neither stubborn Catholic nor fiery Calvinist, neither Arminian nor Presbyterian, but a "middle of the road" Anglican, this would help to explain why he behaved so indecisively and hesitantly during the final months of pre-civil war peace. The contention of one student of Sir Hugh that he "was not vitally interested in the religious question" is, however, misleading.[7] Religion mattered much to him, but because he had no passionate compelling enthusiasm for radical church reform, either Arminian or Presbyterian, he had only negative, not positive, convictions to follow. In 1642, he could not join a king who was surrounded and supported by papists and "souldiers of fortune and/or such as were noe friend to the publicke peace";[8] a year later, he could not continue with a parliamentary cause that now appeared belligerent and revolutionary.

Sir Hugh's hostility to Catholics was one of the main reasons why he could not consider deserting Parliament in London to join the king at York in the summer of 1642. No doubt Charles's dependence on Catholic support was deliberately exaggerated by his enemies for propaganda purposes, but he could not disguise the damaging truth that many of his Yorkshire officers, such as the Eures, the Vavasours, the Constables of Burton Constable and Everingham, and the Methams, were recusants or church papists. At first, Charles tried to cover his recruitment by insisting that commissioned officers took oaths of allegiance and supremacy, but his need was too great to allow such discrimination; he had to allow his general in the North, the earl of Newcastle, to accept Catholics "without examining their consciences". Not that a Yorkshireman like Cholmley would have been fooled: he would have identified many of those who rallied to the king on Heworth Moor in early June 1642 as papist recusants.[9]

If Cholmley's recollections are to be trusted, then during these critical final months of peace he retained a remarkably independent position between king and Parliament, between York and Westminster. During the summer of 1642 it seemed to him that there was a conspiracy of extremists on both sides intent on "fomenting disstractions". As he wrote, quoting Psalm 120, "I am for peace but when I speake they are for warre." On the one hand, he objected to Parliament's Militia Ordinance of March 1642, not because it lacked royal assent, but because "to draw the trayned bands together and to oppose the K[ing] in all things . . . were to beginne the warre which I intended not". Though in May Sir Hugh agreed to act as one of Parliament's commissioners along with Lord Howard of Escrick, Ferdinando, Lord Fairfax, Sir Philip Stapleton and his brother, Sir Henry, to meet the king at York, he refused to comply with the instructions drawn up by Pym and redrafted them in more conciliatory terms. As for the Nineteen Propositions, Cholmley refused point blank to read them to Charles because, in his own words, they were "the most unjust and unreasenable ones as ever I thinke was made to [the] King". On the other hand, in retrospect, Cholmley condemned those members of the House of Lords and Commons, such as Lord Keeper Littleton, who left London and gathered round the king at York: "my oppinion was they had ruined booth the King and Nation by quitting the Parla[men]t as I told many of the[m], in w[hic]h I proved propheticall".[10]

If, therefore, Cholmley heartily disapproved of the extremists on both sides, why did he not take a neutral stance when the war began in August 1642? In Yorkshire as a whole, neutral or passive gentry families were only slightly outnumbered by active Royalist; and in the North Riding, there were more neutrals than Royalists. Nevertheless, towards the end of August 1642, after first refusing it, Sir Hugh accepted the commission offered by the earl of Essex, Strafford's replacement as Yorkshire's Lord Lieutenant, to secure Scarborough with his old regiment of the local trained band.[11]

Sir Hugh had had to make a hard choice: it was impossible for him to opt out and leave the country like George Wandesford or John Evelyn, to name two runaways. First of all, he was head of a large and vulnerable family with a responsibility to protect it and his children's inheritance. He had named his reliable brother Henry and his Twysden brothers-in-law trustees of the Whitby estate on behalf of his wife, sons and daughters. Before he went north from London to Yorkshire in September his eldest son, William, now nearly 17 years old, was granted a Speaker's pass to cross over to France accompanied by two servants; but William's inheritance, the Cholmley properties, were now threatened. Reports of Cavalier attacks on the undefended homes of Yorkshiremen, such as that of George Marwood at Nun Monkton near York, which was made known to the Commons on 18 August, must have given Cholmley good reason to accept Essex's commission. Even if he had no appetite to fight for Parliament or against the king's forces, he had a primary duty to defend his land, his tenants and his friends.[12]

As for Sir Hugh's relatives and friends, by September 1642, nearly all of them were already committed to Parliament. His brother Henry had been named as Parliament's colonel of one of Yorkshire's trained band regiments and by 26 August his Bluecoats were marching towards Coventry. Before Sir Hugh had even reached Scarborough, the Bluecoats were busy stealing beds and provisions in Northampton on their roundabout route to the first battle of the civil war at Edgehill in Warwickshire. Henry never seems to have entertained his brother's doubts and vacillation. Perhaps the Presbyterian certainties of Sir Philip Stapleton of Warter, Henry's forthright brother-in-law, was a factor in Henry's early attachment to Parliament.[13]

By August 1642 Sir John Hotham was already up to his neck. Having refused to admit Charles into his town on the Hull in April he had been condemned as a traitor. If Hotham had opened the Beverley gate to the royal party and allowed Charles access to the Hull magazine, then Cholmley might have hesitated even longer before accepting Parliament's commission. In the event, after some soul-searching himself, Sir John had held out for Parliament. In July he had asked London to send the Cholmley brothers and Sir Philip Stapleton back into Yorkshire to counter royalist recruitment in the North and East Ridings. Doubtless Sir Hugh was mindful that Sir John was a kinsman who had twice rescued him, once from bankruptcy and then again from Dutchmen, and who had been his principal ally against Strafford.[14]

Moreover, by August 1642, most of Cholmley's other East Riding kin had already thrown their lot in with Parliament. Sir William Strickland of Boynton, a Member for Hedon, had married Hugh's sister Margaret. She had died young, but William, like his father Walter, was a gentleman of strict Puritan principles who patronised Calvinist ministers in his neighbourhood.[15] Of Sir Hugh's mother's family, the Legards, Christopher of Anlaby had had his house pillaged by Cavalier soldiers[16]; and though "uncle John" at Ganton was too old to be active on any side, his nephew must have felt some responsibility for protecting his property. Cholmley owed the Legards debts he could never fully repay.[17]

The one notable exception was the Bellasis family of Newburgh Priory. Thomas Bellasis, the first viscount Fauconberg, had married Barbara Cholmley, Sir Hugh's aunt, so that his eldest son, Henry and Hugh were first cousins and at first good friends. However, during the 1630s, Wentworth's patronage of Cholmley drove them apart. There was bad blood between the Wentworths and the Bellasises. In 1635 Lord Fauconberg would not allow Henry to be a godparent of Henry Slingsby because Hugh Cholmley had already been invited to be another. Then, once Cholmley and St:afford had fallen out, common hostility to the Lord President brought the two families together again. Henry was one of Yorkshire's knights of the shire, and he and Sir Hugh worked closely together in the Long Parliament, particularly to get rid of Strafford. Yet once Strafford had gone the partnership crumbled. The fact that Lord Fauconberg was a "church papist" and Henry a more open Catholic recusant pushed them in the direction of the Royalist party. Henry was one of the first Yorkshire gentlemen to raise a troop of horse for the royal bodyguard and later led a regiment of infantry, paid for by his father, to join the king's army at Nottingham.[18]

As for Sir Hugh's closest relatives by marriage, Sir Christopher Yelverton and Sir Roger Twysden, both were drawn, by different degrees, to side with Parliament. Yelverton was excluded from the Commons after his election to the Long Parliament was declared invalid, but politically he had nowhere else to go. Within little more than a month he was back in the House again with a Cornish seat and occupied it until "purged" in 1648. Like Cholmley and Strickland, Sir Christopher was "bribed" by king Charles with a free baronetcy in 1641 which did not change his preference for Parliament. At the start of the civil war he offered four horses to Parliament's army.[19]

As a "third-generation Puritan" who had resisted Ship Money and had been mulcted by the king's forest fines, Yelverton's commitment to Parliament was never in doubt. Not so Sir Roger's: by 1642 he harboured serious apprehensions about Parliament's increasing trespass on royal prerogative. As a justice of the peace in Kent, he was alarmed by Parliament's growing insensitivity to personal and property rights, and as an Anglican he had begun to fear for the safety of the established church and its doctrine. In March 1642 Sir Roger was imprisoned briefly in the Tower for defending the Anglican clergy and bailed on condition that he remained within 10 miles of the city of London. Cholmley offered him the hospitality of his home at Isleworth which he politely declined. The two shared similar views on church and state; their differences were temperamental, not religious or political. Both dreaded the prospect of civil war and tried to prevent it; both deplored the excesses of arbitrary royal government, yet also had become concerned about the radicalism of Pym's party in the Commons.[20]

If most of Cholmley's friends and family were Parliamentarian, he would also have gathered by August 1642 that his worst enemies had already declared themselves for the King. Sir William Pennyman of Marske and Sir William Savile of Thornhill, Wentworth's "creatures", were both to die fighting for the Royalist cause. There were also lesser but more local men whom Sir Hugh had reason to dislike and fear: the Eures of Malton, the Wyvills of Osgodby and the Conyers of Whitby were all Catholic families that might take advantage of his absence in London. Another North Riding Catholic, Sir Robert Strickland of Thornton Bridge, had been prompt to put his trained band militia at the disposal of the King. It was Strickland's regiment which in June 1642 had attacked the home of Alderman Vaux in York, breaking its windows and pulling up and burning its gate posts. In the house that night were Sir Hugh and the other Parliamentary commissioners. Of more immediate concern, Cholmley was probably informed that as early as 7 July Captain William Wyvill, a Catholic squire from nearby Osgodby, had mustered Scarborough's trained band using a warrant from the earl of Lindsey, the king's general.[21]

In his memoirs Sir Hugh made no mention of his small, vindictive part in the downfall of the earl of Strafford, his erstwhile patron. Nor did he refer there at any point to the fact, which presumably became an embarrassing memory, that he had been one of the material beneficiaries of Strafford's death. Soon after May 1641 he acquired a lease on New Park, a thousand acres of royal forest north-east of York, which had belonged to Wentworth as Lord President. Inside the enclosed deer park a grand hunting lodge had been built for him at a cost of £2,000. When Charles stayed in York in 1633 as Wentworth's guest they went out hunting together in New Park.[22]

In 1649, when a parliamentary survey was made of the late king's royal estate, both Charles and Wentworth had been beheaded, but the deer park, surprisingly, was said to be still largely intact: its fallow deer were valued at £180 and its five thousand trees at nearly £2,500. Though Sir Hugh was still an exile abroad in France, he was described as the tenant until Michaelmas when his lease would expire: afterwards it passed to the Roundhead Colonel Lilburne.[23]

In the circumstances, Sir Hugh could hardly have derived much profit from his park, yet in 1641-2 his lease was another reason why it was in his interest to stick with Parliament. King Charles was not expected to forget or forgive those who had done to death his chief minister and forced him to sign his death warrant. If the King was ever able to revenge Strafford, then Cholmley would surely lose his deer park and much more besides.

In short, Cholmley had much to gain from staying with Parliament and much to lose if the King were ever able to reassert his royal authority and punish his parliamentary enemies. In religious terms, he occupied a middle position between the Anglican polarities of Laudian and Puritan, so that his motives were largely material, not spiritual. He disliked and feared Catholics and he distrusted Scottish Presbyterians. He was a landowning gentleman forced to take up arms, not by his conscience, but largely in self-defence and perceived self-interest. Unlike the Hothams and the Fairfaxes, Sir Hugh had never been a professional soldier and had not the slightest relish for warfare. Though not a great lord like Howard of Escrick or a very rich landowner like Sir John Hotham, he still had substantial territorial interests and important social status locally. His honour was at stake as well as his property. He had never enjoyed the favour of the Court, except indirectly through Strafford; he had never held any lucrative Crown office or sinecure. Nevertheless, his unpopular interventions in the Long Parliament indicated that he still retained a strong affection for the royal family. On the other hand, his membership of the anti-Straffordian conspiracy had put him in harm's way should the Royalists have their revenge; and the destruction of Strafford had provided him with a valuable deer park and an opportunity to take a direct share in the local alum industry.

Finally, given the generally received and accepted view that Cholmley was initially a reluctant Parliamentarian who soon saw the error of his way, it comes as something of a surprise to read that in March 1641 he was one of a number of Commons-men who offered generous loans to Parliament. Sir John Hotham promised £500, Henry Bellasis, £500, Sir William Strickland, £1,000, and Sir Hugh, £1,000. Hotham, Bellasis and Strickland are known to have been rich men, but at that time Cholmley's annual income was estimated to be no more than £1,000. Either he was making an extremely extravagant gesture or he had a source of income far in excess of that from his Whitby estate. If indeed Sir Hugh really did offer a whole year's income, even as a loan, it indicates a commitment to Parliament subsequently denied and concealed in his memoirs and elsewhere.[24]

CHAPTER 9

PARLIAMENTARY COLONEL

The Royalist and future earl of Clarendon, Sir Edward Hyde, was living in Jersey in 1647 when he decided to write his account of the recent civil war in England. Since he knew little of what had happened between 1642 and 1645 in the North, he wrote to another Royalist exile, Sir Hugh Cholmley, then in Rouen, asking for his help. Sir Hugh had held Scarborough and its hinterland first for Parliament from September 1642 until March 1643 and then, after abruptly changing sides, for the King until forced to surrender Scarborough castle in July 1645. With time on his hands and recent events still fresh in his memory, Cholmley was anxious to put the record right and vindicate himself and his friends, especially the Hothams.[1] Consequently, he penned three papers for Hyde's forthcoming history, one on the Hothams, one on the decisive battle of Marston Moor, and a third, "Memorialls tuching Scarbrough". The first two were fairly slight but valuable historical pieces, but Sir Hugh's account of his own war experiences was lengthy, vivid and uniquely informative.[2]

When Lord Clarendon's *History of the Rebellion and Civil Wars in England* was finally published posthumously in 1702-04, it was clear that the once-great earl had made small use of Cholmley's papers, mainly because he had neglected to include them in his baggage when exiled a second time![3] There was no reference to Sir Hugh's initial service in Parliament's army, and after an acknowledgement that Scarborough castle was "a place of great importance to the King" and that Cholmley had discharged his royal commission there "with courage and singular fidelity", Clarendon had nothing more to say about his change of allegiance in March 1643.[4] Moreover, when Clarendon's manuscript sources were published in the 1770s, only Cholmley's essay on the Hothams was considered worthy of print: at the end of it, with insouciant frankness, the editor noted: "It is accompanied by Memorialls touching the Battle of York and the siege of Scarborough, too immaterial to be published."[5] Both languished in manuscript in the Bodleian library, unnoticed and unappreciated, until C H Firth, Regius Professor of Modern History at Oxford, recognised their historical importance and had them printed in the *English Historical Review* in 1904 and 1917.[6]

Cholmley's *Memorialls tuching Scarbrough* failed to make the impact they deserved because in October 1917 the world was preoccupied with far more pressing matters and since then they have been almost forgotten. Also, though Sir Charles Firth was an incomparable editor, the title give to his brief introduction in *EHR,* "Sir Hugh Cholmley's Narrative of the Siege of Scarborough, 1644-5", was both inadequate and inaccurate. Presented with such a title potential readers could be forgiven for thinking that Sir Hugh had written only about Scarborough during the final months of the war there when the North was already lost by the King to Parliament, whereas his narrative covers nearly three years from 1642 to 1645. Also, the siege of Scarborough town and castle did not begin until February 1645.[7]

Nor did Professor Firth seem to appreciate that the manuscripts in the Bodleian library were not written in Sir Hugh Cholmley's own hand: all three papers had been copied in the same skilful, professional style from his originals which were probably destroyed by fire in 1751 or 1752. A letter, dated 7 July 1752, written to Hugh Cholmley (1684-1755), great grandson of Sir Hugh, referred to a recent fire at Lincoln's Inn in London "by which Henry Cholmley lost everything".[8] This misfortune was almost certainly the same as that mentioned by James Schofield in the first edition of his *Guide to Scarborough,* published in 1787. According to Schofield, the Cholmley family had intended "to gratify the curious public" by printing Sir Hugh's manuscripts which included "an exact journal of the siege", but all his precious papers "were entirely consumed" in the fire.[9] Not Sir Hugh's memoirs, of course: Schofield must have known that Nathaniel Cholmley had published these privately in the same year as his own *Guide.* Subsequently, all Scarborough's historians, notably Hinderwell and Baker, accepted Schofield's story that Sir Hugh's "accurate journal" of the great siege of 1645 had been irretrievably lost and were unaware of the Bodleian copy.[10]

Sir Charles Firth was unable to identify the authorship or penmanship of the Clarendon papers because the best example of Sir Hugh's handwriting, the holograph of his memoirs, had been lost at least since 1870 when they last appeared in the form of "a cheap reprint" published in that year at Malton. However, when the holograph was recovered by York Minster library in 1976 and its authenticity verified by chief librarian Mr C B L Barr and Professor G E Aylmer, then of York university, it became clear that the Bodleian memorials had been copied by a secretary, not penned by their original author.[11] All four manuscripts, the memoirs and the three memorials, were eventually published together in one volume by the Yorkshire Archaeological Society in 2000.[12]

Though naturally partisan and self-justifying, Cholmley's *Memorialls tuching Scarbrough* fill a vital gap in his memoirs written a decade later. After describing how and why he accepted a commission from Parliament's general, the earl of Essex, on the next folio he wrote: "How I deported my selfe in these imployments and when how and for what causes I quit it and the Parlament I shall forbeare to speake now but referre the Reader to the Accoumpt I have given booth of that and the seage of Scarbrough together. . ."[13] Clearly, Cholmley expected Sir Edward Hyde to make sooner and better use of his memorials on Scarborough.

However, just as Sir Hugh's memoirs reveal very little of his active career as a member of the Long Parliament between 1640 and 1642, so his memorials are predictably brief on his record as one of Parliament's colonels during the first six months of the civil war that followed. If he was retrospectively ashamed of the part he had played in the pursuit to the death of Strafford, subsequently he was also embarrassed by his Roundhead past. He would have his reader believe that he was always a reluctant and conditional Parliamentarian soldier, dragged into the war against his instincts and wishes. Moreover, his memory of recent past events was especially selective and defensive because he was writing to a fellow Royalist for a Royalist version of history. As a result, Cholmley's report for the months between September 1642, when he arrived in Scarborough, and March 1643, when he defected to the King, occupied little more than a single side of foolscap paper.[14]

Cholmley's written recollection of his military service to Parliament is not merely brief and reticent, it is also tendentious and unconvincing. Obviously he was most anxious to convey the message that his attachment to Parliament was always unwilling, unhappy and mistaken; that he never regarded himself, whatever others might allege, as a rebel against the Crown; and that during these six months he conducted himself honourably, independently and entirely in conformity with his conscience. He was able to convince himself that with a sword in his hand he would be "in better capacity to promote peace, having noe other end then to preserve the libertie of the subiect and to render the duties to his majestie". Only when he came round to realise that Parliament, not the King, was the greater threat to "the libertie of the subiect" was he able, in conscience, to change sides.[15]

At the outset, Sir Hugh contended that his colonel's commission came not from Parliament but from the earl of Essex, who was Lord Lieutenant of Yorkshire, "with the kings consent and approbation". But in fact Essex was Parliament's appointed general of its armed forces and he had been already condemned by Charles as a traitor. In truth, Cholmley's commission rested insecurely on Parliament's Militia Ordinance, which the king had denounced as fraudulent and invalid in his proclamation of 27 May 1642. According to this royal pronouncement, trained band regiments raised on the sole authority of Parliament's Ordinance had no legal basis; the only legitimate commission was one issued by the Crown under the Great Seal. And Essex was much more than the Lord Lieutenant of Yorkshire: "for the safety of the King's person", Parliament had appointed him commanding general of its entire army. In short, Sir Hugh was trying vainly to maintain a transparent fiction that he was serving both King and Parliament simultaneously when in fact they were already at war with each other. By the time that Cholmley accepted Essex's commission "in the beginning of September", Charles had already flown his battle standard at Nottingham on 22 August.[16]

Sir Hugh's justification that in taking up arms he was "a more indifferent person" was at best disingenuous and at worst dishonest. By accepting the commission he had committed himself unreservedly to one side. As Parliament's own commissioner to the king at York in May-June 1642 he had been rejected by Charles; why he should think that having a sword in his hand would better qualify him as a peacemaker defies logic and common sense.[17]

In fact, Cholmley's strongest reason for taking Essex's commission was, in his own words, "out of indulgencie to his country and desire to preserve the same".[18] By "country" here Sir Hugh meant not England or even Yorkshire but his own immediate neighbourhood in the east of the North Riding. What he had in his mind to defend was his house at Whitby, his landed estate, his family and friends, his property, income and status. Once "divers gentlemen in Yorkesheire" had declared themselves for the King and "were all redy in armes", Cholmley was duty bound to protect his interests against them. With old, implacable enemies such as Sir William Pennyman on the rampage, Abbey House itself was in danger and he had personal experience of what Robert Strickland's hooligans had done to Alderman Vaux's home in York.[19]

Cholmley's instructions were to mobilise his old trained band regiment, drawn from Ryedale, Pickering Lythe and Whitby Strand wapentakes, and bring it into Scarborough to secure town and harbour. He was also ordered by Parliament's Committee of Safety to take control of Scarborough castle which overlooked and dominated both. With such a range of authority he would wield even greater local power than he had done before the breach with Strafford.[20]

However, according to his own later account, Sir Hugh was unwilling to occupy the castle: as he pointed out to the Committee, it no longer belonged to the Crown, but was now privately owned by "one Thompson, a Burgher of the Towne". Since Parliament "att that time" was "nise to take any mans inheritance from him by force", Cholmley was told therefore "to use his interest with Thompson" to persuade him to put the castle into his hands "for service of king and Parliament". Presumably, if Scarborough castle had still belonged to the Crown there would have been no need to seek the king's permission![21]

From London Cholmley arrived in Scarborough with only a troop of horse. En route at Hull he had been promised a reinforcement of 200 infantrymen, but Sir John Hotham, the governor there, could not spare them. Though Wyvill had left Scarborough with what troops he could recruit there, Cholmley found Stephen Thompson "verie much affected to the kings cause". Nevertheless, without "Thompsons good will", he was able to bring most of his regiment into the town and acquire "the keyes of the Casstle" for his garrison.[22]

Cholmley's achievement in taking over Scarborough without resistance was remarkable. Many of the militia he would have expected to lead into the town were at that time marauding their way through the Midlands under the command of his brother, Sir Henry. Apart from being one of the borough's burgess representatives at Westminster, Sir Hugh had slight claim on the loyalty of Scarborians. He had no property in the town and had spent very little time there. As a resident of Whitby, where he was lord of the manor and chief patron, he would have been regarded with suspicion if not hostility by Scarborough's mercantile oligarchy who dominated its borough chamber on Sandside. There was no love between Whitby and Scarborough; and Whitby's recent growth as an alum, coal and ship-building port served only to intensify a traditional rivalry. Despite Scarborough's opposition to it, but thanks to Cholmley's initiative and influence, Whitby's harbour had been much improved by its new west pier. In contrast, Cholmley had done nothing for Scarborough: as its Member in the Commons he had been entirely absorbed in national and personal, not local, issues.

In all but name, Scarborough was then a Thompson town. For the past four decades they had dominated its Common Hall. During the last four years in succession, 1638, 1639, 1640, and 1641, four Thompsons, Christopher, Timothy, Richard and Francis, had held the highest office in the borough as senior bailiff. The political and judicial power of the family reflected and was a product of their landed and commercial wealth. Stephen owned the castle and its grounds and the rectory of St Mary's parish church; his father, Francis, was the richest merchant in the town.[23] However, Stephen seems to have been more "affected" to making money than "to the kings cause": he was not bullied into surrendering his castle, but willing to sell it to Cholmley for £800 or lease it to him at a rent of £50 a year. Sir Hugh wrote nothing about the terms by which he secured the castle, but according to Stephen's later testimony before the Committee for Compounding with Delinquents in January 1646, by July 1645 Cholmley was in arrears for only £90, so he must have paid at least £60 in castle rent.[24]

Whatever the Royalist inclinations of the Thompsons or other leading Scarborians, it seems that they were perfectly willing to remain in a town now under Parliament's military occupation. At the end of September 1642, when the Common Hall held its annual elections, all five Thompsons retained their seats in the First Twelve out of its 44 members. Perhaps the Thompsons expected that Cholmley's presence would be short-lived and were prepared to tolerate him in the meantime. Certainly, Sir Hugh did not trust them: in a letter to London he described Francis as a "malignant man", a term usually reserved by Roundheads for active Royalists, and his son, Christopher, as no better. They had recently sent a ship carrying arms to the Royalist port of Newcastle.[25]

In both memorials and memoirs Cholmley asserted that during his "5 mounthes spaice" in Parliament's service he received no money from London. Again his memory was at fault and is contradicted by his own words in correspondence. Writing to John Pym on 3 November 1642 from Stamfordbridge, Sir Hugh reported that he had given £100 to Captain Alured, who commanded one of his foot companies, and that he had lately spent another £200 repairing and strengthening Scarborough castle. My "money slips fast away," he continued, "and yet I am as careful as if it went out of my own purse, and I am both Paymaster and Commissary".[26] Clearly, by this time, Cholmley had taken in several hundred pounds from somewhere and someone. A few weeks later, a House of Commons order revealed one of his sources. Acting on behalf of Parliament, it seems that "the earl of Danby"[?] had forwarded £523 to Cholmley out of his own pocket.[27]

Another major source of assistance, which Sir Hugh failed subsequently to acknowledge, came from the residents of Scarborough. Though the Thompsons were very rich, locally powerful and predisposed towards the King's cause, Scarborough's borough records provide no evidence that they offered any resistance to Cholmley. Not only did they hand over the castle to him, as leaders of the Common Hall, the town's governing body, they contributed substantially to the borough's military defences. Richard, younger brother of Francis and uncle of Stephen Thompson, was one of the signatories to the order of 16 October which placed the town's trained band under Sir Hugh's command, provided that he paid its expenses. Before the end of that month, two new pairs of gates were made at the Newborough and Oldborough land entrances and a watch of 18 townsmen set up every night. Each household was expected to contribute to the watch or suffer a fine. The fines were to buy powder and shot. The whole town was assessed at £50. In November, 28 of the 44 members of the Common Hall agreed to raise and pay for a company of dragoons. Francis Thompson volunteered a man and a horse, his brother Richard gave £5 and his son Christopher, another £5. Altogether the councillors offered Cholmley four men, five horses and £55 15s. 4d. in money.[28]

In neither memorials nor memoirs did Cholmley give any explanation of the crucial strategical importance of Scarborough when he arrived there in the autumn of 1642. If he understood that his bloodless take-over of Scarborough town, castle and harbour was a serious blow to the King's overall plan to defeat Parliament he did not admit it in writing.

Early in 1642, King Charles had decided to use force to bring his rebellious English subjects to heel. Since London and the south-east showed little affection for him and even less for his wife, he would move North to York and there recruit a royal army from amongst his more loyal people. Meanwhile, Henrietta Maria would sail to Holland with their daughter Mary and the crown jewels. Princess Mary was already betrothed to the son of the Prince of Orange, reputedly the richest ruler on the continent; and the Jewish bankers and diamond merchants of Amsterdam were expected to advance great sums of money on the security of the jewels. Having raised sufficient silver, bought arms and hired mercenaries, the Queen would return with them to re-join her husband and his army in Yorkshire.

However, Charles's recruitment drive in Yorkshire was a big disappointment to him. In May 1642, when he told a well-attended meeting of the county's gentry at York that he intended to form a royal bodyguard, he succeeded only into splitting them into three groups: about a third, already called "Cavaliers", led by Sir Francis Wortley and Sir Robert Strickland, promised every help within their power, a smaller group, soon to be dubbed "Roundheads", headed by the Fairfaxes of Denton, Sir William Constable and Sir Matthew Boynton, denied that Charles needed a guard; and a majority agreed to form a guard only if it excluded Catholics and was approved by Parliament. As one of Parliament's commissioners, Sir Hugh was present at this meeting and was clearly identified with the "Roundhead" group.[29]

Sir Hugh was also present on Heworth Moor outside York on 3 June 1642 when the King made his personal appeal to Yorkshire's freeholders and copyholders. Again, from a Royalist point of view, though well-attended, the gathering was far from successful. Instead of loyalist support, Charles encountered only confusion, division and disorder. Beside shouts of "God blesse the King", there were also cries of "God unite the king and Parliament" and even "God turn the King's heart".[30] When early in August a meeting of all Yorkshire's militia was summoned to York, "not one in sixty appeared".[31]

Worst setback of all for Charles was his abysmal failure to secure Hull. His town on the river Hull was an essential key to his strategy: its defences were the strongest of any port in the kingdom; its arsenal of arms was second only in size to that of the Tower of London; and it was perfectly situated to receive the Queen when she was ready to sail from Holland. All the other coastal harbours further south and closest to the continent were now Parliament's. Thanks to the daredevil exploits of Sir Hugh's cousin, Captain Browne Bushell, even Portsmouth had been lost to the King. Twice Charles had tried to enter Hull: in April, Sir John Hotham had shut the gates in his face and openly defied him, and the following July he had suffered another humiliating defeat when he attempted to take the town by force.

Without Hull, the King's need for an east-coast substitute had become imperative. Bridlington, or Bridlington Quay as it was then called, lacked defences and was too close to Hotham's hostile force at Hull. Whitby's harbour was too remote, inaccessible from the land and easily blockaded by Parliament's warships at its river mouth. Newcastle and Sunderland were even further away from York and dangerously vulnerable to another Scottish invasion. If Charles could not have Hull then Scarborough was his next best choice.

Scarborough had a safe, pier-protected anchorage, an impregnable castle overlooking it, and it was so open to the North Sea that a naval blockade would be difficult to maintain in summer and impossible in winter weather. And Scarborough was less than 40 miles from York, only a day's journey away even for heavy wagons over a level, lowland road. These were the reasons why both King and Parliament set great store by Scarborough and why Cholmley was sent north to secure it.[32] When Parliament already held Hull it had no use for Scarborough, but to hold its harbour and castle meant that both were denied to the King.

Yet Sir Hugh's service to Parliament during the first few months of hostilities went far beyond his brief. Though predictably there is no mention of it in either his memorials or memoirs, far from sitting safely in Scarborough's reinforced castle, as early as November 1642 Cholmley ventured boldly and deeply into Royalist territory. If he was a reluctant Roundhead, as subsequently he wanted Clarendon and his descendants to believe, there is not much contemporary evidence of it.

On 3 November 1642, Cholmley wrote to John Pym from Stamfordbridge. Since his arrival in Scarborough only six weeks earlier, he had brought together 400 militia men from the immediate neighbourhood, spent £200 on repairs to the castle walls and gates, and strengthened them with cannon and platforms. The castle was not yet quite ready to withstand a siege: he still needed another two or three hundred pounds to stock it with powder, ammunition and food; but if victualled and fully garrisoned, his captains assured him, it could hold out against any number of attackers.[33]

But what was Sir Hugh doing at Stamfordbridge, only five miles from Royalist York and more than 30 miles from his base at Scarborough? By his own admission, Cholmley's captains had tried to dissuade him from leaving Scarborough town, which was not yet fully defensible, to venture dangerously deep into Royalist territory. He had left behind only 112 men at the castle and brought only 300 foot soldiers with him. Even when reinforced with 220 infantry and two troops of cavalry from Hull, Cholmley's force was still greatly outnumbered by a York garrison thought to be 2,000 strong. Sir Hugh's only excuse for such rashness was that Sir John Hotham at Hull had "much importuned him" to march from Scarborough towards York.[34]

For a so-called reluctant Roundhead, Cholmley had made an amazingly belligerent demonstration, for which he had no authority from London. And this demonstration was all the more astonishing in view of the fact that at the end of September Ferdinando, Lord Fairfax, Parliament's general of its northern forces in Yorkshire, had signed a pact of neutrality with the King's commanding general at York, the earl of Cumberland. Though this treaty of Rothwell was immediately denounced and rejected by the Hothams and subsequently repudiated by Cumberland and Pym, it showed that even at this late stage there were Yorkshiremen on both sides genuinely unwilling to strike the first blows.[35]

Nevertheless, Stamfordbridge was a well-chosen position, astride the river Derwent and adjacent to the main routes into York from Hull and Scarborough. If the Royalists sallied out from the city, Cholmley could retire to the east bank of the Derwent. Though the enemy was much superior in cavalry, he would have some difficulty launching a surprise attack through the forest of Galtres which covered Cholmley's right flank. However, since the Royalist garrison of York seemed more concerned to provision their quarters than to come out of them, Sir Hugh resolved to move his men closer to the city walls. Accordingly, he sent a request back to Scarborough for "a great ordnance", broke all the millstones along the banks of the Derwent to deprive the Royalists of their flour supplies, and prepared to advance into York's suburbs.[36]

At this moment, Sir Hugh received alarming letters from Lord Fairfax and Captain John Hotham, telling him that the earl of Newcastle was about to cross into Yorkshire from Durham with a Royalist army of at least 8,000 well-armed men, a quarter of them cavalry. Suddenly, the balance of military power in the county was about to be reversed. Captain Hotham's feeble attempt to prevent the Royalist crossing of the river Tees at Piercebridge was easily brushed aside. Parliament's militia of Richmondshire under Sir Edward Loftus and those of Cleveland under Sir Henry Anderson disbanded and went home. On 3 December Lord Newcastle led his triumphant army into York where he was warmly welcomed by the city corporation. The tables had been turned. As Lord Fairfax himself put it: "the enemy is mighty and master of the field".[37]

With not many more than a thousand soldiers at Tadcaster to bar the entrance to his West Riding heartland, Lord Fairfax was vastly outnumbered. At this critical moment he ordered Cholmley to bring his forces westwards to link up with him at Tadcaster. Not only did Sir Hugh ignore the order, he turned round his men, 300 foot and 40 horse, and took them all back to Scarborough in the opposite direction! Since Cholmley defected to the King only four months later, his defiance of Fairfax, Parliament's appointed general in the North, was later regarded as a certain sign of his dishonesty and disloyalty.[38]

Yet Cholmley's retreat to Scarborough was neither cowardly nor rebellious: in the circumstances, there was no sensible alternative. To reach Tadcaster he would have had to make a wide, semi-circular movement to the south of York, crossing the swollen river Ouse by boats. Guarding the bridge over the river Wharfe with only a thousand men, nearly all infantry, Fairfax would still not have stood against Newcastle's advance for more than a few hours. If Cholmley had crossed the Ouse he would have put the Royalists as well as the river between himself and his home base; the whole of the east side of York all the way to the coast would have been at the mercy of Newcastle's troopers. Since Sir Hugh's only commission was to hold Scarborough for Parliament, to abandon town, harbour and castle there would have constituted an act of reckless betrayal.

Even so, despite these compelling arguments, Cholmley might still have hazarded a march to Tadcaster, but he was persuaded otherwise by his junior officers. From the outset, they had been nervous about leaving Scarborough: now, a month later, and many miles from home in winter weather, they were anxious for the safety of their families. Besides, Sir Hugh was running out of money: he had only one more week's pay for his trained band. So he went back down the road to Scarborough and Sir Matthew Boynton returned to Hull with his men after he heard of Fairfax's forced retreat from Tadcaster.[39]

Lord Fairfax was angered by Cholmley's disobedience; the House of Commons rebuked him for it; and the Royalist press rejoiced that Yorkshire's Roundheads were now split into three separate, uncooperative forces under Fairfax, Hotham and Cholmley. When, soon afterwards, Lord Newcastle secured the castles at Pontefract and Newark, the Royalists controlled all the major river-crossings on the principal north-south routes. If the Queen landed in Yorkshire she would be able to bring her arms and mercenaries to the aid of her husband at Oxford.[40]

Yet Cholmley had done the right thing; and events of the previous two months had demonstrated not his incompetence but Fairfax's excessive caution. Between 16 August when Charles had left York finally for Nottingham and 3 December when the earl of Newcastle entered it, Parliament had the opportunity and the means to capture the nation's second city. Neither the Royalist governor and general, the earl of Cumberland, nor the city's aldermen had any stomach to withstand a siege and would probably have surrendered if they had been hard pressed.[41] It was Fairfax's fault that the opportunity was wasted, not Cholmley's. Sir Hugh had advanced to the outskirts of York, some 40 miles from Scarborough, with only one troop of horse and after only six weeks in the county. In contrast, with far richer potential for recruitment in the West Riding, Fairfax started out from Leeds only to halt at Tadcaster, nearly ten miles short of York.

Nevertheless, soon after his return to Scarborough, Sir Hugh received a letter from John Pym which annoyed and upset him. He was again reprimanded for not joining his forces with those of Lord Fairfax and for giving far too much importance to the security of Scarborough, "a place to be conceived not to be very usefull". Both his judgement and his honour had been questioned.[42]

Consequently, on 9 December, Cholmley wrote a letter in reply to Speaker Lenthall and with it enclosed another from and signed by his junior officers. First, he offered to resign his commission: "If I have fail'd in my duty," he wrote, "I am unworthy to be employ'd longer in public service." There then followed a list of complaints against his masters at Westminster, excuses for his recent conduct, and finally, in the tail, an implied threat. He had not been supplied with the money and ammunition promised and therefore lacked both essentials. He had never received any specific orders from Parliament and had been left without support at "an out angle". He had nothing to gain personally from taking up arms: his desire only was "to contribute ...to the setling the truth of the Gospel, liberty of the subject, and peace of the kingdome...with as much honour as possibly may be to his Majesty". However, if Parliament and the King did not soon come to "a good understanding", he concluded, "to my judgement the kingdome is in danger to bee ruined".[43]

Along with Colonel Cholmley's explanation and justification of his own conduct since accepting Essex's commission, there came a pithy statement written by Captain John Legard. The statement was signed by Sir Hugh's junior officers, who included Lieutenant-Colonel Launcelot, a veteran of the battle of Edgehill, and Captain Browne Bushell, who had recently arrived in Scarborough after performing daring deeds for Parliament at Portsmouth. Legard advanced four main reasons why Scarborough was "a place of very great consequence". First, the castle there dominated the harbour and constituted a formidable presence in the neighbourhood. Second, Scarborough harbour was best placed to receive arms and ammunition from Holland or Denmark "in despite of any Navy on the sea". Third, even in the depth of winter, ordnance and carriages could pass without difficulty from Scarborough to York "which cannot be done from Newcastle". And, finally, from Scarborough "pinnaces may upon every occasion make out and hinder the bringing of arms and ammunition from Holland or Denmarke". No better appreciation of Scarborough's strategic importance in the Civil War has ever been written.[44]

Both Lord Fairfax and the House of Commons soon accepted the validity of these persuasive and perceptive arguments. Fairfax realised that without Cholmley's presence at Scarborough the whole of the length of Yorkshire's coast from Whitby to Bridlington would be open to Royalist reinforcements from the continent. He no longer demanded Sir Hugh's assistance in the West Riding.[45] Parliament also changed its tune: it authorised a grant of more than £500 and later resolved, "That Sir Hugh Cholmley shall be required to employ his best endeavours in the charge and custody of Scarborough castle." He had won the argument.[46]

At Christmas 1642 Sir Hugh and his officers and men enjoyed a brief, deserved respite in Scarborough. Thankful for their return, the corporation treated them to a venison feast: including the vintner's bill, and the money paid out to "the bringers of the venison", it cost the Common Hall £3 2s. 4d. No doubt everyone there thought the cost worthwhile.[47]

Yet it was never Cholmley's intention to immure himself in the castle or to prolong the comforts of town life even in mid-winter: before the New Year he took the road westwards in the direction of the enemy. Not only was Sir Hugh anxious to prove himself an entirely trustworthy servant of Parliament, he knew that it was vital to keep Newcastle's cavalry a harmless distance from the coast. As early as 29 December, Fairfax reported that Cholmley's soldiers were active in the area of Malton where they had robbed Royalist recruiters of their money. Soon afterwards, the earl of Newport's Royalist troopers were driven off by Cholmley's own cavalry outside the same town.[48]

On 8 January 1643, Sir Hugh was at Malton when he was told that Colonels Robert Strickland and Guildford Slingsby had reached Guisborough and were recruiting there for the King's army. More alarmingly, it was reported to him that they had ordered the town of Whitby, only "sixteen miles away", to be ready to receive a Royalist garrison. Cholmley reacted with decisive speed: leaving a small company at Malton under Captain Browne Bushell to guard the main road from York to Scarborough, he led two troops of horse and 130 foot northwards over the North York Moors. The only details we have of the ensuing battle of Guisborough are to be found in Cholmley's official report to Speaker Lenthall written that same evening, 16 January. The Royalists had stationed their musketeers about a mile outside the town "under hedges in places of advantage". The engagement lasted about two hours before the Royalist retreat turned into a running rout. Sir Hugh took over 100 prisoners, who included Colonel Slingsby, but, "praised be God", lost not a single soldier of his own. Slingsby, who had been Strafford's devoted secretary, bled to death after three days: amputation of both his legs above the knees failed to save his life.[49]

Guisborough was a one-sided victory and it was Cholmley's first experience of the battlefield. Yet what might have been an encouraging and satisfying baptism had the opposite affect. The sight of so many dead, dying and mutilated clearly distressed him, not least the agony of young Slingsby, a "fellow countryman". There was no triumphalism in his letter to Lenthall: on the contrary, there was a repeated warning that without "supply" from London "all will dissolve instantly". He had received £200 of his brother Henry's rents, but his forces were quite inadequate should the earl of Newcastle decide to move eastwards out of York where he was wintering. Above all, now that he had witnessed civil war with his own eyes and heard the cries of the wounded, the prospect of further battles filled him with anguish:

> I confess it grieves my heart to see how these calamities increase and how I am forced to draw my sword not onely against my countrymen but many near friends and allies some of which I know both to be well affected in religion and lovers of their liberties.

He then went on to say that for him issues of constitutional power and even civil freedom were not paramount: Parliament, he thought, ought to give way to the King on every outstanding disagreement except religion. He believed that it was better "to let go some things that in right belong to the subject" as long as "our religion be but firmly settled". Though he assured Lethall that nothing could divert him from "serving the Parliament with all fidelity" whilst he was "in their imployment", here was a clear monition that his "fidelity" was conditional. Even at this late hour, it seems that Cholmley could still delude himself that an all-out civil conflict might be prevented, if only Parliament made some concession to the King.[50] From Guisborough he returned to his Scarborough base with a heavy heart.

Fairfax's victories at Bradford in December and Leeds in January induced the earl of Newcastle to withdraw most of his Royalist troops from the West Riding back to York. Papers from the earl found in the possession of Guildford Slingsby indicated that his priority was now to establish a secure base for the Queen whose arrival from Holland was imminent. If Strickland and Slingsby had intended to hold Whitby as an entry port for Henrietta Maria, then Cholmley's swift and effective reaction at Guisborough had put paid to such a plan. The Queen would have to sail as far north as the Tyne to be sure of a safe landing.

This was the route forced upon the next major importers of arms from Holland. At the end of January 1643, George, Lord Goring brought 4,000 horse arms, 20 pieces of artillery, 200 officers and £20,000 in cash safely to the port of Newcastle. When Sir Hugh heard that the Royalist convoy was about to cross the North Riding on its way to York, he sent a regiment of 400 foot, three troops of cavalry and two cannon to prevent its passage over the Tees at Yarm. The result was disastrous: Cholmley's men were overwhelmed. James King, soon to become Lord Newcastle's Lieutenant-General, and Lord Goring, both veteran, professional commanders, showed no mercy towards Scarborough's amateurs. Most of the 400, including their Captain Medley, were taken prisoner, put in Durham castle, and badly treated there. King and Goring arrived in York with all their wagons and weapons intact.[51] These reinforcements were a welcome addition to Royalist military strength at York, but they were small compared with what the Queen brought ashore at Bridlington Quay on 22 February.

Like her recent predecessors, Henrietta Maria had intended to land at Newcastle, the only friendly anchorage on the North Sea coast. Off Scarborough, however, the wind turned round, blew a gale from the north and forced her fleet into the shelter of Bridlington Bay. Two days later, the Queen dined ashore at the Quay with the earl of Newcastle and General King. Not a Roundhead soldier was to be seen and Parliament's warships had been waiting in vain at Tynemouth. But Henrietta Maria was only just in time. That night Parliament's vice-admiral William Batten arrived with two warships and on the high tide at point-blank range they fired about a hundred shots at the houses on the quayside and the supply vessels in the harbour. The Queen had to run for her life and seek refuge in a ditch. Only when the tide ebbed and her Dutch escort, admiral Van Tromp, threatened to retaliate, did Batten withdraw. The following days the Queen's precious cargo was carried from the transports inland to the safety of Bridlington's priory church. Eventually, loaded on to 500 carts, weapons for 10,000 men accompanied by up to a thousand mercenary soldiers found their way to York via Burton Fleming and Malton. Henrietta Maria was said to carry £80,000 in ready money, raised on her personal and crown jewellery from the merchants of Amsterdam.[52]

All these events underlined the crucial importance of Scarborough and the key role of Cholmley to both Parliament and the King. If the Queen had sailed all the way towards Newcastle her ships would have been intercepted by Batten at the mouth of the Tyne. Bridlington Quay had no defences: its tiny harbour was open to attack from land and sea. The Royalists had been extremely fortunate to avoid the potentially disastrous consequences of not having a protected, deep-water port within reach of York. And it would be hard to exaggerate the value of the Queen's munitions and money to her husband's cause: without them, during the summer of 1643, the King's armies would have been gravely, perhaps hopelessly, short of weapons and ammunition. Even Charles's own position at Oxford was insecure until the Queen's cannon and other arms arrived there from the North. Indeed, the success of Royalist forces in the summer of 1643, the apogee of the King's military fortunes, would have been impossible without Henrietta's courageous enterprise, endurance and good fortune. On the other hand, by denying her Yorkshire's two best sea-ports, Sir John Hotham at Hull and Sir Hugh Cholmley at Scarborough had come close to jeopardising any hope of Royalist victory.[53]

But why did Cholmley allow the Queen to land unchallenged at Bridlington Quay, only 15 miles down the coast from Scarborough? Though he must have known that her arrival from Holland was imminent and probably that her fleet had put into Bridlington Bay, since the events at Guisborough and Yarm he had lost his eagerness for combat. The deaths of his own countrymen had sickened him; and for the ill-treatment of his men after their surrender at Yarm he never forgave General King. The reinforcements brought by Goring and King had greatly strengthened and encouraged the Royalist northern army at York, so that Cholmley withdrew Bushell from his outpost at Malton for fear that he would be surrounded and swamped there. After the painful memory of Yarm, Sir Hugh had no stomach for another encounter with professional Royalist cavalry. Finally, Cholmley now suspected that the Hothams were wavering. Captain John had allowed Goring free passage to Thornton Bridge, the crossing point of the river Swale near Thirsk. Whereas previously he had been aggressive and headstrong, now he was strangely inactive and over-cautious. When news came that the Queen had landed at Bridlington Quay, young Hotham's forces stayed put in Beverley and made no attempt to interrupt or even threaten her convoy's slow passage over the Wolds to Malton. Cholmley's suspicions were well-founded: there was already a secret understanding between Lord Newcastle and the Hothams which left him even more isolated and vulnerable at Scarborough.[54]

CHAPTER 10

CHANGING SIDES

Ever since March 1643, when Sir Hugh Cholmley suddenly and successfully went over to the King from Parliament, ranging from the implausible and romantic to the fatuous and vindictive, explanations for his momentous decision have been numerous and diverse. Predictably, members of the House of Commons were outraged: they resolved that "for falsly and perfidiously betraying the Trust reposed in him by Parliament, falsifying his Protestation, and revolting to the Popish army", Cholmley should be imprisoned for high treason.[1] The Venetian ambassador in London was surprised by the vehemence of this reaction to Sir Hugh's desertion: "parliament," he wrote," is indulging in the utmost severity against sciomle [sic]. He is deprived of his membership and accused of treason, involving the most extreme sentences".[2]

Predictable, also, was the response of Parliament's London press: for his act of treason it attributed the basest of motives. In the words of his most bitter enemies, the *Scottish Dove* and *Civus Britanicus,* "Judas Cholmley" was a "liver-hearted", "cowardly", "rebellious sophister", "perfidious unfaithful wretch", and "apostate". Two years later, after his surrender of Scarborough castle and escape into exile, both newssheets had preferred hanging as a more suitable treatment for such a criminal.[3]

Captain John Hotham, who never much admired his fellow MP for Scarborough, attributed Cholmley's defection to "ambition or lightnesse"; he placed a greater value on his own honour which "like a woman's honesty" was "not to be repayred if once toucht". In one of his many clandestine letters to Lord Newcastle, he wrote bluntly, "... you have gotten by Sir Hugh Cholmley's turning when he could give noe reason for itt but an old castle". Here were the envious words of a secret Royalist who had been in correspondence with the enemy for several weeks and was planning his own desertion of Parliament.[4]

Even some of Cholmley's new allies could find little to say in his favour. One view commonly expressed at the time (and still believed by those who should know better) was that Sir Hugh was infatuated with the Queen and once in her presence he had surrendered Scarborough and himself to her as a gesture of personal devotion. This unflattering explanation of Cholmley's change was hardly any more accurate than the current Roundhead gibe: "Alas, poor Hugh Cholmley, that could turn traitor and sell his honour, for the kiss of a lady's hand"; and "See what a toy took the man in the head, the love of a little court-idolatry put him quite out of his wits, and religion too". Such mocking silliness ought to have been relegated permanently to romantic novels, yet recently it reappeared in a serious historical study of Yorkshire baronets, this time compounded with factual error. According to this fictional version, Sir Hugh was instantly converted to the Royalist cause when the Queen flattered him with a visit to his Whitby home. At no time did Henrietta Maria set foot in Whitby, not even accidently.[5]

One of the many biographers of Queen Henrietta Maria recounted how she had turned her back on Sir Hugh Cholmley when he first came to see her in York.[6] In view of Cholmley's parliamentary and "rebellious" record up to this point and given the Queen's notorious intolerance, such a reaction on her part seems possible. However, the same author then went on to describe in some detail how Henrietta Maria later rode into Scarborough with Lord Montrose at her side, an event as totally fictitious as her visit to Whitby.[7]

The only reasonably reliable reports of their first meeting at York come directly from the Queen herself and later from Sir Hugh in his memorials. In one of her private letters, written at York to her husband in Oxford, Henrietta Maria described how Cholmley had come to York to kiss her hand. In Cholmley's version, he waited until nightfall before he was conducted secretly into her presence by Lord Jermyn. Before he pledged his service to the King, she had given him "a verie satisfactory answeare" to his " two modest requests" that she would not "divert the king from performing those promises hee had made to the Kingdome" and that "shee would endeavour the speedie settling the peace of the Kingdome". Clearly, whatever the value of such promises, Sir Hugh would never have taken the risk of riding out unescorted from Scarborough to York unless he had first received assurances of safe conduct and welcome. Indeed, before he set eyes on the Queen he had already made up his mind to defect.[8]

Having dealt with the frivolous and the fanciful, the more serious, historical explanations of Cholmley's change have now to be examined. First of these is the view of Professor Brian Manning that Sir Hugh deserted Parliament for the King because he feared that the former was fomenting social revolution and political chaos. Though he could find no direct evidence to support this interpretation, he assumed, as others have done since, that Cholmley's motives were similar to those other socially-superior defectors, his blood relatives and political allies, the Hothams.[9]

For the motives of the Hothams' defection there is no shortage of evidence. In secret letter after secret letter, from as early as December 1642, Lieutenant-General (as he became 1 February 1643) John Hotham poured out a continuous flow of doubts and discontents to his "enemy" the earl of Newcastle. He was jealous of the seniority of command of Parliament's Northern army given to Ferdinando, Lord Fairfax, and his son, Sir Thomas. Like his father, Sir John, he was as hostile to the Puritans in Parliament and Fairfax's West Riding army as he was to the papists in Newcastle's Cavalier army. And he was certainly and increasingly alarmed that the war was causing a breakdown in social order and respect for the social hierarchy. To Newcastle, he wrote:" My Lord, there is one thing more which I fear much, that if the honourable endeavours of such powerful men as yourself do not take place for a happy peace, the necessitous people of the whole Kingdom will presently rise in mighty numbers ... to the utter ruin of all the Nobility and Gentry of the Kingdom." He then referred obliquely to the spontaneous rising of the ordinary people of Bradford against an attempted Royalist entry and concluded: "My Lord, necessity teaches us to seek a subsustence, and if this unruly rout have once cast the rider, it will run like wildfire in the example throughout all the counties of England."[10]

Later, Hotham was so outraged by Cromwell's promotion to commissions of mere freeholders and yeomen that he threatened to fire on any of them who trespassed on his territory.[11] Sir Hugh, on the other hand, was far from being a "leveller", but he would not have been in the least offended by Cromwell's principle of rewarding merit rather than inherited social status.

In fact, despite their previous close relationship and enduring friendship, there seems to have been no clandestine collusion between Cholmley and the Hothams. Only three days before Sir Hugh took his famous secret ride to York to see the Queen, the governor of Hull was singing his praises to Speaker Lenthall.[12] When news reached Hull of Sir Hugh's defection, Sir John made every effort within his power to retake the castle and harbour at Scarborough, which he appreciated were great military assets. First, he wrote to Cholmley to try "to disswade him from quitting the Parliament" and, in case this plea should fail, another letter to John Legard, captain of the castle guard, asking him to prevent it.[13] Then he sent Browne Bushell back to Scarborough by sea to recapture it for Parliament during Cholmley's second absence in York. As Hotham gleefully reported to the Commons soon afterwards, Bushell appeared to have succeeded brilliantly: combining subterfuge, guile and boldness, he had restored town, castle and harbour to Parliament's control. Sir John then sent a ship with reinforcements for Bushell and "twenty pound to the souldiers in the castle to drink".[14]

As soon as Hotham heard that Bushell had broken his word and handed Scarborough back to his cousin without a fight, the governor of Hull mounted a joint land and sea attack. By sea he sent two armed "catches" or pinnaces with 80 men on board, and by land he sent his own son at the head of "a chosen group". Pretending friendship, Sir Hugh lured the two catches into the harbour and then seized their crews when they ventured ashore. The ships' cannon he mounted on Ramshill, at the southern entrance to Scarborough, and ambushed young Hotham's party. Twenty of Hotham's troops were killed and 30 taken prisoner.[15]

Far from encouraging the Hothams to follow his example, Cholmley's defection had the opposite affect on them. Having for several months toyed and teased themselves with the thought of changing sides, the Hothams reacted to Sir Hugh's surprising initiative, first with cool indifference and then, after it had clearly worked, with angry hostility. When the Hothams, father and son, finally came out into the open, it was too late for them: hesitation was their undoing.[16] Cholmley's case was different. Even though he shared many of their doubts and fears, he was too much of a civilian to enjoy the discomforts, dangers and brutalities of war. He despised the swashbuckling, daredevil behaviour of young Hotham and detested the cold, calculating professionalism of Cavalier veterans such as Goring and King. Above all, he was not driven merely by jealousy, private pride or misplaced notions of personal honour. Just as he had joined Parliament's side in 1642 in defence of his estate, home and family in Yorkshire, so six months later these same interests were imperilled by rampaging Cavaliers against whom he had no protection. Only in the last few days, again unlike the Hothams, did he practise deceit to conceal his true intentions.

Cholmley had written twice to Speaker Lenthall expressing his misgivings about the war and pleading for an early settlement with the King to end it. In December 1642, he had explained to the Commons that he had taken up arms with the greatest reluctance, not out of self-interest, and only to determine "the truth of the Gospel, liberty of the subject, and peace of the Kingdom".[17] In January 1643, immediately after the battle at Guisborough, the need for "an accommodation between the King and Parliament" had, in his view, become acutely urgent. Peace was now such a priority that Parliament should concede on all outstanding issues "if our religion be but firmly settled".[18] Since these were contemporary, not retrospective, statements, they deserve to be valued as a true reflection of Sir Hugh's mind at that time.

In Cholmley's subsequent and subjective memorials and later still in his memoirs, there was little in his writing that was not special pleading and even self-deception. As he saw it, he had made an honourable contract with Parliament which he, and not it, had fulfilled in full measure. In good faith he had accepted a commission from the king's lord lieutenant of Yorkshire to be colonel of his old trained band regiment. He had carried out this commission faithfully. He had not sought battle and he had not run away from it. From London he had received a minimum of instruction, encouragement and supply. What he had achieved at Scarborough had been done by consent, not imposed by force or threat of it. No subject had been deprived of his liberty or his property. He had disobeyed one order from his superior only because it had been foolish. When his loyalty and competence had been questioned, he had offered to resign his commission. Events had vindicated his decision to fall back to Scarborough and not attempt an advance to Tadcaster. He had denied the Queen a safe anchorage at Scarborough.

By the beginning of March 1643 Cholmley had convinced himself that whereas he had carried out his obligations to Parliament, Parliament's leaders had failed in their duty to him and the nation. Whereas Charles, he believed, had made "faire and reasonable propositions and inclinations to treaty", Parliament seemed stubbornly deaf to concession of any kind.[19] As he described his position in his memoirs:

> I did not forsake them (sic) Parlament till they did faile in performeing those perticulers they made the grounds of the warre when I was first ingaidged *vidz*. the preservation of Relegion, protection of the Kings person and lyberties of the subject, nor did I quit them then for any perticuler ends of my owne, but meerely to performe the duty and allegeance I owed to my Soveraigne, and which I did in such away as was with out any deminution of my honour ether as a gentleman or souldier. [20]

Consequently, Sir Hugh felt justifiably offended by the "sharpe votes in the House of Commons" passed against him personally. He was also angered by the revenge taken against his wife who was still in London. She was "plunder'd ... of her coach horses" and "used coarsely" before being allowed to leave the capital with her two daughters to join her husband in Scarborough.[21]

Cholmley's gloss on his own conduct has won few converts. According to one of the more favourable commentators, compared with the Hothams, Sir Hugh had "the nobler nature" and was "activated by the purer motives"; he was "bitterly disappointed at the failure of the Oxford negotiations to reach any basis of agreement"; and since "he had nothing of the Puritan in him", he felt growing uneasiness with a Parliament that was increasingly radical in religious policy.[22]

Since these were the measured conclusions of the nineteenth-century's greatest Civil War historian, Samuel Rawson Gardiner, they must be treated with respect. It is true that, compared with the Hothams, Cholmley looks like a model of modesty, rationality and unselfishness. As soon as he arrived at the critical decision to desert Parliament, his first action was to send a message to General Essex resigning his commission. From the Queen at York he asked for no reward for himself, only that she would give him the assurances already described. He appears to have taken none of his officers, not even Browne Bushel!, into his confidence; they learned of his defection only when he returned from York. In contrast, when young Hotham met the Queen secretly at Bridlington, he offered to deliver Hull to her on condition that his father was "made a viscount, himself a barron, that they might have twenty thousand pound in money" and Sir John remain governor of Hull for life![23]

Yet this contrast between Cholmley and the Hothams can be overdrawn. Sir Hugh might not have "asked" the Queen for reward, but he readily accepted from her powers far greater than he had held from Parliament. Not only was his colonel's commission retained under Lord Newcastle, he was also made responsible for "all marine affayres with in all the ports from Tease to Bridlington".[24] If he had simply surrendered Parliament's commission and gone into retirement or exile, there would have been no need to ride secretly to York to kiss Henrietta Maria's hand. Though nowhere was it recorded on paper that survives, Cholmley's "reward" must have been guaranteed previously in correspondence with Goring and Newcastle before he rode out of Newborough Bar with a patch over one eye to disguise his identity![25] It was not in Sir Hugh's nature to take unnecessary risks. His audience with the Queen was therefore no more than a polite formality, not abject submission on one side and haughty, gracious pardon on the other.

Cholmley's puritanism, or lack of it, has already been discussed above and a conclusion reached there that is at odds with Gardiner's. On this subject, all that might be emphasized is that "a religious settlement", whatever Sir Hugh meant by that, was the only question on which he insisted Parliament ought not to make concession to the king.[26]

As for the "Oxford negotiations", Gardiner's argument seems to be at odds with the chronology. When Cholmley rode out from Scarborough on 20 March 1643 to offer his allegiance to the Queen at York, Parliament's negotiating committee had not yet arrived at Oxford. When Sir Hugh declared publicly for the King, the articles for an Oxford treaty were still being discussed there. It was not until 15 April, after a twenty-day "truce", that the treaty expired. How much Cholmley, 250 miles away in his Scarborough "out-Angle", knew of these events can be only guessed. Indeed, this goes to the heart of the problem of understanding Cholmley's motives: we have no way of assessing how well-informed at the time he was about what was taking place at Oxford or London and therefore how much he might have been directed by proceedings there.[27]

So, given that Sir Hugh had long harboured sincere doubts about his parliamentary commission, what were the decisive factors that pushed him over the edge? Most commentators on the subject of Cholmley's change, and not just the romantic biographers of Henrietta Maria, have assumed that it was the Queen's arrival at Bridlington Quay and her triumphant progress to York which really brought him over to the Royalist side.[28]

Doubtless, Cholmley was profoundly affected by what had happened at Bridlington: it had taken place on his doorstep and he must have known about it in detail. The Queen had brought a mountain of weaponry and a treasury of money that would sustain the King's field army for the forthcoming campaigns of the summer. Whatever might have recently occurred in the West Riding, the Royalists now had the upper hand in the East and North Ridings. Cholmley must have been demoralised by his isolation and feebleness when he learned of the failure of the Hothams to put up even a token resistance. Even before the Queen's massive reinforcements entered the county,

Sir Hugh had been compelled to withdraw Browne Bushell from Malton.[29] Now he expected Lord Newcastle to launch an offensive against him.

On 11 March, three days after the Queen's huge convoy entered York, Cholmley sent parties out from Scarborough to occupy Pickering castle and destroy the bridges over the Derwent and the Rye at Yedingham and Howebridge; but they were too late. The Royalists had already taken the castle at Pickering and their musketeers were already guarding Howebridge to secure the main road from Malton.[30] Most alarming of all to Cholmley, a troop of Cavalier horsemen had taken the moorland road northwards and plundered Fyling Hall and Hotham's defenceless tenants there. Nearly a week later, writing from Hull, Sir John reported to Speaker Lenthall this first attack on his property:

> The other day, divers Papists, as I have heard, made suit to my Lord of Newcastle to be employed to pillage a little house and [blank] of mine, which accordingly they did and took away all my breed of horses and [blank] that I had there … [31]

Fyling Hall might have been merely "a little house" to the great Sir John Hotham, but it had been Sir Hugh's home for five years and the place where his eldest daughter had died and his youngest son had been born and baptised. Though Captain John Legard rejoiced that Royalist raiders had been routed soon afterwards in a brief action in the main street of Thornton and twenty of them taken captive, this was no consolation to Cholmley. Sir Francis Mackworth, with more than 700 soldiers, most of them cavalry, were now quartered in Thornton, and some of them had taken residence in what was left of Sir Hugh's ancestral home and birthplace, Roxby castle.[32] Thornton was only a dozen miles inland from Scarborough.

With scarcely enough soldiers to defend Scarborough castle and town and none to spare to protect his estate and family home at Whitby, Cholmley must have known that he was at the mercy of Mackworth. Yet "mercy" was the last hope that he could expect from his Cavalier enemies. As Hotham had already complained in another letter to London:

> They [Royalists] have plundered all where they come, but above all Sir William Strickland, and two near kinsmen of his. Sir William had lost above £4000 in his goods and all his evidence seized upon.[33]

Strickland's home, Boynton Hall, was one of the main victims of the Queen's progress inland from Bridlington. Henrietta Maria is reputed to have stayed there one night and left a portrait of herself in the Hall to remind Sir William of his uninvited and unwelcome guest. Abbey House, it seemed, would soon suffer the same callous treatment as Boynton Hall.

At this moment, in the middle of March, Cholmley made his first overtures to the Royalists. On the pretence of only negotiating an exchange of prisoners, who had been "used with all humanity" by Sir Hugh despite "the cruel usage" of his own men at Yarm and afterwards, he began to treat with Generals Mackworth at Thornton and Goring in York. Captain Legard observed that about this time he first heard Sir Hugh speak disparagingly of the armies of the earl of Essex and Lord Fairfax and to compare them unfavourably with those of the earl of Newcastle. Cholmley also now complained

93

to his own officers that Parliament had failed to support and supply them adequately, though he had "several times importun'd them". Soon afterwards, Sir Hugh's cousin, James Cholmley, whose son served in the earl of Crawford's regiment, went off into the country and was away for several days. On his return he claimed to have been captured by Cavaliers, taken by them to York, and from there he had escaped back to Scarborough. Only with hindsight did Legard realise the significance of these hints: at the time he never doubted Cholmley's loyalty to Parliament: "...such was my respect unto him and my confidence in his fidelity [I] did not all this time imagine or conceit that he intended any way to defraud the trust concreded [sic] to him by Parliament".[34]

Not only did Legard place absolute trust in his colonel's attachment to Parliament, to him and the other junior officers it seemed inconceivable that Cholmley alone could plan such a defection:

> ... it could not sinke into our heads that any man of discretion should be so impudent as to betray a Fort, and have no power of the Enemy to joyne with him in case he should find opposition within especially when the cheif officers had not been consulted with, nor their affections tryed, nor any party made amongst the souldiers, to make that good which was intended...[35]

Significantly, of the events leading to his change, little is to be found in Cholmley's own written recollections. Of Newcastle's Royalist army, Sir Hugh noted only that "a great part" of it was "quartered between Scarborough and Yorke". He said nothing of relevant events at Pickering, Thornton, Fyling Hall and Bridlington. Presumably, he wanted his readers to believe that his motives for changing sides were just as personal, principled and disinterested as those that had first pushed him into Parliament's service.[36]

Cholmley went over to the King for reasons which were neither entirely noble nor merely sordid. He was not persuaded by the Queen: she and Newcastle had both given him promises of safe conduct and access to York and a safe return to Scarborough before he passed out of Newborough Bar.[37] Henrietta Maria gave him empty assurances, but by the time of their meeting he had already decided to defect and on terms which had been agreed with Goring. The presence of the Queen was therefore irrelevant: of paramount importance, however, were the psychological and logistical consequences of her arrival in Yorkshire with an enormous supply of arms. If she had come safely ashore at Newcastle, instead of Bridlington Quay, Sir Hugh would still have turned coat, if only a little later. If her expedition had ended disastrously then Cholmley might well have tried to hold out longer against Mackworth, at least until he received reinforcement from London or Hull by sea. In fact, unknown to him at the time, a Parliament ship, loaded with gunpowder, carbines, pistols, swords and match, was heading towards Scarborough.[38]

As they had done so many times before, whether rescuing him from creditors, opposing Strafford and Ship Money, or defying King Charles at Hull, the Hothams played a key role in determining Cholmley's destiny. Now, when their support was again indispensable, they had both deserted him. Sir John had shut himself in Hull, and his son, with about 700 horse and foot, would not stir himself out of Beverley. Their secret understanding with Newcastle in effect meant that they had abandoned Cholmley for the sake of their own skins, families and estates.[39]

The Hothams had good reason to be envious of Cholmley's coup at Scarborough: their only consolation was that most of Sir Hugh's officers and some of their men refused to follow him, quit the town and went home or came to Hull. However, there was no physical resistance. Captain Legard thought first of shooting Sir Hugh in the head, rejected the notion because the colonel's soul was certain to go straight to Hell, and instead settled for a ship to Hull for himself, his family and his household goods. The two Dutch captains, Froome and Vanderhurst, both veterans, brought their own companies of horse and foot out of Scarborough to Hull. Sir Thomas Norcliffe of Nunnington Hall also preferred Hull and led his troop of dragoons there and so did another local gentleman, Lieutenant Thomas Strangeways of Ugglebarnby.[40] In fact, far many more soldiers deserted Sir Hugh than later he was willing to admit. Even his own cornet, Henry Wilkinson, had to be confined because he would not follow his colonel.[41] In the end, blood ties proved stronger than other considerations. Cholmley's own relatives, his cousin James Cholmley, and his Bushell cousins, Browne and Henry, stood by him and carried the day. Apart from Lieutenant-Colonel Lancelot Alured, they were the only senior officers to stay in Scarborough. Yet, astonishingly, there was no violence and not one life was lost.[42]

How had Cholmley managed to carry off his coup so brilliantly? By his own account and that of Legard, the townspeople welcomed the change. According to Sir Hugh, "not above 4 families" refused to stay in a Royalist town.[43] In Legard's words, "The Inhabytants of the Towne were extreme rnalignant."[44] When Cholmley returned from York to Scarborough with the King's commission, "townesmen upon the guarde...expressed great joy to see Sir Hugh and to have him amongst them".[45] Of the ruling town council, only one, senior Bailiff John Harrison, would not cooperate with Cholmley and was imprisoned first in Scarborough castle and later at York.[46]

However, though some were "Malevolents" (as *Certain Informations,* one of Parliament's news-sheets, described Scarborough's civilians)[47] such as the Thompsons, the great majority of the town's leaders were wise enough to appreciate that to go along with Cholmley was the only way to save themselves, their families and their properties from the Cavalier soldiery. Most of the garrison had departed to Hull or returned to their homes; Royalist troops were sweeping towards the coast in overwhelming numbers; and the town had not the means to defend itself against them. After bombardment, assault and plunder would come occupation by hostile, foreign soldiers. Only a resident with radical religious principles such as John Lawson chose to live in exile in Hull rather than under a Royalist regime in his native Scarborough.[48] So, by changing sides in the nick of time, Cholmley had saved Scarborough and Whitby from rapine and ransack. The entry in Scarborough corporation records for 11 April 1643 reads "Omne bene".[49]

Yet credit, if it is due, has to be given to Cholmley: he handled a critical situation with consummate skill and confidence. As Legard wrote afterwards, the announcement of his change of allegiance was so sudden and unexpected that no one was prepared for it and many could not believe it.[50] Indeed, not only did Sir Hugh act almost entirely alone, he refused assistance from his new Royalist allies. The Queen offered him 1,500 cavalry when he returned to Scarborough a second time on 30 March, but he left only a troop of Newcastle's horse at Falsgrave and next day came down to Newborough Bar escorted by only three servants. There, outside the town gates, he was met by Browne Bushell, who had re-taken castle, harbour and town for Parliament in Cholmley's absence. Sir Hugh reminded his cousin of "the favours hee had donn him" and Bushell, who was "of a rash but flexable and good nature", responded by opening the gates and handing over the keys of the castle.[51]

Cholmley had been entirely successful: he had allowed those who wanted, soldiers and civilians alike, to keep their freedom, their families and their goods and go elsewhere, as long as they did not resist him. He had not threatened, badgered or bullied the resident population into submission. On the contrary, he had deliberately kept Royalist strangers out of the town, saving it from any danger of vengeful occupation. Sir Hugh wanted Scarborians to regard him as their guardian, not as their conqueror, and they were grateful for his protection in time of war.[52]

CHAPTER 11

ROYALIST COMMANDER

Cholmley's switch from Parliament to King determined the rest of his life and the lives of his family; whether he ever came to regret it, even in the darkest and most dangerous moments that followed, is doubtful. He had convinced himself that from then on he was fighting on the right side, and that conviction grew in strength in the years to come. Like Browne Bushell, though with much more to lose than him, the more hopeless became the King's cause, the greater his loyalty to it. Whatever Sir Hugh's original motives for changes sides, increasingly it became a matter of honour and pride that he endured its consequences. Yet what had been intended as an act of necessary self-defence led him down a path almost to self-destruction.

The effects of Cholmley's change-over were immediately far-reaching. As Parliament's most northerly, isolated outpost, Scarborough had only negative value: Sir Hugh's commission was simply to deny the use of its harbour to the King. As long as it held on to Hull, Parliament had little use of its own for Scarborough, Bridlington or Whitby; once they were Royalist however, then they, and particularly Scarborough, became the King's most convenient and secure entrance to the North from the Continent. The Queen's convoy of munitions, money and men from Holland was to be the far largest, yet it was not the last. Denied Scarborough as well as Hull, the Royalists had been obliged to depend on the port of Newcastle, though it was always their third choice. When the Scots entered the war as Parliament's ally and invaded England again early in 1644, they soon sealed off Newcastle from the North Sea. Scarborough then became the King's only safe haven on the east coast. As already noted, significantly Cholmley's new commission from the Crown was not only military governor of the town and castle of Scarborough: he was also made responsible for "all marine affayres" in all ports from Tees mouth to Bridlington.[1]

Such vital strategical considerations were ignored by the Royalist mouthpiece, *Mercurius Aulicus*: it welcomed Sir Hugh's "coming over", not because he brought with him "80 horse, and 400 foot, well armed and appointed for present service", but "in respect of his authority in that county, and his being privy to the counsells and designs of the chief actors of this rebellion".[2] In short, Cholmley's material assistance, even when exaggerated, was regarded as less valuable to the Royalist cause than the moral affect of his defection on Parliament and its supporters, especially Yorkshiremen.

There was both hyperbole and wishful thinking in this Royalist report. Parliament's press was much closer to the true figure when it estimated that Cholmley had retained about 150 horse and foot, whereas previously he had commanded upwards of 600.[3] As for Sir Hugh's "authority in that county", whatever titles were bestowed upon him, his writ did not run much inland from the coast. The Hothams were strengthened, not weakened, by his defection, and the Fairfaxes had never received assistance through Scarborough. Lord Ferdinando was forced to retreat westwards from Selby, simply because he was "denyed help & succor" by his "ally", Sir John. The disaster that followed on Seacroft Moor on 30 March demonstrated the weakness of the Fairfaxes in cavalry and well-armed, trained infantry: it had no connection with Cholmley's defection and everything to do with lack of cooperation from the Hothams.[4]

Military historians of the English civil wars have criticised Royalist officers who misemployed themselves, their soldiers and their artillery guarding obsolete castles or country houses without even tactical value; but Cholmley was one Royalist commander innocent of this charge.[5] First as Parliamentarian then as Royalist, Sir Hugh was one of the most mobile, energetic and enterprising of all garrison commanders. Within 30 miles of Scarborough almost every Parliamentarian of means was plundered, driven away, suborned or, in one case, kidnapped.

At the end of May 1643, it was reported to the House of Lords that the earl of Mulgrave, a strong Parliamentarian, had had all his estate and house in the North Riding pillaged and his alum mines and works there confiscated. The Commons granted the earl £50 a week in compensation for what was the work of one or more of Cholmley's long-range raiding parties.[6]

In June, Sir Hugh himself was 60 miles further south in the area of Market Weighton. From there he wrote a friendly letter to Captain William Goodricke, eldest son of William Goodricke of Skidby, colonel of foot at Hull. In it he suggested that Goodricke junior should surrender the castle at Wressle, the only one in the East Riding. Though no evidence of collusion between them exists or has survived, Cholmley was well aware of Sir John Hotham's recent failure to betray Hull to the Royalists, his subsequent flight to Beverley and his violent arrest there. Therefore, to persuade Goodricke to hand over Wressle, Sir Hugh advised him that he would suffer the same indignities and imprisonment now endured by Hotham if he failed to comply. Goodricke's reply was so contemptuous and hostile that the Commons had it printed along with Cholmley's letter.[7] Still the Royalist threat to Wressle was serious enough for Hull to send its garrison a supply of muskets, powder and shot.[8]

Mercurius Aulicus announced on 7 July that Cholmley had taken prompt advantage of the confusion caused by the abortive Hotham coup at Hull "to draw his forces down to Beverly". There he had captured the market place where Sir John had been arrested and chased Parliament's soldiers in the town back "to the Gates of Hull".[9] *Mercurius Aulicus* was invariably Royalist-biased, but not usually inventive; but if its story was true it described only a brief, minor success. According to less partisan sources, as soon as Sir John Hotham was safely dispatched in irons by ship to London, Colonels Matthew Boynton and John Legard (since leaving Scarborough he had been promoted) returned to Beverley from Hull and repulsed the Royalists occupying it.[10] Boynton lost four men, Cholmley at least 24, of whom 13 were buried the following day in the church yard. For the next two months, Beverley was to be the headquarters of Sir Thomas Fairfax's cavalry and from there he led forays as far as Stamfordbridge.[11] Indeed, at this time, Cholmley did not have the strength to hold any forward position in the East Riding beyond Bridlington. After his crushing defeat of the Fairfaxes on Adwalton Moor at the end of June, Lord Newcastle took most of his army southwards into Lincolnshire. He did not return to Yorkshire until the end of August.[12]

None of these sorties north and south of Scarborough was mentioned by Cholmley in any of his reminiscences. Nor did he refer in either memorials or memoirs to his activities as tax collector for the Royalist cause. Earl in April 1643, the earl of Newcastle had assessed Yorkshire at the unprecedented rate of £30,000 a month and apart from Hull, which never came under his control, most parts of the county were burdened until the summer of 1644 with what was called "the great sesse." Fragmentary records show that Sir Hugh made himself responsible for collection of this tax, not only in his own "country", the wapentakes of Whitby Strand and Pickering Lythe, but also deep into the East Riding. For instance, in December 1643, Cholmley was at Burton Agnes Hall, home of the Royalist Sir Henry Griffith, to receive dues brought in by neighbouring constables. Bridlington town and quay paid him £42 10s. which included bread, beef and malt.[13] At the same time, Scarborough town was still paying heavily for its own defences. Before his change of allegiance, Cholmley had passed the port's valuable customs dues to Hull, but afterwards he kept them for his own purposes.

In his memorials on Scarborough, where such matters might have been described, Cholmley dismissed them as "too tedious to relate" and in his later memoirs he passed straight on from his change of sides to his involvement in the second siege of Hull the following autumn.[14] Indeed, whether out of forgetfulness or rank dishonesty, in his memoirs Sir Hugh claimed that, though he lived at Scarborough "in a very handsome port and fashion", it was at his own expense: he received "nether pay nor allowance but maynteined the port of the Governor's place upon my owne purse, not haveing the worth of a chickeing out of the country which I payed not for..."[15] Since Cholmley is known to have received military supplies from the Royalist arsenal at York and from overseas agents in the Netherlands, as well as proceeds from North Sea privateering, such a claim must be disregarded as no more than special and specious pleading.[16]

Even about the siege of Hull, which lasted from 2 September to 11 October 1643, Cholmley had little to say and none of the contemporary accounts of it mention him by name. Lord Newcastle, now raised to marquess by the King, had promoted Sir Hugh to brigadier of horse and put him in command of a third of his cavalry which included Cholmley's own regiment of 300 horsemen. Without any employment of modesty, Sir Hugh described his regiment as "the best in the Army". Out of Scarborough's town garrison he also brought 400 foot soldiers who were led by Launcelot Alured and Browne Bushell.[17]

This third futile attempt by the Royalists to capture Hull was a most unhappy, frustrating experience for Newcastle's soldiers, especially the cavalry. Against well-positioned cannon, trenches and flooded terrain, horsemen were useless. Conditions outside Hull in the wet autumn of 1643 were not unlike those in Flanders during the Great War of 1914-18. It must have been a miserable time for Sir Hugh, which he had no wish to recall, particularly since the siege ended in humiliating defeat and withdrawal.[18] The only Cavalier to profit was Browne Bushell, who on the last day took Colonel Thomas Rainborough prisoner. According to one account, Rainborough was exchanged for a Royalist captive; according to another, Browne demanded and received a ransom of £500![19]

After the siege of Hull was lifted, Newcastle retired his army to winter quarters in York. His troops abandoned the East Riding, devastating the countryside as they retreated. Beverley was reoccupied by the Roundheads; Holderness was cleared of Royalists; Sir William Constable left a garrison at Burton Agnes Hall; Wressle castle was relieved; and Cholmley was forced to make his way back to Scarborough.[20] The military superiority and advantage won by the King's army in Yorkshire at Seacroft and

Adwalton Moor were wasted in the muddy fields on the banks of the Hull and Humber. From now on the Royalists in general and Sir Hugh Cholmley in particular were fighting defensively.

On 19 January 1644 a huge Scottish army of about 15,000 troops crossed the river Tweed into England.[21] Before he died of bowel cancer the previous December, John Pym had negotiated an armed alliance with the Scottish Presbyterians against King Charles and the Scots had been quick to implement its military provisions. Consequently, with about half his field army, the marquess of Newcastle marched northwards out of York to save his namesake city. He left behind an overstretched garrison in Yorkshire, particularly weak in cavalry. The military initiative now passed to Lord Ferdinando Fairfax in Hull.

The first direct challenge to Cholmley at Scarborough came when "Sir William Constable crept out of Hull with their horse, making their carracols upon the Woulds, and was heard of as far as Pickering".[22] "Crept out" was Sir Henry Slingsby's disparaging description of what became a bold raid deep across the East Riding and northwards as far as Whitby. Though places, dates and sequences in this episode remain confused and contradictory, it seems that this extravagant, puritanical and self-impoverished son of Flamborough descended first on Bridlington where he met little resistance. Then, after "Burlington Bay [Bridlington Quay] the furtheste haven towne in the East Riding", Constable crossed into the North Riding, passing through Filey, Potter Brompton and Everley, giving Scarborough a wide berth, before attacking Whitby, "a haven towne in the farthest part of Yorkshire".[23] In the words of a second Parliamentarian version, Whitby "was a very strong garrison of the Earl [sic] of Newcastle", but its 500 soldiers and officers and almost a thousand sailors with 40 ships and 100 cannon in the river were soon subdued! Sir Hugh Cholmley's "great House and Fort on the high cliff" was also taken.[24]

If Whitby did in fact fall to Constable, his success and stay there must have been very brief. Cholmley had nothing remotely close to the figures of soldiers and sailors quoted in the London press, but he had been taken off guard by the speed and audacity of Constable's movement. However, what were presented in Parliament's propaganda as triumphant feats of military skill and courage were no more than lightning, plundering raids. London's news-sheets neglected to report later that Bridlington Quay and Whitby were soon re-occupied by Sir Hugh's troops.

Endorsed by Scarborough's two Bailiffs, John Harrison and Thomas Gill, both Parliamentarians, a draft letter of 1646 condemned the town's former vicar, William Simpson, for being "an inveterate enemye to the Parliament". Not only had he served Cholmley as his domestic chaplain, but from the pulpit of St Mary's, the parish church, he had asked the congregation to "give thanks for that great victorye god hath given us over the rebels att Sandsend ... att the time when Sir H Cholmley tooke Whitbye".[25] It is unlikely that Cholmley had needed to score a "great victorye" two years earlier: by the time that he arrived at Whitby from Scarborough, Constable's cavalry were already on their way back over the moors to Malton, and probably only some few remaining Roundheads were driven off at Sandsend, a mile or so up the coast. We know that Whitby, along with nearby Mulgrave castle, did not fall to Parliament's Colonel Francis Boynton until as late as 17 June 1644.[26]

Bridlington's records are fewer than Scarborough's and more difficult to decipher. Richard Thompson of Kilham, Bridlington's constable, spent five weeks locked up in Scarborough castle, presumably as a punishment for helping Constable's raiders. By the following May, however, Cholmley raised £33 9s. 2d. from the town's residents, though he had to send troops there to collect another £10 that was outstanding.[27]

As the area of Royalist territory shrank and Sir Hugh eventually found himself again isolated by land, his famous "Scarborough Horse" continued to operate, in day and night raids, behind "enemy lines". For instance, early in June 1644, Sir Hugh sent out Major Thomas Crompton with "fiftie of his best horse and choicest men". Their mission was to surprise, capture and bring back to Scarborough Henry Darley, the Yorkshire MP and one of Parliament's commissioners to the Scots. He was then staying at the family home at Buttercrambe. At that time Parliament's Anglo-Scottish armies were just about to complete the encirclement of York, so that Darley, only ten miles from the city and nearly 30 from Scarborough, felt safe enough not to raise the drawbridge over the river Derwent, even at night. Darley was caught in his bed and carried back to Scarborough. Later, Sir Hugh made him into a useful hostage and messenger. Darley's capture was one episode that Cholmley took pleasure in recalling in his memorials, though he shortened the distance between Buttercrambe and York to make the operation appear more hazardous.[28]

These long-range cavalry sorties, sometimes deep into "enemy territory", continued throughout 1644 until Scarborough was eventually closely besieged at the beginning of 1645. In both memorials and memoirs Sir Hugh subsequently claimed that, after the Royalist debacle on Marston Moor in July 1644 and the fall of York, Sir Thomas Fairfax advanced to within five or six miles of Scarborough with a thousand horse and three thousand foot soldiers.[29] But this was another of Cholmley's self-flattering fictions. In August 1644, Sir Thomas was sent by his father to besiege Helmsley castle. There he was shot and badly wounded by a Royalist sharpshooter and had to spend the next three months in York recovering slowly from his injury.[30] Even at Helmsley, 30 miles from Scarborough, Sir Thomas had never more than 300 cavalry and 700 infantry, all badly clothed, equipped and unpaid.[31]

Now desperately short of any encouraging news from Yorkshire, *Mercurius Aulicus* was therefore delighted to report early in October 1644 that Cholmley had scored another daring success. He had sent out a "party of horse to visit the Rebells at Pickering Lithe (14 miles from Scarborough) and there found some Rebell Dragooners, 37 whereof were brought prisoners into Scarborough".[32] Thornton, Cholmley's birthplace, is exactly 14 miles inland from Scarborough in Pickering Lythe wapentake.

Even as late as December 1644, with Parliament's troops now closing in on the town and quartered in most of the villages in the vicinity of Scarborough, thirteen of Sir Hugh's troopers broke through the siege lines and rode 20 miles "into Cleaveland". There they encountered fifteen Scots, killed two of them, and brought the remaining thirteen back to Scarborough with their horses. If we are to believe Sir Hugh, though never more than 200 in number, his cavalry were "verie good men and perpetually in action, and grew soe formidable the enemie durst not stand to looke them in the face under treble the number". Their final foray at the end of the year resulted in the capture of Colonel "Foulthrop" and most of his troop.[33]

However, long before these events, Cholmley's situation at Scarborough had become hopeless. The overwhelming defeat of the Northern army of the marquess of Newcastle by the Anglo-Scottish forces of Lords Fairfax, Manchester and Leven at

Marston Moor on 2 July 1644 was the beginning of the end for the King's military cause. The Royalist army which had dominated most of Yorkshire for the last sixteen months was effectively destroyed; its commander, the marquess, and all of his staff officers gave up the war as lost and fled into continental exile; and York surrendered soon after the battle. In Yorkshire, the King was left only with a handful of isolated garrisons at Tickhill, Sheffield, Helmsley, Sandal, Bolton, Knaresborough, Pontefract, Skipton and Scarborough.

Though Sir Hugh was not present on the battlefield of Marston Moor, his knowledge and understanding of what had happened there were probably clearer and better than most of the Royalist survivors. Indeed, his Memorialls touching the Battle of Yorke, written for but neglected by Lord Clarendon, is the only surviving Royalist account of the battle with much historical value. Lord Newcastle refused to put pen to paper on the subject when asked; the so-called "Rupert's Diary" is no longer regarded as his; James King, Lord Eythin, was too proud to confess or conceal his guilt; and Sir Henry Slingsby's subsequent diary report, both brief and sketchy, does not convince the reader that he was actually present. Other Royalist eyewitnesses conveyed only the utter confusion and complexity of the biggest and bloodiest battle of the civil war fought by at least 40,000 men mainly in half-light.[34] In contrast, Cholmley's own considered analysis was remarkably perceptive, objective and convincing. Unlike the combatants, he had no personal or professional reputation to advance or defend; he was able to envisage the battlefield as a whole; and since his informants were all senior officers he was able to avoid trivial and irrelevant experiences.[35]

On the 3 July, the day after the disaster on Marston Moor, the marquess of Newcastle arrived in Scarborough with his staff officers. In this distinguished party with him were his two sons, colonels viscount Mansfield and lord Henry Cavendish, his brother, Sir Charles Cavendish, Lord Eythin, Sir Francis Mackworth, lords Falconbridge and Widdrington, Sir Edward Widdrington, Sir William Carnaby, treasurer of the Northern army, Sir Walter Vavasour and the earl of Carnwath. The marquess stayed two nights as Cholmley's guest. He told Sir Hugh that all was lost and he should go into exile with them; but his host replied that, though Scarborough was not defensible, he would not desert his post there until he had heard from the King or was forced to surrender it. Cholmley provided the party with two ships, one for Newcastle, the other for Lord Eythin, and they sailed away to Hamburg. For all of them the war was over and lost, but not for Sir Hugh.[36]

Royalist rout at Marston Moor, the desertion and flight of Newcastle and his senior officers and the fall of York to Parliament's armies on 16 July together had a devastating and demoralising affect on Cholmley's garrison at Scarborough. Some of his soldiers procured passes from Sir Hugh to join Prince Rupert, who had gone north to Richmond before crossing the Pennines into Lancashire; others simply drifted way to their homes and families. As he later wrote: "The Generalls departure and gentlemens thus quitting the towne struck soe great a terror into the common soldiors as they ranne away dayly." The town and castle garrison was reduced to 300 foot and 200 horse "and many of those wavering".[37]

In these unpromising circumstances, Cholmley played for time. As usual he pretended to consult and confer when he had already come to a decision. He summoned the principal officers and "some two or three gentlemen of qualitie that remained in the Towne and whoe hee knew [were] verie firme to the Kings cause" and told them that

102

they could not withstand a siege and that therefore he proposed to offer terms of surrender to Parliament. Since this seemed a sensible way of saving Scarborians from the inevitability of Parliament's revenge, "the motion was exceedinglie approved of [by] everyman". Henry Darley was to be given the message to take to London and "greedie of libertie" he was pleased "to undertake the business". However, Cholmley rejected Darley's suggestion that the treaty should be made with Lord Fairfax because his purpose was merely "to gain time" and "a treaty with the Lord Fairefax would bring a short issue".[38]

If Cholmley can be believed, his deception worked well. Darley was duped into thinking that Sir Hugh's terms were genuine and at York persuaded Fairfax to agree to "a cessation for 20 dayes". This respite allowed Cholmley time and space to bring in "400 loades of corne and a good quantity of hay with other provisions" from Scarborough's hinterland. Secondly, his Nineteen Propositions were so devised that Parliament would be able to approve of nearly but not all of them, thereby leaving him grounds for refusal to surrender. Why Nineteen? Did Sir Hugh have in mind the Nineteen Propositions presented to the King by Parliament which he had refused to read out because they were "most uniust and unreasenable"?[39]

At least two of Cholmley's own propositions he must have known were "unreasenable". In article 12 he asked that "the votes passed against the Governor in the house of Commons be revoked, and that hee be put in the same capacitie hee was before they passed". Parliament was willing to allow Cholmley to go free" to what countrie hee please beyond the seas", to let his wife return to their home at Whitby and to order Parliament's soldiers there to remove themselves, but these were the limits of concession. Sir Hugh could not be forgiven for everything. Similarly, though the London committee agreed that neither townspeople nor garrison soldiers should be punished for their loyalty to Sir Hugh and that their replacements would be "att least 2 parts of 3 Yorkshire men", they drew a line through his insistence in article 15 that his brother, Sir Henry, should succeed him as military governor! "As to the fifteenth the Committy thinkes itt not reasonable Sir Hugh Cholmeley name his successor".[40]

Whether Cholmley's Nineteen Propositions were bogus or sincere has been the subject of some historical debate.[41] Bulstrode Whitelocke, who wrote a vivid but partisan account as a contemporary, was convinced that Sir Hugh seriously intended to surrender Scarborough, but when he heard of the King's great victory at Lostwithiel in Cornwall on 2 September he changed his mind. He then wrote to Prince Rupert pledging his continued loyalty and asking for reinforcements.[42] The weakness of Whitelocke's case is that Cholmley's letter to Rupert was dated 4 September, only two days after a battle fought 300 miles away, and he was unlikely by then to have received news of it.[43]

What evidence that we have from sources other than Cholmley's own reminiscences suggests that he never wavered in his commitment and promises to the King. He could so easily have gone with Newcastle and the others who told him that all was lost. Determined to stay put, he sent his two daughters by sea to Holland in the care of the Remmingtons, though Elizabeth would not go with them. Early in August, before he drew up his Nineteen Propositions, he received a personal letter from King Charles then in faraway Trevarrick in Cornwall. In the eyes of the King, the debacle at Marston Moor, the betrayal of Newcastle and the loss of York raised the value of Sir Hugh's faithfulness. In the letter Charles praised Cholmley's past service and promised him reward for it "when God shall enable us". He was concerned to convince Scarborough's governor of the vital importance of holding on to its castle to the "last extremity".[44]

However, Cholmley might well have been puzzled by the reason Charles gave for standing fast at Scarborough as long as it was physically possible. There was no reference in the King's letter to the crucial value of Scarborough harbour as a possible entry port for continental munitions, as a place of refuge for privateers, or as a base for offensive operations. No mention was made of more help that might come there from Holland or Denmark. Instead, the King told him that a prolonged defence of Scarborough would divert Parliament's forces "to give our Nephew Rupert time to make head again". How the prince could "make head again" in the North or anywhere else without new supplies and reinforcements was not explained.[45]

Either the King was badly misinformed or he was just trying to encourage and flatter Cholmley, or both. Nevertheless, Sir Hugh seems to have convinced himself that his stand at Scarborough had special value to the Royalist cause in the North and that his offer of terms of surrender had a major effect on the deployment of Parliament's forces. He believed that when they were assured of the imminent fall of Scarborough Parliament's three victorious armies went their separate ways, the Scots eventually in the direction of Newcastle, Manchester's to the south of the county, and Fairfax's to besiege Pontefract and Helmsley castles.[46]

In fact, Cholmley was deceiving himself: these major decisions of deployment were made weeks before his surrender propositions were known. The "deliverance" of the ports of Sunderland and Newcastle, with their huge stocks of coal on the banks of the Wear and Tyne, was rightly considered to be of far greater priority than the capture of Scarborough. Also, Lord Fairfax showed more interest in the Royalist strongholds at Helmsley, Pontefract and Knaresborough, not because he expected Scarborough to surrender soon, but because Scarborough was too distant and peripheral and its garrison and castle defences too strong for him. After the lengthy and debilitating siege of York and the bloody battle on Marston Moor, the allied troops were weakened by disease and desertion, and after its fall on 16 July, the city offered them neither sustenance nor healthy living quarters.[47] Fear of plague and food shortages drove the three armies out into the countryside to take advantage of the harvest.[48] On Fairfax's part he would have been foolish to commit his depleted forces to the coast leaving Royalist garrisons at Skipton, Helmsley and Knaresborough across their lines of supply. As he told the Committee in London, the best he could do about Cholmley's Royalists at Scarborough was "to restrain their incursions upon the country".[49]

Such considerations explain why the London government, as well as Fairfax, were willing to accept a truce with Sir Hugh and treat his terms with respect. Indeed, Fairfax was urged to come to an agreement with Cholmley as quickly as possible so that later he had to admit that Parliament had made generous concessions to him, rejecting only three of his demands.[50]

If Cholmley was playing for time, then Parliament and Fairfax were content, as yet, to let him have it: they had many other more pressing concerns than Scarborough. The King's victory at Lostwithiel had given him control of the whole of the south-west of England except Plymouth. As winter approached, Parliament was anxious to remodel its armies in time for the spring campaign of 1645. As for Lord Fairfax, perpetually short of money to pay his men and provide them with basic necessities, he was still faced by a number of formidable fortresses which defied his military strength. Even by the end of

1644, the three most vital and defensible castles at Skipton, Pontefract and Scarborough were still intact and defiant.[51]

Whatever the quality of Cholmley's "Scarborough Horse", his commission from the King was to hold the port and castle at Scarborough; and, in Clarendon's words, this service he "discharged with courage and fidelity".[52] However audacious and successful, Sir Hugh's cavalry "incursions upon the country" could never be more than a minor, occasional irritant to Parliament; but Scarborough port was an entirely different matter. As John Legard had written so perceptively and cogently, Scarborough might serve two important wartime purposes: as a place of entry for continental munitions and men and as a safe haven for privateers who might prey upon enemy shipping as it passed up and down the North Sea coast.[53] When Scarborough harbour ceased to have much use to the King in the former role, it soon took on a major function in the latter.

As long as the Royalist army held York and the route to it from the North Sea coast was still open, Scarborough operated as an arms entrepot. The traffic was not always one-way. Soon after Cholmley went over to the King, a Scotsman in Newcastle's employment called Serjeant-Major Rosse brought 200 muskets, 20 barrels of powder and match from the royal arsenal in Clifford's Tower to Scarborough. Rosse carried a letter from Lord Jermyn on behalf of the Queen asking Sir Hugh to provide a ship to carry these munitions on to Scotland. Half of them were intended for the earl of Antrim, the other half for viscount Aboyne. However, at that time, Cholmley himself was so short of essential military supplies that he persuaded Jermyn and the Queen that Rosse's arms would be better employed by him in Scarborough than in Scotland.[54] On the other hand, Cholmley's later assertion that "neither then or at any other time was there any armes or ammunition sent from Scarbrough into Scotland" is flatly contradicted by the earl of Antrim's report that he had received arms via Scarborough.[55]

When arms and ammunition came into Scarborough harbour by sea they were usually kept in store there or sent directly on to York. Cholmley was in correspondence with suppliers and carriers in Amsterdam and Dunkirk and with the commander of the royal magazine at York. Throughout 1643 the traffic in arms flowed freely and in considerable volume. If there was a Parliamentarian naval blockade, its presence was ineffectual. In November, for instance, Sir Hugh signed an order to deliver 62 muskets and bandoliers to Captain Jones at York.[56] The following day, Jacob Williamson, a Dutchman from Amsterdam, arrived at Scarborough in the *Mary* with a shipment of more firearms. Though the figures in the manifest do not quite add up, it seems that on this occasion 884 pair of pistols and 1,390 muskets were landed at Scarborough. From there nearly all of these weapons were distributed to Royalist officers in Yorkshire.[57]

According to the official customs book for the quarter ending 24 March 1643, Scarborough's maritime trade was still largely unaffected by the civil war. Apples and sack came into Scarborough regularly from Ostend and Dunkirk; iron, timber and tar arrived from Norway; raisins and prunes from Rotterdam; and yarn and cloth from Scotland. In return, Scarborough exported beer, barley and malt. After Cholmley's defection, however, no official record of the harbour's trade was kept, or has survived. Scarborough severed contact with Hull and London and, in the name of the King, Sir Hugh took over personal control of the management and receipts of the port. From April 1643 onwards, the only existing description of the harbour's commercial traffic is a carelessly written and incomplete account book kept by Cholmley's agent; and for 1644 there is no record at all.[58]

Soon after Captain Williamson had brought in pistols and muskets, one of Scarborough's own seafarers, William Lawson, arrived with hogsheads of sack and train oil, hundredweights of prunes, sultanas and raisins, and barrels of tar, all from Rotterdam. Between 10 October and 30 December 1643, 23 merchants, three of them known to be of Leeds, paid Cholmley £313 duty on goods imported into Scarborough. The port was profiting from the misfortunes of besieged Hull, which in peacetime took most of Yorkshire's maritime trade.[59]

The letters that passed from Sir William Sandys, the King's chief agent at Dunkirk, in May 1644 to Cholmley indicate how the situation had deteriorated for them even before the disaster on Marston Moor. The Dutch had become less trustworthy; Parliament's warships were now more active and vigilant; and the advance of the Scots southwards had effectively sealed off the hinterlands of the Tees and the Wear, as well as the Tyne. Merchants abroad were no longer willing to take the risks of running guns from the continent. Sandys had sent a shipment of arms to Newcastle in February, but it was taken at sea by Zealanders. Two Danish vessels, also bound for Newcastle with similar cargoes, had been lost to privateers. Sandys had shipped 100 barrels of gunpowder to York via Scarborough, yet had received no payment for them. Two days later, he sent Cholmley a list of arms he was about to dispatch in the *Sunflower,* a Colchester ship with Giles Wigginer of Whitby as its master. The King was now concerned about the safety of Scarborough: he instructed Sandys to arm its garrison. Sir Hugh was to receive 182 rapiers, 142 ammunition belts and 320 muskets with bandoliers. Charles was paying a guinea for every second-hand musket, which Sandys thought a fair price. To protect his merchant ships, Cholmley was advised by Sandys to raise two or three thousand pounds to buy frigate escorts for them. The following day, Sandys wrote to the Dutch admiral Tromp asking him not to interrupt the passage of the *Sunflower* on its way to Scarborough; but there is no record of its fate.[60]

For Cholmley, the worst news came at the end of June 1644. From Amsterdam, John Webster reported that Captain Percy, master of Sir Hugh's "catch", the *Charles,* had betrayed his trust: he had sold the arms cargo he was conveying, worth £4,257 14s. 8d., and also the ship! Webster then complained that he could find no one there willing to insure another of Cholmley's vessels, the *Minnekin,* for £600. Scarborough ships, he wrote, now had a bad reputation in Amsterdam amongst insurers,"these people being very fearful to insure from that port".[61]

If Scarborough-bound ships succeeded in crossing the privateer-infested North Sea, they then had to outwit Parliament's tightening blockade off the Yorkshire coast. Lord Craven, it seems, was lucky. In the words of Agostini, Venetian ambassador in London, "this very rich, devoted servant of the Palatinate House," had "arrived at Scarboro from France with money, arms and officers" early in July. Not that Agostini was always accurately informed: about the same time, the correspondent who spelled Cholmley as "Sciomle" and Hull as "Uls" told his superiors that, after the battle of Marston Moor, Prince Rupert had gone "towards Scarborough to avail himself of the commodities brought there by Lord Crever[Craven]".[62] He was wrong: after his crushing defeat, the Prince never came further east than York.

Finally, if one of Parliament's London news-sheets, *The Kingdomes Weekly Intelligencer,* is to be believed, also in July 1644, a Dutch vessel, carrying 70 barrels of gunpowder and a Royalist colonel on its way to Scarborough, was intercepted and captured by one of Parliament's warships. The Dutchman was probably the frigate, *Utrecht,* and its captor Captain David Brown of the *Sampson.*[63]

The *Utrecht* was possibly the last of its kind: after Marston Moor, the Royalists in the North ran out of money, credit and credibility. If there were any wishful Royalists still coming into Scarborough from abroad after the loss of York, they were greatly outnumbered by defeated and demoralised Royalists leaving the country by this route. From July 1644 Scarborough became an exit into continental exile. Besides, King Charles had now little hope of further substantial assistance from his European cousins in Denmark, Holland or France. Queen Henrietta Maria again left England, this time for the safety of the French court; there she could expect every sympathy, but not "a man or a penny for her husband's cause".[64] She no longer had jewels to pawn and Charles had no hope of raising another field army in the North. Parliament's increasing anxiety to possess Scarborough grew out of a new and dangerous threat that it now posed.

According to one favourite legend, in the middle of the tenth century, Scarborough had been founded as a Viking pirate's nest and named after him, Skarthi's burg; and, for a short time in 1644-45, under Sir Hugh's direction, it resumed the role of a privateers' refuge.

Even when Cholmley held Parliament's commission, he had sent out Scarborough's ships to waylay merchant vessels that were suspected of helping the enemy. Between privateering in wartime and criminal piracy the distinction was thin and blurred. For example, the *Commons Journal* for 4 April 1643 recorded that a corn ship bound northwards towards Newcastle had fallen into the hands of three Scarborough officers, John Legard, John Lawson and William Nesfield. They were then given permission to sell the ship and its cargo to pay for the upkeep of Cholmley's garrison at Scarborough. At that time, London was still unaware of Cholmley's recent defection.[65]

What previously had been done for Parliament could from now on be practised, also legitimately, in the name of the King. As early as June 1643, *Mercurius Aulicus* congratulated Sir Hugh's recent success in bringing into Scarborough harbour "two ships laden with corn and other provisions for the rebels sustenance, which honester men will now make use of".[66]

The Scarborough harbour account book previously referred to is mainly a record of stores bought for and put aboard Cholmley's privateer pinnaces in 1643 and 1644. Of eight ships that can be identified, two were Dutch or captained by Dutchmen, Peter Anderson and Jacob Williamson, who were engaged mainly carrying arms from Amsterdam and Dunkirk and the others were fitted out to prey on Parliament's North Sea traffic. The privateer captains included three cousins of Sir Hugh, Richard and James Cholmley and Browne Bushell.[67]

Captain Browne Bushell, the eldest son of Sir Hugh's aunt Dorothy and Nicholas Bushell of Bagdale Hall, Whitby, came to be Cholmley's most valuable serving officer. During the 1630s he had served the King of Spain at sea and in the Low Countries for nearly ten years. When the civil war began in 1642 he returned to England and within a short time distinguished himself as a most audacious and resourceful soldier, first for Parliament and then for the King. Without his support in March 1643 Cholmley could not have taken Scarborough over to the Royalist side. After the abandoned siege of Hull, Bushell returned to Scarborough where his cousin gave him command of the 12-gun *Cavendish,* referred to in the harbour accounts as "the Great Catch". By 1645, of all the many "sea rovers" and "pyrates" annoying and damaging Parliament's North Sea merchant shipping, none was more feared and hated than "the Bushell", as the London press called him.[68]

Early in 1644 Bushell was recognised at Newcastle by one of Parliament's informants. He had been there for several weeks, probably advising Sir John Marley, Newcastle's Royalist mayor, on the town's defences. No arms had reached Newcastle, now threatened by the Scottish invaders, for ten weeks, other than the 500 muskets brought by Bushell from Scarborough. According to the same source, Bushell had seized the *Ipswich Sarah,* loaded with Necastle coal, and sent it off to Holland to exchange it for arms and ammunition.[69]

Other privateer captains who used Scarborough at this time as a supply base and safe anchorage were John Denton, who like Bushell was to become a professional pirate when there were no more Royalist ports to hide in, Browne Thomas and possibly Ralph Hogg, master of the *Blessing of Scarborough.* From Cholmley's Sandside stores and cellars, managed by Francis Sollitt and Richard Bilbrough, these captains took their ships' provisions of coal, candles, butter, salted beef, vinegar and "soft bread" and received their gunpowder and shot from the same sources.[70]

As the Royalist traffic in arms petered out during 1644, Cholmley's sea captains took to plundering the coastal coal trade. When the King had controlled Newcastle and Sunderland in 1642 and 1643, few colliers had sailed past Scarborough southwards on their way to London. Exports of sea-coal from the Tyne, which pre-war had averaged half a million tons annually, dropped to a tenth of that figure in the year ending Michaelmas 1643 and to a mere trickle of three thousand tons during the following year.[71] As long as Newcastle and Sunderland were in Royalist control, Parliament forbade merchants to trade with them and the King would not sell "his" coal to Londoners. As a result, stocks of unsold coal piled up on the banks of the Tyne and the Wear while London went without fuel. In the capital the cost of firewood soared.[72] In July 1644, the know-all Agostini predicted that there would be riots in the streets of London if there was no great improvement in coal supplies to the capital during the next winter:"the miss of [coal] ... would be unbearable ... as they have felled most of the trees in the neighbourhood", he explained.[73] Nearly all 200,000 Londoners were now dependent on coal for house-warming and food-cooking and brewers, bakers, blacksmiths and brickmakers amongst many other tradesmen used coal as their main fuel. Everyone in the capital dreaded the prospect of a third winter without cheap sea-coal.[74]

As soon as Sunderland was taken by the Scots in April 1644 and the river Wear cleared, Parliament encouraged the coal merchants of the east coast ports to resume their trade.[75] As many as 120 colliers were said to be waiting in Sunderland harbour to load coal from the stockpiles that had accumulated up the river Wear in the Durham coalfield.[76] Similarly, when the Tyne was opened the following October, there were enormous mountains of coal ready to he bought and shipped down the coast. Only Scarborough's "pyrates" now impeded the resumption of full winter coal supplies to freezing Londoners.

Coal, then, or the capital's acute lack of it, explains why Parliament became urgently concerned in October 1644 to rid itself of Cholmley. *Mercurius Aulicus* did not exaggerate when on 11 October it gleefully announced that "the gallant knight [Sir Hugh]" had "taken 22 London coal ships", since one of Parliament's own propaganda sheets, the *Scottish Dove,* had already admitted the loss of "20 saile and upwards...laden with coals to London".[77] It was therefore in direct response to this damaging attack on London's fuel imports that early in November Parliament's Committee wrote to Fairfax "about finding out some way for ships to trade to Newcastle for coals without danger of interruption from Scarborough".[78]

Since Parliament's navy seemed unable to maintain a close, effective blockade of Scarborough harbour, particularly in winter weather, and did not have sufficient warships to escort all the colliers, there was no alternative but to storm the town and seize its harbour and castle from the land. Parliament would have preferred to wait until the spring or early summer of 1645 before mounting such an assault, but the matter had become too urgent to suffer delay. Londoners needed their coal during the coming winter.

Hardly a week passed without the London news-sheets complaining of some further outrage committed by "Scarborough pyrates". Early in February, the *London Post* reported yet another loss: a cargo of coals valued at £10,000 had been taken by Cholmley's pinnaces, not off the Yorkshire coast, but somewhere between King's Lynn and the mouth of the Thames.[79] Soon afterwards, another London paper, *A Diary or an Exact Journal*, rejoiced that at last Scarborough was about to be taken and added, "Indeed the reducing of that place would be a work of great importance, [since] there is almost no day that brings in one complaint or other concerning the pyracies committed by rovers there".[80] A few days later, when Scarborough was overrun by Parliament's troops, there were said to be over 120 ships in the harbour, most of them prizes.[81]

Characteristically, Cholmley never admitted to promoting piracy: he attributed Scarborough's miraculous imports of "coales, salt and corne" to "Devine power and providence". By supplying him with so many valuable windfalls God was not only showing him special favour, He was actually encouraging and helping him to hold out longer against increasing odds. As Sir Hugh later wrote in his memorials on Scarborough: "God having soe plentifully and miraculously furnished them [provisions for the castle] that there were more prises brought into the Harbour in one month past, then ever had beene in all the time Scarbrough was a Garrison".[82] A similar claim, with the same doubtful moral and theological reasoning, was made by Cholmley a decade later in his memoirs when he wrote: "...my wants was [sic] supplyed most miraculously with all necessaryes as if they had bene dropped downe from heaven as I had occation and need...".[83]

Whether the inhabitants of Scarborough town appreciated that they were the beneficiaries of "Devine power and providence" seems unlikely: a few profited from privateering, but the majority who did not leave their homes must have seen their condition and prospects deteriorate under Cholmley's governorship. How did Sir Hugh manage to persuade the townspeople to accept and even support his regime?

Soon after Cholmley changed sides, he made more demands on the pockets of Scarborians. In April 1643 the Common Hall agreed without discussion that "the battrye maid and builded att the southstile shalbe maid and builded att the townes charge, and likewise the sentry house".[84] The South Steel battery, as it is still called, was a fortified enclosure on the cliff overlooking and dominating the harbour. Since heavy erosion has subsequently worn away the ground on which it once stood, it is not possible now to be certain what Cholmley had built there in 1643. However, it seems that steps were cut and laid in stone leading down from the sally port in the curtain wall to a flat promontory where the gun battery was sited; and on the castle-dyke side of this flight of steps a stone wall with musket loops was constructed. Any enemy attempting to negotiate the castle dykes to attack the curtain wall would therefore be exposed to the crossfire of musketeers. South Steel was a perfect position: on its seaward north side the cliff was virtually vertical and unstable and behind and above it, Cockhill or Charles' tower, the last in the curtain wall, provided both look-out and supporting platform fire. Not surprisingly, both besieged and besiegers in 1645 came to regard South Steel battery of crucial importance to the security of the harbour and the defence of the castle.[85]

About the same time that South Steel battery was being built, Browne Bushell was strengthening another possibly weak point of the castle's outworks. He cut a new doorway through the outer wall of the barbican to lead on to a promontory which commanded the main entrance of the castle and afforded over-views of both North and South Bays. Here Bushell placed his cannon and trained local "volunteers" to fire them. "Bushell's Fort" or "Bishop's Fort", as Parliament's news-sheets liked to call it, was soon to figure prominently in the siege of Scarborough castle.[86]

All these works cost money for labour and materials. At the end of May 1643 another assessment of £60 was laid on the inhabitants mostly to pay for improvements to the town's own perimeter defences. Several new sentry houses were built and these had to be provided with coals and candles as well as muskets, powder, match and bullets to arm their watchmen.[87] Buildings of military value in the town were requisitioned by Sir Hugh. The cellar of the Common Hall on Sandside became one of Cholmley's storerooms for ships in the harbour; the schoolhouse standing near the main entrance to the castle became a blockhouse; and even the town prison at Newborough Bar was converted into an artillery post. Councillors pleaded in vain with Cholmley for the return of their Hall cellar and schoolhouse. What happened to the grammar school boys is not recorded, though their master, Mr Peston, still received his half-year salary of £5 as late as September 1644.[88]

Civil-war taxation on the people of Scarborough was unprecedented and excessive. Irregular and infrequent peacetime parliamentary subsidies had been never more than £40; the Ship Money assessment on Scarborough had been only £30; and the annual rent paid to the Crown by the borough for its privileges, the fee-farm, was £40. Yet now the burden was hugely increased and weighed down on most of the community, not just the well-to-do.[89] As the war again came closer to the town and the threat of a siege increased, Cholmley asked for and still got more from its residents. Finally, in February 1644, acting on behalf of Sir Hugh, Captain Richard Legard came down to the Common Hall on Sandside to ask the burgesses to find £30 a week (!) to maintain 300 soldiers in the castle and to choose 100 more townsmen to defend it who would be given "neither billit nor pay".[90]

Throughout the remainder of 1644 the town seems to have kept its promises of payment to Cholmley. About 300 households, more than half the total number, made a weekly contribution to the £30 levy, ranging from ten shillings to threepence each. If there was open resistance to the levy it is not recorded. Even as late as 25 November, when the governor asked the Common Hall to billet 100 men in the town or pay them £10 a week for their lodging, there were no dissenting votes against his proposition.[91]

Even more remarkably, there is no evidence of any breakdown of town administration during Sir Hugh's governorship. Even in 1644, the annual elections of Common Hall members and town officers took place as usual at Michaelmas. Servants of the borough received their annual wages from the chamberlain: the netherd got £2, the keeper of the town bull, £2 5s., and even the gaoler received his salary, though his home had become a guardhouse.[92]

Cholmley's success in keeping the active cooperation of the townspeople was based on their sense of self-preservation and his powers of gentle persuasion. After the headlong flight of the marquess and his entourage, "the gentlemen and straingers then with in Scarbrough ... quitt itt, procuring passes either to goe to Prince Rupert or to live att there owne houses". As for many of "the common soldiers" in Cholmley's garrison, "they ranne away daylay"; but most of the townspeople stayed put.[93] After all, where could they go and how could they abandon their homes, employment and income? Nevertheless, as when he had changed sides 15 months earlier, Sir Hugh allowed all those who would not stand by him to leave the town in peace. Of the 27 of the 44 members of the Common Hall present on 20 July 1644, only two were "licensed to departe" and a third non-member followed them.[94]

From then, apart from the seafaring Puritans such as John Lawson, William Nesfield and John Harrison, who on principle would not live under a Royalist regime, and the three others who went in July 1644, the town's ruling body, though depleted, remained steadfast. Cholmley never tried or even needed to overrule the Common Hall. All but a few of the councillors allowed themselves to be re-elected at the end of September 1644. Despite the radical change of circumstances during the previous 12 months, the First Twelve was virtually unaltered. Once basking in the security of a Royalist Yorkshire, Scarborough had become an isolated, helpless outpost in a Parliamentarian Yorkshire. However, as winter approached, Cholmley's control gradually slipped away. On 23 October a motion to raise another £60 for the use of the governor was only just carried by 22 votes to 16. A month later, on 25 November, when the Common Hall was faced with another of Sir Hugh's proposals that the town should continue to maintain a guard of one hundred at its own expense, the vote was 19 in favour and none against, but ominously there were 22 abstentions.[95]

By this date, Sir Hugh realised that he could no longer depend merely on the majority votes of the Common Hall oligarchy: two days earlier he had broken precedent by calling a meeting of the entire township population.[96] Unfortunately, no record of this extraordinary assembly was kept or has survived. If it did take place it must have been held in one of the two churches, St Mary's on the hill, or St Thomas's inside Newborough Bar. In view of what actually happened nearly three months later when Parliament's troops stormed the town, Cholmley probably assured the civilian community that he intended to spare them the horrors of artillery bombardment, street fighting, plunder and rapine. The town was indefensible and he would retire to the castle. Only those who wished to do so might follow him there. As in March 1643 and July 1644, no one would be forced to take sides.[97]

CHAPTER 12

THE GREAT SIEGE

At ten o'clock in the morning of Shrove Tuesday, 18 February 1645, Scarborough was attacked from the sea and at four points from the land. Under the command of the veteran Scottish general, Sir John Meldrum, a mixed force of 1,200 Scottish and 500 English infantry from the garrisons of Hull and Whitby captured the harbour and overran the town within a few hours. The 200 landsmen and mariners from Cholmley's home town were led by Captain Isaac Newton, Browne Bushell's brother-in-law.

No more than 20, and possibly as few as ten of Meldrum's soldiers lost their lives; of the defenders, only half a dozen were killed. Meldrum took 80 prisoners, 32 cannon, and in the harbour, 120 ships carrying 200 guns. Among the captured Royalists was Sir Jordan Crossland, former governor of Helmsley castle, who had been permitted to join Cholmley after his surrender. Crossland, and most of the other Royalist prisoners, had been taken after heavy hand-to-hand fighting in and around St Mary's church, near the main entrance to the castle. Sir Hugh had tried to escape by sea in a little pinnace which he called his running-horse, but Meldrum's swift advance across the sands of South Bay had cut off his retreat to the harbour. As a result, the governor was forced to retire to the castle which was entirely surrounded and closely besieged.

Such was the news of the fall of Scarborough as reported by all of Parliament's London press. One of the news-sheets, *Mercurius Britanicus,* declared triumphantly that this great victory proved that "God was visible at Scarborough".[1]

Cholmley's own written version of these momentous events differed in several places from those of Parliament's papers. First, he gave Meldrum many more men: in his memorials, he gave his strength as "2000 foot and one thousand horse" when in late January's frost and snow he moved up to Falsgrave village, "not 2 fleete shotts from Scarbrough Towne". To this figure Sir Hugh added another "thousand Scotts" under "Collonel Stewart", who reinforced Meldrum with his Galloway regiment just before the assault.[2] However, in a letter written in the besieged castle only six days after he had lost the town, he gave a more modest and more credible estimate of the enemy's numbers: "Heer are 10 colours of Scots, I imagine, though not above 800 of them: but Meldrum ... had 6 or 700 more of the Lord Fairfaxes Foot".[3] Presumably, after the town was taken, Meldrum's cavalry were sent elsewhere, but the contemporary estimate of 1,500 infantry looks more convincing than the 3,000 recalled by Cholmley two years later. Not surprisingly, there were no references in Cholmley's correspondence or reminiscences to the men from Whitby who had helped to dispossess him of Scarborough town and harbour.

As for the battle for Scarborough, Cholmley emphasized that he never intended to hold the town for long against a siege. Though he understood well enough "what consequence the place was", he did not have enough men to defend its walls and ditches. As he later wrote: "2 thousand men were scarce sufficient to maintaine the towne and there was not 700 in itt with the Townesmen, most of which [were] verie wavering". Accordingly, in the face of Meldrum's great superiority, Sir Hugh withstood a town siege for only three weeks during which time the castle was made ready. When he received warning of a major attack "on Tuesday following", he withdrew all his cannon to the castle the night before, except those in the sunken ship in the harbour which could not be moved. The next morning, as soon as Meldrum's assault began, Cholmley drew all his soldiers into the castle "without making the least shew of opposition".[4]

As with so many other events in his life, Cholmley's memory of them was selective and self-serving. The loss of Crossland and 80 men in the bloody skirmish at St Mary's was conveniently forgotten, even though Sir Jordan's stand there might well have been a courageous rearguard action to cover a headlong retreat of others through the castle gates. If Sir Hugh knew so much in advance of Meldrum's plans, then his own losses ought to have been lighter. Moreover, he also neglected to mention the loss of 32 cannon and all the ships in the harbour.

On the other hand, Cholmley's version makes most sense. The town was indeed untenable with only 700 men to guard the perimeter walls, gateways and ditches which could be easily outflanked from the north and the south by approaches across the sands at low tide. His intention was always to fall back to the strength of the castle; if he had planned to take flight in his "running-horse", he would have done so days, weeks or even months earlier. Secondly, if "most of the Townes men quitt the Governor, except one of the Bailiffs and fower or five others", yet Cholmley still managed to bring "about five hundred, of which three score gentlemen and officers, 250 foot, and the rest Troopers most of them having horses" safely into the castle, then this achievement indicates an orderly withdrawal, not a runaway rout.[5]

Though Sir Hugh never even mentioned the harbour in his memorials, it was its capture and all the vessels in it which most excited the London news-sheets. *The Weekly Account* reported first the taking of "a fort" (South Steel battery?), then "the haven" with its prizes, and finally, almost as an afterthought, the town itself.[6] The same order of importance was also given by *Perfect Passages,* which emphasized that the capture of "one of the Forts" was "very material" because it commanded the harbour below.[7] Parliament too seemed far more interested in Scarborough port than Scarborough town. With some satisfaction it was noted that the merchantman, the *Blessing of Cramond,* which in April 1644 had been lost on its way to Scotland, was one of the many ships re-taken.[8]

Cholmley was now a deeply-detested enemy of Parliament: worse than an ordinary "malignant" Royalist, in London he was regarded as a dishonourable, cowardly traitor. For *Mercurius Britanicus,* the capture of Scarborough town, church and haven, "with six score sail of ships and the castle since block't up" was a "poore prize" because it did not include "Hugh Cholmley's owne person". Soon, it was hoped, Sir Hugh would suffer the same terminal fate as "Sir Hotham".[9] To the *Scottish Dove,* he was "Judas Cholmley" one of those "destroying apostates"[10] and to *A Perfect Diurnall* he was "the cowardly apostate" and the "liver-hearted Cholmley" who one day would have "his just reward at Tiburne".[11] So all partisan London press reports concerning Sir Hugh should be treated with the greatest caution and suspicion. Just as there is no corroboration of the allegation that he attempted to take flight by ship, so there is none for the calumny that the townsmen would have surrendered to Meldrum but "he brought soldiers out of the castle, and compelled the defence to be continued".[12] This last accusation runs directly counter to what is known from Scarborough's own official records of Sir Hugh's relations with the town's inhabitants up to February 1645.

Naturally, the London papers were delighted with the news from Scarborough. Every news-sheet from the *London Post* to the *Scottish Dove* expressed their joy at the "deliverance" of Scarborough and the elimination of its piratical home. The messenger who carried Meldrum's report to London was given £20 by Parliament and the general himself rewarded with a gift of £1,000. Later, after Meldrum had suffered life-threatening injuries trying to take the castle, he was granted another £500, though he never lived long enough to receive it.[13] When thanks were given to God on 12 March for Parliament's latest victories, Scarborough was placed head of the list above Shrewsbury and Weymouth.[14]

Parliament's pleasure soon turned into disappointment when Meldrum failed either to persuade Cholmley to give up his castle or to take it immediately by force. The *London Post* declared that some Royalist gentlemen, "Sir Thomas Ingram, Mr Bellasis and three more" had deserted Sir Hugh and submitted themselves to Lord Fairfax at York, but it was soon ominously clear that there had been no collapse of morale amongst the castle's defenders.[15] Indeed, as *Perfect Passages* had to admit reluctantly, Meldrum might be "within a stones throw of the castle", yet he was having to raise "mounts" and "pieces" to "batter the castle about their eares if they will not yeild".[16] And, a little later, *Perfect Occurrences* informed its readers that Scarborough castle was difficult to approach, that it was founded on solid rock, and that its stone walls were "lined within with earth".[17]

However, Meldrum's problem was not just the natural and Cholmley-made strength of the castle: as he explained to his masters in London, he was short of "men, money, victuals, ammunition and arms" and he warned them of the danger of "mutiny of the soldiers for want of supplies".[18] It was also soon evident to this veteran of many military campaigns and sieges that, whatever *Perfect Passages* might claim, he did not possess the weight of cannon "to batter the castle" into submission. Moreover, Meldrum was aware that Parliament did not attribute the same high priority to reducing the castle as it had formerly done to taking "a den of thieves" and refuge for pirates.[19]

Consequently, since he had neither the ordnance nor the infantry to fight his way into the castle, Meldrum tried to bully his way in. A week after the fall of Scarborough town and harbour, he wrote a haughty letter to Sir Hugh. In his characteristic cryptic and abrupt style, the general told the governor that his position was now hopeless: he had no prospect of relief or even reinforcement by either land or sea. He should surrender at once, otherwise he and his garrison would soon fill the churchyard. The following day Meldrum received a sharp reply from Cholmley. He rebuked the Scotsman for using "the stile of conquerors alone". "'Tis well known", he continued, "I always abhorred whatsoever tended towards tirranie ... though I daily heare of impositions upon men's consciences and personall liberties by your partie". Meldrum's reference to "the Grace of the Kingdome" prompted a brief lesson in constitutional law from Sir Hugh: "all acts of Grace", he pointed out, were "inseparable from the sovereigne power, of which you cannot be ignorante, though perhapps unwillinge to name the Kinge..." Finally, he condemned Meldrum for the damage he had done to St Mary's church by turning it into a forward military strongpoint and warned him that he would find its graveyard useful only "to bury your dead in".[20]

114

Sir John's immediate reply the next day, 27 February, to what he called a "lofty and impertinent answer" to his summons again pointed out the utter pointlessness of Cholmley's resistance. He could expect no help from "the Queen, out of France, from Oxford, or from Newark". Then, in a clever argument which was intended to have the maximum affect on Sir Hugh's conscience, Meldrum drew a distinction between "a moderate and well tempered monarchy" and "a Straffordian ... that is at least cousin german if not worse than anarchy itself". This was a nice touch: he knew of Cholmley's antipathy to Strafford and implied that Charles had been misled by a "viperous brood" of "pernicious counsellors" who had "brought him and his posterity to so low an ebb". Finally, if Sir Hugh was so foolish as to reject his generous terms to surrender, "the castle with all kind of ordnance, ammunition and other provisions for the King and Parliament", he could expect no mercy. "If the Kingdom be put to the trouble of bringing great ordnance ... I will endeavour to make your strong walls spue you out at the broadside". This was the last word in written correspondence between the two adversaries: Cholmley did not respond to Meldrum's dire threats.[21]

In his second summons, Meldrum revealed that he had intercepted and read Cholmley's letters of 23 and 24 February to the King's headquarters at Oxford. In the first of them, Sir Hugh explained that if he did not receive "timely help" Scarborough castle would be lost "and yet I hold myself blameless". He was afraid that if he was taken captive his life would be forfeit and this example of murderous revenge was bound to dissuade others from serving the King "with so little private ends as I have done".[22] Clearly, Sir Hugh had the fate of the Hothams in mind when he wrote these words. A second intercepted letter, "to some commander in the King's army", described how he was "now blockt up close in the castle", that many of his soldiers had deserted and more were expected to follow them, and that he was in need of "speedy supply". He asked to be given hope of relief "from the Queen, or Ireland, or probability of a good issue from the Treaty", yet promised that even if he did not get aid he would not "quitt this trust otherwise than becomes a gentleman, and a good subject".[23] Once he had taken up arms for his family, his friends and his estate; now all that was left to fight for was his honour as a gentleman.

Scarborough castle's walls were indeed "strong" and would require "great ordnance" to breach them. With the professional assistance of Captain Browne Bushell, during the past two and a half years, Cholmley had converted a dilapidated, redundant medieval castle into a formidable, modern fortress. He had foraged over a wide area for timber, lead and iron. Newtondale forest, 15 miles inland from Scarborough, had lost 30 of its trees, "by the instruction of Sir Hu Cholmley for the repair of Scarborough Castle".[24] Pickering castle had not escaped his plundering: the lead, wood and iron of its Diate Tower "was by Sir Hugh Cholmley (as we are informed) carryed to Scarborough Castle".[25] Was Cholmley aware that his great-grandfather, Sir Richard, had pillaged the royal castle at Pickering of its stone and slate to improve his own fortified manor house at Roxby where his great-grandson had been born?[26]

Meldrum had been quick to understand the significance of South Steel battery and had taken it in the first assault; but Bushell's battery, overlooking the approach to the castle's main entrance, remained intact. Its guns had forced the Scots to retreat to the cover of the thick walls of St Mary's church. Behind and above Bushell's cannon, the barbican walls, towers and gates had been strongly reinforced with stones and earth and provided with musketry platforms. Elsewhere, the sea and holms cliffs could not be scaled. Even if Meldrum had enough men and ships to throw a tight net around the castle perimeter, inside the garrison was well supplied with food and ammunition and, for the time being, a reliable source of drinking water. And by now the worst of the winter weather had passed: Cholmley's men could guard the walls and live out in the open without too much discomfort.[27]

So Meldrum had to send to the magazines at Hull and York for his "great ordnance". During the next fortnight there was a lull as both sides made their preparations for battle. By sea, from Hull, came several demi-cannon and demi-culverin. The largest of these, called the Queen's pocket-pistol, fired a 36-pound bullet. By land, from York, came the heaviest piece of artillery in the entire kingdom, a whole cannon or cannon-royal, which fired a huge missile weighing more than 60 pounds. Over firm, level ground it required 16 horses or 90 men to haul it. During the siege of York in June 1644 the cannon-royal's long-range fire had demolished at least two church steeples. Now, in the middle of March 1645, under the cover of darkness, this three and a half ton monster was brought through the west door of St Mary's, dragged down the long, central nave, and mounted at the far east end of the chancel. From there it was positioned to fire over the former altar, through the great east window, at the castle keep only 200 yards away, at "point-blank range".[28]

The Royalists as well as Parliament attached high value to the castle and harbour at Scarborough. They made several recorded attempts by sea to relieve Cholmley, or at least keep him stocked with essential munitions. In April 1645, a Dunkirker carrying gunpowder and weapons, failed to pass through Vice-Admiral Zachary's sea blockade.[29] In June, there was a report that one of the King's few remaining warships, the *John,* under Captain Mucknell, was sailing northwards up the east coast towards Scarborough. Zachary was warned that "Captain Mucknell may be disposed to relieve Scarborough castle" and ordered to keep a sharp look-out for him.[30]

Meanwhile, Scarborough's pirates, John Denton, Browne Thomas and the most infamous, Browne Bushell, though now deprived of their home base, were still active at sea. Parliament's worse fear was that the impudent Bushell would try to rescue his cousin in the beleagured castle. In the same issue that it announced the fall of Scarborough to Meldrum, *A Perfect Diurnall* revealed that it had received letters from Holland relating that the "perfidious apostate", Bushell, was at sea in command of a squadron of freebooting warships.[31] Three months later, *Exchange Intelligencer,* another London news-sheet, declared that Bushell had lately come out of Dunkirk at the head of 15 ships and that he was "now a robbing up and down our coasts". With more indignation than wit, it concluded:" the Bushell is almost heap't up: and he is, likely to be measured according to his deserts".[32] By the beginning of July, some alarm was expressed by the London press that Bushell was about to break through the sea blockade at Scarborough. In the words of *Mercurius Veridicus,* "Brown Bushell looks big, and threatens much with his little squadron, if he comes we have four stout ships in harbour [at Scarborough] to welcome him".[33]

In the event, Browne Bushell never made an attempt to return to Scarborough, though from Dunkirk, Ostend and Boulogne his squadron terrorised the sailors of other east-coast ports and preyed on their vessels.[34] Nevertheless, Scarborough harbour remained an indispensable refuge for coastal traffic, particularly unarmed colliers out of Newcastle and Sunderland; and as long as Cholmley held the castle and from there could direct cannon fire down on to the pier, it could not be regarded as a safe haven. For this reason, as early as March, even before his "great ordnance" had arrived, Meldrum had written to Hull, Boston, King's Lynn, Yarmouth and Ipswich, asking for their assistance. He told them that though he held the town and pier of Scarborough with 1,600 soldiers he lacked "victualls and amunicon" for them beyond six days. If he did not soon receive money and provisions he would be compelled to abandon Scarborough which was "a Receptable for the Enemyes of the Kingdome and an obstruccon to the Northerne Trade". This astute appeal to their "perticuler interests" in their "Comon Trade" was instantly rewarded: four of the five ports sent Meldrum much-needed aid. Hull gave him £240, King's Lynn, nearly £400 in provisions, Yarmouth, £234 10s. in ready money, and Ipswich collected £140 in voluntary subscription.[35] If Cholmley had been informed of Meldrum's correspondence and its postive outcome, he would have had all the more reason to stand fast at Scarborough castle to the "last extremity".

On the other side, against all the odds and facts, Royalists still deluded themselves that Scarborough could be retaken or rescued by help from the continent. Writing to Lord Digby, the King's secretary of state, from exile at St Germain, Lord Jermyn explained that the Queen now placed her faith in aid from the King of Denmark: "If he could be prevailed on to give us an army, its descent on Scarborough or Burlington [Bridlington Quay] would give a new turn to all".[36] In faraway France Jermyn did not know that Cholmley had surrendered Scarborough castle the day before he wrote these wishful words. Yet even after the loss of Scarborough castle was known everywhere, including Paris, the Yorkshire coast was still regarded as the most promising landing-place for Royalist arms and agents. As late as 9 August, Lord Digby implored Jermyn, "For God's sake hasten gunpowder and match in plenty to the northern coast, and what muskets and pistols you can, but ammunition in the first place; let these be directed to Burlington or Whitby, for Scarborough is lost ...".[37] By this time, Cholmley was an exile in Holland and the whole of the Yorkshire coast was securely Parliament's.

Parliament's appreciation of Scarborough's potential value to its enemies sharpened after Meldrum's failure to take its castle and secure its harbour. The London committee came round to realise that of all the other sieges then taking place in Yorkshire, principally at Pontefract, Bolton, Sandal and Skipton, that of Scarborough castle ought to be given their highest priority.

As a result, on 1 May 1645, the Committee of Both Kingdoms in London ordered Lord Fairfax "to send a sufficient force to take in Scarborough". In a covering note that was also conveyed to Meldrum, the Committee provided a succinct explanation for the order:

...Scarborough Castle is not so effectively besieged as were necessary for the carrying of a place of so great concernment to the public. All the ports on the east and south sides of the kingdom from Berwick to Topsham [near Exeter], with the sole exception of Scarborough are already in the power of Parliament. If this also could be taken there would be no place left along all the coast for the enemy to retire unto and from whence they may be able to interrupt and hinder the whole trade of the coast wherein the City is deeply concerned. We consider the taking in of that castle to be of greater consequence than any inland fort whatsoever can be, and therefore especially recommend to you that the siege may be carried on with effect. Send thither what foot forces you can spare, as they could nowhere be employed to greater advantage.[38]

Even if Sir Hugh had written nothing else about himself and his extraordinary life, historians would still be grateful to him for his vivid, robust and uniquely informative account of the siege of Scarborough castle.[39] In addition to its recognised military importance, the siege was one of the most dramatic, intense and active of the English civil wars. Other Yorkshire "leaguers", such as those at Pontefract and Skipton, lasted longer, but they were usually little more than prolonged, sporadic blockades, whereas that at Scarborough, which occupied 22 weeks from 18 February to 25 July 1645, was exceptional for its destructive scale. Losses of men and material on both sides were enormous. Until the final surrender there were no truces and no quarter was asked for or given. Other sieges involved hundreds of soldiers; that at Scarborough castle engaged thousands of infantry, the heaviest artillery in the kingdom and a squadron of blockading, bombarding ships.

The London and Oxford presses showed the greatest interest in what was happening at Scarborough in the spring and summer of 1645, but less understanding of it. Some of their reports are difficult to interpret because they were written at second or third hand and considerable distance without knowledge of location and topography. Subsequently, antiquarians and historians relying on these news-sheet descriptions have been handicapped by the same ignorance and, as a result, many misunderstandings have gone into print and been accepted at face value. In contrast, Cholmley's "Memorialls Tuching Scarbrough" was written by a principal participant very soon after the event and though naturally partisan, unlike other versions, both contemporary and subsequent, makes almost perfect sense.

For example, Cholmley cannot be blamed for the misunderstandings of the chronology of the castle siege which have arisen and are still repeated. Using the Old Style calendar convention, Sir Hugh gave the date of the beginning of the siege as February 1644, but this has often been read as a New Style date, thereby extending the duration by an extra 12 months! Instead of February to July 1645, the dates of the castle or castle and town siege have been stretched from February 1644 to July 1645![40] Later, in his memoirs, when Cholmley wrote that the siege lasted "for about 12 monthes" and "above 12 monthes", he was referring to that of the town and castle, not of the castle alone, and he was elongating the truth by pre-dating its start to July 1644, when the first Roundhead soldier appeared outside Scarborough. In his memorials, Cholmley made it clear that Meldrum did not advance to Falsgrave village on the outskirts of Scarborough until the end of January 1645 and that the close siege of the town took place during the next three weeks. Nevertheless, some later commentators have taken Sir Hugh's words literally and carelessly and assumed that the castle was surrounded for a full year. Even Professor Firth was misleading the readers of the *English Historical Review* if he was responsible for entitling the memorials as "Sir Hugh Cholmley's Narrative of the Siege of Scarborough, 1644-5".[41]

Royalist reports of the siege are almost worthless. The castle was effectively cut off from the outside world and even Cholmley's letters were intercepted. Consequently, in the absence of news from the garrison, the Royalist propaganda sheet, *Mercurius Aulicus,* was obliged to invent it. Early in March 1645, it announced that Meldrum had raised the castle siege and marched away from Scarborough "bag and baggage to patch up with Lord Fairfax". A month later, it reported the death of Meldrum, "some weeks since being hurt by a shot from the garrison of Scarborough". This second piece of "news" was just as untrue as the first. Meldrum had never broken off the siege and he had been injured by a fall down the castle cliff and had recovered from it. It was left to *Mercurius Rusticus,* which specialised in retailing stories of alleged Roundhead atrocities, to inform its readers that Sir John had died on 11 May as a result of wounds received in a battle for the castle gatehouse.[42]

Cholmley's memorials, therefore, constitute the only Royalist corrective to Parliament's own propaganda newsprint which otherwise would command a monopoly of primary evidence for the siege. As the weeks then months of the siege passed, the prejudices of the London press gradually got the better of factual reporting. Meldrum, and later his successor, Sir Matthew Boynton, were always heroic and Cholmley, invariably, the villain. The former were incapable of cowardice or dishonourable conduct, the latter incapable of anything else. Parliament's soldiers always acted bravely, whereas Sir Hugh, it was alleged, had to make his men mad with drink before they would sally out to do battle. Only Royalists committed barbarities. Gallant Lieutenant-Colonel Francis Stanley, one of Meldrum's Yorkshiremen, was taken prisoner during an assault, but "basely slaine...by a Blackamore" who "stabbed him to the heart" and then threw his corpse over the castle wall! Cholmley's garrison was always on the verge of capitulation: they had no drinking water; their towers and walls were all broken down; they lacked fresh meat; and they never had hope of rescue.[43]

Of course Cholmley would have written nothing of Royalist atrocities even if they had occurred, and all his men fought bravely. Nevertheless, without his memorials we would be left with a colourless, inaccurate, one-sided picture of the castle siege of 1645. For example, *Perfect Diurnall* reported that on Monday, 24 March "Sir John Meldrum, that brave commander, hath had a fall from a rocke by a violent guste of winde, going to view a place to plant his cannon against Scarborough castl[e]; which hath much bruised him, but (tis hoped) not mortally."[44] This was the fullest news-sheet description of Meldrum's near-fatal accident at South Steel battery; yet it compares unfavourably with Sir Hugh's own colloquial, entertaining version of this event in his memorials:

> Beeing to plant these ordnance neere to the sea cliff for more advantage to batter, Meldrum there in person giving directions about them, his hatt blowes of[f] his head, and hee catching to save that, the winde beeing verie great blowes his cloake over his face, and hee falls over the cliff amongst the rockes and stones att least steeple height. Itt was a miracle his braines were not beaten out and all his bones broaken, but itt seemed the winde together with the cloake did in some sorte beare him up, and lessen the fall. Yet hee is taken up for dead, lyes 3 dayes speachless, his head opened and the bruised blood taken out, though a man above threescore yeare old, recovered this soe perfectlie that with in six weekes hee is on foote againe, and beginns to batter the Castle.[45]

During the six weeks it took the tough, old Scotsman to recover, there was a pause in attacks on the castle. Sensing that something was wrong with Meldrum, but at the same time not knowing precisely what had happened to him, Sir Hugh sent out Captain William Wickham at the head of 50 men to make a surprise sortie against the Scots manning South Steel battery. Though it was midday, the Scotsmen were taken off guard; many of them jumped from the rock into the sea, "whoe thincking thereby to esscape fire died by water". Captain Wickham, yet another of Cholmley's many cousins, returned triumphantly with 20 prisoners. We do not have to believe Sir Hugh's exaggerated claim that he had "left a hunderd killed and wounded".[46] However, it must have been from Wickham's prisoners that Cholmley learned the details of Meldrum's spectacular accident. Needless to say, there was no mention in the London papers of Wickham's audacious and successful raid.

By the time of Meldrum's recovery at the beginning of May all was in place to batter the castle with "great ordnance". Again we are dependent on Cholmley's memorials for a detailed explanation of the consequences of the bombardment that followed. The cannon-royal directed its fire at Henry II's keep through St Mary's east window. For three days, time and again, its 60-pound shot hit the masonry of the west wall. Though 15-feet thick with central newel staircase and mural chambers, on the third day, this wall suddenly collapsed. As Sir Hugh later described this dramatic episode.

> ...in 3 dayes the great Tower splitt in two, and that side which was battered falls to the ground, the other standing firme beeing supported by an arch of stone that went through the midst; there were neere 20 personns upon the topp of the tower when itt cleft, yett all gott into the standing parte, except 2 of Captaine Richard Ledgard's servants which were in the turrett where there maister lodged. ... The fall of the Tower was a verly terrible spectacle...[47]

No contemporary account of the destruction of Scarborough castle's keep was published. In contrast to Sir Hugh's later vivid details, *Perfect Passages* recorded vaguely on 6 May that "Sir John had made a breach into one of the towers".[48] If Sir Hugh's own unique description of the fall of the keep had been more widely known, then many subsequent histories of the town and castle would not have been so misinformed. For instance, without the benefit of Cholmley's memorials, Hinderwell and Baker were not entirely to blame for believing that Parliament had "slighted" the keep with gunpowder charges after the castle was surrendered a second time in 1649; but this story was inexcusably endorsed later by the Department of the Environment and its successor, English Heritage.[49] From subsequent records it is clear that, far from destroying the castle, Parliament spent considerable sums on its repair and the order to "slight" was never carried out. From May 1645 until the present day, Henry II's magnificent keep has been eroded only by weather and neglect.[50]

Similarly, it is still commonly believed that Cholmley's retaliatory gunfire from the castle destroyed much of St Mary's church which has never been repaired; whereas a careful reading of Sir Hugh's memorials indicates that the major damage to the eastern end of the parish church was caused by the vibration and recoil of Meldrum's cannon-royal. As Cholmley explained, the castle was so high above and so close to St Mary's that the Royalist guns could not be depressed sufficiently to hit other than its upper roof parts, central tower and parapets. In his words: "...though the Castle could make shotts into the Church and the workes about itt, yett they laid soe lowe the execution was not much, nor the preiudice answerable to the expense of powder".[51] In other words, Sir Hugh had no scruple about bombarding the parish church: in this case, it was simply not a worthwhile target. In fact, neither side showed the slightest respect for the fabric and furnishings of St Mary's: Meldrum used it as a forward blockhouse and his soldiers gutted its contents; and Crossland had occupied it as an outlying defensive work.[52]

Only in Cholmley's memorials is there a clear explanation why the fall of the keep, instead of weakening the resistance of the defenders, actually strengthened it and thereby prolonged the siege. The three-storey tower was no longer habitable and so "the Governor, his ladie, and most of the gentlemen and officers of qualitie... were forced to betake themselves to poore Cabbins reared against the walls and banckes in the Castle yeard".[53] However, this was a relatively minor inconvenience in early summer weather compared with the unexpected bonus given to the castle's defences. The west wall, roof and two west towers of the keep had collapsed outwards and downwards on to the narrow, main entrance below, completely blocking it. Though Bushell's battery and the barbican beyond and outside the drawbridges became battlegrounds, there was now no way that Meldrum or Boynton could break into the heart of the castle by this route. Twelve weeks later, at the time of the surrender, the castle was still so "barracadoed" with fallen rubble from the ruined keep that a new exit had to be cut into the curtain wall to allow the defenders to pass out. During those 12 weeks the debris from the collapsed keep had provided not only cover but also deadly ammunition for the Royalist garrison. "The stones from the falne Tower were thrown freelie amongst them [the attackers] and did the greatest execution", wrote Sir Hugh.[54]

From February until June 1645 Cholmley's garrison did much more than just shut themselves in the castle and wait for relief or reinforcement: their defence of it was spirited, enterprising and aggressive. Though always outnumbered, they were rarely outfought in pitched battles. Repeatedly, they sallied out to dislodge the enemy from advantaged positions and even, on more than one occasion, to take them completely off guard.

After the fall of the keep, Bushell's battery (or "Bishop's Fort", as some London papers liked to call it) and the gatehouse barbican behind it were fiercely contested in close combat and changed hands more than once. According to Sir Hugh, so heavy was the fire of artillery and small arms from both sides that for ten days no one dared to occupy this battered, hazardous battle-zone. Finally, when Meldrum managed to plant some of his own guns on Bushell's hill, Cholmley ordered a counter-attack to neutralise these two demi-cannon, each firing a 34-pound ball. With 60 picked men, Major Thomas Crompton of Driffield led a desperate onslaught. The operation was a brilliant success. Meldrum's soldiers were beaten out of "three severall strong woorkes", each occupied by 80 men, the two cannon were dismounted and their carriages broken.[55]

Even Parliament's partisan reporters had to concede the success of Crompton's sortie which had occurred in the evening of Saturday, 10 May.[56] The high number of officers killed or wounded on Parliament's side suggests that Cholmley was probably not exaggerating when later he wrote that Meldrum's soldiers had taken flight and had to be rallied by their leaders. "Crompton had soe maulled and frightened those upon guard as the rest with in the towne were readie to runn away, probable if it had beene a little darker they had donne soe, and as it was the officers had much to doe to keepe the soldiers together."[57] A Perfect Diurnall and Mercurius Civicus attributed the extraordinary courage of Crompton's men to their drunkenness; Perfect Passages said "the pangs of death" were upon the Royalists who were "desperately mad" as well as the worse for drink.[58]

Cholmley now ordered Crompton to pull back from the ruins of Bushell's battery to the shelter of the keep's rubble. The following day, Sunday, 11 May, was the bloodiest of the whole siege. The two sides fought each other for several hours for possession of the barbican and drawbridges. There was savage, bloody hand-to-hand fighting as cannon and musket fire rained down from opposing positions. Casualties were heavy; no mercy was shown by either side. As usual, Meldrum was in the thick of it.

Parliament's dead included two lieutenant-colonels, Francis Stanley, a veteran of many recent battles, and Henry Vickerman of Fraisthorpe, "one that Sir John Meldrum loved dearly", Major John Dent and a Captain Pearson, all Yorkshiremen. Many others had been maimed and badly cut by stones thrown down by Cholmley's defenders. Sir Hugh lost nine officers, one of them Lieutenant John Gower, a distant kinsman. One other Royalist casualty reported was "Sir (sic) Michael Wharton, a gentleman that was in the castle worth £4000 per annum ... killed with one of our cannon shot as he was standing by Sir Hugh Cholmley".[59]

Though reports disagreed about the number of casualties, they all agreed that General Meldrum had been severely wounded. During what Cholmley later described with understatement as a "scuffle", "the old knight" had taken "a shott in att the bellie and out of the backe".[60] Naturally, the London papers offered an optimistic prognosis: *A Perfect Diurnall* said that his wound was definitely "not mortall".[61] With added medical detail, *Mercurius Civicus* concurred: the general had received a brush neere his bellie with a bullet, a shot in the thigh, and another flesh wound with a sword, but his hurts [were] not mortall"![62] *Perfect Occurrences* assured its anxious readers that "none of his guts [was] touched".[63] Yet even Sir Hugh did not expect his opponent to die since previously he had recovered "perfectlie" from his cliff fall and from a battle injury when he had been "shot through the Codds".[64] But die he did, six days later, on 17 May, and his corpse was carried to Hull and interred in the parish church there.[65]

Meldrum's death was a terrible blow to the morale and confidence of the besiegers which even the London press could not conceal. Even before news of it reached the capital, *The Moderate Intelligencer,* in a rare moment of sanity, had suggested that it might be wiser to starve rather than storm a determined garrison of "300 souldiers and well nigh 100 officers" who were "stout and resolute".[66] Several other London news-sheets admitted that to make good its losses it had been necessary to call up reinforcements from York.[67] *Mercurius Veridicus* took an uncharacteristically pessimistic line: the garrison, it pointed out, had enough ammunition as well as bread and wine; they lacked only water and fresh meat. Should they exhaust their shot, they still had plenty of stone to annoy and hurt the besiegers.[68]

With hindsight it becomes clear that Meldrum's departure was a turning-point in Parliament's conduct of the castle siege. He had been the bravest example and an inspiration to all his officers and men. Cholmley had to admit that Sir John had been a formidable adversary: "Hee had often both in woords and letters protested [that] hee would either take the Casstle or lay his bones before itt, and though hee dyed with in six dayes of this wound, hee before had esscaiped verie great dangers..."[69] After the "bones" of the old, gallant knight had been given "honourable interrement" at Hull, his successor was named as Sir Matthew Boynton (1591-1647). Boynton was from Barmston in the East Riding and well known to Cholmley; he had served under him and fought at Guisborough under his command.

From now on, for the next ten weeks, in Cholmley's words, there were no more "actions of consequence".[70] The castle was tightly enveloped and continuously harassed by gunfire from land and ships at sea, but Boynton made no more infantry assaults on the walls. As *Mercurius Veridicus* reported towards the end of June, "little is said of Scarbrough but onely that it is besieged, the Enemy not makeing many sallyes forth, nor the besiegers any late attempts".[71]

Against the odds and the evidence, Sir Hugh continued to believe in the possibility of rescue. Reference has been made already to several Royalist efforts to bring him succour and the troublesome piracy of Browne Bushell's squadron at large in the North Sea. Overall Royalist defeat was still far from certain in the first half of 1645. In Scotland, Montrose was winning battle after battle against the King's enemies there. At the end of May, Rupert had taken Leicester. At the time, to Royalist optimists, even the defeat at Naseby in June did not seem irreversible. And in Yorkshire, Bolton, Pontefract, Sandal and Skipton still held out for Charles.[72] But not for very much longer: Pontefract castle fell to Parliament in July; Sandal surrendered on 2 October; Bolton yielded on 5 November; and Skipton castle held out until just before Christmas 1645.[73]

The total silence of the Royalist press and the general indifference of Parliament's news-sheets mean that for the last weeks and conclusion of the castle siege we are almost entirely dependent on Cholmley's Scarborough memorials. Fortunately, Sir Hugh provided Sir Edward Hyde with a marvellous account of these events which fills the historical hiatus.

Without any previous warning, on Tuesday, 22 July 1645, *Mercurius Civicus* announced "a confident report of the surrender of Scarbrough castle to Colonel Boynton".[74] A day later, *The Scottish Dove* confirmed this news from Scarborough and, by way of explanation, added briefly that the Royalist garrison was "sick of the scurvie ... and many of Cholmley's officers are dead of it, himselfe sick". Sir Henry Cholmley, who had recently received the surrender of Pontefract castle, was said to be on the road to Scarborough to treat with his brother.[75] Further references in the London papers gave no more than the terms of Cholmley's surrender and the stock of arms handed over to Boynton.[76]

In marked contrast to these threadbare reports from London, Sir Hugh's own description of his capitulation ran to nearly three folios. Naturally, he was anxious to justify his conduct so that some allowance has to be made for his exaggeration of the extreme plight of the garrison. The reader is invited to believe that Cholmley had held out as long as it was humanly possible in fulfilment of his promises to King Charles. Sir Hugh denied that the news of the utter defeat of the King's field army at Naseby on 14 June had undermined the morale of his officers and men. When the Roundheads outside the walls had "solemnised" the victory with bonfires, cannon fire and "huge acclamations of joy", the Royalists inside replied with trumpets, drums and muskets and "made such cryes and hollowing as they caused the enemie to decist from there jolletie". Cholmley and his troops were reluctant to accept that Naseby had been such a military disaster to their cause and they held out for another six weeks (not "8 weekes", as Sir Hugh later wrote) in the hope of better news. Cut off from the outside world, they had no means of knowing for certain "how affaires went with the King".[77]

Later, Cholmley gave three main reasons why he and his officers finally accepted Colonel Boynton's terms: lack of food, lack of water and lack of gunpowder. For once, *The Scottish Dove* was right: of the many privations suffered by the besieged, the worst was scurvy. As Sir Hugh himself described the situation:

… halfe of the soldiors were either slaine or dead of the scurvy, of which disease neare the other halfe laid soe miserable handled they were scarce able to stirr hand or foot. There was but 25 of the common soldiors able to doe dutie, and the gentlemen and officers which were glad to undertake it in there roome, were almost tiered out of there skinns. There dyed tenn in a night, and manie layed two dayes unburied for want of helpe to carrie them to the grave.[78]

Only about 60 defenders were able to walk unaided out of the castle; and most of them were gentlemen and officers. Of the remaining 180 survivors, most were carried out on stretchers and in blankets through the rubble, and some of them died before they reached the town below. So, by Cholmley's reckoning, of the 500 men and women, soldiers and civilians, who had taken refuge in the castle in mid-February, fewer than half of them came out out of it five months later, and all of them weak and diseased.[79]

Other contemporary sources confirm the toll of scurvy. Quoting an unsigned letter from Hull, dated Saturday, 26 July, the day after the surrender, *An Exact Relation* related that "scurvey made such a mortality among the soldiers... that Sir Hugh hastened to make conditions".[80] One of the more reliable London sources, *Parliament's Post,* admitted that it did not know whether Cholmley had gone to Newark or Holland, but in Scarborough he had left behind "100 sicke of the scurvy".[81] Much later, when Scarborough's resident spa physicians came to recommend the local waters to visitors, they claimed that they had provided a speedy and perfect cure of scurvy for the Royalist survivors of 1645. In his *Scarbrough Spaw,* first published in 1660, the earliest of these physicians, Dr Robert Wittie, wrote of the town's medicinal spring water:

> It purifies the blood and cures the *Scurvy,* even such as have been tainted with it in a high degree, a large triall whereof I had in the late wars, when the Garrison that was kept by Sr Hugh Cholmley on the top of this Castle hill, after a few weeks siege, whither from the air of the Sea, or a bad dyet, or want of exercise, were most of them fallen into *Scurvy,* especially the *Country Gentlemen* who had fled in thither, as many of them drank of the *Spaw Water* were perfectly and speedily cured, which some of them used without any other means.[82]

According to Cholmley's own account, another "miserie" of the beleaguered Royalists was shortage of water. The castle had two wells: one very deep in the inner bailey, which by 1645 was already dry, and a shallow well of Our Lady, close to the edge of the sea cliff. By mid-summer the latter must also have failed and the garrison had to take its water from springs at the base of the sea cliff "though with much paines, difficulty and perrill".[83] As early as 14 May, one of London's news-sheets asserted that, "All supplies of water are stopt from Scarbrough [castle] except a well which is called our Ladyes well that affords but little."[84] However, as the garrison grew weaker and the naval blockade intensified, even the sea cliff springs became inaccessible. There was scarcely sufficient drinking water for the human inmates and none at all to spare for the animals, "soe that manie horses had beene with out water for seaven dayes together, which occasioned contagion amongst them alsoe".[85]

The Royalists had plenty of grain, but there was no one strong enough "to make the mills goe", so that most of them "had not eaten a bitt of bread for divers dayes before the render". To get himself flour for bread-making, Sir Hugh had to turn the mills himself.[86] So, as "scurvie ... grew to be as contagious as the Plague", those who did not suffer from it were debilitated by thirst and hunger.[87] As a result, "in lieu of guards there were not persons with in the walls able to stand sentynells, and in a weeke longer probable there would scarce have beene one able to looke over the walls".[88]

However, whereas Cholmley's two "miseries", a "reign" of scurvy and a lack of water, were corroborated by Parliament's news-sheets, his third, "want of poother [gunpowder]", was challenged by all of them. More than once in his memorials Sir Hugh referred to his shortage of gunpowder which meant that, after the death of Meldrum, the defenders could not make full use of their artillery and this permitted "the enemie to make there approaches verie neare". Without fear of a counter-barrage from the castle, Vice-Admiral Zachary was able to bring his squadron close to the headland and fire on Cholmley's men as they tried to bring up fresh water from the undercliff. According to Cholmley, eight weeks before the surrender the defenders were reduced to only two barrels of gunpowder and at the surrender "less than halfe a barrell" remained.[89]

Yet, when Major-General Poyntz (who had succeeded Lord Fairfax as commander of Parliament's Northern Association army) sent in his report of the capture of Scarborough castle to London, it stated that Boynton had taken five brass and 30 iron pieces of artillery, a thousand small arms, and "a great quantitie of Powder, Match, Bullets and other Ammunition".[90] Predictably, these "official" figures were repeated word for word in several London news-sheets, such as *An Exact Journal* and *Mercurius Civicus*;[91] but not in other less partisan and usually more trustworthy "government" sources. *Parliament's Post* and *The Weekly Account* reduced the number of cannon taken to 25 and mentioned only arms and ammunition, not gunpowder.[92]

In all probability, Poyntz and Boynton, his informant, were merely parroting a familiar formula to enhance the military value of the victory and Cholmley, as he so often did, was only exaggerating his predicament to justify his surrender. If the castle had indeed been so short of gunpowder during the final two months of the siege, then Boynton should have taken it by storm instead of relying on attrition. On the other hand, Boynton might well have been unaware of Cholmley's weakness, or he was under orders not to spend any more lives in direct, infantry assaults. All that can be said with some certainty is that Meldrum would not have been so cautious and patient.

Finally, Sir Hugh and his officers conceded defeat because they were given such generous terms by fellow Yorkshiremen, terms which were deeply resented in London. *Mercurius Britanicus* was certain that Cholmley would not be allowed to go freely into exile: "What a thing 'tis that Hugh Cholmley should get such good conditions at Scarborough! Treachery hath shackled him to another destiny in England ... He had best hie him into Holland."[93] Always one of the most outspoken enemies of Cholmley, *The Scottish Dove* did not attempt to conceal its displeasure that Sir Hugh had been allowed to go to Holland; it would have much preferred him to have "cut a caper on an English tree" and been "drawn on an English oak rather than a Low Country waggon".[94]

Indeed, considering the blood and treasure Cholmley's defection and then prolonged, stubborn resistance had cost Parliament during the past 28 months, he was extremely lucky to keep his freedom as well as his life. Boynton offered him much more than he had the right to expect. Yet far from acknowledging the extraordinary leniency of Parliament's terms, Sir Hugh had the temerity to suggest in his memorials that he might have concluded a better bargain had not one of his own unnamed negotiators "disclosed the weake esstaite of the besiedged".[95]

What greater concessions could have been offered to Cholmley are hard to imagine. Article 3 permitted him and all his officers and men to go peacefully to Holland or the nearest Royalist garrison at Newark. Article 5 granted Lady Cholmley leave to return to her home at Whitby with two male servants and two horses and to "enjoy such parte of her estate as is allowed by ordinance of Parliament". Like all other Royalists in arms, Cholmley could hardly expect his property to be exempt from sequestration or his wife and children benefit from more than a fifth of its income.[96] Sir Hugh was fortunate not to share the same fate as his Hotham cousins: in Parliament's view, all three were traitors who had broken their vows and gone over to the enemy. If Meldrum had lived to dictate the conditions, they would surely have been much harsher. Colonels Matthew Boynton, Francis Lascelles and Simon Needham, who negotiated for Parliament, were all Yorkshiremen. Not only did they grant magnanimous terms, afterwards they made sure that, in Cholmley's words, they "were verie justlie observed".[97]

So, at noon on Friday, 25 July 1645, three days after Sir Hugh's 45th birthday, the great siege of Scarborough castle came to an end. The main gateway was so obstructed with debris that a new exit had to be cut through the curtain wall into the dykes. Sir Hugh brought up the rear. According to the governor, only 180 had survived the ordeal and most of them were so sick that they had to be carried out.[98] According to *An Exact Relation,* "there were about 200 in the castle and 100 came into Parliament", though most of the latter must have been the sick and wounded unable to travel any further.[99] A more reliable report from London was that 160 men and women had taken the road from Scarborough to Newark, led by Cholmley.[100]

Several of London's news-sheets alleged that Cholmley needed physical protection when he emerged last out of the castle ruins: in the words of one of them, *An Exact Relation*: "The women in Scarborough could hardly be kept from stoning of Sir Hugh Cholmley".[101] By holding out for another six months in the castle, Cholmley could be blamed for inflicting even more sufferings on the townspeople ranging from food rationing and forced billeting to cannon bombardment. Their parish church, St Mary's, had been wrecked: its northern aisle, north transept and chancel were in ruins and its central tower so undermined that it collapsed in a gale in 1659. Despite a national appeal for repair funds made in 1660, St Mary's was never restored to its former size. What remains of it today stands as a constant reminder of civil-war destruction. The twelfth-century church of St Thomas the Martyr, just inside Newborough Bar, had become a horse stable and a military magazine; five years later it had to be demolished. There was no reprieve for Scarborough's grammar school either: Sir Hugh had converted it into a guardhouse and it never recovered from the experience. The boys and their master did not return to it; instead they had to make do with the undamaged south transept of St Mary's as a "temporary" substitute for the next two centuries.[102]

Outside the immediate battle zone, there was other evidence of the grievous affect of the siege. The town windmill, which Meldrum had used as an observation tower, and the three water mills in Ramsdale, had been "totally pulled down". The mile-long lead pipes which supplied the town with water from Falsgrave springs had been unearthed and made into ammunition. Ships had rotted on the beach; their cables, sails, anchors and furniture were taken away as prizes; and their owners were forced to pay for their recovery. Shipping losses alone were valued at £3,000. The town subsequently claimed that altogether it had been impoverished by the sum of £5,000. It could not even find a salary for the new preacher at St Mary's who replaced the Royalist vicar, William

Simpson. Sir Hugh might once have been welcomed as Scarborough's guardian; now he was cursed and denounced as its worst enemy.[103] Not surprisingly, Sir Hugh never set foot in Scarborough again and after 1645 his descendants, generation after generation, were shunned there.

Cholmley himself put no figure on the number of survivors of the siege who decided and were able to march on Newark. He intended "to go immediatlie to his Majestie", but when the party reached Selby he changed his mind. The King, he heard, was "then in the remoatest part of Wales", a Scottish army stood across the route there, and now he felt too ill and weak to undertake such a long march or join another Royalist garrison. Transferring leadership of the column to Colonel Sir Jordan Crossland, Sir Hugh turned round and, accompanied only by Major Crompton, headed for Bridlington Quay. From there he boarded a ship bound for Holland.[104]

Cholmley was ruined, a sick and broken man. He was practically penniless. When he walked out of the castle his brother Henry was there to lend him £200, but this he distributed "amongst the officers and souldiers to releve their necessityes". When he said goodbye to Elizabeth she had "not above £10 in her purse" and, after he had paid for his sea passage, he was left with only about five pounds.[105]

At Selby, Sir Hugh convinced himself that he had done as much as honour and duty demanded of him: he now had to think first of his own family. His eldest son and heir, William, was now 20-years-old and an exile somewhere in Italy. Sir Hugh had received no communication from or about him for over a year. Young Hugh had been left behind as a boarder at St Paul's school in London when his mother went north in 1643. Though the boy had not suffered ill-treatment from his father's enemies, his parents were naturally concerned for the 13-year-old's welfare. Finally there were the two girls, Ann and Elizabeth, already in Holland with the Remmingtons. It would take Sir Hugh two more years to bring them all back together again as one family.[106]

Elizabeth had refused to go to Holland with her girls and stayed with her husband throughout the castle siege. After her death, ten years later, Sir Hugh wrote his memoirs as a tribute to her courage and devotion. As he wrote, "She would nether before nor in the seage be perswaded to leave mee, though dureing that tyme she endured much troble and inconvenience..." When the keep was brought down and became uninhabitable, "she was forced to lye in a little Cabin on the ground, sevrell monthes together".[107] Earlier, in his memorials, Cholmley had described these makeshift shelters as "poore cabbins reared against the walls and banckes in the Castle yeard".[108] As a result, not only did Elizabeth suffer from scurvy like the others, she also "tooke a defluction of rume upon one of her eies which trobled her ever after..."[109] Nevertheless, despite these hardships, "though by nature according to her sex tymerous", she would not be daunted and "shewd a courridge even a bove her sex". When Meldrum threatened "not [to] give quarter to man or woeman but put all to the sword", Elizabeth implored her husband not to submit to such menaces on her account, since this would be to prejudice his honour and the King's interest.[110] During the siege she had visited and tended to the sick and injured. When one of her maids attempted to desert but turned back when challenged by "the enemies gardes", Lady Cholmley forgave her "there being not persons in health to attend the sicke".[111]

In the words of Article 5 of the terms of rendition, "Ladie Cholmeley shall have libertie to live att her owne house att Whitbie".[112] However, Abbey house was already occupied by a captain of Parliament's town garrison and he "liked the place soe well he would not out…"[113] Consequently, Elizabeth had to lodge with one of Sir Hugh's old friends, Christopher Percehay, at his home at Ryton, near Malton. She was still there early in 1646 when she was told that the captain had abandoned her home after one of his servants had died of the plague there. Though it was still mid-winter and the North York moors were under deep snow, with only one maid and Thomas Knowles, the family cook, as her companions, she travelled the 30 miles to claim back her Whitby home. Abbey house had been plundered and she spent a very cold, hard time there, "the saddest and worst tyme of her life", until her two girls came back from Holland to join her. Nevertheless, in the words of her doting husband, "her sperret would not submit to make complaint and application to the Parliament's committee at York, as most others did, who disposed all my esstate".[114]

News of the fall of Scarborough castle was received in London with pleasure and relief: the siege had been costly, frustrating and prolonged. The loss of Meldrum had been a great blow and so had the death of Vice-Admiral Zachary, commander of Parliament's blockading squadron. In addition, according to Cholmley, nine other of Parliament's senior officers, "the meanest beeing a captaine", had forfeited their lives as well as "manie common soldiors".[115] As many as 16 of Parliament's warships had been engaged in the sea blockade at one time or another and for about six months upwards of 2,000 of its troops had been committed there. Meldrum had been obliged to call up the heaviest of siege artillery from Parliament's arsenals at Hull and York. With never more than 500 soldiers at his disposal, Cholmley could not have served the King's cause to greater effect; on the battlefields of Marston Moor or Naseby they would have made no difference to the outcome.

On 19 August 1645, the Journal of the House of Commons recorded that three days later there would be an official "thanksgiving to Almighty God for his late mercies vouchsafed to the Parliament's forces in the taking of Scarborough castle, and some other places". The "other places", the towns of Bath and Bridgwater and Sherborne castle, were not, it seems, to be compared with that "place of so great concernment to the public".[116] For Sir Hugh Cholmley, the day he surrendered Scarborough castle was one of the greatest concernment to him: it was the last day of his public career.

CHAPTER 13

EXILE, HOMECOMING AND DEATH

In his memorials on Scarborough, Cholmley ended by explaining that after his surrender of the castle he and Major Crompton "went for France".[1] Though these words were written in 1647, only two years later, Sir Hugh's memory was faulty: as he later recalled in his memoirs, from Bridlington Quay he had sailed first to Holland and only later from there to France.[2] But why did he choose Holland first?

Primarily, his concern was for the welfare of his daughters, Ann, not yet eleven, and Elizabeth, only six years old. As soon as he found them there in the care of the Remmingtons, he arranged for their return by ship to Bridlington. However, "a great and dangerous tempest" blew their vessel off course and they were forced to land at Grimsby. Whether Elizabeth went to greet them in Lincolnshire or whether they journeyed to Ryton to join their mother there, Sir Hugh did not say; but at least he soon had the comfort of knowing that mother and daughters had been re-united in Yorkshire. Secondly, Cholmley might have had a financial motive. Three years earlier, Queen Henrietta Maria had gone to Amsterdam to pawn her jewels and probably this was Sir Hugh's destination with the same purpose in mind. With his "jewels", and whatever other valuables he might have been carrying, he was able "by gods providence" to raise £600, a sum sufficient to support him for some time in foreign exile.[3]

After two or three weeks in Holland, where he visited the Hague, Amsterdam and "some other good townes", he went on to Flushing and from there took a ship to Calais. From Calais he went by coach on the main road to Paris. On the way, at Montreuil, the coach was "allarmed by 500 Spanish horse which followed us", and Cholmley was afraid that he might lose the £300 in English gold he was carrying. No harm came to him or his money, but he realised that in future it would be safer to travel with bills of exchange rather than coin.[4]

In Paris, Sir Hugh at last heard from his eldest son, William. He was in Italy and desperate for cash. Unless his father sent him "spedy supply" he would have "to turne souldior and trale a picke in Catelonia for his subustance". In other words, he would be compelled to join the Spanish army that was quartered there.[5] To prevent such an appalling fate for an English Protestant, Sir Hugh sent William enough money to pay his travel costs to Paris. At the same time, Sir Henry Cholmley was asked by his elder brother to provide for young Hugh's passage from London to Paris. As a result, before the end of 1645, all three, father and two sons, were reunited in Paris.[6]

From Paris the Cholmleys travelled to Rouen where they met two of their Twysden relatives, Elizabeth's younger brother, Doctor John, and William, son of Sir Roger, her nephew. In February 1646, Sir Hugh sent his eldest son, William, back home to Whitby to care for his mother and sisters and manage the family estate. With the help of his uncle, Sir Henry, William was able to secure a fifth of the estate's income for his mother and begin negotiations for his father's sequestration and composition fine.[7]

In April the two Cholmleys and the two Twysdens journeyed to Tours. Sir Hugh stayed there until July before going alone to Paris where he lived until March 1647. Presumably, he was in contact with other English Royalist exiles at this time, but none of them are referred to by name in his subsequent memoirs. Finally, in May 1647, the whole Cholmley family was re-united in Rouen where Sir Hugh had taken a house. All six of them, parents, two sons and two daughters, lived handsomely and comfortably there for the next year and a half and it was here and then that Cholmley wrote his three memorials for Sir Edward Hyde.[8]

In previous chapters repeated references have been made to Sir Hugh's "Memorialls Tuching Scarbrough", which are the bedrock of our knowledge and understanding of his and Scarborough's experience of the civil war of 1642-5. The other two essays he wrote in exile in 1647-8, "Some Observations and Memorialls touching the Hothams" and "Memorialls touching the Battle of Yorke", were shorter pieces, though still revealing historically and biographically.

Cholmley's brief paper on the Hothams, father and son, was the only one of the three selected by the editors of the *Clarendon State Papers* for their second volume published in 1773.[9] The editors were aware of the existence of two more papers of the same date and written for the same purpose by Sir Hugh, but rejected them for publication on the astonishing ground that they were "too immaterial", whereas the essay on the Hothams contained "some particulars ...omitted in [Clarendon's] *History of the Rebellion*". From a different perspective however, of the three, "Observations" on the Hothams is of least value to a historian and lacks the objectivity of Sir Hugh's account of the battle of Marston Moor.

In simple terms, Cholmley's account of Sir John and his eldest son, "Captain" John, was slanted in several ways. Firstly, Sir John was a blood relative, a valued friend and a valuable political ally and Sir Hugh tried his best to defend and excuse his conduct. To suggest that Sir John might have been "a faithfull and serviceable person" to the King and Queen if they had shown "grace and favour" towards him, ignores the course of events which led to his defiance of Charles at Hull's Beverley gate in March 1642.[10] By that time Hotham had made himself a prominent and troublesome opponent of the King: he had led resistance to Ship Money in the East Riding; he had obstructed the King's efforts to raise the Yorkshire militia against the Scots; in the Short Parliament he had been so outspokenly critical of government policy that the Privy Council had sent him to the Fleet prison; and during the summer of 1640, along with Cholmley, he had been author of three county petitions which so angered Charles that he threatened to have him hanged if he wrote any more.

As a result of all these persistent misdemeanours, Hotham had been deprived of all his commissions only to be restored by order of Parliament to be governor of Hull. Finally, it is clear that Sir John would never have been given the crucial responsibility of holding Hull unless Parliament had not had total confidence in his trustworthiness.[11] In short, Hotham's commitment to Parliament in 1642 was just as strong as Sir Hugh's, but, in retrospect, such an admission by the latter had become too embarrasing.

Whereas Cholmley tried to excuse or justify the elder Hotham's conduct, he did not have a single word of mitigation for his son. Sir John resented but tolerated being made subordinate to lord Fairfax, whom Parliament chose as commanding general of its Northern Association army, but young Hotham showed open disrespect for the Fairfaxes, father and son, even though he had been given the rank of Lieutenant-General and "rainged the Country with out controwle".[12] Young Hotham was also the first to start a correspondence in secret with the earl of Newcastle; it was his fault that General Goring was allowed to pass through Yorkshire to York with his vital supplies; and it was he who, insteading of challenging the Queen's progress from Bridlington to York, went secretly to Lord Newcastle to offer him Hull in return for titles, money and offices for himself and his father.[13]

For much of this we have only Sir Hugh's biased testimony. Cholmley was deeply annoyed by Goring's successful journey from Newcastle to York in February 1643, not least because his own regiment under Captain Medley had been badly beaten at Yarm attempting to prevent his crossing of the Tees. Yet instead of blaming himself for sending out such an inadequate, inexperienced force against professional veterans, he was annoyed by Hotham's failure to stop Goring crossing the Swale at Thornton Bridge.[14] Similarly, whatever young Hotham's extravagant terms for changing sides, which seem far-fetched, he did not have the military means to disrupt Henrietta Maria's escorted convoy as it passed over the Wolds to Malton. He certainly did not have "above a thousand horse and Dragooners", as Cholmley alleged.[15] Moreover, it is not true that the Royalists were diverted northwards by Hotham's assurances. During the winter weather of February-March it made good sense to take a more northerly route to York via Malton rather than risk the greater gradients of the higher Wolds.[16]

When he came to the Hotham defection, Sir Hugh was unable to resist the temptation to compare their prevarication, dishonesty and failure with his own brilliant, honourable and bloodless coup. He had taken Scarborough over to the King without a shot being fired; he had carried the townspeople and the garrison with him by his fairness and popularity. In the sharpest contrast, the Hotham plot to betray Hull was blown before it was hatched. Sir John ran off towards his home at Scorborough but was seized by force at Beverley. Both he and his son were shipped in irons to London, stood trial for treason, and were executed on consecutive days in January 1645. No wonder Sir Hugh was smuggly superior!

Several of Sir Hugh's so-called "Observations" were as much grounded on his own experiences at Scarborough as Sir John's at Hull. One of the reasons he gave for Hull's attachment to Parliament was the strong influence there of "the seamen" who, as in other "maretine townes", preferred Westminster to Whitehall. Probably, Cholmley was mindful that at Scarborough the only truly committed Parliamentarians whom he could not win over to the King's side, such as the Harrisons, Nesfields and John Lawson, were all God-fearing seafaring men.[17]

Though Cholmley believed that Sir John had fallen out with his masters in London for the same reasons that had prompted him to defect, in his opinion there was one vital difference between them. Hotham did not like Puritans and they did not like him. What Sir Hugh called "the Presiser cleargie", by which he meant the Puritan preachers and clergymen who had sought refuge in Hull when Yorkshire and Lincolnshire had been overrun by Royalists in 1642-3, had informed against Hotham to Parliament and conspired against him.[18] Also, though Sir John had powerful Presbyterian friends such as Sir Philip Stapleton of Warter Priory who was MP for Boroughbridge, his "mortall enemies" were the Independents in the House of Commons. Notable amongst these Independent members was Oliver Cromwell, who twice led the party that refused to grant a reprieve to him.[19]

Nevertheless, Sir Hugh's sympathies were clearly with his old friend and blood relative. Cholmley admired a kinsman who was valiant, honourable and "loved libertie"; who had good understanding and "ingenuitie"; and whose only faults were "a rash and hasty nature" and too great a concern for his own interests. Above all, in Sir Hugh's opinion, he had genuine affection for the King's cause and the peace of the kingdom and, unlike his son, he was not moved merely by political self-interest.[20] Even under sentence of death, according to Cholmley, the father showed more courage than the son, though both denied that they were guilty of treason. Always conscious of his own, similar situation and action, Sir Hugh agreed that "they were both convicted meerely [!] for treating with the ennemie and having an intention to deliver up the towne of Hull".[21] How he could think that conspiring secretly with the enemy in wartime and plotting to hand over a place of great strategic value, whether Hull or Scarborough, was anything but treasonable shows just how unrepentant and Royalist Cholmley had become.

Needless to say, Clarendon did not accept all of Cholmley's views on the Hothams, particularly his favourable bias towards the father. According to his *History*, which he resumed writing in 1668, the elder Hotham was "without any bowels of compassion or the least touch of generosity" and he was both deceitful and untrustworthy. On the other hand, he agreed with Cholmley that by nature Sir John was conservative and fearful of social disorder; that he favoured the established church and state; and that the main reason for his ruin was his "great covetousness ... and great ambition" - though unacknowledged, almost word for word from Cholmley's "Observations".[22]

If Cholmley's essay on the Hothams was marred by prejudice and special pleading, his account of the biggest and bloodiest battle of the civil wars was a model of objectivity.

Not even a southern historian can doubt the crucial military importance of the battle of Marston Moor. With the possible exception of the battle at Towton of 1461, also fought near York, that on 2 July 1644 was the largest ever held on British soil. Estimates of the number of soldiers engaged range from 36 to 46 thousand and the number killed in little more than two hours from four to six thousand. It was also one of the most decisive and one-sided battles of the civil wars of the 1640s: Royalist casualties exceeded Parliamentarian losses by as many as ten to one. The Royalist debacle ruined the marquess of Newcastle and effectively destroyed for ever his field army in the north of England. He and his senior officers took no further part in the war and abandoned the King. Thereafter, Charles's military support in most of the North was reduced to a scattering of isolated, besieged garrisons of towns and castles. The King lost York, which fell soon afterwards. Prince Rupert, hitherto the most successful and feared of his Royalist generals, suffered his first overwhelming reverse; his reputation and nerve never completely recovered from his humiliation on Marston Moor. On Parliament's side, Oliver Cromwell's fame as a brilliant leading commander was firmly established, though it was greater than his real contribution to victory. And finally, Parliament's military alliance with the Scots had proved to be of inestimable value.

In these circumstances, it therefore comes as a surprise to discover that the events of the evening of 2 July 1644 on Marston Moor remain, even today, far from clear and uncontroversial. Military historians muddy their boots treading on the battle ground and argue amongst themselves about the roles of individual officers and, above all, about how and why the Royalists threw away vital, initial advantage and turned it into utter defeat. To this debate, though often ignored or underestimated, Sir Hugh's "Memorialls touching the Battle of Yorke" made an important historical contribution.

As Professor Firth pointed out more than a century ago, Royalist accounts of the battle are much fewer and less informative than those available from the other side.[23] The Royalist mouthpiece, *Mercurius Aulicus,* was eager to report Prince Rupert's relief of besieged York, yet reluctant to concede that a crushing defeat had been suffered soon afterwards. At first, it admitted that only 600 of the King's soldiers had died on Marston Moor,[24] and the following week owed most of its news to the brief, official dispatch of the Allied generals to Parliament.[25]

Even the leading Royalist participants had little or nothing to say or write. The so-called "Prince Rupert's Diary" is no longer regarded as authentic. Lord Newcastle, a very proud but broken man, refused Hyde's invitation to set down his side of the story. James King, created baron Eythin in 1643, a professional Scottish soldier and veteran of the continental war, who was Newcastle's General of Foot, was too overwhelmed by a sense of guilt to defend himself.[26] Twenty years later, Newcastle's doting duchess wrote a version of events, but it was little more than a ridiculous apology for her husband.[27]

Indeed, all the first-hand Royalist narratives are seriously flawed. Sir Henry Slingsby's diary is usually regarded as the best Royalist source, yet we do not know whether he was actually present on the battlefield, even though only a few miles from his home it was terrain he knew well.[28] The remaining Royalist eye-witnesses were even less forthcoming and reliable. Ogden's short letter contains the amazing conclusion: "More of the Enemyes slayne then of ours ... and soe few killed".[29] Sir Philip Monkton, who rode in the van of Goring's famous cavalry charge, conveyed only the confusion and chaos of a widespread battle fought out in clouds of smoke and growing darkness.[30] And finally, Arthur Trevor's letter merely clarified the deployment of the Royalist armies on the eve of the battle.[31]

With Sir Hugh's willing assistance, Clarendon might have been expected to have presented a reasoned and accurate anaylsis of the battle, but in Professor Firth's word, what he actually wrote in his celebrated *History* was "worthless".[32] For this there were several reasons other than his notorious ignorance of the North and dislike of Yorkshiremen. In the first place, in his narrative, Clarendon did not reach the events of June-July 1644 until his second exile a quarter of a century later; secondly, when he went abroad to France he neglected to bring Cholmley's manuscript with him; and thirdly, what he called "that unfortunate battle" so saddened him that he chose to pass over it without a "full relation"![33]

So though they ran to only three foolscap folios, Sir Hugh's memorials have a unique historical value, not least because he was not himself present on Marston Moor. As related in chapter 11 above, the marquess of Newcastle accompanied by about 70 senior officers in his Northern Royalist army, stayed two nights, 3 and 4 July, as Cholmley's guests in Scarborough before departing for Hamburg.[34] From these leading officers, Sir Hugh must have heard several eye-witness versions of what had just occurred on Marston Moor. Later, other high-ranking Royalists, such as Henry Constable, viscount Dunbar, who had fought in the battle, took refuge with Cholmley in the besieged Scarborough castle.[35] Clearly, all these defeated and despondent gentlemen would have denied personal responsibility for their defeat, but Cholmley himself had no personal record or reputation to justify. On the contrary, because he was not in the thick of the bloodbath he was able to take an overall as well as a dispassionate view of it. The principal weakness of his viewpoint was that he had listened to the stories of only Northern army officers: Rupert and his officers never passed through Scarborough. At one point, Sir Hugh wrote: "I have heard the Prince in his owne private opinion ...", but there is no evidence that before he penned his memorials he had ever encountered Rupert or any of his officers who were on Marston Moor.[36]

However, in recent years, Cholmley's memorials on the battle of Marston Moor have been awarded more recognition by historians. In 1978, Dr Peter Newman, then the acknowledged authority on the battle, almost ignored Sir Hugh's manuscript when writing about the historical sources. "He [Cholmley] adds little of interest to a revision of the sources...", was his dismissive comment in a footnote.[37] Yet, only three years later, in his lengthier and wiser treatment of the battle, Newman gave much greater credit to Sir Hugh's literary contribution: his pendulum had swung to the opposite extreme. Now he wrote that Cholmley's memorials were "crucial", since he had "no political or personal axe to grind" and he had benefited from the unique privilege of listening to Royalist generals only hours after the battle had been lost.[38] Since then subsequent historians of the period have paid suitable homage to Cholmley's work. John Barratt's *The Battle for York* (Stroud, 2002) cited Sir Hugh six times in one chapter; Charles Spencer in his life of Prince Rupert quoted him three times in his biography of 2007; and in her life of Lord Newcastle, *Cavalier,* also published in 2007, Lucy Worsley gave him the tribute of nine references.

None of these were more than Cholmley deserved: his memorials provide abundant and convincing explanation for Royalist defeat on Marston Moor. First of all, Sir Hugh was sharply aware of the vital significance and potentially fatal consequences of the failure of the York garrison to join Rupert on the battlefield on the morning of 2 July. His own explanation for this disastrous delay was probably as fair, factual and balanced as anyone could expect. Though Sir Hugh bore a justified grudge against James King, Lord Eythin, mainly because of the ill-treatment he had meted out to Cholmley's militia men after their surrender at Yarm, he refrained from the temptation to blame Newcastle's general entirely for the delay.

Though there is no surviving evidence to corroborate or deny it, according to Cholmley, Rupert had been given "a supreame commission above the Marquess, so that his forces came very untowardlie out of Yorke". Newcastle was a very proud aristocrat of ancient lineage and he had wielded "absolute power" as commander of the royal army in the North, so that he was sure to resent any subordination of his authority even to a prince of the royal blood. Indeed, Cholmley went so far as to suggest that the marquess was so disgruntled that he had decided "to quitt his imployment and the kingdome" even "though the Prince should have the day" in the forthcoming battle.[39] Whatever the truth of the difference between Rupert and Newcastle, it was a serious omission of the King not to make it clear to both of them who was the senior.[40]

Yet it seems that Lord Eythin, who had an old but festering quarrel with Rupert, was even more reluctant to follow the Prince's orders which were to bring his foot soldiers out of York by four in the morning of 2 July. Subsequently, Eythin was named as the chief culprit because he had said that his garrison could not march out of the city until they had first received their pay. Sir Hugh admitted that Eythin had denied that he had issued such an order, even though it was in fact pay day. Secondly, in fairness to Eythin, Cholmley also pointed out that many of his troops were busy "plundering in the enemies trenches where they found good bootie".[41] Nevertheless, as Cholmley well knew, whoever was responsible, with the help of Newcastle's infantry, Rupert might have taken the initiative on Marston Moor before the allied army had time to turn around and face him; but instead he was forced to wait until the following day when they did not arrive in time.[42]

By nine o'clock, when Newcastle finally arrived on the battlefield in his coach and escorted only by his lifeguard cavalry, the Prince was growing increasingly impatient. Newcastle himself was already five hours late and his 4,000 infantry nowhere in sight. When at last the two of them came face to face, Rupert said to Newcastle: "My Lord, I wish you had come sooner with your forces, but I hope we shall yet have a glorious day." Cholmley is our only authority for these words. Clarendon's shorter and much less revealing version of the Prince's greeting: "My Lord, I hope we shall have a glorious day," fails to convey the weight of Rupert's controlled but real annoyance that he had lost the advantage on the field which he had gained by rapid and unexpected manoeuvre. Unfortunately, some historians have quoted Clarendon's, not Cholmley's, version.[43]

Finally, about four o'clock in the afternoon according to Cholmley, Eythin came on to Marston Moor with the York infantry. They were 12 hours late. For what Eythin and Rupert then said to each other, we have only Cholmley's own account:

> The Prince demanded of King how hee liked the marshelling of his army, whoe replide hee did not approve of itt beeing drawne too near the enemy, and in a place of disadvantage. Then said the Prince, "They may be drawne to a further disstance." "Noe sir," said King, "it is too laite".

At this point, with total tactlessness, Lord Eythin reminded Rupert that six years earlier in the Palatinate the Prince's "forwardness" lost them the day and brought about his own capture.[44] Eythin's undiplomatic reference to the battle of Lemgo fought in 1638 was probably his retaliation after the Prince had rebuked him for arriving so late. Given the well-known ill-feeling between the two, Sir Hugh's report of their meeting sounds all too credible.

Prince Rupert has been criticised by military historians for not pressing home his early advantage and for allowing the allies to recover the intitiative by attacking him after he had decided the battle would have to be delayed until the next morning. However, Sir Hugh's essay makes plain that both Newcastle and Eythin were unwilling to commit the Northern army to battle and left the prince no choice. Indeed, Cholmley's account does more credit to the prince than to either the marquess or to the baron. When Rupert's own cavalry regiment broke and scattered under the impact of Cromwell's charge, he tried unsuccessfully to rally his horsemen. "Swounds, doe you runne, follow mee," he cried as he led a counter-attack. Later, the following morning, when Rupert thought of gathering the defeated Royalists to "attempt some thing upon the enemie", he was again overruled by General King (Eythin) who pronounced the situation as hopeless. Since at that moment the Royalist command was unaware of the extent of their defeat and the loss of all their artillery and baggage, King's counsel was wise; but the suspicion remains that both he and Newcastle had been altogether negative, obstructive and defeatist.[45]

Apart from this damaging disunity of command, Sir Hugh provided another pertinent reason for Royalist defeat. Whereas the Parliamentarian cavalry on the allied left-wing under Cromwell and Leslie retained their discipline and order after they had routed the Prince's forces, at the other end of the battlefield, Goring's horsemen dissipated their triumphant charge plundering the enemy's baggage train.[46] This contrast between the self-imposed discipline of Cromwell's "Ironsides" and the helter-skelter, devil-may-care Cavalier cavalry of Rupert and Goring can be exaggerated, but Cholmley was right to appreciate its significance on Marston Moor.

In summary, the battle of Marston Moor was one of exceptional size in men and terrain and extraordinarily complex and confused. It was not until 3 July that both sides began to realise the enormity of its decisiveness. Lord Fairfax had spent the night at Cawood believing that the Royalists had won; even Rupert took some time to grasp the extent of his losses. Cholmley's concise but considered attempt to explain, clarify and interpret what had happened on 2 July 1644 is especially valuable because it offers credible evidence of the disastrous discords that undermined the Royalist army. In the absence of written testimony from Newcastle, from Rupert, from Eythin, or from any other senior Royalist commander, based on his privileged conversations with several of them within hours of the battle, Sir Hugh's memorials fill vital gaps in the primary evidence. Moreover, despite his own natural partisanship, Cholmley was able to find a commendable degree of fairminded objectivity. Though he might have exaggerated Eythin's part in persuading Newcastle to desert the King's cause and the country, unlike Clarendon, he seems to have made a genuine effort to check his prejudice against Scotsmen.[47]

After Cholmley had written his three memorials and sent them off to Hyde, an outbreak of plague there made Rouen too dangerous. So the Cholmleys moved to Gaillony, about 20 miles to the south-east, until it was safe to return. Early in 1649 news of the execution of King Charles I led to anti-English demonstrations in France and the Cholmleys were about to be stoned until Sir Hugh persuaded a mob that he was of "our Kings party".[48]

By February 1649, Sir Hugh's "moneyes" were "falling short" so it was decided that all would return to England except the two Hughs. Lady Elizabeth sent ahead "some household stuffe", which she had brought with her into France, but crossing the Channel the English "bottom" was lost to "an Ostend man of warre". Unaware, it seems, of his own double standards, Cholmley later noted scornfully that the Ostend "pirat" had "pretended a commission from the King of England". For the previous six years Scarborough ships, often under his direction, had plundered English east-coast traffic in the name of the king, first Charles I and then Charles II, and now the Cholmleys themselves were the victims of this practice. In fact, though captain Browne Bushell had recently been caught and was now a prisoner in Windsor castle awaiting trial, other Scarborough pirates who had operated out of Ostend and Dunkirk, such as Francis Fawether, William Cooper and John Denton, were still at large and still active at sea.[49] The Ostend "pirat" could have been one of them. Soon afterwards, along with the two girls and the two Twysdens, Elizabeth left Dieppe for England. For this journey, "a very great storme at sea" might, in Sir Hugh's view, have "deliver[d] them from the danger of being taken by a Pirat". Another silver lining to a black cloud.

Sir Hugh and young Hugh followed them by ship from Calais to Dover in June 1649. Parliament's Committee for Compounding with Delinquents had examined Sir Hugh's case and allowed him to "compound" for the restoration of his estate. If he paid the composition fee, swore never to assist the royal cause again and took the

Presbyterian National Covenant, he could return permanently to England and resume ownership of his home and land. Sir Hugh's composition fine had been fixed at £850, a very small sum for a Royalist combatant with so much pre-war wealth. The reason for this apparent leniency was that in June 1640, long before the outbreak of hostilities, Cholmley had taken the wise precaution of placing the bulk of his landed estate, estimated to be worth £1000 a year, in the care of three trustees, his brother Henry, his brother-in-law, Sir Roger Twysden, and Sir William Strickland. For himself, Sir Hugh had retained only the manor of Fyling, valued at £170 a year. Consequently, in accordance with the rule of the Committee, Cholmley was required to compound only for an estate of only £170 and his other properties were discharged "for the use of his eldest son and younger children". Once £450 had been paid in as the first instalment, Sir Hugh was free to return to Whitby and as early as 11 February 1650 the Committee was informed that the remaining £400 had been received.[50]

In June 1640, after his return from the Short Parliament, Cholmley had safeguarded his family's inheritance against Strafford's revenge. At that time he could never have imagined that within less than twelve months the great earl would be disgraced and dead. Even less could he have foreseen that soon afterwards he would be deeply and damagingly engaged in a civil war that would endanger all that he possessed. When later in his memoirs he wrote that he had taken out this insurance policy "upon foresight of these trobles" he was flattering himself with a vision he did not have. In the event he would have been more honest with himself and his readers to attribute this fortunate escape from ruin to "gods providence".[51]

On the other hand, Sir Hugh did admit that he owed his deliverance to his brother Henry who testified on his behalf and produced the necessary deeds of proof. With some justification the London Committee was suspicious of the Yorkshire County Committee which showed undue generosity towards Royalist Yorkshiremen and even resented sending composition fines from York to London. However, the London Committee was finally satisfied that Cholmley's deeds were genuine and that the rents from most of his estate were going to the trustees on behalf of his children. Nevertheless, suspicions remained, and as late as June 1650, James Cholmley of Cramlington, County Durham, and William Noble of Whitby were required to testify on oath that they had been witnesses to the deed of 1640 sealed "when the King first went against the Scots, in the parlor at Whitby".[52]

There was yet another piece of "good fortune" waiting for Sir Hugh when he returned finally to Whitby in August 1649. The death of Charles I earlier that year and the abolition of the monarchy in effect meant that the royal monopoly on alum mining, manufacture and domestic sale had ceased. The Cholmleys were now free to exploit directly the mineral potential of their own lands whereas previously they benefited only indirectly from the local alum industry. This was surely the greatest of all ironies in Sir Hugh's life: that the man who had jeopardised everything for the sake of the King should eventually profit handsomely from that same king's execution and the republican regime that ensued. Even before Sir Hugh reached Whitby his brother Henry had already entered into partnership with Sir Nicholas Crispe to start a new alum mine and works at nearby Saltwick Bay. Subsequently, Sir Hugh and his son William made a bargain with Sir Nicholas whereby he leased a third of the new works for 21 years at a rent of £200 annually. A further sixth share was given to Henry "in retorne of all his kindnesses" for 26 years which was then sub-let to Crispe for £150 a year.[53]

Very little is known about the early history of alum mining at Saltwick. Locally, the alum industry was by then nearly half a century old, but hitherto it had been confined to the coastal areas north of the Esk belonging mainly to the Chaloners of Guisborough and the Sheffields of Mulgrave. The potential profits to be made by the industry were enormous. Foreign imports of manufactured alum were banned; the home demand for this essential mordant for fixing dyes in textiles and leather and its use in a wide variety of medical and cosmetic products continued to grow; the Crown and its farmers had a monopoly; and a ton of alum which could cost about £10 to produce might fetch any market price between £18 and £26. However, it took decades of costly experimentation and repeated failure to convert mountains of grey shale into the precious white crystals of finished alum. Until the nineteenth century there was no understanding of the process: only then did chemistry succeed alchemy and science replace trial and error. Secondly, the costs and materials involved in manufacture were colossal. The main fuel, coal, had to come by river and sea from Durham to Coatham and Whitby; human urine, known as chamber lye, arrived in barrels by sea from London and was collected in the streets of Whitby and its rural hinterland; and seaweed was harvested from the coastal rocks or scarrs. At least 50 tons of shale, cut out by pickaxe and carried in wheelbarrows, a ton of coal, threequarters of a ton of seaweed ash and 20 gallons of urine were needed to produce one ton of alum.[54]

The timing of Sir Hugh's direct investment in the alum industry was also providential. Once the civil wars were over and the Commonwealth navy had secured the North Sea coastal trade, there was no further interruption of coal supply from Durham or alum shipments to London. Even during the first naval war with the Dutch between 1652 and 1654 the Admiralty was able to supply effective protection to convoys of English colliers and alum-carriers.

To serve his new works at Saltwick, Cholmley first built a new staith and coalgarth at Spital Bridge on the east side of the Esk. Not until 1673 did Sir Hugh junior secure a licence to build a new wharf and port at Saltwick Bay itself,[55] but during his last years Sir Hugh senior had begun to insist that his new tenants should include their urine as a rental contribution and this became standard practice. For example, on 5 November 1658, Mark Trewhitt secured a one thousand year lease on a tenement in Fylingthorpe for which he was obliged to pay sixpence, two good hens, and the urine of his house to be delivered every Michaelmas to William Cholmley's alum works a Saltwick.[56]

Finally, there is no doubt that after four decades of trial and error there was much better understanding of the alum-making process than when it was pioneered by the Chaloners at the beginning of the century. This acquired knowledge and lengthy local experience might well explain why Sir Hugh and his descendants did not trust the final stage of the manufacture to take place at Saltwick. Not until as late as 1770 was there a boiling house there: until then the alum liquor was shipped out to South Shields for evaporation.[57]

Yet even back at his home at Abbey House, Sir Hugh was not entirely safe from those who wished him harm. One Sunday afternoon as he came out of church to return home, an attempt was made by six soldiers to arrest him. It seems that during his exile in France an alderman of York called Taylor had sued him for failure to pay £800 for pigs of lead brought up to Scarborough castle "in tyme of the seage". When one of the soldiers laid his hand on Sir Hugh's shoulder and the others drew their swords menacingly, Cholmley's companions, his two sons, Richard Trotter, his nephew, and a

French servant responded by drawing their swords. When he saw one of the soldiers running towards young Hugh, Sir Hugh also drew his sword. At this moment there might have been an awful blood-letting in Abbey House courtyard, but Sir Hugh knew that whatever the outcome he would be judged in the wrong, so he "renderd" himself to the soldiers without further resistance.

Since the soldiers would not accept bail from him, Sir Hugh was forced to go with them to York. The following day the party set off, Sir Hugh attended only by his faithful French servant, but determined to give his captors the slip before they reached York. He had provided the six soldiers with five "ordnary country horses so that two roade duble" whereas he rode on "a little galloway". He bided his time until they were "a quarter of a mile" beyond Malton when suddenly he jumped his horse over a roadside ditch and spurred it up to Hildenley. It was a hamlet that he knew well: Roger of Roxby, his ancestor, had once owned it and now it was part of the estate of his brother-in-law, Sir William Strickland. Sir Hugh got clean away: once in prison he feared that he would be the victim of more legal actions and that he might never be free again.[58]

To clear his name against Taylor's accusations, Cholmley went immediately to London where his lawyers assured him that the alderman's writ was invalid because it omitted his title of baronet. However, Taylor was not to be outplayed so easily: he now began an action against young William. Once again six soldiers came up Whitby's East Cliff one Sunday and this time arrested William in his own bedroom. Again they would not take bail and, not to be outwitted a second time, compelled William to walk all the way to York, "in very wet unseasenable wether, useing him both uncyvelly and barberously". At York the sheriff bailed William, but the court found him guilty of being an accomplice to his father's escape from custody. He was fined £400. However, when William brought a counter action against alderman Taylor for the way that he had been arrested and forced to walk the 50 miles to York, the jury awarded him £600 in damages! The result, according to Sir Hugh's memory, was that Taylor agreed to pay the Cholmleys £300 in ready money and drop all suits and actions against father and son. Not only was Taylor's money very welcome, but the whole affair deterred others from bringing similar actions against Sir Hugh when he had been governor at Scarborough, "for which", he wrote later, "let my heart never forget to prayse the Lord all the dayes of my life".[59]

In the late autumn of 1650, from London Sir Hugh moved south to lodge with Sir Roger Twysden at his home, Roydon Hall, near East Peckham in Kent, while the rest of his family, except Ann, spent the next winter in Whitby. After the Scots had crowned Charles II as their new king in January 1651, the Commonwealth government in London feared another Royalist rising. As a result, none who had previously fought for Charles I was allowed within ten miles of the capital and Northern Royalists like Cholmley were regarded with the greatest suspicion. It was to allay such suspicion that Sir Hugh stayed with his brother-in-law in Kent throughout the winter of 1650-1. However, both he and Sir Roger were so deeply distrusted that at four o'clock in the morning of Saturday, 26 April 1651 government troopers descended on Roydon Hall. They came, they said, in search of arms and incriminating letters, but though they found none they still arrested Cholmley and Twysden and took them away to Leeds Castle near Maidstone. Here they were joined by other prisoners, notably the 72-year-old Lord Astley, formerly Sir Jacob Astley, one of the king's most distinguished field army commanders, and Sir John Culpepper, formerly the king's chancellor of the exchequer. Sir Roger was allowed out on 2 May; but Sir Hugh was not released until 16 June and only on condition that he entered into bonds to appear before the Council of State at 10 days' notice if required.[60]

After his release, Sir Hugh summoned Lady Elizabeth from Whitby. The family now had no coach horses of their own and even if they could have paid for their upkeep "they would have bene taken for Armyes services". So Elizabeth came south by sea. Previously, in 1643, she had come to Yorkshire from London by ship and resolved to repeat the journey in the opposite direction regardless of the hazards. However, though the season was mid-summer, the "wether" was so "ruffe" that the passage from Whitby to Gravesend took "10 or 12 dayes" and so she swore "never to passe that way againe". Sir Hugh went to meet her at Gravesend and brought her safely to her old home at Roydon Hall. Here the whole Cholmley family, Sir Hugh, Lady Elizabeth and their four children were reunited under the Twysden roof. Sir Hugh insisted on paying their household expenses along with those of their three servants at a rate of £12 a month for the next 12 months.[61]

From July 1652 until June 1653 all the Cholmleys were living at Abbey House, Whitby. As Sir Hugh explained: "my intention was to live retyredly". The alum works at Saltwick were now beginning to produce profits and, clear of all their remaining debts and free of malicious creditors, the Cholmleys were able to refurnish and replenish their home after its mauling during the civil wars. Elizabeth employed her considerable domestic skills "addorneing and fitting" the house and once again the family was able to entertain guests and employ servants on a scale almost comparable with the pre-war standards of the 1630s. At this time Sir Hugh described his "famuly" as "small" yet wrote that it was "neare 30 persons".[62]

In July 1654 the Cholmleys returned to London to witness the wedding of Ann. She was married to Mr Richard Stephens, eldest son of Mr Nathaniel Stephens of Gloucestershire. After the ceremony, Elizabeth took lodgings at Westminster near to her newly-married daughter while Sir Hugh returned to Whitby.

The following August William Cholmley was married to Katherine Hotham of Fyling Hall, the youngest daughter of Sarah Anlaby, the fifth and last wife and now widow of Sir John Hotham. The marriage alliance with his Hotham cousins must have been pleasing to the bridegroom's father. What dowry the bride was able to offer William was not reported by Sir Hugh: given the sad circumstances of the Hothams after the 1645 it could not have been more than minimal. In his memoirs Sir Hugh mentioned that one of the distinguished guests at the marriage of William at Whitby was Lady Leppington, then a widow of substantial means. Only from young Hugh do we learn that despite the discrepancies in age and fortune he pursued this lady in vain. Soon afterwards, Lady Leppington took Lord St John, the future Marquess of Winchester, as her second husband.[63]

At Michaelmas 1654 the Cholmleys returned to London intending to spend the winter there. They took lodgings in Russell Street, next door to the Reindeer Inn, until in February 1655 Sir Hugh was obliged to travel back to Whitby on his own. Lady Elizabeth first went to Chiswick to stay with the two Cholmley widows, one the second wife of Sir Hugh's father, the other, the wife of his half-brother. Confusingly, both their husbands were called Sir Richard Cholmley. However, not feeling well, Elizabeth decided to go up to London to see her daughter Ann who was with child; but while she was staying with the Lady Katherine Moore in Bedford Street, Covent Garden, "she fell into a feaver there of which [she] dyed, the 17 of April..." Sir Hugh heard the news of his wife's sudden death at Whitby. Three or four days later, "not able to endure the sight of those rooms and places in which [he] used to enioy her company", he left Abbey House, never to return.[64]

Lady Elizabeth's unexpected demise was the final, fatal blow to Sir Hugh: not even in death could he bear to be far apart from his dear wife. Though he could not be present at her funeral and interment, he spent the rest of his life as close as possible to her grave. She was buried near the south wall of the chancel of St Michael's church in East Peckham, close to the graves of her parents. On the wall Sir Hugh put up a plaque engraved with his and her arms and inscribed with the words:

> Deposited
> The body of Elizabeth the daughter of
> Sr. William Twysden of East Peckham in the county
> of Kent Knt & Bart, wife to Sr Hugh Cholmeley of
> Whitby in the county of Yorke Knt & Bart. She dyed
> the 17th of April 1655 and was aged 55

Underneath the same wall, on a black marble floor tablet bearing the Cholmley family crest, Sir Hugh had the following words inscribed:

> Deposited
> The body of the Lady Cholmeley, Elizabeth
> daughter of Sr W Twysden of Peckham in
> the county of Kent, Kt & Baronet, wife to
> Sr Hugh Cholmeley of Whitby in the county
> of Yorke Kt & Baronet by whome she had
> six children. She was very beautiful, of great
> inienuety, a discerning judgment, in
> great dangers had a courage above her sex,
> of a most noble and sweet nature, compassionate
> to all in distress, a vertuous chast loving
> wife, indulgent parent & true friend, and
> w[hi]ch was above all a most pious religious
> person & in belief and assurance of salvatio[n]
> & eternal life by the death & merritts
> of Christ Jesus dyed the 17th April an dom
> 1655 in the 54th yeare of her age after she
> had bene married 32 yeares

The black marble stone slab is now badly damaged and cracked and the church of St Michael has been redundant for some time.

Sir Hugh never again left Roydon Hall where he wrote his memoirs as a tribute to his wife and where he died in November 1657. Before his own death he decided that he would not be buried at Whitby but would share Elizabeth's grave. Accordingly, adjacent to her gravestone are the following words which he probably composed:

Hier also lyes

The body of Sr Hugh Cholmeley her husband who for the great love
he bore [her] the virtue & worth he found in the said Elizabeth declined the being
interred in his own country among his ancestors, and chose to be laid heer beside
her, by whom he had six children Richard and Elizabeth deceased young,
William, Hugh, Ann and Elizabeth did survive at his death which hapned the 30th
of November 1667 (sic) & in the 57th yeare of his age.

Also buried later in St Michael's were Sir William, Hugh's heir, who died in
1663; his grandson, Hugh, the third baronet, who died in 1665 in his third year; and
Elizabeth, his unmarried daughter, who lived until 1699. Elizabeth's tablet on the north
wall of the chancel reads that it was "according to her own desire" that she "was layd
nere the remains of her parents, from whom she did not degenerate being a very worthy
person & of a pious and virtuous life".

Eleven days before he died, Sir Hugh had dictated his last will: "considering the
certainty of death, and the uncertainty when it may happen, [I] doe therefore for the
better quieting my mind, and setling of my estate, make and ordaine this my last
will..."[65] His body was to be buried "without pompe, or more than necessary charge, in
the Quier belonging to the family of the Twysdens, in the church of great Peckham in
Kent, as neare as conveniently may bee to the place where my deer wife lyeth interred,
between her, and the chancel belonging to the saide church".

Three days earlier Sir Hugh had signed an indenture passing his manor and
lordship of Aislaby to three trustees, his brother, Sir Henry, his brother-in-law, Francis
Twysden, and his son-in-law, Richard Stephens. Aislaby in the North Riding had been
once monastic then royal and finally became Cholmley property sometime during the
early 1650s. In 1640, it was said to be worth £1000 when it was described as 16
messuages, one cottage, 300 acres of arable, 200 of meadow, 300 of pasture and 100 of
woodland.[66]

During his last stay in Whitby, on the 5th of May 1655, Sir Hugh had also
entrusted the same three men with the manor and lordship of Daletown, another of his
acquisitions. This outlying part of the Cholmley estate was to pay a debt he owed of
£800 to his brother-in-law, Dr John Tywsden, and its remaining value to maintain Sir
Hugh's unmarried daughter, Elizabeth, who was then 19, and provide her with a
marriage portion of £2,500 to be paid at 21 or on the day of her marriage. If, however,
Elizabeth should die before she became 21 or never marry, the £2,500 should be divided
between Sir Hugh's daughter, Ann Stephens, and his two Sons, William and Hugh. In
the event, Daletown was sold to Thomas Bellasis, Viscount Fauconberg, as early as 19
January 1658, for £2,950, which would have left Elizabeth with a dowry of only
£2,150.[67]

As for Sir Hugh's personal possessions, to his "deare brother", Sir Henry, he left
his "bay Bald Barbary mare called Spanker"; to Richard Stephens, his three-year-old
stone colt then in Whitby's manor house park; and to Francis Twysden, his chestnut
gelding. A plain gold ring worth 13 shillings with the motto "Ex eadem radice" was to
go to each of his four children, Sir Henry's two children, and to Margaret and Ursula, the
daughters of his deceased half brother Richard. This Sir Richard (1617-44) was the son
of Sir Hugh's father's second wife, Margaret Cobb, and much admired by his half
brother. In his memoirs Sir Hugh had described him as "a handsome proper gallant

142

gentleman" who had been knighted by Charles I for his service in taking Exeter. Subsequently, he had been killed in the siege of Lyme Regis "shewing more vallour then became a person haveing the commaund". According to Hugh, Richard "was exceeding beloved and lamented by his soldiers, and after by the King himself..."[68]

To his son Hugh, Sir Hugh gave all his books that were at Whitby, in London and at Roydon Hall. To his daughter-in-law, William's wife, he bequeathed the "green cloath hangings" at Abbey House which Lady Elizabeth and her servants had made. To his grandchildren, Nat, Dick and Betty Stephens, he gave £5 each and the same sum to his favourite aunt, Mrs Dorothy Bushell, Browne's widowed mother. To Mrs Jane Twysden, wife to serjeant at law, Thomas, he left "a little gold pott of tenn pounds price, with hearty thanks and acknowledgements for her many favors and kindnesses to my selfe and children".

To Francis Comyn he gave his "dunn mare". Francis was the son of Timothy Comyn of Durham, second husband of Margaret Cholmley, one of Sir Hugh's many aunts. George Coward, his "trusty servant", was to have the handsome reward of £40 and, if he wished, a house and farm at Aislaby at a rent of £16 a year. Thomas Huntrods could have £10 to buy himself an apprenticeship. Mr Crosby, Whitby's parish church minister, was to have £5 to buy himself a gown and 20 nobles (£6 13s. 4d.) for the poor of Whitby to be dispensed by William. The poor of East Peckham were also to receive £5 to be dispensed by Sir Roger.

As for Sir Hugh's executors, Sir Henry Cholmley and Richard Stephens, they were to have the remainder of his goods and any remaining interest in his lease of the rectory of Whitby. After Sir Hugh's debts and expenses had been paid, any money left over was to go to young Hugh, while William was to have all the family household furniture at Abbey House and the gatehouse, paying the executors £100 for it. Finally, the supervisors of Sir Hugh's will, Sir Roger, Thomas, John and Francis Twysden were each to have a gold ring 20 shillings in value.

Less than a year after his father's death, William Cholmley placed his inheritance in the hands of trustees. The four Cholmley trustees were named as Sir Henry, son of Sir Christopher Yelverton of Easton Mauduit in Northamptonshire, William, son of Sir Roger Twysden, John Savile of Methley in the West Riding, and Richard Stephens of Eastington in Gloucestershire, the husband of William's sister, Ann. The deed of trust of 1658 is particularly valuable and enlightening because it is the only comprehensive description of the Cholmley estate at the end of Sir Hugh's tenure of it.[69]

Despite the heavy losses forced on Sir Hugh in 1638-9 and 1653-4, there were still substantial rents coming to Abbey House in 1658 from the family's Whitby town shops, tofts and half tofts. Though these rents were not specified in the deed, evidence from later sources demonstrates their importance. For example, the Cholmleys still had four shops at the east end of Esk bridge, near the junction with Bridgegate and Grape Lane. In 1661, these were sold by William for £180 and a Michaelmas rent of fourpence halfpenny.[70] Even as late as 1679, Sir Hugh, William's younger brother who had succeeded to the estate, had 20 shops and stalls in Whitby's market-place and shambles which were worth to him £18 a year in rents.[71]

At the same time, the 36 burgage tenancies belonging to the Cholmleys in 1626 had been reduced to only 13 during the next 40 years, but their rents had been greatly increased. Sir Richard had charged only a flat, uniform rate of only one shilling a year in rent; but his son collected four times as much altogether from far fewer properties. For instance, Robert Norrison and Robert Bushell were each paying as much as 16 shillings and eightpence for their town tofts.[72]

The deed of 1658 also referred to other sources of Cholmley land income. Sir Hugh had retained the horsemill at the south-east end of Baxtergate and the windmill on the top of East Cliff; both dated from monastic times. He had also kept the very valuable watermills at Ruswarp along with the fishing rights from there down to the mouth of the river Esk. In 1678 the mills had an annual rental value of £80 and in 1682 the Cholmley fishing rights were sold for £500 by his younger son.[73]

To his pier tolls, harbour dues and court perquisites, Sir Hugh had added an entirely new source of income from his post-war investment in the alum industry at Saltwick. Since 1649, for his third share, Sir Nicholas Crispe had been paying him £200 a year.[74] After the death of Sir Nicholas, his son Ellis was granted a renewal of his lease for 21 years at an increased rent of £300 per annum from 1 April 1657. Then, when the Crown had reasserted its former rights to alum mining and manufacture in 1665, Saltwick was conveyed to Charles II on a 21-year lease for an annual rent of £1,500.[75] To his heirs Sir Hugh also left his new riverside wharf at Spital Bridge which he had constructed to supply and serve the Saltwick works. Though not recorded in the deed, there is evidence that by 1658 adjacent to Spital Bridge staith there were rope-making, salt-panning and lime-burning industries belonging to the Cholmleys. Finally, it is also evident that the owners of the alum works at Sandsend, Mulgrave and Peak were paying rent to the Cholmleys for harvesting their seaweed-bearing off-shore scarrs.[76]

Without any definition of location or extent the deed of 1658 also referred to the "Great Park". According to Lionel Charlton, writing about a century later, Sir Hugh's deer park had been allowed to decay after the death of his son Hugh in 1689. The deer disappeared and the park reverted to farmland. Clearly, Charlton was not writing about the old monastic deer park at Fyling, which Sir Hugh had long since sold to the Hothams, but to an undefined enclosure near Whitby.[77]

Unlike Fyling Park, Sir Hugh's Great Park did not have the impressive and distinctive stone walls to mark its perimeter, yet it must have been quite extensive and must have been surrounded by high walls or fences. The deed of 1658 noted only that the park was let to Francis Dickinson. Twenty years later, when the park was no longer leased, its annual value was quoted as £300. By comparison, the Lesser or Cow Park, which was also then without a tenant, was 13 acres in area and worth only £20 a year.[78]

Later documents indicate that this Lesser Park was immediately south of Abbey House above Boulby Bank. Since both the Great and Lesser Parks were tenanted in 1658 it seems unlikely that they were then being used as deer enclosures. Twenty years later, however, when both were unlet and the Lesser was known as the Cow Park, the probability is that one or the other or both were game reserves and stocked with some deer. By 1666 the Great Park was said to consist of Stripes farm, Robin Hood stones, Stumpe closes, Jackcroft and Cross Flatts. All of these lands can be identified and some of these names have survived to the present day. All were originally part of the abbey demesne, a mixture then of arable, meadow and pasture of several hundred acres between what became Hawsker Lane and Stainsacre Lane.[79]

Subsequently, when in 1685 Nathaniel Cholmley bought the family estate from his father-in-law, Sir Hugh, the younger, the Great Park was then said to consist of the Abbey Garth, Ston'd Horse Park, Cow Park, Pettlington Fields, Bushell's Flatts, New Garden House and Close, part of Moorgate Lees and lands formerly belonging to

Richard Dickinson's farm. Presumably, Richard Dickinson had succeeded Francis as tenant of the Great Park. In other words, the Great Park was not so great in area as it had been 20 years earlier: it now stretched southwards only as far as Moorgate Lees or Lathes.[80]

In and around the outskirts of Whitby town, William Cholmley inherited a number of valuable properties from his father. The deed of 1658 identified Cholmley closes at Haggerlythe, in Almshouse field, at Spital Bridge and Salt Pans on the east bank of the Esk, and Wheeldale, Highfields and Windmill Flatts, between Hawsker Lane and the sea coast. Southwards in Whitby Laithes, the Cholmleys retained their rights in the coastal "scarrs lying on the seaside" and to several farms inland outside the Great Park called Highgate, Haggit Howe, Oldstead and Beacon Hill in High Whitby. Further south still, Cholmley lands were now fewer and well scattered. Eight farms in Stainsacre, not recorded in the deed of 1658, were let out in 1679 and sold in 1707 by Sir Hugh's great-grandson for £3,475. By 1658, the Cholmleys had little left in Hawsker, and only four of the 40 cottages they had once held in Robin Hood's Bay. In Fyling manor, they retained only the Ness, two corn mills in lower Ramsdale at Boggle Hole; some enclosed commons and wastes on the moor called Billery Fields; an eight-acre farm at Normanby; and Southward or Southwell Houses.[81]

Only an approximate estimate can therefore be made of Sir Hugh's legacy from the deed of 1658. No rents or capital values were quoted in the document or any other of the same kind until as late as 1678. In that year total rents for the whole year came to £1,112 and harbour dues, tithes, market stalls and court receipts brought in an additional £730. After his premature death in 1663, William's widow was to receive £100 a year out of the estate, his daughter £160 for her education and maintenance, and a further £3,000 at the age of 21 or as a marriage portion if she married earlier. Unfortunately, the deed of 1658 says nothing about the entitlement of his younger brother Hugh, since the estate was expected to pass to Sir William's own son, another Hugh Cholmley.[82]

Events proved the wisdom of Sir Hugh's purchase of both Daletown and Aislaby. Daletown was as valuable as he had anticipated and sufficient to endow Elizabeth's dowry.[83] As for Aislaby, whatever its true market value, his younger son seems to have sold four closes there for less than he might have asked. In 1679, Richard Woodhouse, a mariner of Aislaby, bought them from him for only £80, only to sell the same two years later for £110. By 1700 their market price was put at £156 and by 1735, at £220.[84] Why they should have appreciated so much in only half a century cannot be expained for certain, but they probably contained excellent building stone.

CHAPTER 14

THE FATHER OF WHITBY?

Though Sir Hugh chose to be buried 300 miles away and not in Whitby "among his ancestors", and though he spent very little time during his 57 years at Abbey House, nearly all historians of the town since have agreed in print that he was its greatest benefactor.

Whitby's first historian, Lionel Charlton, described Sir Hugh in superlative terms as "the father of Whitby" and its "continual benefactor".[1] To the Reverend Dr George Young, another Whitby resident, historian and polymath, Sir Hugh was a paragon of virtue - prudent, pious, hospitable, generous and brave. "The whole vicinity", he wrote, "enjoyed the advantage of his residence there [Whitby]" and in him "the laurels of a hero [were] entwined with the graces of a Christian".[2]

Charlton and Young lived in a town that was still under the shadow of the Cholmleys, but by the time Robert Gaskin's work appeared in 1909 the family had long since moved from Abbey House. Nevertheless, the author of *The Old Seaport of Whitby* was only slightly more restrained than Dr Young: in his curious words, Sir Hugh was "an English gentleman of the olden time ... whose memory will be kept green by all who have affection for Whitby and its past". With Young he agreed that this "good" Cholmley had been a "wonderful" improver of his estate and a "beneficial influence" on the whole locality. He had promoted trade, set up alum works in the neighbourhood and aroused the apathetic people of Whitby "to the necessity of public improvements". To Gaskin, as to Charlton and Young, he was the "brave Sir Hugh" whose life had been both "useful and honourable".[3]

Since Gaskin, not much has appeared in print to question or even qualify these eulogies written by Charlton, Young and Gaskin. In the 1950s Percy Shaw Jeffrey and F R Pearson, both admired local authorities, were content to endorse the received dogma that Sir Hugh Cholmley was indeed "the father of Whitby". The former noted that he had built a drawbridge over the river Esk to link the east and west banks and stressed the contribution of his harbour improvements and alum works to Whitby's success as a sea port. The latter referred glowingly to his "civic foresight and philanthropic zeal". Shaw Jeffrey concluded in familiar terms that "Sir Hugh was probably the greatest of all Whitby's benefactors". His only points of censure in this otherwise impeccable testimonial were that Cholmley had pillaged the stones of St Mary's abbey to build Abbey House and that during the Civil War he had stripped the lead from the roof of its church "to provide his garrison with shot and shell".[4] Presumably this was not the same lead that Henry VIII's men had taken away when the abbey was dissolved in 1539.

Against this deafening chorus of praise of Sir Hugh Cholmley only one dissonant Whitby voice has been found in the printed word. William Chapman (1713-93) was a Quaker master mariner of Whitby who in 1786, the year before Cholmley's memoirs were first published and seven years after Charlton's *History* appeared in print, began to write down his own family history and personal memories. The Chapmans were well-known for their longevity: William himself was then 73 and his maternal grandfather, William Linskill, was 93 when he died in 1747. With the aid of distant family perspective, William could look back over a century and a half during which Whitby had "advanced from a mere fishing town to be a place of opulence and of great note for shipping as any on this side the Island, London excepted". And how and why had this bountiful transformation happened? Chapman's own explanation was simple and singular: the people of Whitby had imitated the Dutch "in building a great number of ships for other ports as well as their own, and by their being common carriers from the Baltic, White Sea, Norway, Sweden and other places to most parts of the ports of England and Ireland". Though the Cholmleys had been a dominant influence in Whitby during the last two centuries, there was no reference to them in Chapman's explanation of his town's growing prosperity.[5]

Chapman also recalled that the lords of the manor of Whitby had effectively inherited the powers of their abbot predecessors, who had once ruled over an area 20 miles long and seven miles wide as "absolute princes". As an example of the anachronistic and vindictive tyranny of such secular lords, Chapman cited the case of two local men who in 1660 were unjustly convicted of "capital" crimes because the unnamed lord of the manor "wanted" them both "removed". As a result, these "poor fellows" were hanged in a field just outside the town boundary ever since known as Gallows Close.[6]

Since the oldest surviving records of Whitby's court leet date from 1684, there is no way that Chapman's grim story can be verified. Nevertheless, whatever the truth of this particular example, Chapman was right: the secular lords of the manors of Whitby and Fyling had much the same supreme authority in the wapentake of Whitby Strand as the Benedictine abbots had once wielded there. However, Chapman's attitude to these lords of the manors was exceptional: for him the "industry" and "frugality" of Whitby's inhabitants were sufficient to explain their increasing affluence during the seventeenth and eighteenth centuries. Far from owing everything to such lords, Chapman implied that their influence on the town and port was at best negative and at worst oppressive and cruel. Indeed, he could not bring himself to pen the name Cholmley and his implicit hostility to that family was in the sharpest contrast to the deferential eulogies of other contemporary and later Whitby men. In 1660, Sir Hugh's eldest son, William, was then lord of the manor.[7]

There can be no doubt that Whitby enjoyed a spectacular growth of commerce and industry during the first four decades of the seventeenth century. In 1600 the town was little more than a fishing village with a population counted in a few hundreds. After the dissolution of the abbey in 1539, Henry VIII was reputed to have spent "great somes of money" on Whitby's river harbour, but the best description John Leland could write of it in the 1540s was "a great fischar toune".[8] Like Scarborough, Whitby was ignored and neglected by the Tudors, perhaps because they regarded it as too remote and inaccessible by land. Even North Riding magistrates showed little concern for it: in 1608 the vital river bridge that linked east and west sides was said to be "in great ruine and decay".[9] By 1640, however, the town and port had profited conspicuously from a generation of economic development. Its annual exports of butter to London had increased from just over 100 to more than 6,500 firkins. In 1614 there had been only two Whitby vessels carrying trade abroad; by 1640 there were 19. Shipments of fish to the capital increased ten fold. Above all, the nearby alum works at Sandsend and Asholme, opened about 1607, had transformed the west bank of the lower river Esk with its coal garths, landing staithes and shipyards. Whitby had become a major coal-carrying, alum exporting and ship-building port. Despite several visitations of the plague, probably brought in from the Continent, the town's population had more than doubled to nearly 2,000.[10] So to what extent, and in what ways, was Sir Hugh Cholmley responsible for any of this steep upward curve of prosperity?

All commentators, native and foreign, contemporary and historical, concur that it was alum mining and manufacture that gave Whitby's economy its kick start. The works on the nearby Mulgrave estate were serviced and supplied almost entirely through the port of Whitby. As Thomas Hinderwell, Scarborough's historian, wrote in 1798: "The important discovery of the alum mine[s] in those parts ... was the original cause which raised Whitby from its obscurity, and by opening a channel for commerce enabled the town gradually to obtain a degree of maritime importance."[11] As a former master mariner writing about Scarborough's traditional commercial rival, Hinderwell's recognition of Whitby's success was predictably grudging, understated and envious, but his explanation of it hit the mark. The impact of this new industry on Whitby's west bank was dramatic. Colliers came in from Sunderland loaded with coal from the Durham field. Human urine was shipped in from London in Whitby butter barrels. Hundreds of men were employed at the mines and works and thousands of pounds invested in raw materials, equipment and transport. From Whitby's coal yards and storehouses along the staithes everything needed at Mulgrave and Sandsend had to be carried by packhorse and wagon up the steep hills out of the town and all the alum produced went by sea from Whitby in Whitby-built boats.

Yet none of these earliest mines and alum works were on Cholmley land and there is no evidence that the Cholmleys invested directly in them. The original landlords and patentees were the Chaloners of Guisborough and the Sheffields of Mulgrave. Later, rich speculators, such as Sir Arthur Ingram and Sir Thomas Wentworth, risked their capital in what was an extremely unpredictable business adventure. Not until 1649, when the royal monopoly had gone and Sir Hugh returned from exile, did the Cholmleys open their own mine and works on their own land at Saltwick. By that time the local industry was more than 40 years old and its expensive teething-troubles were mostly in the past. Shaw Jeffrey was correct when he wrote that Whitby's "prosperity as a sea-port dates from the opening of the alum works"[12], but he had the wrong works in mind. Mulgrave and Sandsend first made Whitby wealthy, not Saltwick.

On the other hand, long before 1649, the Cholmleys had become principal beneficiaries of the local alum industry. As lords of the manor and port of Whitby they were required to set up navigation beacons at the mouth of the river Esk. As early as 1584, the narrow, perilous channel into and out of Whitby lower harbour was marked by what the French edition of Waghenaer called two "baques ou marques d'osieres".[13] The Cholmleys were also expected to maintain mooring posts along the riverbanks and "bushels" for measuring cargoes of coal, salt and corn. In return for these services, they were entitled to collect customs and dues from all shipping using their harbour. When Robert Fotherby, master of the Whitby ship, *Diligence,* refused to pay these dues, in 1655 he was sued by William Cholmley, acting on behalf of his absentee father. In court it was stated that every vessel in Whitby port was liable to pay twopence for every chaldron of coal landed, fourpence for "beaconage", fourpence for "plank-laying" from ship to shore, and fourpence for the use of the lord's measures. The Cholmleys won their case, even though a Commonwealth court was clearly reluctant to concede it to Royalists. They were awarded twopence in damages and forty shillings costs.[14] Much later, during the protracted legal dispute between Sir Charles William Strickland, then lord of the manor of Whitby, and the Crown, which lasted from 1884 until 1907, and concerned rights to the port and the North Sea foreshore, Strickland's lawyers quoted the Fotherby precedent. Amongst many other harbour dues traditionally collected by the manor lords, it seems that the Cholmleys had also taken a "launching" fee when a Whitby boat first put to sea.[15]

As the alum industry grew, Whitby harbour dues must have become increasingly valuable to the Cholmleys. The works at nearby Sandsend and Mulgrave received all their coal and nearly all their urine, timber, iron, lead and seaweed through the west bank port of Whitby. Port Book evidence for Whitby in the early years of the seventeenth century is disappointingly slight and random, but sufficient to indicate the volume and trends of commercial traffic. As early as 1612, 46 colliers from Sunderland and seven from Newcastle brought 925 chaldrons, more than 2,300 tons, of coal into Whitby. The following year, during the seven months from 28 March to 31 October, 1036 chaldrons, or more than 2,500 tons, of coal were carried up from west-side Whitby to Sandsend and Mulgrave. Even this heavy traffic was less than half of the 2,311 chaldrons landed at Whitby "for the allom workes" between 31 March and 14 February 1614.[16]

The alum industry was very vulnerable to a volatile market and the whole process was very difficult and unpredictable. There were many points of potential failure and failure was frequent and costly. Land slides, droughts, frosts and floods were just some of the natural hazards encountered. Bankruptcy was a constant threat; workers went months without a penny in wages. Nevertheless, despite many setbacks, the industry continued to grow. In 1633-4, 2,450 chaldrons of coal were landed at Whitby "for his Majesties allome works". The Civil Wars of the 1640s interrupted coal imports from Sunderland and disrupted the coastal trade in alum, but they seem not to have done any lasting damage to the industry. On the contrary, the end of the royal monopoly in 1649 led to the opening of several new mines. Between April and October 1651, 3,182 chaldrons, nearly 8,000 tons, of coal were brought into Whitby.[17]

Cholmley income from Whitby's increasing coal trade did not end with their landing duty on it: the family also owned some of the riverside staithes and storage places. Though the Cholmleys did not own the alum garth, coal garth and storehouse below Burtree Crag on the west bank which supplied the works at Mulgrave and Sandsend, Sir Hugh did have at least one coal yard at Hagglesgate until 1638. In that year, the "old coalgarth", as it was then called, was sold to Isaac Newton of Bagdale Old Hall for an undisclosed sum on a thousand year lease. Four years later, the lease passed to two Whitby master mariners for £40. This particular coal yard probably served the fuel needs of Whitby's west-side householders and craftsmen.[18]

There was at least one other coal yard on the east bank of the river near Awders or Alders Waste which belonged to the Cholmleys. When describing his confrontation with the Dutch seamen at the riverside in 1635 Sir Hugh referred to this particular coal storage depot above the bridge. Only as late as 1679 did Sir Hugh junior sell the lease on this third yard to Thomas Shipton junior, whose father of the same name had been steward to the second Earl of Mulgrave and manager of his alum works.[19]

The Cholmleys profited from the local alum industry indirectly in other ways. "Country urine" was never sufficient in quantity to supply the works with all their needs, but it was far cheaper, and some thought of better quality, than imported "London urine" brought up to Whitby by sea from the capital. Tenants of the Cholmleys were sometimes expected to make their household contributions to the "vasae urinae" provided by their landlord. In at least one case recorded, a Fylingthorpe farmer bought a thousand year lease from the Cholmleys for seven pounds with an annual rent of sixpence, two good hens and the urine of his house to be delivered to Sir William Cholmley's "allome workes if demanded at Michaelmas". The usual price of a full barrel of human urine was fivepence with an extra three farthings for freight when carried from Whitby port to the inland works.[20]

Human urine or "chamber lye" was used to produce ammonium alum. When soda or potash alum was being made, burnt seaweed ashes took the place of urine. Both kinds of alum were equally commercial. The seaweed or kelp was harvested in vast quantities: it took a hundred tons of wet seaweed to yield one ton of potash alum. Here again, as hereditary lords of the port of Whitby, the Cholmleys held exclusive rights to the shore and off-shore seaweed-bearing rocks or scarrs. And "the port of Whitby", as confirmed in an Exchequer ruling of 1729, extended from Huntcliff, eleven miles west of Whitby Bar, to Peasholm Beck, eleven miles south of it, up the river Esk as far as Ruswarp mill and dam, and fourteen fathoms out in the open sea.[21]

Though no records of scarr rentals have survived for the early part of the seventeenth century, it would be surprising if Sir Hugh allowed his "seaweed gardens" to be harvested without payment. In the earliest known rent book of 1678 "the scarrs" were then said to be worth £25 a year, which compares with the £9 in annual rents derived then from 20 market shops in Whitby town owned by Sir Hugh Cholmley junior.[22]

Even ships seeking shelter in Whitby harbour from storm, fog or privateers were obliged to pay the Cholmleys for the privilege. No account of harbour dues of Sir Hugh's time had been found, but at York assizes in 1765 it was stated in evidence that Nathaniel Cholmley then took eight pence from every English vessel and one shilling and fourpence from every unladen foreigner sheltering there. Though Sir Hugh's charges would have been lower, clearly he must have benefited financially from the enormous increase during his lifetime of North Sea coastal, especially coal, traffic. The upper harbour, above the bridge, was one of the safest anchorages along the whole coast from Newcastle to London. The Cholmley rent roll for the year 1678, when the North Sea was temporarily free of Dutch warmen and Dunkirk privateers, shows that harbour dues were worth £30 to Sir Hugh junior.[23]

The most important by-product of the alum industry was the stimulus it gave to ship-building along the west bank of the lower river Esk. As early as 1612 several Whitby-built, owned and mastered colliers were carrying coals regularly between Sunderland and Whitby. Judging by the weight of their cargoes they must have been roughly of the same capacity, from the smallest carrying 45 tons to the largest with 62 tons of coal onboard. With crews of five, six or seven, they were purpose-built craft designed specially for the river and coastal trade. By 1661, Whitby port was said to have above 60 vessels, and by 1701, more than 100.[24]

Yet there is evidence that as early as the 1620s Whitby's ship-builders were constructing more than small, coastal colliers. The *Neptune,* intended to make a trans-Atlantic voyage to New England, had already cost its Whitby builder £1000 in 1625.[25]

Soon afterwards, Trinity House certificates were granted to three warships, all built at Whitby though owned at other ports: the *Margaret* of Queensferry and the *Love's Increase* of King's Lynn were 110 tons and the *Pelican* of Newcastle 170 tons.[26]

If Whitby ships were carrying more and more coal, alum and butter up and down the East coast, then between 1614 and 1640 they had also captured Whitby's growing foreign trade from foreign carriers. In the former year, of 24 vessels entering and leaving Whitby from and to overseas ports, only two of them belonged to Whitby. In the latter year, of the 21 ships engaged in Whitby's foreign commerce, all but three of them were Whitby's own.[27] Also, almost entirely because of the presence and success of the neighbouring alum works, Whitby's overseas exports had grown enormously in value. In 1609, Bridlington Quay, Scarborough and Whitby were all minor ports: the values of their foreign exports were £210, £124 and £92 respectively. By 1640, Whitby had surpassed all its Yorkshire rivals except Hull: in that year its exports abroad were worth £12,795, whereas Bridlington Quay and Scarborough lagged far behind at about £500 each. All seven ships that year sailing out of Whitby and bound for the Continent carried alum, all seven had been built in Whitby, and their combined cargoes of 500 tons constituted all of England's exports of alum for that year.[28]

In short, Whitby's extraordinary development in the first half of the seventeenth century owed very little to the Cholmley lordship: it derived almost wholly from the alum mines and works at nearby Sandsend and Mulgrave which sucked in huge quantities of coal, timber, iron and lead, stimulated the growth of a ship-building industry and provided employment and income for hundreds of Whitby men and their families. Apart from the sea, river and land carriers, alum mining and making gave work to diggers and barrowers, coopers, masons, bricklayers, plumbers, carpenters, smiths, not to mention customers for a multitude of many different provisioners.

Lionel Charlton's bold assertion that the first Sir Hugh Cholmley made Whitby into a maritime town can therefore be dismissed as preposterous; but the common, received view that he was personally responsible for the lower harbour's earliest permanent pier has to be taken seriously.[29]

Reference has been made already to a pier or quay at Whitby at the time of the Dissolution in 1539 and there is evidence that a solid structure existed there long before. However, the location, length, form and purpose of such a pier or quay remain matters of continuing controversy. None of the royal grants of quayage, from Edward I's in 1307 to that of 1424, when the quay was said to be "decayed and broken down", identifies its position or describes its construction. Yet both Charlton and Atkinson, who disagreed about most things, thought that Whitby's oldest port was on the east side of the Esk near the bridge. Since the purpose of the earliest medieval quay would have been to serve the abbey and the lower end of the east bank would have been too exposed to the open sea, their assumptions make sense. In 1520, the abbot permitted a local mason to take building stone "between Byker Stone and Saltwick", provided that he did "not hurte the pere nor the clyf". Since Byker Stone and Saltwick were both on the east side of the mouth of the Esk, this places "the pere" approximately south of this area.[30]

That richer Whitby burgesses were contributing to the great costs of port maintenance right up to the Dissolution is attested by the contents of their wills. For example, in 1530, John Ledum, a very wealthy merchant, left 40 shillings "to the peir if it go furtherwordes". Six years later, John Skelton gave 6s. 8d. "to the peyre or haven" at Whitby. However, even the "great somes of money" which Henry VIII was alleged in

1545 to have "imployede" for "the Peyr against the See at Whitbye" seem to have been misused or insufficient. According to George Conyers, then bailiff of the town, in 1544 Whitby had no ships of war for the King's service because its harbour was "in great decaie". If, on the other hand, the port was "amended", there was no better place for the "savegard of shippes from Humber to the Firthe" than Whitby. In other words, if Henry wanted a secure haven for his warships he would have to pay for it: he could not expect Whitby men to bear the costs. In fact, none of the Tudors after Henry appear to have shown the slightest interest in Whitby harbour.[31]

In 1626, Trinity House Corporation certified that the "piers and jetties" at Whitby were in a state of decay, but if repaired the harbour there would be very suitable as a place of safe refuge for shipping.[32] This certificate bears almost the same date as a letter written at Whitby on 1 February 1626 by Hugh Cholmley addressed to the bailiffs and burgesses of Scarborough. Cholmley was about to set off for London having been chosen recently for the third time to represent the borough of Scarborough in the second parliament of Charles I. He told the bailiffs that it was not his intention to visit their town en route. Instead, he had sent his footman with the letter to inform them that he carried a petition to Westminster "for some releife towerds the repaireing the Peer" at Whitby which was "lately much indamiged and in short tyme like to be absolutely ruined". Similar representations had been made to the Commons by his father, Sir Richard, since 1621, but they had come to nothing. Now he appealed to Scarborough's "neighburly affection" and commiseration for "a poor towne", particularly since "it being not long since yo[u]r own cases".[33]

Cholmley's letter contains a wealth of hidden, subtle meaning. It is true that in November 1621, while he was wasting his time pretending to study law at London's Gray's Inn, his father, then MP for Scarborough, had suggested to its Common Hall, his electors, that Whitby would benefit from a strong harbour pier like theirs. Scarborough's medieval timber and stone pier had become derelict in the 1540s and then rescued from extinction 20 years later by a grant from Queen Elizabeth of £500. However, after a great sea storm of 1614 had punched holes in it, a parliamentary order had guaranteed the pier's survival and permament endurance. After petitions from almost every East-coast port that Scarborough harbour was an indispensable place of refuge for the growing number of colliers sailing between Newcastle and London, Parliament agreed to a levy on this traffic to finance its vital pier. Since Whitby by 1621 had a coal trade even greater than Scarborough's and potentially a safer haven, presumably Sir Richard had made out a similar rescue case for his own port. However, Scarborians had never been known to grant favours to Whitby, particularly when such favours might be self-damaging to their own commercial interests. In the bluntest terms, Scarborough's ruling burgesses told Sir Richard that he could not count on their support.[34]

In his letter Hugh was trying to disguise his own vital interest for fear of upsetting his electors. He understood well enough the native hostility of his constituency town to his home town and therefore minimised any threat that Scarborians might feel. His father had spoken only of a new pier at Whitby whereas Hugh wrote of "repaireing the Peer". And both to engage sympathy and to allay worries of competition, Hugh described Whitby as "a poore towne". Finally, Hugh was at pains to emphasize that Whitby's petition came from that "towne and country" and that he was merely the conduit "doeing publicke and good service" by carrying it to London. There was no hint in the letter that a pier at Whitby, new or repaired, would serve Cholmley's own self-interest.[35]

Memories are notoriously fallible and self-misleading and the story as told by Sir Hugh about this episode in his memoirs 30 years later was very different. If he ever presented the petition from Whitby nothing at the time came of it. After Parliament was sent packing in June 1626, Hugh withdrew from all public affairs and devoted himself, in his words, to his own "perticuler profitts". Only when his estate was safe from bankruptcy did he return in 1632 to the subject of Whitby's pier.

According to his recollection, Sir Hugh went up to London in Easter term 1632, having with some "troble & difeculty" persuaded Whitby's townsmen to petition the Privy Council "for obteyneing some thing for reedifieing the peers at Whitby". However, only with the personal and powerful favour of "the Earl of Strafford" was he able to secure a licence to collect money throughout England and even then he was unable to persuade a single Whitby man to involve himself in the project. Only with the assistance of two "honest neighbours" from Fylingdales, John Farside and Henry Dickinson, was £500 gathered. As a result, the west side pier was built which saved a great part of the town from being flooded and kept the harbour open in bad weather. In short, without his initiative, concern and public spirit, Whitby would never have enjoyed a commercial prosperity which owed nothing to its slothful, indifferent inhabitants.[36]

That was all that Cholmley had to write about Whitby piers and it has been accepted ever since at face value, from Charlton to Pearson, without question or qualification. But as far as the paucity of evidence allows, the truth of the matter is very different from his version. Fragments of the Strafford-Cholmley correspondence reveal that it took many years after 1632 to find the necessary money and finish the pier. In a letter from Whitby, dated 18 May 1635, Sir Hugh told the Lord Deputy in Ireland that he hoped that half of the west pier would be completed by Michaelmas. Serious obstacles had been encountered in the raising of contributions. Some money taken in had been in counterfeit or invalid coin; some English counties had offered nothing at all. To renew the briefs for these counties a new application to the Lord Keeper would have to be made.[37]

Three years later all the money needed had still to be brought in. In September 1638 the Lord Deputy told Cholmley that he had "recommended" to the Lord Keeper "the Peere of Whitby". It seems that six years after the Privy Council had first issued a licence there were still some writs to be issued and others had not been received.[38]

Cholmley's harbour pier was eventually constructed and today forms the backbone of the southern end of Whitby's great west pier, but dispute remains about when, exactly where and how it was built. Charlton's initial contribution to this debate was unhelpful. First, he took Sir Hugh's own account as factual and accepted that his work was on the west side of the river mouth at the "north end of the harbour". Later, he flatly contradicted himself by adding "there is little reason to doubt but that it was the burgess pier that was then built". Now better known as Tate Hill Pier, Burgess Pier is on the east bank of the Esk![39]

As always, the Reverend Dr Young was more circumspect and sensible. He could not be sure of the site of the pier mentioned by Leland in the 1540s and allegedly repaired at great expense by Henry VIII soon afterwards, but in his opinion Sir Hugh had re-built a ruined pier on the west side of the river at the mouth of the outer harbour.[40]

If Cholmley's pier was a reconstruction, at least in part, was it made of timber, of stone, or a mixture of both? If it was on the west side did it continue northwards along the line of the shore or run north-east across part of the harbour mouth? Pearson argued unconvincingly that Sir Hugh had a new wooden pier built, 200 yards long, from Scotch Head, under West Cliff, towards Spa Ladder on the opposite bank of the Esk. Subsequently, one of the anonymous authors of the reputable *Survey of Whitby*, published in 1958, stated, without reference to sources, that in 1632 Sir Hugh had begun to build a new west pier in stone with timber protection in front of it on the seaward side.[41]

In fact, most of the answers were supplied by Sir Hugh's younger son, the fourth baronet, in his "Account of Tangier", published along with his father's memoirs in 1787. Young Hugh was not born until 1632, appropriately the same year that his father made the journey to London to renew Whitby's case "for reedifieing the peers", so he could not have been aware at the time of any pre-war building. However, when the Cholmleys returned to Abbey House in the 1650s we know that young Hugh was with them, though how much of the new pier was finished by Sir Hugh's death in 1657 cannot be said. Yet in 1664 Hugh was appointed Surveyor-General of Tangier with the colossal task of designing and constructing a great sea mole to protect England's new African colony. It seems therefore that by that year Hugh's unique knowledge and experience of sea-pier building at Whitby had given him the reputation of the foremost authority on the subject.[42]

As Sir Hugh junior explained in his 'Account of Tangier", "the pier...at Whitby...was the first that gave me insight into this sort of work". Because at Whitby the pier was pounded by violent high seas it could not be secured simply by dumping stones. Even when heavy blocks of masonry were encased in stout timber frames and bolted with iron the worst storms still made breaches in it. Cholmley's solution was to reduce the full force of incoming waves by planting lines of timber posts in the water to act as breakwaters. It was this successful experiment of his at Whitby that he re-employed on a greater scale at Tangier.[43]

The final part of young Hugh's account established clearly the extent and location of his father's Whitby pier. Having stated that it was 200 yards long, he continued: "the work at Whitby, although it lies with the broadside exposed to an open north-east sea, did never receive any considerable damage but what came from the north-west, against which it seemed in good measure to be land-locked and protected".[44] In other words, before the East Pier was built early in the next century, Cholmley's west pier would have been almost entirely exposed on both sides to the North Sea. However, Sandsend Ness to the north-west gave the pier little protection from the rage of the sea from that direction, so Cholmley's breakwater posts were placed on that outer side where they could not obstruct the harbour entrance.

To summarise: though Sir Hugh's west pier was the long-term result of his enterprise and friendship with the Earl of Strafford, it is doubtful whether it was completed much before his death and ultimately it owed its endurance to the engineering skills and ingenuity of his younger son.

Yet, strangely, no historian of Whitby has thought fit to challenge Sir Hugh's version of events or examine his motives. Why did he go to so much trouble and presumably some expense to construct a west-side pier and why were the burgesses of Whitby so indifferent to his scheme? The truth is that the new pier was intended to protect Sir Hugh's own property interests and plans for the commercial development of the *east* bank of the river Esk. The western riverside where, by the 1630s, there were coal garths, alum houses, landing staithes and boat-building yards, had no need of artificial defences against the open sea: it was adequately sheltered by Burtree Crag and West Cliff. In contrast, the east bank of the river underneath East Cliff was fully exposed to the high tides driven by north-westerly gales. Whitby's commercial elite, the Newtons, Shiptons, Bagwiths and Bushells, had nothing to gain from a west-side pier on their side of the river, whereas the opposite east bank, Kirkgate, Sandgate and Bridgegate and the site of the new market, were all Cholmley territory. Much of the east side was still worthless mudflat and sandbank: if guaranteed security from the highest tides, it was ripe for development. Significantly, John Farside and Henry Dickinson were two of Cholmley's east-side tenant farmers with no direct interest in alum, coal or shipping. So what has been uncritically regarded as benevolent philanthropy was largely motivated by Sir Hugh's material self-interest.

From Charlton onwards all of Whitby's historians agree that Sir Hugh Cholmley moved the town's main, permanent weekly market from the west to the east side of the river. They also agree that about 1640 he had a tollbooth built for the new market which was not replaced until 1788 by Nathaniel Cholmley's "elegant town-hall".[45] Though evidence concerning the tollbooth is thin and conflicting, and the year 1640 seems improbably late, the market transfer certainly took place in Sir Hugh's time and must have been his doing. The question is, What were his motives?

Young conceded that the site of the old market where Flowergate, Baxtergate and Haggleseygate met near to the bridge and St Ann's Staith made perfect sense, but argued that, though the new market place was less conveniently located, it suited the demands of a growing population. Whitby had outgrown its small, medieval market. An alternative explanation, less complimentary to Sir Hugh, is that except for the upper end of Flowergate, the Cholmleys had few remaining properties in west-side Whitby, which was dominated by the port's commercial and ship-building families such as the Newtons and the Wigginers. By 1638, Sir Hugh had only one messuage left in the old market place, whereas the new site was entirely his.[46] Since the new market stalls and shambles would now be on his land he would receive rent from them as well as dues as lord of the manor. Moreover, the Cholmley estate, now mostly in Whitby Laithes, Stainsacre, Hawsker and Fyling, would be better served by an east-side market for its butter, cereals, meat and fish. So much for Cholmley altruism.

The most ill-informed, though often repeated, claim made for Sir Hugh has been that he was responsible for the construction of a new (or even the first) bridge over the river Esk at Whitby.[47] In fact, Whitby has had a bridge at about the same place where the river channel narrows since at least the fourteenth century and probably long before. Since there were early settlements on both sides of the lower Esk and the Abbey had land and possessions on the west as well as the east bank, it would have been very surprising had there not been a permanent crossing centuries before Sir Hugh came on the scene. As early as 1327, a burgess of Ravenserodd referred in his will to ten shops "at the bridge foot of Whitby".[48] By 1351, the bridge was old enough to need repairs: in that year a royal charter authorised the collection of tolls to finance its maintenance. Significantly, the grant was given not to the abbot but to the "King's beloved bailiffs and proved men of the towne of Whiteby".[49] Significant also was the assumption that the bridge was sufficiently substantial to carry cartloads of produce not merely horses and pedestrians. Ten years later, another grant described the bridge as "lying across a certain arm of the sea leading itself through the middle of the town". Similar grants of toll to pay for the upkeep of the bridge were made in 1371, 1383 and 1391.[50]

During the fifteenth and early sixteenth centuries, it was the custom at Whitby to bequeath money for bridge repairs. For example, before and immediately after the Dissolution, a succession of members of the Conyers family, Christopher, Thomas, Gregory and James, all left substantial bequests "to the repair of Whitby Brig".[51] In the meantime, the Statute of Bridges of 1531 had made each county responsible for its own bridges. Bridge surveyors were chosen from local men and justices of the peace were authorised to levy rates to pay for bridge maintenance. During Elizabeth's long reign, at least £128 was raised in the North Riding for the bridge at Whitby, yet by 1608 it was said to be "in great ruin and decay". It was no longer a question of maintenance: the bridge had to be re-built before it fell down. Justices sitting at the Helmsley sessions in July asked the question: "Who oght truely to beare the charge thereof?". Amongst them that day was Sir Richard Cholmley and no doubt his reply was that the whole of the Riding had to pay: the bridge was not Whitby's or his liability.[52]

Accordingly, at the next quarter sessions, held at Malton in October 1608, with Sir Richard again present, it was agreed by the Bench that the North Riding would raise £110 for a new wooden bridge at Whitby. Altogether 60 oaks were used and the cost rose to £140. Assisted by four leading Whitby burgesses, Sir Richard accepted responsibility for the future upkeep of the new bridge.[53]

Sir Richard might have accepted responsibility, but he abused it and his son, Sir Hugh, neglected it. In 1629, five Whitby men petitioned the magistrates sitting at Helmsley against Sir Richard's misbehaviour. They alleged that he had ousted their two elected bridgemasters, put his own men in their places, who had then handed over the tolls and rents to their master. The sums involved were not inconsiderable: shops and houses on the bridge yielded rents of £5 a year; tolls raised another £6; and land bequeathed to the bridge was worth another ten shillings.[54] Sir Richard's claim to the rents was strongly denied by all the witnesses called before the next sessions at Thirsk in April 1629: he was clearly in the wrong. The bridge did not belong to the lord of the manor: it had been "lately built at the charge" of the town and the county. Nor did Sir Richard have the right to appoint bridgemasters: they were chosen by Whitby's burgesses to collect and spend the tolls for the benefit of the bridge.[55]

Matters did not improve when Sir Hugh replaced his father on the North Riding Bench. In 1634 Whitby bridge was reported to be "very ruinous and in great decay"; it could not be crossed "without great danger to life". Yet, neither as magistrate nor as lord of the manor, did Sir Hugh fulfil responsibility for bridge safety and repairs. The same description as that of 1634 occurred again in 1640 and 1642.[56] Time and time again the North Riding Bench had assigned money for repair work but either it went uncollected or it was misspent. In 1629, Sir Richard's theft of bridge income was explicable if inexcusable: he was drowning in debt. But his son, who claimed to have mastered his inherited debts, might have done something for Whitby's vital artery. The truth was that Sir Hugh did not care much for Whitby's west side: his interests and plans were concentrated on the opposite bank.

Whitby's historians might well proclaim Sir Hugh Cholmley as the town's greatest benefactor, yet there is plenty of evidence that contemporary residents thought otherwise of him and his family. Whitby's alum lobby, for instance, regarded the Cholmley lordship as a major impediment to its enterprise and profit.

Unlike the royal corporation of Scarborough, which controlled most of the borough's commercial and judicial affairs, Whitby was one of the five mesne towns in

156

the North Riding with only the slightest autonomy. For centuries past, Whitby had been under the abbot's thumb; after the Dissolution it answered to his secular successors, the Cholmleys. Even when a Cholmley sat in the House of Commons, he represented Scarborough, not its chief rival Whitby, which had no separate say in Parliament. After Sir Hugh stood down, in the Parliament of 1628-9 Whitby lost any claim to representation: Scarborough borough's Members, were Sir William Constable of Flamborough and John Harrison, one of its own merchants.[57]

As a result, in January 1630, "the burgesses and commons" of Whitby presented a petition to King Charles. They pointed out that Whitby was an "ancient borough and haven town". For hundreds of years it had been a port of refuge and a great fishing town and in more recent times it had become indispensable for "the forwarding of His Majesty's alum" and many other commodities from its hinterland to London. However, "of late years", the port was much decayed and in danger of ruin because its inhabitants did not have the power "to make ordinances and wholesome laws within themselves for the well ordering of their town and river". There was no mention of the need for a new quay or pier.[58]

The petitioners did not refer specifically to the Cholmley lordship, but resentment of it was implicit in every word. In effect, the petitioners were asking the Crown for the liberties and privileges of a royal borough which would have swept away the irksome and restrictive control exercised by the lord of the manor and replaced it with a governing body of elected burgesses. If the petition had been granted in full, the Cholmleys would have been dispossessed of their courts, their jurisdiction of the river and the harbour, and all the seignorial rights once held by Whitby's abbots and transferred by the Crown to Sir Richard Cholmley in 1555. Instead of the lord of the manor's chosen 24 burgesses, the petitioners asked to be governed by their own elected aldermen, eight burgesses and 16 assistants. They also asked for the exclusion of North Riding magistrates and the right to choose their own justices with power to commit offenders to the town gaol. As inducement, the Crown was offered an annual fee-farm rent of 20 nobles or £6 13s. 4d., a paltry sum compared with Scarborough's payment to the Treasury of £40 a year.[59]

Since it was published in full more than a century ago in Gaskin's *Old Seaport,* the Whitby petition of 1630 is well enough known. Yet neither Gaskin nor his successors appear to have appreciated the significance of the petition and in particular its connection with the alum industry.[60] Five days after the receipt of the petition in London, a certificate in its support arrived there signed by Sir Thomas Brooke, William Turner, Edward Smythe, George Lowe, Sir Thomas Jones, John Coventry and Thomas Russell. With one possible exception, all seven signatories were directly involved in the alum industry.[61]

The immediate reaction of Whitehall to the Whitby petition was predictably favourable. The Crown had its own financial stake in the alum industry and therefore in the port of Whitby. Lord Keeper Coventry and Attorney-General Sir Robert Heath recommended to Charles that incorporation should be granted to the town. They did not warm to the idea that Whitby should be independent of the jurisdiction of the North Riding, but otherwise they agreed that its port, river, courts and prison should be under locally-elected burgess control.[62] Consequently, in May 1630, the King wrote to the Attorney-General authorising him to proceed with the grant of incorporation. He was instructed to insert a clause in the charter exempting Whitby townsmen from county jury service and licensing them to purchase land in mortmain up to the value of £40.[63]

The alum lobby had won and the Cholmleys had been dealt a mortal blow - or so it seemed. Yet, for reasons which are unrecorded, nothing more was heard of Whitby's incorporation. No letters patent were issued. Whitby remained securely under the thumb of Sir Hugh Cholmley. Though there is no concrete evidence even to suggest it, Sir Hugh's champion and rescuer on this as on other later occasions was probably Thomas, Viscount Wentworth. The two were now close friends, distant relatives and political allies. In December 1628 Wentworth had been appointed Lord President of the Council in the North and less than two years later he had entered the Privy Council, the inner circle of royal advisers. More to the point, only a week after the King's letter to his Attorney-General, Wentworth had received from the Crown a promise of a future lease of the north Yorkshire alum works.[64]

As revealed in a case quoted by Gaskin from Exchequer Depositions at York at Michaelmas 1635, the ancient form of Whitby's unreformed government by county and manor courts did in fact handicap its commercial progress. Only 24 burgesses were permitted to buy and sell goods brought into the port by sea and all 24 were chosen by the lord of the manor. All other residents of Whitby were allowed to buy only for their own use and not to trade.[65] The case at York had arisen because one of the "commonalty" of Whitby, Francis Winn, though a resident gentleman, was not one of the privileged 24 and was therefore forbidden to trade in seaborne goods.[66]

In medieval times and for two or three generations after the Dissolution, Whitby's maritime trade, apart from fishing, was probably so insignificant that two dozen merchants were sufficient to handle it. However, since the advent of the alum industry in the second decade of the seventeenth century, anachronistic custom must have become an intolerable strait-jacket on Whitby's commerce. And out-of-date regulation hampered more than just the alum business. For instance, by the 1630s Whitby had become the county's biggest exporter of butter to the capital and there were many cases brought before the North Riding sessions of Whitby men accused of buying and selling this commodity illegally. Several of these illegal traders of butter were prominent Whitby merchants with names such as Newton, Wigginer and Shipton.[67]

Unfortunately, no records of Whitby's manor courts have survived for these years. The Court Leet, held twice a year after Easter and at Michaelmas, is unreported before 1684; the proceedings of the Court of Pleas are extant only from 1676; and Fyling's court rolls date only from 1681. The two Whitby courts, which were often held together, were presided over by the Cholmley steward and both had juries of 15, or not fewer than 12, all members of the town's 24 burgesses chosen by the Cholmleys. Therefore, in the absence of such potentially rich documentary evidence, dependence on a scattering of quarter sessions is unsatisfactory but unavoidable.[68]

For what they are worth, quarter sessions records indicate that whatever Sir Hugh's relations might have been with the people of Whitby, his father made many enemies there. As early as 1606, the North Riding Bench was told that Sir Richard, himself one of the justices, had been publicly insulted by a Whitby trader called John Boyes. The court ruled that it was "not fitting that such contemptes and abuse committed by inferiour persons against men of his authoritie and place should escape unpunished..." John was put in Whitby stocks for a whole market day.[69]

158

Richard Wigginer was another Whitby merchant who quarrelled with Sir Richard. In 1608 he was also condemned to the stocks for accusing the lord of the manor's son of "injustice and partiality". When arrested he had declared that Sir Richard "might as well bind all the men in the towne" since "he did it for no other cause but for getting of fees". Wigginer was ordered to go down on his knees and beg Sir Richard for his forgiveness. Twenty years later, Richard Wigginer was one of the signatories of a petition against Sir Richard, accusing him of stealing Whitby bridge rents and tolls.[70]

Several members of the Noble family nursed grudges against the Cholmleys. William testified on behalf of Sir Thomas Hoby against Sir Richard in their dispute concerning rights in Whitby Strand.[71] John, a tanner by trade, was accused of unlicensed brewing and contempt of the Court Leet. When Sir Richard's notorious bailiff, William Heron, came to arrest John, his wife Jane assaulted him. Even after John's death, Jane Noble and her daughters continued to defy the Court Leet. Finally, at the Helmsley sessions in January 1637, James Cholmley, one of Sir Hugh's many "cousins", accused the three Noble females of having threatened him and his children with "bodily violence".[72]

So did Sir Hugh Cholmley do anything good for the inhabitants of Whitby? One of the more modest and credible claims made on his behalf concerns the New Gardens.

In 1652, during his last, lengthy stay with his wife at Abbey House, Sir Hugh enclosed an area of the Cholmley demesne in the Great Park on the north side of Spital Vale. This piece of land is still called New Gardens. No documentary confirmation of this event has been found, but there remains an inscription on its north boundary brick wall which reads:" I Sr Hugh Cholmeley Kt & Barronet & Elizabeth my deare wife (daughter to Sr Will: Twysden of Great Peckham in ye county of Kent, Kt & Barronet) built this wall & planted this orchard. Anno Domini 1652". Below it are the arms of the Cholmley and Twysden families and, now almost entirely eroded, the lines:

Our handy worke like to the Frutefull tree
Blesse thou o Lord; let it not blasted bee.

Several commentators have contended that Sir Hugh's purpose in enclosing and planting this protected site was to provide the undernourished people of Whitby with fresh fruit and vegetables.[73] If this was true and not merely wishful, then the Cholmleys were making a wise, considerate and humane gesture. If, on the other hand, Sir Hugh and Lady Elizabeth, who came from the garden county of England, intended the New Gardens to supply the kitchen and table needs of Abbey House, only half a mile away, and to sell surpluses from it in their Saturday market, then they were acting out of sound self-interest. In 1652 it is unlikely that they were aware of the nutritional value of five daily portions of fruit and vegetables. As in other cases where motives are unfathomable, altruism and self-interest were probably both at work. In his memoirs Cholmley never referred to the New Gardens.

It has been implied, though never explained how, that Sir Hugh's re-building and enlargement of Abbey House during the 1630s benefited Whitby.[74] Presumably, the underlying implicit assumption is that the work on the house and grounds must have provided temporary employment and income for many local masons, carpenters, plasterers, plumbers, gardeners and so on. Also, if Sir Hugh's household, or "ordnarely famuly", as he called it, then expanded to as many as 30 or 40 and, with summer guests added, to perhaps 50 or 60, this number must have included and required a large number of domestic servants locally-recruited.[75]

Yet it could hardly be argued that Sir Hugh's purposes were mainly to create employment for the locality. After many years in the cramped quarters of Abbey gatehouse and in the damp rooms of Fyling Hall, Cholmley wanted a conspicuous residence that demonstrated his solvency and elevated status. The new Abbey House was meant to show off the Cholmleys, not to serve the residents of Whitby; if they benefited that was an incidental by-product not an exercise in philanthropy. In his memoirs Sir Hugh made no attempt to disguise his pride that he lived in a house and grounds "more then all [his] Ancestors" and "in a handsome & plentyfull a fashon … as [any] gentleman of my ranke in all the country". Having once been perilously close to ruin, he now employed a full-time domestic chaplain and "a Porter who merely attended the gates".

The only direct evidence of Cholmley charity is also derived from Sir Hugh's memoirs. "Twice a weeke," he wrote, "a certaine number of old people widdowes or indigent persons were served at my gates with bread and gud pottage mad of beefe." In case his readers should find reference to such generosity as too pious, Cholmley excused himself by explaining that he hoped that this tradition would be continued by his descendants.[77] As successors to the abbots of Whitby, Sir Hugh believed that his family had inherited an obligation to dispense alms in the monastic tradition. If he needed any reminder of this medieval custom, the field between Abbey House and Whitby town was, and still is, called Almshouse Close.

Whether Sir Hugh's foundation of a correction house in Whitby was further proof of his charitable concern is less certain. Correction houses were agencies of stern social control and sources of cheap labour, not merely refuges for the destitute and disabled. Again, the probability is that Sir Hugh's motives were mixed.

A poor house is thought to have existed in Whitby under the patronage of the Cholmleys as early as the seventeenth century, but no documentary trace of it has been discovered. The poor-rate records for Whitby go back only as far as 1697 and, according to them, the town had no pauper or workhouse until as late as 1726-7. The Seamen's Hospital on the east side of the river for "distressed and decayed" mariners and their dependants was founded in 1675-6 and financed and run by the town's burgesses who were masters and owners of the port's shipping. The Cholmleys appear to have played no part in its establishment.[78]

The first reference to Whitby's house of correction is to be found in an order of the North Riding justices issued at Malton in July 1636 when Sir Hugh was one of them present. The order stated that "a multydute (sic) of poore" had been created when "the trade of fishing failed" during the winter months in the four neighbouring parishes of Whitby, Lythe, Sneaton and Hinderwell. Since the only county poorhouse was then at Richmond, too distant and too small to accommodate so many new paupers, another was to be set up "neare them".[79]

The two magistrates authorised to establish this new house of correction in Whitby were Sir John Hotham and Sir Hugh Cholmley, but it was only the latter who seems to have been involved. In a very short time, by Michaelmas 1636, the house was already open and growing so rapidly that its master's salary was doubled and the whole of the North Riding, not just the original four parishes, was required to contribute to its upkeep.[80]

It was due mainly to Sir Hugh that Whitby got its house of correction so promptly and cheaply. The building was converted property on one of his burgage tofts on the west side of upper Flowergate.[81] The first order for a levy of £200 would have been an unsupportable burden on the four impoverished parishes, and Cholmley seems to have saved his countrymen from carrying the entire costs. In fact, the four parishes raised £55 for "convenient stocke" and the remainder, including the master's salary, became the liability of the whole Riding.[82] Whether Cholmley charged the county rent for the use of his property is not recorded. After the house was closed in 1658 his son, Sir William, sold one-thousand-year leases on the land and buildings for £95.[83]

Whitby's house of correction had a brief life. Shortly after Sir Hugh's return from exile in 1649, the house in Flowergate was vacated and its stock and furniture removed to a new house of correction at Pickering.[84] The reasons for this transfer were political, not economic. The Whitby area had not recovered its prosperity and Pickering had not abruptly succumbed to destitution and crime. Once Sir Hugh had been removed from the scene by his royalism and defeat, the house at Whitby lost its patron and its purpose. Hotham was dead and Cholmley would never again become a North Riding magistrate. Pickering was preferred because this was now the seat of the new political regime in the region under the republican leadership of Luke Robinson, who had also replaced Sir Hugh as one of Scarborough's MPs. If there had been an alarming rise in unemployment and distress in Whitby during the winter of 1635-6, it was not caused by the "failure of fishing". Winter was never the time for fishing. In fact, these were bad months when seaborne and local trade in such commodities as butter, coal and alum were seriously interrupted by the Dutch-Spanish naval war fought in the North Sea and yet another visitation of plague, both temporary "nuisances".[85]

In all the many deferential tributes to Sir Hugh Cholmley there have been none to suggest that he was responsible for improvements to local roads; yet such a claim carries far more weight than most of the others that have been made for him. Sir Hugh first sat on the North Riding Bench in January 1632 which coincided with a petition from Robin Hood's Bay complaining that its coastal road was being constantly flooded and eroded by the sea. George Conyers, Henry Dickinson and John Farside, all tenants and associates of Sir Hugh, were each allowed six pounds by the court to mend the protective sea wall.[86] From then on, hardly a year passed without some complaint being made about the poor state of public highways in Whitby or Fyling parishes. In 1634, the main Whitby-Hawsker road was said to be in "such decaie as that his Majesties subjects cannot pass that waie without great danger".[87] Subsequently, the people of Whitby were threatened with a fine of ten pounds if they failed to repair the road immediately.[88] Four years later, Sir Hugh was on the Bench when both Whitby town and Fylingdales were censured at the sessions for neglecting their highways.[89]

When Sir Hugh wrote in his memoirs: "The country beeing destitute of a Justice of peace I put my selfe in to the commission of peace" and later, "The country suffering much for want of a Justice of peace there not beeing any with in 12 miles of Whitby", one of the issues he must have had in mind was the unsatisfactory condition of the public roads in his neighbourhood.[90] However, there is no evidence that during his time on the North Riding Bench these roads were actually repaired. For example, 18 months after they had been threatened with punishment, the townspeople of Whitby had still not mended the north end of Kirkgate and were duly fined ten pounds.[91]

All that can be said with certainty is that the roads mentioned in the North Riding court reports crossed and served the Cholmley estate, so that Sir Hugh had everything to gain and nothing to spend by insisting on their maintenance. Here again was a happy coincidence of public service and self interest. Even Kirk Lane, or "Donkey Road" as locals still call it, which runs down the very steep East Cliff from Abbey House grounds to Tate Hill and the north end of Kirkgate, was maintained by the inhabitants of Hawsker and Stainsacre, not by the Cholmleys who had most to gain by its good condition. The best that can be claimed for Sir Hugh on the matter of public highways is that in his role as county magistrate he insisted that parishioners performed their statutory duties.[92]

Finally, there is still a common misunderstanding in Whitby that Sir Hugh Cholmley's long leases, amounting in effect to sale of freeholds, opened up the town's river fronts to occupation and commercial development. Part of the explanation for this fundamental error rests on a gross exaggeration of Cholmley property possession and Cholmley economic enterprise before the 1630s.

Ever since Lionel Charlton's pioneer history of Whitby was published in 1779, local assumptions about the town's past have been determined, inevitably, by both the patchiness and the partiality of the surviving documentary evidence of it. Most of the historical information about Whitby's property since the Dissolution was, and still is, drawn from the surviving records of the Cholmley family. As a result, the influence and importance of the early Cholmleys in general, and Sir Hugh senior in particular, in Whitby's history have been greatly exaggerated at the expence of the experience of other families and factors.

In Whitby's case, as elsewhere, it was conveniently concluded that in the absence of other readily-available and accessible sources, no evidence other than that concerning the Cholmleys had been overlooked. For example, Charlton assumed that Baxtergate was unoccupied waste until the late sixteenth century because he could find no reference to it in Cholmley deeds before that time. Young made fewer errors of this kind because Cholmley papers were not put at his disposal and he had to search out alternative sources.[93] Atkinson's mistakes were the least excusable since he had the most plentiful sources and yet made poor use of them. Though he was the first of the locality to consult the abundant Dissolution documents, principally the *Valor Ecclesiasticus* and the accounts of the Augmentation Office, unlike Young, he assumed wrongly that even as late as 1539 all the land in Whitby town belonged to the Abbey. If Charlton had depended too heavily on the Cholmley archive, to which he had privileged access, Atkinson was totally at the mercy of the official state papers. For instance, because he could not find reference to "Sandgate" in the Ministers' Accounts, he concluded that in 1540 it did not exist! In its place, on his map of Whitby c.1540, he substituted "Greffergate", even though he must have known that the town never had a house of Grey Friars. In fact, the "Greffergate" named in the Ministers' Accounts was in Scarborough, not Whitby! Atkinson openly acknowledged that there were many "old deeds, old leases, old memoranda, old plans or maps" which he had not examined, yet this did not deter him from publishing a town map complete with street names and property boundaries, as "it certainly was" in 1540.[94]

Atkinson's over-estimate of Abbey lands and his underestimate of Whitby's size have together seriously misled subsequent writers. In broad, simple terms, like Charlton before him, though not so extravagantly, Atkinson believed that Whitby town had been little more than what its monastery had made and owned of it; that the Dissolution was therefore an economic disaster to the town and port; and that due to the patronage, foresight and enterprise of the first Sir Hugh, Whitby's prosperity and prominence were restored after a century of decline and decay.

If Sir Hugh was only a latecomer to Whitby's most important alum industry but an indirect beneficiary of it, he seems not to have engaged directly in any other local industry, except corn-milling and salt-panning. He was not a ship builder or a ship owner. In 1548, Sir Richard, the "great blacke knight of the North", did not live in Whitby, yet he owned there a five-man fishing boat of 28 tons called the *Margaret*.[95] But there is no evidence seen that his great-grandson, who lived above the port, was a shareholder in fishing boats or carrier ships. This is most surprising since virtually all the well-to-do residents of Whitby, not just mariners and boat-builders, and some of quite modest means, had investments in local shipping. It seems that contemporary Whitby families, with names such as Haggas, Wigginer, Newton, Bagwith, Bushell and Shipton, and not the Cholmleys, were the ones who invested and took their risks in Whitby's maritime commerce.[96]

Secondly, the former Abbey properties bought by Sir Richard in 1555 constituted only a part, albeit a major one, of the town on both banks of the river. After 1555, no more land in Whitby town came into the hands of the Cholmleys. On the contrary, after that high point, the number of tofts and crofts belonging to the Cholmleys was steadily eroded. What Hugh inherited from his father in the 1620s was much less than what his great-grandfather had bought. In 1540, the Crown had annexed 90 cottages from the Abbey in Whitby town; in 1626, the Writ of Extent listed only 56 tenants of Hugh's father living there.[97]

Of all the former religious properties in Whitby, the Cholmleys eventually acquired only those that had belonged formerly to the abbot; the others were annexed by the Crown. As late as 1586, Queen Elizabeth gave five burgage tenements, two houses, two closes of meadow and a garth, all in Whitby town, to an officer in the Court of Augmentations. In 1599, these valuable but unidentified properties passed to John Radcliffe. None of them had ever been part of the Cholmley estate; all of them were former chantry or guild possessions. Similarly, a deed of 1624 reveals that a cottage and garth on the north side of Baxtergate had once belonged to Grosmont priory and never to a Cholmley.[98]

As far as Baxtergate was concerned, the Newtons of Bagdale Hall had a greater property stake there than Sir Hugh. Only six domestic plots can be positively identified in Baxtergate which were once part of the Cholmley inheritance (nos. 9, 12, 22, 39, 40, and 48), and all of them were sold by Sir Hugh. At the end of his tenure, all he held in this area of the west side was the old horse mill behind Blackwell Staith; the rest belonged to a variety of tradesmen, merchants, mariners, shipbuilders and the schoolmaster.[99]

Other occupied properties on the west side of Whitby were also conspicuously free of the Cholmleys. They appear to have owned little land on the north side of Flowergate between Cliff Lane and St Ann's Staith and the full length of south side Flowergate from Skate Lane top down to Golden Lion Bank is almost entirely absent from the Cholmley lease book. During Sir Hugh's lifetime the tofts and long garths running down steeply from Flowergate to Baxtergate were held mostly by Whitby's leading merchant families such as the Newtons, Wigginers, Bowers and Mersingales. In the sharpest contrast, west of Cliff Lane in uppermost Flowergate was nearly all Cholmley's until the avalanche of sales in the 1630s.[100]

St Ann's Staith and its continuation northwards along Haggleseagate was also not part of the Cholmley town estate. Only four properties along this river front are recorded in the Cholmley lease book: Isaac Newton bought their old coal garth in 1638 (no.27); William Dodds paid £24 for the Well garth below Burtree (Buttery) Crag three days later (no.26); John Woodhouse paid £61 for the burgage tenement fronting St Ann's Staith in 1639 (no.30); and it cost William Pearson £20 for a Cholmley stable on half a toft at the south end of Haggleseagate later that same year (no.44). Yet this same stretch on the west bank of the Esk was already well settled and usefully employed. James Strangeways, lord of the manor of Sneaton, had a "mansion house" fronting St Ann's Staith which was still there in 1642. The Crown also owned property here held by Henry Awder, a compass maker, and Henry Pearson, a stringlayer or maker of ships' ropes.[101]

Througout Sir Hugh's lifetime, the south side of Baxtergate running down to Walker sands was a hive of growing industry and enterprise. Next to the Cholmley horse-mill near Blackwell Staith was a neighbourhood of houses, taverns and river side storehouses known as the Callis. In 1607, half of the Callis was bought by Christopher Newton, and the other half by another local merchant, John Glover. By 1638 they had both been bought out by the alum leaseholders, William Turner and George Lowe, two of the signatories of the Whitby petition of 1630. Subsequently, this valuable site was sold to John Turner of Kirkleatham, another business man deeply engaged in the alum industry.[102]

An inventory of the goods of James Harrison, the coble-wright from Robin Hood's Bay, who had bought a toft and a half on the south side of Baxtergate in 1617, suggests that the Walker sands alongside Bagdale Beck (The Slike) had become boat-building yards. By 1644, Harrison had a substantial house and a well-stocked workshop on this sheltered frontage.[103]

Other occupants of these south-side tofts which ran from Baxtergate down to Walker sands included a mason, a blacksmith, a mariner and Christopher Bagwith, a prosperous ships' carpenter. Finally, there was Anthony Arundel, who also had extensive estates in Stakesby, Staintondale and at Peak (Ravenscar) and was described as a gentleman of Whitby. Mr Arundel lived in the last burgage tenement in Baxtergate where it joined the foot of Skate Lane (Brunswick Street).[104]

Just outside Whitby's town boundary in the parish of Ruswarp was Bagdale Hall, the oldest, stone-built mansion in the area. Originally, it had been built, owned and lived in by the Conyers family, hereditary bailiffs of Whitby Strand and, notoriously, frequently at odds with the Abbey. The Conyers held farming land in Stakesby, shares in Whitby boats, and several houses and shops in Whitby town. In 1596, Nicholas Conyers sold Bagdale Hall to Nicholas Bushell, the youngest of four sons born to Robert Bushell, a prosperous merchant of Ruswarp.[105] The Bushells had held land, buildings, mills and Esk-river fishing rights from the abbot and probably profited from the Dissolution.[106] In 1601, Nicholas Bushell married Dorothy Cholmley, one of Sir Henry's many younger daughters. The discrepancy in their ages was so great that Lady Margaret Hoby at Hackness thought it fit to record the event at Whitby in her diary: "...we hard also of Mr Busshup mariag to Mr Cholmeles Daughter, beinge about 14 years olde and himself fiftie".[107] The results of their marriage were four surviving children, Browne, the eldest son, born in 1609, Michael, Dorothy and Hester.[108] So Mrs Bushell was Sir Hugh's favourite "Ant Dorothy" who made several appearances in his memoirs and Browne Bushell was to become the infamous privateer who figured so prominently in the civil wars on land and at sea.

However, though Nicholas might have been considered a suitably wealthy husband for a Cholmley daughter in 1601, when he died in his eighties in 1632 he had lost the means if not the title of a gentleman. Leonard Bushell, his elder brother, had inherited much of the Bushell estate including the new Ruswarp Hall, whereas Nicholas had been obliged to sell and sell again mostly to the Newtons. During the 1620s, Christopher Newton and his young son, Isaac, had accumulated a considerable property portfolio in the Whitby neighbourhood. In 1621 from the Cholmleys they had bought Normanby Hall; in 1627 and 1628 they paid more than £600 for Nicholas Bushell's pastures in Ruswarp and Stakesby; and finally, for £1,862, they acquired Bagdale Hall and dozens of closes with it. By that time Isaac had married Hester Bushell and moved into the Hall. Effectively, Browne Bushell was disinherited by a feckless father and had to seek his fortune at sea and abroad as a mercenary in the pay of King Philip of Spain.[109] Consequently, along with the Shiptons, Bagwiths, Wigginers and Haggases, the Newtons had become another powerful, propertied local influence to challenge the overmighty Cholmleys. Significantly, Captain Isaac Newton was the leader of the Whitby militia and mariners who stormed Scarborough in February 1645 and besieged Sir Hugh in his castle.[110] Following his loyal and distinguished civil-war service for Parliament, Isaac Newton became a North Riding magistrate and an early Quaker convert. After the wars there was no reconciliation between Sir Hugh and Isaac and ill-feeling between their families continued well beyond the Restoration.[111]

In short, Sir Hugh Cholmley's personal interest in west-side Whitby was minimal. There the alum industry had transformed its river front into boat-building yards, coal garths, storehouses and landing staithes to serve the works at Mulgrave and Sandsend. There the alum lobby predominanted. In contrast, the east side of the Esk was relatively untouched by industrial and commercial development. From Haglithe under East Cliff southwards to Spital Bridge there were mainly only mudflats and sandbank wastes, all belonging to the Cholmleys. In this context, Sir Hugh's purposeful strategy makes sense. He promoted the west-side pier because it protected his lower east-side possessions against high tide surges of the North Sea. He transferred the weekly market across the river from west to east. He showed no interest in keeping the river drawbridge in good repair. The attempt to deprive him of his lordship rights came from the west-side alum lobby, whereas his allies were east-side farmers and landowners such as John Farside and Henry Dickinson, who also had no investment in coal, ships or alum. When roads needed to be mended, they were on the east-side running through and linking Cholmley properties. The New Gardens were on the east side outside the town boundary in Hawsker. Finally, Sir Hugh's Saltwick alum works reinforced his east-side commitment: to serve them he had a new staith built on wasteland at Spital Bridge on the east side of the upper harbour.[112]

So what remains factually of the grounds on which so many sweeping claims have been made for Sir Hugh Cholmley's vital contribution to the growth of seventeenth-century Whitby? One indicator of Whitby's prosperity during Sir High's lifetime would be demographic, but estimating the town's population during these years encounters several obstacles. Not until the time of the Commonwealth in the 1650s does the parish register distinguish clearly between Whitby town and Whitby parish. The parish of Whitby, which included the townships of Ruswarp, Stakesby, Newholm, Hawsker and Stainsacre, covered an area of 14,000 acres, whereas Whitby town was little more than a mere 78 acres. Secondly, there is no record extant of baptisms, marriages and burials at Whitby parish church until 1608 and none at all for the years of civil war during the 1640s.[113]

Further doubts about the completeness and accuracy of Whitby's parish register arise because of the extraordinary extent of the parish, the poor conditions of its roads, its extreme winter weather, and its daunting steep hills. Whitby's parish church was, and still is, infamously inaccessible even from the town, 199 steps below it. Whitby parish also contained a high proportion of religious nonconformists. In 1627, 25 Catholic recusants were counted there and by 1641 this number had risen to 59. From the 1650s Whitby became a place where Protestant nonconformity and Quakerism found ready refuge. Finally, a significant excess of female over male deaths suggests that many Whitby men were buried abroad and at sea.[114]

Nevertheless, Whitby's parish register, whatever its defects, contains unmistakable proof of population growth during the lifetime of Sir Hugh. The average number of annual baptisms recorded in the second, third and fourth decades of the seventeenth century rose from 45, to 53, to 63. Apart from the plague years of 1635, 1636, 1647, 1648 and 1655, baptisms always exceeded burials. Furthermore, whereas the fertility rate of 15 per hundred households was an urban average at the time, Whitby's mortality rate of 13 per hundred was exceptionally low.[115]

Both the Hearth Tax returns of 1673-4 and the Compton Census of 1676 suggest that the population of Whitby parish had by then grown to 2,500. Half a century earlier it was about a thousand fewer. As for Whitby town, when the Hearth Tax list was drawn up it had 347 households, or about 1,500 inhabitants. Forty years later, in 1713, Whitby town had nearly 500 households or more than 2,000 residents.[116]

If Sir Hugh's purpose was to increase the wealth and enhance the property values of east-side Whitby, population figures suggest that he was successful. The Hearth Tax returns for 1673-4 reveal that the east side was catching up on the west. At that time the west side had 184 occupied homes, 374 taxed hearths and 30 houses with four or more chimneys, whereas the east side's comparable figures were 150, 321 and 22 respectively.[117] Yet by the time of the first surviving poor rate list of 1713, the west bank's households outnumbered the east bank's by 201 to 175.[118]

Indeed, Sir Hugh's sale of long-term leases which reached a peak between October 1638 and September 1640 shows that the east side was already by that time experiencing the benefits of his policy. The 32 conveyances recorded for this two-year period raised £1,183 10s. and 20 of them were for land on the east side of the river. More to the point, all these plots were already built upon and commercially exploited so that the high prices placed upon these tofts and half tofts indicate both their market value and the affluence of their purchasers. Where status or occupation of purchaser are given, there were at least four gentlemen, a clothworker, two tailors, a butcher, a smith and a boatwright. Nearly all were Cholmley's sitting tenants. William Jackson, a clothworker, paid £95 for his plot on the corner of Grape Lane and Bridgegate. At the same time, Sir Hugh was taking advantage of the growing wealth of the west-side merchants, boatbuilders and alum profiteers. Christopher Bagwith, for instance, paid him £80 for his lease in Baxtergate and Robert Mason, a gentleman, found £86 13s. 4d for his site on St Ann's Staith which today is occupied by Woolworth's store.[119]

Sir Hugh's post-war sales of land in Whitby, which raised a more modest £728 on 21 properties, followed the same pattern. All the town tofts sold were already occupied and most were bought by or on behalf of sitting tenants. The buyers who can be identified by occupation included two master mariners, a tailor, a tanner, a smith, a whitesmith and a mason. On the east side, John Wilkinson, the tailor, paid £70 for his Kirkgate property; Francis Garland, a master mariner, £60 for his in Grape Lane; William Ventriss, described as a labourer, £50 for a tenanted toft in Southgate; and Sir Hugh's old friend from Fylingdales, Henry Dickinson, gave him £44 for a half toft on the corner of Southgate and Brewster Lane and £50 more for another on the west side of Kirkgate. Of the commercial properties so described, there was a butcher's shop, a blacksmith's forge, a bakehouse and the former house of correction, now converted to streetfront shop, living rooms behind and above, and a garth at the rear.[120] Only in the final month of his father's life, did William Cholmley sell "waste" land in Whitby, though even Tentergarth, on the west side of Cliff Lane, was already enclosed and shared by eight tenants.[121]

So commercial use and domestic occupation had nearly always preceded Cholmley's sale of long-term leases. Because trade and industry had already created and enhanced property values during the previous three decades, by 1638 Cholmley's tenants and merchant townsmen had the ready cash or credit to buy and Sir Hugh had the incentive to sell. Though his grandfather and father had needed to convert their inherited estate into money, they had been able to sell only farm and moorland in Ryedale and Fylingdales where land values were a small fraction of what Whitby's tofts were worth by Sir Hugh's time. In other words, the Cholmley estate was a principal beneficiary of Whitby's extraordinary economic growth. The Bushells, Shiptons, Newtons, Bagwiths and Wigginers et al were unwitting agents in the rescue of Sir Hugh Cholmley from reduced circumstances or even poverty; it was their capital and enterprise that helped to pay indirectly for his expensive improvement of Abbey House and his "handsome" lifestyle. As far as the alum industry and its by-products were concerned, Sir Hugh reaped where he had not sown until profit was virtually guaranteed. Even then there was no investment in an alum house at Saltwick; to save himself expense in coal and kelp he had the alum liquour shipped to South Shields for evaporation.[122] Nor does he appear to have risked his money in shipping or trade. On the contrary, as lord of the manor of Whitby, Sir Hugh's seignorial strait-jacket was more of an obstruction than a stimulant to the town's commercial activity. In a royal chartered borough like Scarborough, Whitby's residents and investors might well have prospered more than they did under Cholmley's restrictions; and many were aware of the handicap they suffered.

CHAPTER 15

CHOLMLEY'S MEMOIRS

Sir Hugh's most valuable legacy was neither land nor alum works: though his memoirs were intended by him to be read only by his own family, they have become his most enduring, precious gift to historians of the seventeenth century.

After the sudden and shattering death of his wife, Lady Elizabeth, in April 1655, what was left of Cholmley's world fell apart. At that time there seemed no prospect of the downfall of Cromwell's Protectorate and the return of the monarchy. The exile of Charles II in France looked permanent. Sir Hugh had no further wish to live in Whitby and Abbey House and preferred instead the company of his Twysden in-laws at Roydon Hall in Kent. Since there seemed little for him to do or hope for, his thoughts turned increasingly towards his own death and to posterity. By the end of the following year, the first rough draft of his memoirs was almost finished.

Sir Hugh's original intention had been to praise his wife; or, as he explained in a preface, "to imbalme her great virtues and perfections to future generations". However, as he gave more thought to his purposes, the scope of the work widened. To single out only his "deare wife" for commendation would mean excluding or devaluing all those other females in his family who also merited recognition and approbation. He could hardly describe the "prime flower" without reference to "the Garland". Moreover, as he explained, in his time, men had the "greatest honour & reverence ascribed to them" and were "commonly ... the princypall Actors in the seane," so his male forebears could not be left out either. Therefore, what had set out as a dirge, written out of grief and gratitude, developed and expanded into a family history of the Yorkshire Cholmleys.[1]

Though "history" was a word that flowed naturally and easily from Sir Hugh's pen, it was not a word that he chose to describe his own memoirs. When he started to write the final section on his own biography, at first he wrote:"Beeing to write a History of my selfe and my owne life". Then, on second thought, he crossed out "History" and substituted "story".[2] For Cholmley, history was an important subject for serious study and it was about the remote, not the recent, past. Though he wrote nothing of his own reading and we know little of the books in his library, he was clearly proud that Lady Elizabeth's "cheife delight was in her booke, being addicted to reade and well versed in history".[3] Similarly, of his father, Sir Richard, he recorded that he "was noe great scoller yet understood latin and [was] well red in History".[4]

Cholmley's lively awareness of history and the importance he attached to ancestry reflect the contemporary obsession of his gentry class with genealogy and family kinship. Between 1530 and 1666, the years approximately covered by his memoirs, there were no fewer than four major heraldic visitations of Yorkshire. It was an age when rank and precedence were clearly established and respected and society strictly stratified. One of the purposes, therefore, of Cholmley's memoirs was to confirm his distinguished ancestry and describe his illustrious kinship. As the author himself explained, without benefit of punctuation, of his forebears he intended to record their "births matches fortunes and tymes of their deaths ... since there planting in Yorkesheire" because this information might "bee usefull for pedegrees and evidenceing of titles".[5] Even the most remote and tenuous ties of blood and marriage were regarded by Sir Hugh as significant. To him, kinship was a blood bond that conferred both advantage and obligation. As the historian of Yorkshire's gentry during this period has written: "... this concept of clan solidarity was an important factor not only in normal social intercourse but also in public life".[6] In Sir Hugh's own case, for example, the Cholmley-Wentworth connection was the source of great pride and value to him and, when it was broken, of much pain and regret.[7]

Sir Hugh's sharp sense of biological inheritance is evident through his autobiography. He was immensely proud that his male ancestors were tall, sturdy men. His great-grandfather, Sir Richard, had been "tall of stature, and with all big and strong made haveing in his youth a very active able body, bold and stout".[8] Richard's eldest son, Sir Francis, was "a tall blacke man much after the make and proportion of his father, a valliant and complete gentleman in all points".[9] At considerable length, Sir Hugh then listed his own father's exceptional physical features:" He was of the tallest stature of men about the height of his father but slender and well shaped."[10] Later still, he went into further detail: "the skinne of his body was passeing white and of a very smouth graine and he had a most incomparable sweet breath, in soe much at many tymes one would have thought it had carried a perfume or sweet odarifferus smell with it". Sir Richard had chestnut brown hair, curly but not frizzled, grey eyes, a long face with "a handsome Roman nose". He also had "a very wining aspect, a most manly and gracefull presence" and a sweet, strong singing voice, "all of which rendered him favoured amongst the femall sex".[11] In similar glowing terms, Sir Hugh described his half-brother Richard as "a proper man as tall as his father, slender and well shaped ... a kind well natured man and loving trew friend, valliant and ingenious and a good solliscitor in law businesses".[12] Clearly, we are meant to believe that the Cholmleys were pedigree stock.

Not to be outshone, nearly all of the females in Sir Hugh's family had been beautiful. His great-grandmother, Lady Katherine, "was tall and a very beutifull person, of fayre and ruddy complection, her haire light flaxon with a little inclynation to yellow, which she tooke not of the Cliffords whu were blacke but of her Mother being a Percy". Indeed, she was so attractive that her first husband, Lord Scrope, refused to bring her to the royal court lest she fall prey to Henry VIII's lust. The king was so angry that he banned Scrope from his court.[13] Sir Hugh's own mother, Susannah Legard, "was tall something above the middle stature of woemen, slender and well shaped, her haire a light chestnut, her eies gray, a slender well shaped face and though she passed under the notion of a browne woeman she had a very cleare complection booth for white and red, soe that she was by every one accounted very beautifull".[14]

Unfortunately, Sir Hugh refrained from describing his own physical features, except to lament that poor nutrition in his earliest weeks of life had robbed him of that tall, sturdy stature of his forebears which he so envied. Otherwise, "I verely beleive," he wrote, "I should have bene as able a man of body as most in the Nation".[15]

However, genealogy for Cholmley was not only a matter of physical inheritance: he thought that behavioural traits were passed down from father to son. At several points, he implied that his family's men had a strong, natural inclination towards wildness and irresponsibility; that they had short, sometimes violent, tempers; that they were prone to idleness, extravagance and frivolity; and that they were particularly amorous. The one weakness of his great-grandfather, "the great blacke knight of the North", was that he was "exstraordnarely given to the love of woemen", so much so that for a time his second wife, Lady Katherine, banished him from her bed.[16] As for Sir Hugh's father, Richard, at the age of 16 he was so besotted with his 18-year-old bride that he refused to return to Trinity College Cambridge to continue his studies there.[17]

But this Richard's worst weakness was not for women, even though he had an "amerous humeur":[18] Sir Hugh's filial loyalty could not conceal his father's notoriety for "a hauty sperret naturally cholericke", for using "harsh langwidge", and for "an ill custome to sweareing esspetially in his anger or sportts when they went crosse to his mynde".[19] Even more damaging to his family was Richard's extravagance and his addiction to alchemy. Young Hugh was astonished that his father had reached the age of 47 and still believed that pewter could be transformed into gold and was foolish enough to pay charlatans hundreds of pounds for the "phlossopher stone".[20]

Hugh had little to write about his grandfather, Sir Henry, and even less that was complimentary. Henry had at least been wise enough to turn overtly Protestant when to have remained overtly Catholic would have been fatal, but he was "much given to the pleasure of hunting and esspetially with fleet hounds" at the expense of his estate. That he should have died at the age of only 56 as a result of a fall from his horse "at the leape of a hedge" seemed only fitting and perhaps even deserved to his grandson.[21]

In contrast, with the exception of Joane Cholmley, who "over topped" her husband, Francis, and outraged the Cholmleys by burying him in Beverley and then marrying a commoner,[22] all the females in Sir Hugh's family according to him were paragons of virtue as well as stunningly beautiful. Lady Katherine, his great-grandmother, was "of very great wisdome and piety".[23] Susannah Legard, his mother, was "a very vertus relegious woeman, a loving wife and wise and understanding in the mannageing of her husbands affayres booth domesticke and with out doores in his absence". Whether she would have been able to prevent the sale of so many Cholmley lands if she had lived longer was a questionable claim made by her son.[24] And, of course, Sir Hugh had nothing but admiration and praise for his own wife whose death had driven him to take up his pen.

Of himself, Sir Hugh confessed that he had shared or inherited many of the sinful weaknesses of his forebears. He had misspent his youth, wasted his education, and sometimes given way to acts of violent temper even in maturer years. He had been a heavy drinker and gambler; he had neglected his studies for sports such as bowling; he had piled up debts; and even at the age of 17 he had spent his time in "hunting, hawkeing and horse rases" with his father.[25] However, of other unspecified "exstraviganses" he was "temperate".[26] Did he inherit the "amerous humours" of his father and great-grandfather? He does not say.

Finally, are we to believe Cholmley that sometime in his mid-twenties he recognised the foolishness of his ways and became sober, responsible, industrious and public-spirited? There were certainly many influences at this time of his life pushing him towards reformed maturity. First of all, his marriage to Elizabeth at the age of 22 brought him into close contact with a family very different from his own. Clearly, his wife was an improving influence: she was clever, religious, strong-willed and proud, and Hugh was soon devoted her. Indeed, the whole Twysden family came to exercise an influence on him that proved entirely beneficial. No doubt, also, the Yelvertons, another well-educated, puritanical lot, played their part in transforming Hugh from spendthrift play-boy into respectable and respected gentleman. But it was probably the shock of discovering that his father was on the sharp edge of imminent ruin and that he was about to lose his inheritance that jolted Hugh into reformation.

So Hugh's memoirs began modestly as a farewell tribute to Elizabeth Twysden from her bereaved husband, broadened into a family saga of the Yorkshire Cholmleys, and ended with a reformed hero, the author himself. Consequently, the memoir was enlarged into a moral tract aimed at his descendants who he believed were certain to inherit some or all of the family's past failings but might learn better ways from his example. Cholmley's "discourse" was therefore dedicated to his two "dearely bloved sonnes William and Hugh" and their yet unborn progeny. It was meant to be read as a guide, a warning and an inspiration, a sort of private family bible. He took the risk of being accused of casting dust in the faces of his ancestors or defiling his own family nest, but unless the truth was told his work would lack moral value as well as credibility. It was not a matter merely of holding up good examples to be followed: folly had to be exposed and recognised as such if it was to be avoided by future generations of Cholmleys.

Since he had no wish to broadcast his family's weaknesses and failures more widely than was necessary, Hugh's manuscript was not to be published or passed outside the Cholmley circle. Confident therefore that the privacy of his frank revelations would be respected, he was able to "performe the duty [of] a Historian, which is to expresse all things with as much truth and clearenesse as may bee".[27] In short, since no one outside the Cholmleys would ever be allowed to set eyes on his manuscript, he could write freely and critically without fear of being disloyal to his ancestors and relations. The human memory is famously fallible and invariably self-regarding even in the privacy of a diary, but Sir Hugh's memoirs, for these reasons, lack the worst features of most published memoranda.

In obedience to his wishes, Sir Hugh's memoirs remained in manuscript in the possession of the Cholmley family at Whitby and Howsham for the next 130 years. Then, in 1787, Nathaniel Cholmley, Hugh's great-great-grandson decided to publish it along with some of the manuscripts of his great-grandfather, Sir Hugh, the fourth baronet. Altogether the reminiscences of the son, concerning mainly his experience as surveyor-general of the harbour works at Tangier, running to more than 300 printed pages, far outweighed in bulk those of the father, which ran to little more than 90 pages. Nevertheless, because of the public perception that the latter contained matters of far greater historical importance, national and local, than the former, they have received much wider attention. Whereas the greater causes of Sir Hugh the elder eventually triumphed with the restoration of both monarchy and church of England only three years after his death, his youngest son survived only to see his massive and hugely costly works come to nothing. The mole at Tangier, a much enlarged version of Whitby's west pier, was deliberately demolished and Tangier itself was forever abandoned by the English. As for Tangier Cholmley's "Banqueting Hall" on Whitby's East Cliff, a storm blew away its roof and the family left it as a derelict shell.

The lives and works of the two Hugh Cholmleys, the first baronet and the fourth and last, had little in common. Their memoirs, the one short and more or less finished, the other a disconnected collection of lengthy rambling pieces, were published together in the same volume partly because by 1787 the manuscripts were in poor and deteriorating condition and Nathaniel was concerned to preserve their contents in print.

Besides, by 1787, the issues that had so preoccupied and perplexed these two men were now historical and no longer bitterly divisive. More than a century later, no one much cared about the personal and moral dilemmas that had dominated their lives and almost ruined their fortunes.

Nevertheless, Nathaniel respected the confidentiality of the elder Sir Hugh: he had all the manuscripts printed together in one handsome, leather-bound, but private, volume. At his expense, only 100 copies were made. In the words of the *Gentleman's Magazine,* which reviewed the book in 1788, it had been printed "for private use".[28] Most copies, therefore, remained in the possession of the numerous members of the Cholmley-Strickland family and more than two centuries later the 1787 edition is extremely rare and usually quoted or mis-quoted at second hand. For instance, in his book on the social history of early modern England of 1987, J A Sharpe twice referred to the same passage in the elder Sir Hugh's memoirs yet attributed it wrongly to "Sir Richard Cholmely".[29]

It seems more than likely that Lionel Charlton was employed by Nathaniel Cholmley to prepare the manuscripts for the printer, though his name did not appear as editor. Charlton's own *History of Whitby* was published in 1779, eight years before the memoirs, yet it contained a summary of Sir Hugh senior's private work. Also, a significant number of errors in the printed edition of the memoirs, caused by careless or unskilful reading of the manuscript, first appeared in print in Charlton's *History*. For example, when relating Sir Hugh's confrontation with armed Dutch seamen in Whitby harbour, which actually occurred in December 1635, Charlton began by accepting Cholmley's own wrong date of "about June 1637", and then, almost word for word, repeated his account of it. However, where Sir Hugh had written "advised", Charlton substituted "ordered"; where he wrote "I gave him charge", Charlton added "strict" between "him" and "charged"; and for Cholmley's "drink", Charlton preferred "dine". All these minor alterations had the effect of making Sir Hugh's behaviour even braver than he had described himself and suggest deliberate falsification.[30] Other mistranscriptions in the printed edition might well have been the outcome of Charlton's inability to read "the old writing" well.[31]

The earliest printed guide to Scarborough was produced by James Schofield, the town's leading bookseller, and published at York in 1787. Whether Schofield actually saw the Cholmley manuscripts, as he claimed, is most doubtful. He described the work of the elder Sir Hugh as "a curious and valuable remain" and expressed his debt "to the most obliging condescension of Nathaniel Cholmley Esq. ... by whose favour we are enabled to present it to the public".[32] Though here there was no reference to a printed edition of the memoirs, it is clear that Schofield's source was in fact the publication of 1787. For instance, Sir Hugh had strongly condemned leading members of both houses of Parliament who, in the summer of 1642, left London to join the Cavalier court at York. Such men, he wrote, had "ruined booth the King and Nation"; but in Charlton's printed transcription the harshness of "ruined" was softened to "misled".[33] It seems that Charlton was determined to present Sir Hugh as a true Royalist, only temporarily diverted from his natural allegiance by honest misunderstanding: he could never have been a committed Parliamentarian who changed sides to save his skin. As Charlton himself put it in his *History*: "... being deluded with the specious pretence of the Protestant religion being in danger, and that the King's design was to subvert the rights and liberties of the nation, he [Sir Hugh] opposed the measures of the court for some time, but was at length fully convinced that the parliament was resolved not to act honourably with his Majesty...”[34] So Charlton found that “misled” rather than “ruined” suited his view rather than Cholmley’s and Schofield obediently followed suit.[35]

Thomas Hinderwell, Scarborough’s earliest historian, was heavily indebted to both Charlton and Schofield without explicit acknowledgement. All three editions of his history of 1798, 1811 and (posthumously) 1832 quoted lengthy passages from the 1787 publication without reference to it.[36] On one occasion, Hinderwell copied one of Scholfield’s own mistakes. Sir Hugh had been proud to recall that during the siege of Hull in the autumn of 1643 the marquess of Newcastle had given him command of a whole brigade of the Royalist cavalry. These horsemen he described in a marginal note of the manuscript as “a terse of the Army”, meaning a third of it. In Schofield’s Guide, “terse” became “curse” and, until revised to “flower” in the 1832 edition, the word remained “curse” in Hinderwell’s two earlier editions of 1798 and 1811.[37]

George Young followed Charlton with his own *History of Whitby*, published in 1817. There is evidence that this Presbyterian minister and distinguished amateur historian made painstaking preparations before writing his major work. Among the abundant manuscript collection of Whitby’s Literary and Philosophical Society there is a bound notebook into which Young had carefully copied the first 242 pages of the 1787 edition of the Cholmley memoirs. The pages of the notebook are water-marked “C WILMOT 1815” and “C WILMOT 1816” indicating that he had transcribed the text as part of his pre-publication work.

Where he believed the published print to be factually inaccurate or incomplete, Young added his own corrections in brackets and with historical names and events he was invariably right. He knew, for example, that Sir Richard Cholmley (II) had bought the Whitby estate from Sir John, not from “Sir Edward” Yorke[38] that the Hothams lived at Scorborough, not in Scarborough. Where there were blanks in the text, sometimes he supplied the missing information. He knew that the church in Micklegate, York, where many of the early Cholmleys were buried, was dedicated to St John, whereas Sir Hugh had not been able to recall the name.[39]

None the less, like Schofield and Hinderwell before him, Young did not enjoy the advantage of seeing the original Cholmley manuscripts. In his *History of Whitby* he was obliged to rely entirely on his own copy of the printed work of 1787 and his own historical knowledge of its context. That he had taken so much time and trouble to write out his own copy suggests that he had to borrow but did not possess even one of the hundred printed versions. Young’s handicap was therefore the same as Hinderwell’s: the seventeenth-century holographs were still jealously guarded family properties, inaccessible even to reputable historians, and even the printed memoirs were still reserved “for private use”.

Cholmley’s memoirs were printed again at Malton in 1870. This time only the work of the father and not that of the son was offered to the public. In outward appearance this selder volume looks like a cheap reprint. This was the conclusion of the author, T H Brooke, of an Oxford university thesis on Sir Hugh completed in 1937. Brooke found the volume in the Bodleian library, where it is correctly identified in its catalogue, but still managed to misdate it to 1890. However, though this second edition was sold to the public, it seems that only 100 copies were ever printed, along with three superior versions on Whatman’s fine, hand-made drawing paper. Consequently, the Victorian edition is now almost as rare and nearly as valuable as its 1787 predecessor.[40]

The anonymous editor of the 1870 memoirs claimed in the preface that the text was "taken from the original manuscript, in his [Sir Hugh Cholmley's] own Handwriting, now in the possession of Nathaniel Cholmley of Whitby and Howsham". On its title page the book carries the date MDCCLXXVII (1777) which presumably was meant to be MDCCLXXXVII (1787), the year of the first edition. Since Nathaniel Cholmley had died in 1791 and there was no acknowledgement of his publication, such careless claims to authenticity naturally stretch the reader's credulity. Only when the book is examined closely in detail and compared with that of 1787 and with Cholmley's holograph does it become certain that its editorial claims were genuine. Whoever was responsible for the 1870 "reprint" must have seen Sir Hugh's manuscript. At many places, he or she had read the manuscript differently from and more accurately than Charlton had done nearly a century earlier. Only a few examples can be quoted here, but enough, it is hoped, to establish that these discrepancies were deliberate and significant, not accidental or merely trivial.

Usually Charlton inserted Cholmley's marginal afterthoughts into the body of the text; but there was one notable exception which the editor of 1870 noticed and put right. After Sir Hugh had explained that his father and mother had spent seven years with the Legards at Ganton and then, in 1608, gone to live at Whitby, down the left-hand margin of the folio he added the following detail about Sir Richard's estate:

haveing all the demeynes of Whitby Hausker Staneseker
and Southward Howses for present maintnance which were
alsoe his wifes oiynture, And though of good vallew
gave then but small rent ...[41]

Not a word of this additional note was included in the text of 1787, whereas in 1870 these words were printed as a footnote. Unfortunately, by transcribing "then" as "them", the editor missed a key point. Sir Hugh was trying to say that these Cholmley lands were worth far more than the rents charged for them at that time.

Some of the corrections made in 1870 could have been guessed without the benefit of Sir Hugh's holograph. One of the daughters of his grandfather was named as "Hilday" in the manuscript, but became "Kilday" in 1787 and altered to "Hilda" in 1870. The 1870 edition never made the mistake of confusing Scorborough with Scarborough. Cholmley had explained that his third son, Hugh, had been "baptised in the great chamber at Fyleing hall" by "Mr Reming[ton] the Minister then preacher at Whitby". Not happy with "chamber", Charlton had substituted "church", but in 1870 the original word was restored.[42]

Other errors in the 1787 text could have been detected only by careful examination of Cholmley's holograph. For example, describing how his wife was so weak after giving birth to her eldest son Richard, he wrote:"she could not move from her bed to the pallett but as I carried her in my armes". In 1787, "pallett" was unacccountably transformed into "toilet" and rendered correctly in 1870.[43] Similarly, when complaining that impoverishment had driven away his family's supporters, Sir Hugh's own phrase, "this tyme of collaption of friends", in 1787 became "this time of defection of friends" until reinstated as "collaption" in 1870.[44]

However, having said so much in defence of what was clearly not a "cheap reprint", the 1870 edition still contained numerous misspellings of key names. Sir

Hugh's uncle was "Mr Jo. Legard" not "Mr George Legard" who did not exist; he wrote "Sr Will Sayvell", not "Sir William Cayvell", another invention; "Skelton Castle", not "Skilton castle"; and "Pexton Moore", which still exists, not "Paston Moore" or Paxton Moor", which never did. Sir Hugh's memory was fallible, but there is no evidence that he suffered from Alzheimer's disease.

Some printed mistakes were more serious than misspellings. Sir Hugh had written of events in 1649 when he returned home from French exile "tuching the ~~bet~~ erecting an Allome woorke". If he had intended to write "better" he had stopped at the first "t" and then crossed out all three letters. Nevertheless, in both printed texts, we find "touching the better erecting my allum works", though Sir Hugh wrote neither "my" nor "works" in the plural. The effect of these inaccurate transcriptions was to imply that an alum mine already existed in 1649 at Saltwick before Sir Hugh returned to Whitby when there is no evidence elsewhere to confirm this.[45]

Some eighteenth-century editing intended to play down the Catholic commitment of the Tudor Cholmleys also found its way into the 1870 "reprint". Whatever his own anti-Catholic prejudice, Sir Hugh was at least honest enough to admit that in his grandfather's time during the 1590s Abbey House had been a refuge for seminary priests entering the country illegally from the continent.[46] But when he wrote that his great-grandmother had, on her death bed, asked for the "preists" to be put out of the house, the editors of 1787 and 1870 substituted "priest" in the singular. Similarly, though Sir Hugh wrote that three or four Catholic priests at any one time had been hidden, fed, clothed and sent on their missionary way with horses at "Sir Henryes charge", the phrase was altered to "at his ladyes charge".[47] So the blame for harbouring papist clerics became a Babthorpe rather than a Cholmley crime.

Though Sir Hugh never concealed the help he and his wife and family received from his brother after the fall of Scarborough castle in July 1645, the generosity of Sir Henry appeared far greater in the printed than in the manuscript memoirs. What had been written by Sir Hugh as "my good brother Sir Henry Cholmeley had lent mee £200 at my comeing out of the castle" was printed in 1787 and again in 1870 as "Sir Henry Cholmley had sent me 200£".[48] Was "lent" innocently misread as "sent", or was the alteration deliberate?

If the printed memoirs are a little less frank and sometimes more self-defensive than the holograph about the Catholic sympathies of Sir Hugh's family, they are also less "Puritan" in expression. Hugh's own phrase, "if the Lo[r]d Jesus had not bene with mee" in print became "if the Lord had not been with me".[49] Later in the manuscript, "let my heart never forget to prayse the Lord all the dayes of my life" was altered in both printed editions to "Let my heart never forget to pray to the Lord all the days of my life".[50] Since Cholmley's religious outlook is a matter of some importance and debate among historians, such slight but significant changes to his words are not without interest.

No published historian until recently has written at greater length about Sir Hugh Cholmley senior and his family than Robert Tate Gaskin. Charlton's quarto volume gave inordinate space to the medieval history of Whitby and its abbey and disappointingly little to post-Dissolution events. Dr Young's two-volume work was also much concerned with the town's earlier history: the Cholmleys were relegated mainly to a 12-page biographical appendix at the end of the second volume. Even Canon Atkinson, whose knowledge of the area's history and understanding of its available documentary sources were then unrivalled, never wrote a continuous, narrative account of Whitby's past.

Gaskin also did not claim to have written a full history of the town since his *Old Seaport of Whitby* (1909) was subtitled "Chapters from the Life of its Bygone People" and was more biographical than historical. However, in a book of 450 pages, Gaskin devoted as many as 87 entirely to the Cholmleys and more to matters that involved them indirectly. Gaskin was also the first historian to write about Tangier Cholmley in his chapter called "Whitby in Morocco".[51]

It would be reassuring therefore to discover that Gaskin had consulted the Cholmley manuscripts; but his book contains nothing to indicate that he ever saw any of them. Though he had the critical sense not to accept Sir Hugh's memoirs at face value, all his explicit references were to the printed edition of 1787. However, on close examination of his text it is evident that he had used a copy of the 1870 edition without acknowledgement of its existence. For instance, at one point, he noticed a discrepancy between the two printed texts. After listing his father's many attractive physical qualities, Sir Hugh had concluded with the meaningful comment: "all w[hic]h rendered him favoured amongst the femall sex". In 1787, Charlton had changed "favoured" to "famous", but the anonymous editor of 1870 had restored the correct adjective. In Gaskin's own version, "famous" is immediately followed by "favoured" in brackets with a question mark inside them (favoured?).[52]

Nevertheless, unlike the editors of 1787 and 1870, Gaskin's familiarity with the locality and its past saved him from misspelling family and place-names in almost every case, thereby correcting Sir Hugh's errors and omissions. Consequently, even without direct access to the Cholmley manuscripts, a century ago Gaskin succeeded in producing the most accurate rendition of them in print up to that time.

In the late 1930s, when T H Brooke wrote his Oxford university thesis on the memoirs of Sir Hugh Cholmley, he seems to have been entirely at the mercy of the 1787 edition. He dismissed the 1870 version disparagingly as a "cheap reprint" without being aware of its merits. Mistakenly, he also assumed that Sir Hugh's holograph could not be found. He was prepared to accept that it was lost or destroyed or buried in some private family archive. On the other hand, to be fair to Brooke, there was a note of cautious scepticism in his parting comment on the memoirs: "... all attempts to trace the original manuscript have proved vain. According to the possessors of such family records as exist, the memoirs have been 'lost', a rather remarkable fate for such a bulky document."[53] Whether Brooke really did make exhaustive efforts to trace the manuscript(s) cannot be said, but it seems that, like the present author, he received little help or encouragement from the surviving members of the Yorkshire Cholmleys. Consequently, Brooke had no choice but to quote the 1787 edition with only his own minimal corrections as an appendix to his thesis.[54]

Brooke was able to convince himself that the only major inaccuracies in the printed memoirs concerned sums of money, such as debts, incomes, portions, fines and land values. His "irresistible conclusion" was that Cholmley had consistently inflated the figures or that the editor of 1787 had brought them up to match contemporary values. Again, Brooke was mistaken: all but one of Sir Hugh's figures had been printed as he had written them. What Brooke failed to appreciate was that Sir Hugh had sometimes translated values from past into contemporary terms which, with inflation, appeared to exaggerate them. Otherwise, Brooke comforted himself (and persuaded his examiners) with the wishful thought that "the manuscript would probably add nothing to Sir Hugh's account of his own career".[55]

Sometime during the 1950s a manuscript came into the hands of Percy Burnett, secretary and librarian of Whitby Literary and Philosophical Society. He felt certain that it was the original holograph of circa 1656. How he acquired the manuscript and later, after his death in 1972, how it was disposed of, remain unsolved mysteries. Unfortunately, Burnett did not possess a copy of the printed work of 1787 and therefore had to rely on the Society's 1870 "reprint". He also had access to Young's manuscript, though he did not know that it was a perfect copy of Charlton's text. Moreover, though he noted the many discrepancies between the manuscript before him and the histories of Young and Gaskin, he did not appreciate that Sir Hugh's manuscript had been declared "lost" by Brooke in his unpublished thesis.[56]

The document copied meticulously by Percy Burnett more than half a century ago was almost intact: its folios had been bound together in red leather covers which had helped to preserve them. Some of the folios had been trimmed at the edges and had lost their bottom lines of script, but Burnett found that his 1870 edition indicated what words had gone. In a few places there were alterations or insertions in another, later hand, but most of Sir Hugh's own gaps were still blank. No sheets were missing; all of them were legible; the ink had not faded much or spread. Whole sheets had been crossed out, re-written or repeated later, indicating that this was a first rough draft, not a finished, polished work.[57]

Percy Burnett spent the greater part of his productive life copying out primary historical documents concerning Whitby and its neighbourhood. He was an untrained, amateur expert, a self-educated antiquarian, qualified only by high intelligence, inexhaustible industry, patience and long practice. All his work in the keeping of the library of Whitby Literary and Philosophical Society, which runs to more than 70 foolscap volumes, was thorough, painstaking and totally accurate. His attention to the smallest detail was astonishing and admirable; his stamina was extraordinary; and his hand-writing immaculate. All historians of his locality owe him a huge debt. His copy of Cholmley's manuscript, which he recognised as Sir Hugh's holograph, was word for word, letter for letter. He never knowingly changed a pen mark; he rarely made a mistake; he copied everything just as it was written. The absolute reliability of number 4328 in volume 41 of Burnett's huge collection of transcripts is therefore guaranteed.[58]

Some 20 years after Burnett wrote his transcript, the holograph of Sir Hugh Cholmley's memoirs re-surfaced. In September 1976, Professor G E Aylmer, then at York University, and Mr C B L Barr, then chief librarian, examined a manuscript which had been recently bought by York Minster library from a local antiquarian bookseller. To both of them the document seemed to be "the original holograph copy by Sir Hugh ... showing signs of revision", but written on paper and in a script of "the mid-seventeenth century". They decided that the manuscript had been badly treated in its early life, rather crudely repaired, and then bound in red leather covers, probably about the time of the first print in 1787. Gold letters on the outside of the spine misleadingly described the contents as "Memoirs of Sr Hugh Cholmley 1600". Inside the covers were 32 folios of foolscap size written on both sides in a mixture of late secretary-hand and italics. As conclusive proof that this was indeed the same work as that transcribed by Percy Burnett, inside the front cover, in his unmistakable hand, were written the figures "4328", his reference number.[59]

Burnett's perfect transcript had been timely and providential: 50 years older than when he saw it, the manuscript is now in poor condition. Some of Sir Hugh's sheets are now so worn and the ink so faded that it would be impossible to improve on Burnett's transcript, even with the aid of ultra-violet light enhancement. Nevertheless, with the original, albeit decayed, holograph, and with Burnett's meticulous copy of it when it was in better condition, it is still possible to re-produce a faithful, full facsimile of what Sir Hugh wrote at Roydon Hall in 1656. Consequently, in the year 2000, the Yorkshire Archaeological Society published a volume in its Record Series which contained the text of Cholmley's memoirs along with his three memorials on the Civil War.[60]

When in 1937 T H Brooke satisfied himself wishfully that the manuscript which he had not found "would probably add nothing to Sir Hugh's published memoirs," he was a little wide of the mark.[61] Apart from all the many factual inaccuracies, careless misreadings and, more seriously, the deliberate falsifications in Charlton's text of 1787, there was one erased paragraph in Sir Hugh's hand that had never benefited from publication. Immediately before announcing his marriage to Elizabeth Twysden, he wrote:

A little before my leaveing Grayes In, one Mr Lovesesse
a Kentis gentleman brought mee acquainted with my deare wife
by an accydentall meeting in Hide parcke with some other
friends of his. I liked her well as theire was good cause yet
noe Motion set on foote but the suppreame wisdome who
orders all things and disposeth all things haveing determined
it should bee [a ma]tch betweene produced.[62]

At no other place in his manuscript did Sir Hugh even hint that he had met Elizabeth in advance of their wedding. So why did he cross out the whole paragraph? There seems no reason why he should have deleted a passage which expressed his conviction that "the suppreame wisdome" had determined he should marry a Kentish lady who lived 300 miles away from his home. However, suspicion soon gathers that Sir Hugh did not act as censor himself and that the paragraph was deliberately erased by Charlton, the editor. It is the only deleted part of the manuscript that the author did not re-write. And it is the only passage so strongly crossed out by horizontal wavy lines that it has become very difficult to decipher. Sir Hugh's own corrections were indicated by two or three parallel diagonal lines and remain perfectly legible.

So the puzzle remains: why was this passage omitted from both the 1787 and the 1870 publications? As Cholmley himself readily admitted, his marriage was pre-arranged. His father was then desperately short of money and deeply in debt so that Elizabeth's dowry of £3,000 in ready cash was most welcome.[63] The missing paragraph contains nothing that might have embarrassed the Cholmleys or the Twysdens. On the other hand, it is interesting to learn that Sir Hugh believed that the "match" owed its arrangement not merely to two earthly fathers but to some higher planning authority. Whatever his many disappointments and misfortunes, to the end Cholmley was convinced that his life had been determined by the benevolence of "gods providence".

POSTSCRIPT

TANGIER CHOLMLEY

In addition to his literary memoirs and memorials, Sir Hugh Cholmley's legacy also included his younger son of the same name, who has been unfairly overshadowed historically by his much better known father.

The neglect of the younger and the excessive attention and praise given to the elder Sir Hugh date hack to 1787 when Nathaniel Cholmley (1721-91) had their manuscripts printed together in a single volume. Though the father's printed memoirs ran to fewer than a hundred pages and the whole volume was 320 pages long, its title referred only to the former and ignored the greater remainder. Later, in 1870, when a second publication was released, the elder's manuscript alone was printed and his son's work entirely ignored.

Yet the publication of 1787 opened with a preface written by the younger Sir Hugh, the fourth and last Cholmley baronet. Clearly, it had been written about a century earlier and intended to serve as an introduction to a full-length autobiography which was never written or has since been lost. The preface started with Hugh's birth and ended in December 1653 when its author was only 21-years-old. It petered out in a trivial miscellany of letters and poems concerning his fruitless attempt to woo and win a certain Lady Leppington, a friend of the family. If young Hugh had inherited his antecedents' "amorous humour", then it seems that he had less success than they had satisfying it.

This so-called preface of 15 pages was then followed by his father's memoirs, dedicated to him and his elder brother, William. As explained above, these memoirs were written in 1656 at Roydon Hall in East Peckham in Kent, the home of the Twysdens, and not intended to be seen outside the two families. Sir Hugh's holograph was clearly only a rough, first draft and its author died before he could revise or add to it.

After a brief summary of Cholmley family history from the death of the first baronet in 1657 to 1689, the year of the death of his younger son, the next section in the publication of 1787 was headed: "An Account of Tangier". This consisted of three disjointed parts. First, "A Discourse of Tangier", ran to nearly 100 pages, and described in detail, geographically and historically, events there from 1661, when it was acquired by the Crown, until 1672, when Sir Hugh returned to England from his third visit there. This general account was then followed by Sir Hugh's own personal journal for the years 1669 to 1672, in which he recounted his journey from London to Tangier with his wife and daughter by way of France and Spain and his return home by sea. This third visit to Tangier took up 130 pages of text. Finally, in the next 50 pages, Sir Hugh gave an account of his engineering work on the great mole at Tangier "from the beginning unto 1 August 1670".

It appears that all three parts were written separately at different times and consequently there is much repetition and overlap between them. Presumably, Sir Hugh intended eventually to conflate them into one continuous narrative, but a century later the three manuscripts must have remained in their original form. Also, if any of them have survived today they are not in the public domain. A copy of some of Cholmley's journal recounting his overland journey to Tangier was recently discovered by Sir Frederic Strickland-Constable in his mother's knitting drawer, and another distant descendant of Sir Hugh, Richard Marriott of Boynton Hall, possesses a bound manuscript of his Account of Tangier.[1]

Finally, the 1787 printed memoirs contain the texts of seven speeches delivered by Sir Hugh in the House of Commons, all made in 1679 during the time of the Popish Plot and the impeachment of the earl of Danby. They bear no relation to Sir Hugh's other narratives and seem to have been added only as makeweights. The same could be said of the verse Prologue of the Conquest of Mexico, acted at Whitby, Shrove Monday and Tuesday, 10 and 11 February 1683, which brings the volume to an end.

Fortunately, much more of Tangier Cholmley's personal record has survived in manuscript and much of it is still accessible to the curious reader. When he was surveyor of Tangier from 1664 until 1676, Sir Hugh carefully preserved most of the letters which he wrote to and received from his many contacts, friends, relatives and agents. This huge correspondence provides a detailed and thorough picture of Sir Hugh the man and his work at and about Tangier and adds to his later Account of Tangier printed in 1787. Four of Tangier Cholmley's letter-books and his books of accounts concerning the great mole are kept by the North Yorkshire County Record Office at Northallerton.[2]

Moreover, the fourth baronet was a methodical manager of his Whitby estate. For example, before he set out in 1669 on his third journey to Tangier, he arranged that full accounts of the estate should be kept in his absence. As a result, for the years 1670, 1677 and 1687, just before his death, there are written lists of rentals, dealings with individuals and stewards' accounts all copied into foolscap volumes which are also in the care of the County Record Office.[3]

Thirdly, several important documents, which have not found their way to Northallerton, were copied by Percy Burnett and are stored in the library of Whitby literary and Philosophical Society amongst his manuscripts. These documents include a detailed summary of all the money received by Sir Hugh from Thomas Povey and Samuel Pepys, the Crown treasurers, for the city, port and garrison of Tangier from 1663 until 1676. Also in the Burnett collection are other carefully copied pieces such as the will of Lord Teviot, one of Sir Hugh's original partner contractors, Sir Hugh's military commissions and Inspeximus rolls of the Whitby estate dated 1674 and 1679.[4]

In short, there is no justification for the historical neglect of Tangier Cholmley, the fourth and last baronet: the sources of evidence about him and his career that have survived are many and weighty. For his work at Tangier alone, in the words of one of our leading historians, "the man deserves a modern biography".[5] In her brilliant book, *Captives: Britain, Empire and the World 1600-1850,* published in 2002, Linda Colley wrote a lengthy, opening account of England's first, failed African colony and described Cholmley there in glowing terms for his extraordinary but doomed "masterwork" of the great mole. Nearly 500 yards long, more than 100 feet wide, the pier rose 18 feet above the Atlantic low-tide and carried shops, store-houses, barracks and cannon batteries. At that time it was the largest civil engineering structure ever raised by the English. Yet, as Professor Colley also noted, "that strange, maniacal imperial projector and builder" has never featured in the history books and is absent even from the *Dictionary of National Biography.*[6] Even less excusable is Sir Hugh's omission from the new *Oxford Dictionary of National Biography,* published in 2004, two years after Colley's pioneer publication.

Her only explanation for this common neglect was that historians of the British empire have preferred to expunge "early disasters and retreats" from national memory and Tangier Cholmley has been one of the victims of this prejudice.[7]

To add insult to injustice, even when historians have taken notice of Tangier Cholmley, they have not taken the trouble to record his life accurately. At Abbey House, Whitby, in the so-called "banqueting hall" built by Sir Hugh during the 1670s and now "restored" as a museum by English Heritage, several references to him are factually incorrect. For instance, young Hugh is there credited with climbing the spire of St Paul's cathedral. In fact, old St Paul's spire was destroyed by a lightning strike and fire in 1561 and his feat was performed on the outside of the spire of St Paul's school where he was a pupil in the 1640s. Perhaps even less pardonable, in a recent article published in the *Yorkshire Archaeological Journal,* Sir Hugh's dates of birth and death were wrong.[8]

Even in his own time, Sir Hugh was never justly rewarded or appreciated for his loyal service to the country and the Crown. Like many other Royalists he suffered from the amazing ingratitude of Charles II, who frankly admitted that after the Restoration he needed to win over former enemies with undeserved favours, whereas Royalist supporters did not have to be bought. For his father's and his family's sacrifices, Cholmley had to be content with the sinecure post of gentleman bedchamber groom to the Queen. Whereas his investment in Tangier and its mole was total, tireless and honest, others engaged in the enterprise, such as Samuel Pepys, saw the colony only as a money-making opportunity for themselves. In the end, Sir Hugh fulfilled what should have been an impossible commission against overwhelming odds, but when Tangier was abandoned and its mole destroyed he was blamed unfairly for this costly and catastrophic failure.[9]

The moment of truth came at Windsor in 1673 when King Charles in person rejected Hugh's proposal to complete the harbour at Tangier within the next three years, if he was made governor there as well as surveyor-general of the works. Charles would not agree to concentrate so much power in the hands of only one man, especially a commoner: the governorship went to Lord Inchiquin and Cholmley was replaced by Henry Sheeres, his rival engineer.[10] Ten years later, Cholmley's great mole was demolished and Tangier evacuated and abandoned: the event must have been a grievous blow to him.

Yet even at Whitby the younger Sir Hugh came to be regarded as an impractical, grandiose visionary, whose ambitions far exceeded his means to fund them. When it was built in 1672, Cholmley's so-called banqueting house with its "massive, fantastical facade of eleven bays" was one of the most expensive buildings of its kind and time in England. As Simon Jenkins has written of it: "this was clearly built for splendour rather than comfort and was rarely used".[11] During his travels through France and Spain, Sir Hugh had seen, admired and later attempted to emulate on East Cliff the royal palaces of Versailles and Fontainebleau and of Retiro and Aranjuez with their ornamental gardens, fountains and statues; but the investment was out of place and beyond his modest income.

Some indication of the scale of Cholmley's enlarged Abbey House is provided by the Hearth Tax returns. In 1662, Sir William Cholmley was assessed there for 19 chimneys; in 1675, Sir Hugh was reported to have 39 hearths, a number greater than any other home in north-east Yorkshire.[12] Sir Hugh Cholmley senior would have been astonished not just by the scale and grandeur of his son's extension of Abbey House, but also by the magnitude of his financial affairs. The family's properties in the Whitby estate were still worth about £2,000 a year in rents, harbour dues, tithes and court receipts, and income from the mine at Saltwick yielded a similar annual amount. But these figures were dwarfed by the huge sums received and spent by Cholmley as surveyor-general of the Tangier mole. Altogether, between 1663 and 1676, when the work was finished, the Treasury advanced £243,897 5s. 4d, most of it passing through his hands.[13] As surveyor-general his annual salary was fixed at £1,500 in 1669 and backdated to 1663, but for a final settlement of his financial claims against the Treasury he had to wait for reimbursement until as late as 1681. As for the property in Tangier he had lost as a result of the evacuation, he received only as little as £12 as late as 1685.[14]

By the beginning of the 1680s, with only one teenage daughter and no resources free to provide her with a sufficient and suitable dowry, prospects for Sir Hugh Cholmley and his heavily-indebted estate seemed unpromising. It was at this late hour that a saviour appeared out of the East. In 1683, a diamond merchant called Nathaniel Cholmley, a distant relative, who had made a fortune in India and retired to England, offered himself and his money. Mary Cholmley was still only 16 and the bridegroom in his late forties, but the offer was irresistible. A match was made. In effect, Nathaniel handed over £26,000 for his bride and her inheritance to Abbey House and the Whitby estate.[15]

The deeds of 15 and 16 June 1685 conveyed in fee simple to Nathaniel Cholmley the manors of Whitby and Fyling, the manor house at Whitby, and all the rights of manorial jurisdiction in return for £14,404 - £4,000 owed to Lady Norcliffe; £2,000 to the daughter of Sir William Cholmley; £250 to Lady Strode, formerly wife of Sir William; and £80 owed to Dr John Twysden. By two more deeds signed the following month, the manors of Stakesby and Whitby Laithes and all Sir Hugh's other lands were conveyed as security for his debts. Mary was made tenant of the Whitby estate for life.[16]

After he had cleared his debts, Sir Hugh had invested his remaining cash in government loans. The Treasury Books record a loan from Cholmley to the Customs of £5,000 in 1683 and another one of £11,000 to the Exchequer a year later. Before the creation of the National Debt in 1692-3 and the Bank of England in 1694, loans to the government were not guaranteed by parliamentary taxes, but instead were tied to unreliable sources of royal revenue such as customs and excise. Consequently, though Sir Hugh seems to have received interest due on the loans to Charles II, a principal sum of £10,000 was not re-paid to him until after his brother succeeded in 1685.[17]

The succession of James early in 1685 and the suppression of the Monmouth rebellion against him must have brought great relief to Sir Hugh. As the Tory Member of Parliament for Northampton, a seat secured for him by his Yelverton cousin, Sir Henry, Cholmley had spoken and voted against the Bill to exclude James from the throne. However, though the succession of James secured Cholmley's financial investment, during the next three years the king's conduct forfeited Sir Hugh's loyalty. Though elected MP for Thirsk with the support of the Catholic Lord Bellasis in the new parliament of 1685, by 1688 Sir Hugh was so distrusted by the royal government that he was deprived of all his county offices and suspected of planning rebellion. When the Revolution came he welcomed it but did not live long enough to enjoy its fruits. He died on 9 January 1689 and was buried at Whitby.[18]

One old tradition Sir Hugh had carried to the grave was the unpopularity of his family with many leading Whitby families, particularly the Newtons of Bagdale Hall.

The intense rivalry between Abbey House on the East Cliff and Bagdale Hall on the west side came to a climax in 1685. As usual, and especially since the Newtons had become Quakers, they and the Anglican Cholmleys found themselves on opposing religious and political grounds. During the Exclusion crisis, Sir Hugh was employed in his offices as deputy-lieutenant and justice in the North Riding to search for the arms of suspected rebels. According to one report, his men discovered a case of pistols and an old musket in Bagdale Hall and confiscated them.[19] Ill-feeling between the two families reached a climax in the summer of 1685 when Sir Hugh's gamekeeper seized a greyhound belonging to Captain Isaac Newton and hanged it in public. In retaliation, Isaac placed a notice on Whitby bridge which described Sir Hugh as "a base, cowardly rascal" and continued:"Whitby men, beware of these people, who on one day may have no more esteem for you than they now have for dogs". Isaac and his son Ambrose were subsequently fined five shillings by the court leet for fixing this "scandalous libel" on the bridge. Later, Cholmley sued Newton in the Court of King's Bench, but the outcome is not known.[20]

In October 1685, the North Riding magistrates' court meeting at Thirsk was informed of an assault by Isaac Newton on William Wigginer and Robert Bland, Sir Hugh's "tythingman" and his servant. Wigginer, an old decrepit man with only one good leg, had been knocked to the ground and his lame leg broken. Newton had drawn his sword on them. Here was one local Quaker who not only refused to pay tithes but carried a weapon and was prepared to use it![21]

However, the final words go to James Grysedale, a Whitby innkeeper, who was brought before the quarter sessions at Thirsk in April 1685. He was indicted for declaring in public that Sir Hugh Cholmley was "a thicke, idle, sappheaded, sleepy drone"![22] Grysedale's punishment for uttering such an outrageous slander is not recorded, but the incident provides further evidence that in their own time the occupants of Abbey House made many enemies living below them in the town, whatever their reputation elsewhere. Still, what the historical record of Sir Hugh reveals of his intelligence, diligence, honesty and creativity suggests that Grysedale's calumny was merely personal and malicious. A better judge of character, Samuel Pepys, wrote that Tangier Cholmley was "a fine, worthy, well-disposed gentleman".[23] The lady was surely right when she said that "the man deserves a modern biography".[24]

SIR HUGH CHOLMLEY'S FAMILY TREE

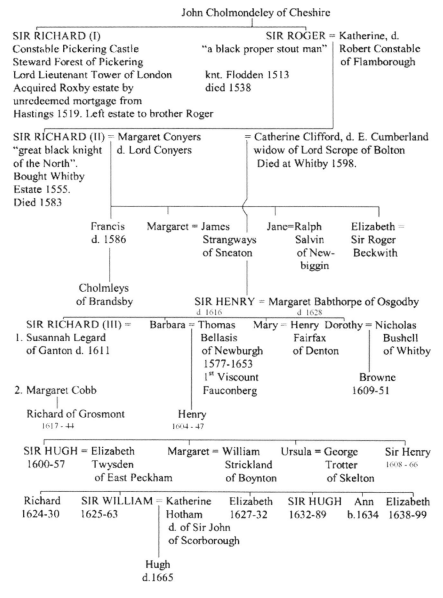

John Cholmondeley of Cheshire

SIR RICHARD (I)
Constable Pickering Castle
Steward Forest of Pickering
Lord Lieutenant Tower of London
Acquired Roxby estate by
unredeemed mortgage from
Hastings 1519. Left estate to brother Roger

SIR ROGER = Katherine, d.
"a black proper stout man" | Robert Constable
of Flamborough

knt. Flodden 1513
died 1538

SIR RICHARD (II) = Margaret Conyers
"great black knight | d. Lord Conyers
of the North".
Bought Whitby
Estate 1555.
Died 1583

= Catherine Clifford, d. E. Cumberland
widow of Lord Scrope of Bolton
Died at Whitby 1598.

Francis
d. 1586

Margaret = James
Strangways
of Sneaton

Jane=Ralph
Salvin
of New-
biggin

Elizabeth =
Sir Roger
Beckwith

Cholmleys
of Brandsby

SIR HENRY = Margaret Babthorpe of Osgodby
d 1616   d 1628

SIR RICHARD (III) =
1. Susannah Legard
of Ganton d. 1611

2. Margaret Cobb

Richard of Grosmont
1617 - 44

Barbara = Thomas
Bellasis
of Newburgh
1577-1653
1st Viscount
Fauconberg

Henry
1604 - 47

Mary = Henry
Fairfax
of Denton

Dorothy = Nicholas
Bushell
of Whitby

Browne
1609-51

SIR HUGH = Elizabeth
1600-57   Twysden
of East Peckham

Margaret = William
Strickland
of Boynton

Ursula = George
Trotter
of Skelton

Sir Henry
1608 - 66

Richard
1624-30

SIR WILLIAM = Katherine
1625-63   Hotham
d. of Sir John
of Scorborough

Elizabeth
1627-32

SIR HUGH
1632-89

Ann
b.1634

Elizabeth
1638-99

Hugh
d.1665

Sir Henry d 1616 was the eldest son of Sir Richard (II)
and his second wife, Catherine Clifford

APPENDIX 2

SIR HUGH CHOLMLEY'S DESCENDANTS

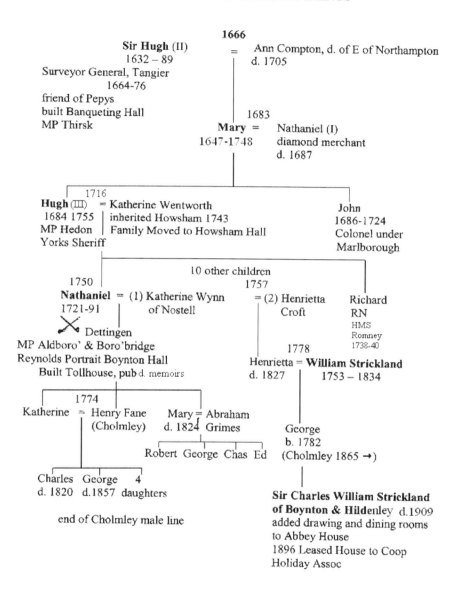

1666

Sir Hugh (II)
1632 – 89
Surveyor General, Tangier
1664-76
friend of Pepys
built Banqueting Hall
MP Thirsk

= Ann Compton, d. of E of Northampton
d. 1705

1683
Mary =
1647-1748

Nathaniel (I)
diamond merchant
d. 1687

1716
Hugh (III) = Katherine Wentworth
1684 1755 | inherited Howsham 1743
MP Hedon | Family Moved to Howsham Hall
Yorks Sheriff

John
1686-1724
Colonel under
Marlborough

10 other children

1750
Nathaniel = (1) Katherine Wynn
1721-91 | of Nostell

Dettingen
MP Aldboro' & Boro'bridge
Reynolds Portrait Boynton Hall
Built Tollhouse, pub d. memoirs

1757
= (2) Henrietta
Croft

Richard
RN
HMS
Romney
1738-40

1778
Henrietta = **William Strickland**
d. 1827 | 1753 – 1834

1774
Katherine = Henry Fane
(Cholmley)

Mary = Abraham
d. 1824 Grimes

George
b. 1782
(Cholmley 1865 →)

Robert George Chas Ed

Charles George 4
d. 1820 d.1857 daughters

end of Cholmley male line

Sir Charles William Strickland
of Boynton & Hildenley d.1909
added drawing and dining rooms
to Abbey House
1896 Leased House to Coop
Holiday Assoc

185

APPENDIX 3

SIR HUGH CHOLMLEY 1600 – 1657 CHRONOLOGY

1600   Born 22 July at Roxby castle, Thornton-on-the-Hill

1603-7   At Ganton, home of uncle John Legard.
             At the age of seven survived a riding fall on Pexton Moor.

1608   On his eighth birthday at Whitby saved from a fierce sow by the butler.

1611   Entered Beverley Grammar School as a boarder. His mother died of a fever caught from him at the home of the Hothams at Scorborough.

1613   Went up to Jesus College, Cambridge with his tutor, Mr Petty.

1617   On the death of Sir Henry, his grandfather, he left Cambridge and returned to Yorkshire for a year.

1618-21 Three years spent wastefully at Gray's Inn. Lodgings in Fleet Street.

1622   Marriage arranged with Elizabeth. daughter of Sir William Twysden.

1624   Sat as Scarborough's MP in last Parliament of James I. Richard, his eldest son, born.

1625   Returned again for Scarborough to sit in first Parliament of Charles I. William, his second son, born.

1626   Took over his father's indebted estate and came North to live in Whitby Abbey gatehouse. Re-elected MP for Scarborough. Knighted.

1627   His daughter, the first Elizabeth, born.

1629   Sir Hugh and his family moved into their new home, Fyling Old Hall.

1630   Death of his eldest son, Richard.

1631   Death of his father, Sir Richard.

1632   Became JP for the North Riding. Successful petition for a new west pier at Whitby. Birth of his third son, Hugh after death of his first daughter, Elizabeth.

1633   Returned to Fyling after winter at Langton on the Wolds.

1634   Sold Fyling Old Hall and deer park to Sir John Hotham. Birth of daughter, Ann. Family moved back to Whitby Abbey gatehouse until main house improvements were finished.

1635   Confrontation at the Malton quarter sessions with Sir Thomas Hoby. Dunkirkers and Dutchmen at Whitby

1636   Family moved into Abbey House. Sir Hugh became deputy-lieutenant of the North Riding and commissioned colonel of the trained bands of Whitby, Scarborough, Pickering and Ryedale.

1638   Birth of daughter, the second Elizabeth. Family stayed with the Yelvertons at Easton Maudit in Northants.

1639   First Bishops' War. Incident on Pexton Moor.

1640   Elected to Short Parliament as MP for Scarborough. Outspoken protest in the Commons against Ship Money and militia charges. Open quarrel with his former patron, Earl of Strafford. Dismissed from all commissions and summoned before Privy Council. Assigned all Whitby estate except Fyling to trustees. Leading Yorkshire petitioner during second Bishops' War. Elected to sit in Long Parliament.

1641   Sir Hugh's family came south from Whitby to live in London while he attended the House of Commons. Active in the trial and condemnation of Strafford.

Voted for the Grand Remonstrance but against root and branch reform of the Church of England. Created first baronet.

1642   One of Parliament's Commissioners to King Charles at York. Accepted Parliament's commission to hold Scarborough. Advanced to Stamford Bridge, but refused to join Fairfaxes at Tadcaster.

1643   Won battle at Guisborough, but changed sides and took Scarborough with him after the Queen had landed at Bridlington.
        Lady Elizabeth and two daughters arrived at Scarborough from London.
        Cholmley commanded cavalry in the unsuccessful royalist siege of Hull.

1644   Cholmley refused to go into exile with the Marquess of Newcastle after royalist defeat at Marston Moor.

1645   Two daughters sent to safety of Holland. Scarborough town and harbour lost to Parliament's troops under Sir John Meldrum. Cholmley held castle for the king from February until surrender in July.
        After surrender Lady Elizabeth stayed behind in Yorkshire while Sir Hugh went abroad, first to Holland, then to France.
        Young Hugh left St Paul's school to join his father in Paris. William arrived in Paris from Italy.

1646   Sir Hugh moved to Rouen. William returned to Whitby to manage estate.

1647   Whole Cholmley family reunited at Rouen. Sir Hugh wrote his three Memorials on the Civil War for Sir Edward Hyde.

1649   Sir Hugh followed his wife back to London and in the summer returned to Whitby. New alum works opened at Saltwick Bay. Composition fine of £850 paid in full. Sir Hugh arrested at Abbey house on charge of debt but escaped at Malton and travelled to London.

1650   Charges against Sir Hugh dropped. His son William awarded damages for ill-treatment.

1651   Cholmley took up residence with his brother-in-law, Sir Roger Twysden, at Roydon Hall, East Peckham in Kent.
        Eight weeks imprisoned in Leeds castle.

1652-4 Summers spent at Whitby. New Gardens enclosed and planted.

1653   William married Katherine Hotham.

1654   Daughter Ann married Richard Stephens.

1655   Death of Lady Elizabeth. Sir Hugh left Whitby for last time.

1655-6 Sir Hugh wrote his Memoirs at Roydon Hall.

1657   Died 30 November and buried next to Elizabeth in St Michael's at East Peckham.

187

REFERENCES

Preface

1   L B Larking (ed.), Sir Roger Twysden's Journal, *Archaeologia Cantiana,* 1 (1858), 189
2   J Binns (ed.), *The Memoirs and Memorials of Sir Hugh Cholmley of Whitby 1600-1657,* YASRS CLIII (2000)
3   Bod. Lib., Clarendon MS 1809, *Clarendon Papers,* ii (1773), 181-6; Clarendon MS 1764, *EHR* V (1890), 347-51; Clarendon MS 1609, *EHR* XXXII (1917), 569-87

Chapter 1

1   The Cholmeleys usually wrote their name with this spelling until Nathaniel (1721-91) dropped the first letter 'e'. I have used the shortest, modern version throughout.
2   *CPR 1485-94,* 176, 299, 454, 478; Ibid, *1494-1509,* 213, 233, 269, 312; *CFR 1485-1509,* 378
3   NYCRO, ZPK 1,2
4   *ODNB* 11,505
5   NYCRO, ZPK 3
6   Monument to Sir Marmaduke Constable, who died in 1520 aged 77, in St Oswald's church, Flamborough. YML, Add. MS 343, f.2r.
7   YML, Add MS 343, ff. 2v., 3r.
8   *L & P.* xii (1), 393. "Mr Chamley's house" was misplaced at Roxby "between Whitby and Loftus" in R W Hoyle, *The Pilgrimage of Grace and the Politics of the 1530s* (Oxford, 2001), 227. The "Mr Chamley" was probably Richard, not knighted until 1544, not his elderly father, knighted in 1513.
9   WLPS, PB 1548
10 Charlton, 292-4; Young, ii, 930-1
11 *L & P,* xix (1), 328-9; BL, Harleian MS 6063
12 *L & P.* xix (2), 168, 322, 326; Add. MS 32, 656, f.7; Gaskin, 79-81
13 NA, Patent Rolls, C66/759, 778; *L & P,* xx(1), 128, 244
14 *CPR 1547-8,* 92; Ibid. *1547-53,* 316
15 *CPR 1548-9,* 133
16 Ibid, 135-6
17 *YAJ* xxxiv (1939), 151-69
18 *CPR 1550-3,* 394; Ibid, *1553,* App., 354
19 *CPR 1547-53,* 40
20 WLPS, PB 2018; *Feet of Fines, 1486-1571,* YASRS, ii, part 1
21 WLPS, PB 2018; *CPR 1554-5,* 257-8
22 S T Bindoff (ed.), *The House of Commons, 1509-1558,* 3 vols (1982), i, 642-4; *CJ,* I, 47

23   *APC 1556-8,* 254
24   Rowntree, 215-16
25   *CPR 1555-7,* 54
26   *APC 1556-8,* 396
27   Charlton, 300-2
28   *CPR 1563-66,* 206; Charlton, 300-2
29   Cartwright, 67; Aveling, *NR,* 418, 426, 427
30   Aveling, *NR,* 182, 194
31   *CSPD, Addenda 1547-65,* 567. For "Chamberlain" read "Cholmley"; *CSPD, Addenda 1566-71,* 96
32   NRRS, NS, i, 205, 207 seq.; *CSPF 1562,* 5, 33
33   *APC 1558-70,* 231, 233; *CSPD 1563-9,* 159-60, 165; R R Reid, *The King's Council in the North* (1921), 201, 202
34   *APC 1558-70,* 301
35   Ibid
36   *CPR 1568-9,* 431; *CSPD, Addenda 1547-65,* 359, *567; YASRS* XCVI (1938), 18,19
37   *CPR 1569-72,* 224
38   *CPR 1572-5,* 204-5
39   *CPR 1572-5,* 446; Ibid, *1575-8, 45;* Ibid, *1578-80,* 123
40   YML, Add MS 343, 2v.
41   Ibid, 4r.
42   Ibid, 3r.
43   Ibid; E Watson, "A Stiff-Necked, Wilful and Obstinate People": The Catholic Laity in the North York Moors c.1559-1603, *YAJ* 77 (2005), 194
44   YML, Add MS 343, 3v.; NA, Inquisition Post Mortem, C142/214/157; NYCRO, ZPK 4; WLPS, PB 2018

Chapter 2

1   WLPS, PB 585; *Feet of Fines,* YASRS V, ii (1888), 132; Aveling, *NR,* 181
2   YML, Add MS 343, 3v.
3   Ibid
4   Ibid, 4v.
5   Ibid, 5r.
6   NYCRO, ZQC, MIC 1456
7   YML, Add MS 343, 5v.
8   J & J A Venn (eds), *Alumni Cantabrigiensis* (1922), pt.1, vol.1, 334
9   *Lincoln's Inn Register 1420-1893*(1896), 55; YML, Add MS 343, 15v.
10   J Strype, *Annals of the Reformation* (Oxford, 1824), vol. ii, pt. II, 341-2; iii, pt.I, 73
11   YML, Add MS 343, 5r.
12   Aveling, *NR,* 182, 194
13   Ibid, 182; YML, Add MS 343, 5v.
14   Reid, *King's Council,* 230-2
15   Cartwright, 166
16   HMC, *Salisbury,* X, 9,11; XI, 214, 456
17   NA, StaC 5/H50/4

18   YML, Add MS 343, 5v.
19   E Peacock (ed.), *A List of Roman Catholics in the County of York* (1872), 109-10
20   WLPS, PB 814, 2889
21   J Rushton, *The History of Ryedale* (Pickering, 2003), 201
22   WLPS, PB 872
23   WLPS, PB 885; *Feet of Fines,* IV, 29, 47, 144; *Yorkshire Fines for the Stuart period 1603-14,* YASRS LIII (1915), 31, 69
24   WLPS, PB 666
25   YML, Add MS 343, 5v.
26   YML, Add MS 343, ff.6r., 7r.
27   NA, StaC 5/H16/2, H22/21, H50/4
28   Ibid
29   Ibid, 5/H50/4
30   HMC, *Salisbury,* IX, 68
31   HMC, *Salisbury,* XI, 39, 214; *APC 1600-01,* 160, 261, 488
32   HMC, *Salisbury,* IX, 149; XI, 11-12
33   Meads, 149-65
34   Ibid, 197-8; NYCRO, *Journal,* 7, 50-1; J D Legard, *The Legards of Anlaby and Ganton* (1920), 30-1
35   Meads, 197-8
36   Aveling, *NR,* 183, 185
37   M Y Ashcroft (ed.), *The Memorandum Book of Richard Cholmeley of Brandsby 1602-23,* NYCRO, 44 (1988), *passim*
38   Aveling, *NR,* 183, 423
39   Ibid, 423
40   YML, Add MS 343, f.6r.
41   Ibid, ff.6v.-7r.
42   *NRQSR,* NRRS, I, 36, Thirsk, 29 Apr. 1606
43   Ibid. 133, Malton, 4/5 Oct. 1608
44   *APC 1600-01,* 160
45   HMC, *Salisbury,* XI, 39
46   Aveling, *NR,* 121
47   *APC 1600-01,* 261, 488; HMC, *Salisbury,* XI, 214. In his memoirs, Sir Hugh wrote that the fine was £3,000 (YML, Add MS 343, f. 6r.)
48   W A Shaw (ed.), *The Knights of England,* ii (1906), 100-01, 113; YML, Add MS 343, f.6r.
49   This Star Chamber case is examined in detail in G C F Forster, Faction and County Government in Early Stuart England, *NH* XI (1976), 77-9
50   NA, StaC 8/12/11
51   Ibid, StaC 8/110/23, 12/11, 104/15
52   G W Boddy, Players of Interludes in North Yorkshire in the Early Seventeenth Century, NYCRO,7 (1976), 109, 121-3
53   *NRQSR,* NRRS I, 204; Ibid, NRRS II, 64
54   *NRQSR,* NRRS I and II, *passim*
55   HMC, *Salisbury,* XI, 39
56   *CSPD 1603-10,* 502, 516
57   WLPS, PB 1462

58   NYCRO, ZF 1/12/5,6; WLPS, PB 1460
59   WLPS, PB 1460
60   W Page (ed.), *VCH, Yorks NR,* II, 504; *CSPD 1611-18,* 126
61   WLPS, PB 1462-6; *VCH, NR,* II, 504; NYCRO, ZF 1/12/8,9
62   YML, Add MS 343, f.8r.
63   Ibid, ff. 8r.-8v.
64   Ibid, ff. 8v.-9r.
65   *CSPD 1619-23,* 168; Reid, *King's Council,* 388
66   NA, StaC 8/104/15. This Star Chamber case has been examined more fully in Forster, *NH* XI, 80-2.
67   *NRQSR,* NRRS, III, 134-46
68   Ibid, 313
69   YML, Add MS 343, f.7v.
70   Ibid, f.7v.
71   Ibid
72   The best, brief account of the life of Sir Thomas is to be found in Hasler, iii, 323-4
73   J C Hodgson (ed.), *North Country Diaries,* Surtees Society cxxiv (1915), 6
74   Knowler, ii, 108
75   YML, Add MS 343, ff6r., 6v.
76   Ibid, ff.8r.,llr.
77   Ibid, f.l0r.
78   Ibid, f.8v.
79   Ibid. f.llv.
80   Ibid, ff.8r.-v.
81   Ibid, ff.8v.-9r.
82   Cartwright, 220-6
83   YML, Add MS 343, f.9r.
84   Ibid, f.9v.
85   Ibid, ff.9v.-l0r.
86   Ibid, f.9v.
87   WLPS, PB 878, 883
88   YML, Add MS 343, f.5v.
89   Ibid, f.l0r.

Chapter 3

1   YML, Add MS 343, f.14v.; NYCRO, Thornton Parish Register, PR 806, 27 Jly 1600
2   YML, Add MS 343, f.14v.
3   Ibid; PR 806, 6 Mar 1603
4   YML, Add MS 343, f.14r.
5   Ibid. ff.14v.-15r.
6   Ibid, f.15r.
7   C Webster (ed.), *Health, Medicine and Mortality in the Sixteenth Century* (Cambridge, 1979), 65
8   YML, MS 343, f.15r.
9   L Stone, *The Family, Sex and Marriage in England 1500-1800* (1980), 64-5

10   NYCRO, DC/SCB, B1, General Letters, 19 Jly 1619

11   A M W Stirling, *The Hothams,* 2 vols (1918), i, 24

12   BIHR, V37, f.273; Scarborough Central Library, Scarborough Wills, 3 vols, III, 650

13   A F Leach (ed.), *Early Yorkshire Schools,* YASRS XXVII (1899), 121-7; G Poulson, *Beverlac* (1829), 452

14   YML, Add MS 343, f.14r.

15   Venns, *Alumni,* pt.1, vol.1, 334; YML, Add MS 343, f.6r.

16   Cliffe, *Yorks Gentry,* 74

17   Ibid, 74, 266-7; G Ridsdill Smith, *Without Touch of Dishonour: The Life and Death of Sir Henry Slingsby 1602-58* (Kineton, 1968), 16; F W Jessup, *Sir Roger Twysden 1597-1672* (1965), *15*

18   Bursar's Book, Jesus College, Cambridge (A/c 1.3)

19   For all these details of Jesus men I am indebted to the former College archivist, Mr E F Mills.

20   YML, Add MS 343, ff. 15r.-v.

21   D Howarth, *Lord Arundel and his Circle* (1985), 127-30. Unfortunately, Mr Howarth misread Hugh's own account and confused Petty with first the College debaucher and then Hugh's father, Sir Richard!

22   *Alum. Cantab.,* iv. 88

23   YML, Add MS 343, ff. 15r., 15v.

24   Ibid. 15v.

25   *Alum. Cantab.,* pt.1, vol.i, 334; YML, Add MS 343, 5v.

26   YML, Add MS 343, f.15v.

27   Jessup, *Twysden,* 16

28   Cliffe, *Yorks Gentry,* 248

29   YML, Add Ms 343, ff. 15v., 16r., 22v.

30   Ibid, 16r.

31   Ibid

32   Ibid, 16v.

33   Jessup, *Twysden,* 10; J Newman, *West Kent and the Weald* (1976), 268-9

34   YML, Add MS 343, ff. 4v., 14v.

35   Ibid, 9v., 16v.

36   Jessup, *Twysden,* 13; YML, Add MS 343, 15w.

37   Jessup, *Twysden,* 13

38   YML, Add MS 343, f.19v.

39   Jessup, *Twysden,* 81, 178 *et seq.*

40   Ibid. 14-16

41   YML, Add MS 343, ff. 16v. -17r.

42   Ibid

43   Ibid, f.17r.

44   Ibid

45   Ibid

46   Ibid, ff.17r.- 17v.

Chapter 4

1   YML, Add MS 343, ff. l0r., 17r., 17v.

2   Ibid, f.17v.
3   NYCRO, DC/SCB, B1, 17 Jan 1628
4   YML, Add MS 343, f.18r.; WLPS, PB 878
5   YML, Add MS 343, ff. 18r.-18v.
6   Ibid
7   Ibid, f.18v.
8   Ibid
9   NYCRO, ZPK 12, 13
10   YML, Add MS 343, ff. 17v., 18v., 19r.
11   WLPS, PB 1773, 1788, 1772, 879; YAS, Fairfax Evidences, MS 41, 28
12   WLPS, PB 1774, 6019
13   WLPS, PB 739, 923, 924
14   Whitby parish register, baptisms, 1608-38, 21
15   YML, Add MS 343, ff.18v., 20r.
16   Ibid, f.20v.
17   Ibid, f.l0v.; Whitby parish register, burials, 1608-38, 103
18   YML, Add MS 343, f.21v.
19   Ibid
20   Ibid, f.22r.
21   Ibid, ff.20r., 22r.
22   Ibid, f.22r.; Hull University Library, Cholmley papers, DCY/19/2
23   Whitby parish register, baptisms, 1608-38, 29
24   YML, Add MS 343, f.22v.
25   Ibid, ff.22r.-v.
26   Ibid
27   WLPS, PB 5939/NYCRO, ZCG (MIC 1343/272); YML, Add MS 343, ff. l0v.,
        15r.
28   WLPS, PB 1779, 869, 1094
29   *M & M,* 176-7, 180-1
30   WLPS, PB 1783
31   For a fuller, critical account of Sir Hugh Cholmley and Whitby see below in
        chapter 14.

Chapter 5

1   *NRQSR,* NRRS III, 324
2   YML, Add MS 343, f.22v.
3   *NRQSR,* NRRS III, 329, 331; YML, Add MS 343, f.21v.
4   YML, Add MS 343, f.22v.
5   *NRQSR,* NRRS IV, 34
6   Hackness parish register, 1557-1783, 60. The burial monument to Lady Margaret
        is on the south wall of the chancel of St Peter's church, Hackness.
7   *YAJ,* 17 (1903), 72-93
8   Ashcroft, i, 225, 227, 229, 230, 232, 233
9   YML, Add MS 343, f. 24v.
10   NYCRO, DC/SCB, BI, 1 Feb 1626
11   *APC 1613-14,* 417-18; Ashcroft, i, 53-4
12   YML, Add MS 343, f.21v.

13 *APC 1630-1,* 248-5, 259, 271, 285, 292-3, 318, 345-6, 373; Reid, *King's Council,* 414-16; Cliffe, *Yorks Gentry,* 298; Wedgwood, *Wentworth,* 106-7
14 Cliffe, *Yorks Gentry,* 298; Sheffield Archives, WWM, Strafford Papers, xvi, 23 Sept 1631
15 Sheffield Archives, Strafford Papers, xv, 76
16 *NRQSR,* IV, *passim*
17 YML, Add MS 343, f.22v.
18 Ibid
19 Ashcroft, i, 290-1
20 Knowler, *Strafford Correspondence,* ii, 94, 108
21 YML, Add MS 343, f.22v.
22 *YAJ,* 17, 81-4
23 *CSPD 1634-5,* 273, 294; Ashcroft, i, 274-6
24 YML, Add MS 343, ff.23r.-v.
25 *CPPD 1635,* 322-3, 549, 572
26 YML, Add MS 343, f.18r.
27 *CSPD 1631-3,* 370
28 Ibid, 375
29 *CSPD 1634-5,* 242-3
30 Cliffe, *Yorks Gentry,* 304
31 C*SPD 1635,* 479
32 NYCRO, DC/SCB, H1, 6 Dec 1635
33 *CSPD 1636-7,* 96; K R Andrews, *Ships, Money and Politics: Seafaring and Enterprise in the Reign of Charles I* (Cambridge, 1991), 155
34 Jessup, *Twysden,* 30, 31, 38
35 Ibid, 27, 29; YML, Add MS 343, ff. 22r., 24r., 17r., 18r.; WLPS, PB 1775, 880, 1799
36 Jessup, *Twysden,* 20-1
37 Ibid, 17-18
38 YML, Add MS 343, f.15v.
39 Jessup, *Twysden,* 182; V H Galbraith, *English Historical Scholarship in the Sixteenth and Seventeenth Centuries* (1956), 118
40 HMC, *Denbigh,* 280a.; G Isham, *Easton Mauduit and the Parish Church of SS. Peter & Paul* (1974), 2-4; M F Keeler, *The Long Parliament 1640-1* (Philadelphia, 1954), 403
41 YML, Add MS 343, ff. 20v., 21v., 24r.
42 *CSPD 1635,* 470; Ibid, *1635-6,* 421; NA, SP 16, 378/94
43 Keeler. *Long Parliament,* 403; Cliffe, *Yorks Gentry,* 315
44 *CSPD 1639-40,* 185; Ibid, *1640,* 126, 147; NA, SP 16, 314/97/1, 445/51/1; Rushworth, iii, 991
45 Knowler, *Strafford Letters,* ii,193
46 Ibid, ii, 193-4; Cliffe, *Yorks Gentry,* 311; HMC, *Coke,* ii, 189
47 Sheffield Archives, WWM, Strafford Papers, 10 (2/4)
48 Ashcroft, i, 327-9
49 Ibid, 330; Chapman. iii, 112
50 YML, Add MS 343, f.24r.
51 Ibid

52   Ibid
53   Ashcroft, i, 335
54   Clarendon, *Rebellion,* v, 105
55   Legard, *Legards,* 105. This volume contains the only known photographs of the portraits of Sir Hugh and several of his ancestors which at the time were in Howsham Hall. For a full catalogue of these Howsham portraits see *TERAS,* X (1903), 41-61.
56   YML, Add MS 343, ff. 22r., 23v.
57   Sheffield Archives, WWM, 16, 13 Jan 1636
58   Knowler, *Strafford Letters,* ii, 288
59   Cliffe, *Yorks Gentry,* 305
60   Clarendon, *Rebellion,* iii, 164, 185; Cliffe, *Yorks Gentry,* 382; Stirling, *Hothams,* i, 21, 25-6
61   Knowler, *Strafford Letters,* ii, 288, 310, 307-8
62   Reckitt, 7
63   *Cliffe, Yorks Gentry,* 314
64   Ibid, 315

Chapter 6

1   NYCRO, DC/SCB, B1, 8, 12, 13, 26 Dec 1639, 24 Feb, 19 Mar 1640
2   YML, Add MS 343, f.24r.; Cliffe, *Yorks Gentry,* 315
3   YML, Add MS 343, ff.25r.-v.
4   Wedgwood, *Wentworth,* 281-3
5   E S Cope & W H Coates (eds), *Proceedings of the Short Parliament of 1640,* Camden, 4th series, xix (1977), 161, 162, 194
6   *CJ* ii, 4, 12, 18
7   Cope & Coates, *Proceedings,* 161
8   Ibid, 194; J D Maltby (ed.), *The Short Parliament (1640) Diary of Sir Thomas Aston,* Camden, 4th series, xxxv (1988), 129, 132, 140, 142-3
9   *LJ* ix, 81
10   *CSPD 1640,* 154-5, 166
11   YML, Add MS 343, f.24v.
12   Cope & Coates, *Proceedings,* 161, 162, 194; Maltby, *Aston Diary,* 17, 18, 129, 132, 140
13   YML, Add MS 343, f.24v.
14   *Calendar of the Proceedings of the Committee for Compounding 1643-60,* Part iii, 2062; YML, Add MS 343, f.28v.
15   *CSPD 1640,* 120, 222-3, 308, 586; Cliffe, *Yorks Gentry,* 318
16   YML, Add MS 343, f.24v.; M D Gordon, The Collection of Ship Money, *TRHS,* 3rd series, 4 (1910), 161
17   Cliffe, *Yorks Gentry,* 318
18   YML, Add MS 343, f.24v.
19   *VCH, Yorks,* iii, 418
20   *CSPD 1640,* 585-6, 588
21   NA, SP 16/456/38; YML, Add MS 343, f.25r.
22   Rushworth, iii, 1215; *CSPD 1640,* 595-7
23   YML, Add MS 343, f.25r.

24   Skipton Library, Petyt Collection, S.t.b., T1540A
25   *CSPD 1640,* 34-5, 54
26   Knowler, *Strafford Letters,* ii, 393, 408
27   Ibid, ii, 411; C*SPD 1640,* 67, 68, 69
28   YML, Add MS 343, f.25r. Cholmley got only four names right of the 12 peers who signed this petition. Southampton, Bristol and "Claire" were not signatories. Surprisingly, he omitted the two Yorkshiremen, Mulgrave and Howard of Escrick, as well as Saye, Brooke, Mandeville, Rutland, Bolingbroke and Exeter.
29   YML Add MS 343, f.25r.
30   What Cholmley could not have known then and still did not appreciate 15 years later was that the majority of these 12 peers, namely Warwick, Bedford, Essex, Mandeville, Saye, Brooke and Essex, were in active, secret collusion with the Scottish Covenanters to force Charles to call a new parliament. J Adamson, *The Noble Revolt* (2007), 46-56.
31   YML, Add MS 343, f.24r.
32   *CSPD 1640,* 626, 629, 630, 637, 642, 649; Rushworth, iii, 1230-1, 1235
33   YML, Add MS 343, f.25r.
34   Ibid
35   *CSPD 1640-1,* 47
36   *CSPD 1640,* 624-5; NA, SPI6/467/54, f.100; YML, Add MS 343, f.25v.
37   *CSPD 1640,* 624-5
38   YML, Add MS 343, f.25v.
39   Ibid
40   *CSPD 1640-1,* 56-7, 61-2; D Parsons (ed.), *The Diary of Sir Henry Slingsby* (1836), 56-8; Rushworth, *Collections,* iii, 1264-5; Rushworth, *The Trial of Thomas, Earl of Strafford* (1680), 603, 613-15
41   YML, Add MS 343, f.26r.
42   Adamson, *Noble Revolt,* 563, fn.145
43   Ibid, 38, 47, 60, 61
44   For a fuller treatment of Yorkshire's dissident nobility and gentry see D Scott, Hannibal at our Gates, *Historical Research,* 70 (1997), 269-93
45   Adamson, *Noble Revolt,* 40, 50-1, 151
46   Scott, 293
47   Rushworth, *Collections,* iii, 1295-6

Chapter 7

1   Cliffe, *Yorks Gentry,* 323-5; NYCRO, DC/SCB, B1, 25, 29 Sept 1640
2   Keeler, *Long Parliament,* 74, 75-6
3   YML, Add MS 343, ff.26r.-v.
4   Ibid, f.26r.; *LJ* iv, 366
5   YML, Add MS 343, f.26r.
6   *CJ* ii, 20, 31, 39, 45, 47, 50, 52, 57, 58, 60, 79, 81, 115, 136, 185, 196, 223, 235, 414, 463, 510, 547, 552, 663
7   W Notestein (ed.), *The Journal of Sir Simonds D'Ewes* ... (Yale, 1923), 104-5, 151
8   Ibid, 151-2
9   Cliffe, *Yorks Gentry,* 91; Wedgwood, *Wentworth,* 341-2; Turton, *Alum Farm,* 162

10   *CJ ii,* 142
11   Adamson, *Noble Revolt,* 249, 627-8, n.87
12   Notestein, *Journal,* 322-3, 326, 329; Cliffe, *Yorks Gentry,* 324, n.3; *CJ* ii, 78, 192
13   Clarendon, *Rebellion,* ii, 205. On the other hand, Cholmley expressed no wish to penalize Wentworth's family for his misdeeds: on 14 April 1641 he had moved in the Commons that "his blood may not be attainted, that his ancient inheritance may descend". *Proceedings,* iii, *553*
14   Hotham and the Cholmleys had been nominated by Pym to attend Strafford's trial daily *(Proceedings,* 2 Apr 1641). Rushworth, *Trial,* 14, 44, 600
15   Rushworth, *Trial,* 603, 613-15, 617-20
16   Ibid
17   Ibid. 613; Snow & Young, *Private Journals,* 218
18   Rushworth, *Trial,* 611-13, 629-32
19   Johnson, *Fairfax Correspondence,* ii, 81
20   Cliffe, *Yorks Gentry,* 328; Rushworth, *Trial,* 59; *CJ* ii, 123-5; Wedgwood, *Wentworth,* 367-8
21   Clarendon, *Rebellion,* i, 315-16
22   Notestein, *Journal,* 382; *Proceedings,* ii, 502
23   Notestein, *Journal,* 43; *Proceedings,* i, 131, 132, 138, 141
24   Notestein, *Journal,* 324; *Proceedings,* ii, 365; Rushworth, *Collections,* iv, 169-70; E B G Warburton, *Memoirs of Prince Rupert and the Cavaliers* (1849), ii, 129
25   Coates, Young & Snow, 54; Fletcher, *Outbreak,* 236; *CJ* ii, *375*
26   Coates, Young & Snow, 63-5
27   Ibid, 69
28   Fletcher, *Outbreak,* 55, 57; *CSPD 1641-3,* 24
29   *LJ* v, 15; Snow & Young, 217-18; Cliffe, *Yorks Gentry,* 331-2; *CSPD 1640-1,* 62
30   Coates, Young & Snow, 193
31   Ibid, 240; *CJ* ii, 407
32   *ODNB*
33   Aveling, *NR,* 423, 426, 412
34   Notestein, *Journal,* 461
35   Woolrych, *Britain in Revolution,* 197
36   Coates, Young & Snow, 38; *CJ* ii, 371
37   T Fuller, *Church History of Britain* (Oxford, 1845), iv, 327
38   Adamson, *Noble Revolt,* 90-1
39   Maltby, *Aston Diary,* 91
40   Gardiner, *Docs,* 57
41   Coates, *D'Ewes Journal,* 152; *CJ* ii, 317
42   Ibid
43   YML, Add MS 343, ff. 6v., 7r., 24r.
44   Ibid, ff.6v., 10v.
45   Cliffe, *Puritan Gentry,* 12
46   *CJ* ii, 86; Notestein, *Journal,* 256
47   Cliffe, *Yorks Gentry,* 345-6, 261
48   Bod. Lib., Clarendon MS 1809, ff. 239r., 240r.
49   Cliffe, *Yorks Gentry,* 261
50   BIHR, PW, V.38, ff. 625, 626

51   Marchant, 46-7
52   YML, Add MS 343, f.8r.
53   Ibid, ff.20v., 21v., 28r.; Bod. Lib. Clarendon MS 1669, ff.13r., 13v.; Marchant, 271, 453
54   YML, Add MS 343, f.54r.
55   Keeler, *Long Parliament,* 135; Gardiner, *Civil War,* i, 122

Chapter 8

1   Cliffe, *Yorks Gentry,* 343
2   Fletcher, *Outbreak,* 346
3   J Morrill, The Religious Context of the Civil War, *TRHS,* 5th series, 34 (1984), 178
4   Gardiner, *Civil War,* i, 9
5   Adamson, *Noble Revolt,* 518
6   Cliffe, *Yorks Gentry,* 344-8; Aveling, *NR,* 306-7
7   Brooke, thesis, 87
8   YML, Add MS 343, f.26v.
9   Aveling, *NR.* 306-9; P R Newman, Catholic Royalists of Northern England, 1642-6, *NH* xv (1979), 88-95; J L Malcolm, A King in Search of Soldiers, *HJ* 21 (1978), 255; *LJ* v, 107
10   YML, Add MS 343, ff. 26r.-v.
11   Bod. Lib. Clarendon MS 1669, f.8r.; Cliffe, *Yorks Gentry,* 336, 338; YML, Add MS 343, f.26v.
12   G E Aylmer, Royalist Attitudes, *TRHS,* 5th series, 37 (1987), 2: *CJ* ii, 763; *LJ* v, 302
13   *CSPD 1642,* 366, 379, 387; G Duckett, Civil War Proceedings in Yorkshire, *YAJ* vii (1882), 67
14   Clarendon, *Rebellion,* ii, 251-67; HMC, *Thirteenth Report,* Appendix 1, 41; Ibid. *Fifth Report,* Appendix, 191; Cliffe, *Yorks Gentry,* 334; YML, Add MS 343, ff. 19r.-v., 22r., 23v.
15   Cliffe, *Yorks Gentry,* 268
16   Ibid, 335
17   YML, Add MS 343, ff. 7v., 14v., 18v.
18   Cliffe, *Yorks Gentry,* 297-8, 334, 345; J Moone, A Brief Relation of the Life and Memoires of John, Lord Belasyse, HMC, *Ormonde,* New Series, ii, 379
19   Keeler, *Long Parliament,* 403-4
20   Jessup, *Twysden,* 31-2, 42-3, 45-60
21   Cliffe, *Yorks Gentry,* 333, 342-3; Fletcher, *Outbreak,* 231; Duckett, *YAJ* vii, 75-6; NYCRO, DC/SCB, Bl, 7 July 1642
22   Willan, *YAJ* xxxi, 187-9, 266-7; *VCH, Yorks NR,* ii, 197
23   Ibid
24   Notestein, *Journal,* 438-9; Cliife, *Yorks Gentry,* 382; J W Clay (ed.), *Yorkshire Royalist Composition Papers,* 3 vols, ii, YASRS xviii (1895), 221-2; *CPCC,* iii, 2062

Chapter 9

1   *EHR* xix (1904), 46-8, 52
2   All three manuscripts were copied for Clarendon's papers in the Bod. Lib., shelf
    marked 22:
    Some Observations & Memorialls touching the Hothams, MS 1809
    Memorialls touching the Battle of Yorke, MS 1764
    Memorialls tuching Scarbrough, MS 1669
3   *EHR* xix, 49, 52, 54
4   Clarendon, *Rebellion,* vi, 267
5   *Clarendon State Papers* ii (1773), 186
6   *EHR* v (1890), 145-51; Ibid, xxxii (1917), 568-87
7   *EHR* xxxii, 568
8   WLPS, PB 571
9   J Schofield, *Guide to Scarborough* (York, 1787), 86-7
10 Hinderwell, 70; Baker, 74
11 YML, Add MS 343
12 J Binns (ed.), *The Memoirs and Memorials of Sir Hugh Cholmley of Whitby 1600-
    1657,* YASRS clii (2000)
13 YML, Add MS 343, f.27r.
14 Ibid, ff.8r.-v.
15 Scarborough Memorials, f.8r.
16 Ibid; Gardiner, *Documents,* 245-7, 248-9, 261; Wedgwood, *King's War,* 117
17 YML, Add MS 343, ff.26r.-v.; Scarborough Memorials, f.8r.
18 Scarborough Memorials, f.8r.
19 YML, Add MS 343, 26v.; Duckett, *YAJ* vii, 75-6
20 Scarborough Memorials, f.8r.
21 Ibid
22 Ibid; YML, Add MS 343, f.26v.
23 Hinderwell, 162; Ashcroft, ii, 5, 272-8
24 *YRCP,* YASRS xv, 7-8
25 Ashcroft, ii, 18-19; HMC, *Bouverie,* x, pt.6 (1886), 90-1
26 HMC, *Bouverie,* x, pt.6, 90
27 *CSPD 1625-49,* 644, 650
28 NYCRO, DC/SCB, Common Hall Minutes & Orders, 1642-9, 16 Oct 1642; Ibid,
    Common Hall Memoranda, 1497-1737, 21 Nov 1642
29 *CSPD 1641-3,* 322-3; Cliffe, *Yorks Gentry,* 332-3; Rushworth, *Collections,* iv,
    615-17, 620-1; *LJ* v, 61
30 *YAJ* vii, 64-6; *LJ* v, 107
31 Malcolm, *HJ* 21, 257-9
32 J Binns, Scarborough and the Civil Wars 1642-51, *NH* xxii (1986), 100-02
33 HMC, *Bouverie,* x, pt.6, 90-1; BL, TT, E85(17), Two Letters from Sir Hugh
    Cholmley, 18 Jan 1643
34 BL, TT, E85(17)
35 BL, TT, E119(29), Fourteen Articles Propounded by the County of York; J Batty,
    History of Rothwell (Rothwell, 1877), 280-7
36 BL, TT, E85(17); HMC, *Bouverie,* x, pt.6, 90
37 Rushworth, *Collections,* v, 78; *Fairfax Correspondence,* i, 25-30

38   Bell, *Fairfax Memorials,* i, 26; BL, TT, E85(17)
39   BL, TT, E85(17)
40   *CJ* ii, 891, 893; *Mercurius Aulicus,* 8 Jan 1643
41   A Hopper, *"Black Tom"* (Manchester, 2007), 35
42   *CJ* ii, 891, 893; BL, TT, E85(17)
43   BL, TT, E85(17)
44   Ibid
45   *CJ*, ii, 891, 893; BL, TT, E84(15)
46   *CSPD 1625-49,* 644, 650; *CJ* ii, 926
47   Chapman, iii, 114
48   BL, TT, E84(15); HMC, *Portland* I, xiii, app.1, 90-1; Rushworth, *Collections* v, 125
49   HMC, *Portland* I, 90-1; G Ridsdill Smith, *Slingsby,* 67
50   HMC, *Portland* I, 90-1; *CJ* ii, 938
51   HMC, *Hastings* II, 92; BL, TT, E90(3); Ibid, E95(9); *Mercurius Aulicus,* 8, 15 Feb 1643
52   Slingsby, *Diary,* 87-91; J R Powell & E K Timings (eds), *Documents Relating to the Civil War1642-1648,* Navy Records Society (1963), 60-7; *Mercurius Aulicus,* 27 Feb, 10 Mar 1643
53   M D G Wanklyn, Royalist Strategy in the South of England, 1642-44, *Southern History,* 3 (1981), 56-60
54   Slingsby, *Diary*, 87-8; *CJ* ii, 993, 1000; Bod.Lib., Clarendon MS 1809, ff.238r.-v

Chapter 10

1   *CJ* iii, 28
2   *CSPV 1642-3,* 263-4
3   BL, TT, E95(9); Ibid, E270(33); Ibid, E294(20)
4   HMC, *Portland* I, 90
5   M Bence-Jones, *The Cavaliers* (1977), 159; Warburton, *Rupert* ii, 129; Roebuck, 18
6   BL, TT, 252(24), *A Perfect Diurnal ...* (1644), 259
7   C Oman, *Henrietta Maria* (1976 edn) 145, 148
8   BL, TT, E296(1); Scarborough Memorials, f.8v.
9   B Manning, The Outbreak of the English Civil War, in *The English Civil War and After 1642-58* ed. R H Parry (1970), 18. See also, A J Hopper, "Fitted for Desperation", Honour and Treachery in Parliament's Yorkshire Command, 1642-43, *History* 86 (Apr 2001), 138-54
10   HMC, *Portland* I, 80, 81-2, 83-4, 87, 89, 90, 99, 109, supp. 701
11   Wedgwood, *King's War,* 217
12   HMC, *Portland* I, 104; *CJ* iii, 10
13   Scarborough Memorials, f.9r.
14   BL, TT, E95(9); Rushworth, *Collections* v, 264-5
15   *Mercurius Aulicus,* 16 Apr 1643; Wildridge, *Hull Letters,* 151; T Gent, *History of Hull* (Hull, 1735), 150; Scarborough Memorials, f.l0r.
16   HMC, *Portland* I, 105, 109, 702
17   BL, TT, E85(17)
18   HMC, *Portland* I, 90

19   Scarborough Memorials, f.8v.
20   YML, Add MS 343, f.27r.
21   Ibid, 27r.
22   Gardiner, *Civil War,* i, 121-2
23   Hotham Memorials, 238v.; YML, Add MS 343, f.27r.; Slingsby, *Diary,* 91-2
24   YML, Add MS 343, f.27r.
25   Scarborough Memorials, f.8v.
26   HMC, *Portland* I, 90
27   Clarendon, *Rebellion,* iii, 1-13
28   *DNB,* iv, 268-9; Wedgwood, *King's War,* 180; Young & Holmes, *Civil War,* 104
29   BL, TT, E95(9); HMC, *Portland* I, 102
30   BL, TT, E95(9); HMC, *Portland* I, 104
31   Bod. Lib. Nalson MS,2, n.173. Unfortunately, Hotham's letter is badly damaged
      and, in the words of assistant librarian, Steven Tomlinson, to whom I am grateful,
      "the blanks cannot be filled".
32   BL, TT, E95(9)
33   HMC, *Portland* I, 102
34   BL, TT, E95(9); Rushworth, *Collections* v, 264
35   BL, TT, E95(9)
36   Scarborough Memorials, f.8v.
37   Ibid
38   BL, TT, E292(27); Ibid. E95(9)
39   HMC, *Portland* I, 102; Hotham Memorials, f.238v.
40   BL, TT, E95(9); Scarborough Memorials, ff.9r.-v.
41   NA, SP28/129/6, f.9
42   BL, TT, E95(9); Rushworth, *Collections* v, 265
43   Scarborough Memorials, f.9v.
44   BL, TT, E95(9)
45   Scarborough Memorials, f.10r.
46   Ashcroft ii, 166
47   BL, TT, E97(3), *C(ertaine) I(nformations),* 13, 10 Mar -1 Apr 1643
48   *ODNB* 32; J Binns, Sir John Lawson: Scarborough's Admiral of the Red, *NH*
      xxxii (1996), 94
49   Ashcroft ii, 23
50   BL, TT, E95(9)
51   Ashcroft ii, 165-8; Scarborough Memorials, f.10r.
52   BL, TT, E97(3)

Chapter 11

1   YML, Add MS 343, f.27r.
2   *M(ercurius) A(ulicus),* 26 Mar 1643
3   BL, TT, E95(2), *K(ingdomes) W(eekly) I(ntelligencer),* 110, 14, 28 Mar -4 Apr
     1643
4   *YAJ* viii, 211
5   P Young & W Emberton, *Sieges of the Great Civil War 1642-46* (1978), ix, 7
6   *LJ* vi, 70; *CJ* iii, 111
7   YML, CWT, 43-07-12/ BL, TT, E60(4), Two Letters ... 12 Jly 1643

8   Wildridge, *Hull Letters,* 158, 159
9   *MA*, 7 Jly 1643
10   Reckitt, 85
11   ERRO, PE1/257/7; HMC, *Seventh Report,* Lowndes MS, 567
12   For the best account of the battle of Adwalton Moor and its significance, see D Johnson, *Adwalton Moor 1643* (Pickering, 2003)
13   M E Ingram, *The Manor of Bridlington* (Bridlington, 1977), 56-7
14   Scarborough Memorials, f.l0v.; YML, Add MS 343, 27v.
15   YML, Add MS 343, ff.27r.-v.
16   HMC, *Portland* I, 113, 116-18, 121; Ashcroft ii, 33; *CSPD 1644,* 157-9
17   YML, Add MS 343, f.27v.
18   Reckitt, 96; BL, TT, E59(11)
19   *CJ* iii, 302; HMC, *Portland* I, 138; BL, TT, E59(11); Ibid, E71(12)
20   HMC, *Seventh Report,* Lowndes MS, 568
21   Reid, *King's Armies,* 108-9
22   Slingsby, *Diary,* 103
23   *CJ* iii, 394, 29-30 Jan 1644; Vicars, ii, 154
24   Vicars ii, 156-7; BL, TT, E33(25), 20 Feb 1644
25   Ashcroft ii, 75
26   BL, TT, E53(12), 1-3 Jly 1644
27   Ingram, *Manor of Bridlington,* 56-7
28   Scarborough Memorials, ff.l0v.-llr.; BL, TT, E50(30), *E(xact) R(elation)* ... 12 June 1644; *CSPD 1644,* 203; *CJ* iii, 532
29   Scarborough Memorials, f.12r.; YML, Add MS 343, 27v.
30   BL, TT, E254(28), *P(erfect) O(ccurrences),* 30 Aug -6 Sept 1644
31   *CSPD 1644,* 447; Bell, *Memorials* ii, 121-2
32   *MA,* 11 Oct 1644
33   Scarborough Memorials, f.14v.
34   Binns, *Memoirs & Memorials,* 133-4
35   For a fuller analysis of Cholmley's own account of the battle of Marston Moor, see below chapter 13.
36   YML, Add MS 343, f.27v.: P Young, *Marston Moor 1644* (Kineton, 1970), 160
37   Scarborough Memorials, f.12r.
38   Ibid; YML, Add MS 343, f.27v.
39   Scarborough Memorials, ff.12r.-14r.; YML, Add MS 343, f.26v.
40   Scarborough Memorials, ff.12r.-14r.
41   For example, see Newman, thesis, i, 464-72
42   B Whitelocke, *Memorials of the English Affairs* ... (1732), 105
43   BL, Egerton MS 2884, f.47
44   Ibid, f.41
45   Ibid
46   Scarborough Memorials, f.12v.; YML, Add MS 343, f.27v.
47   *CSPD 1644,* 366
48   Ibid, 246, 422-3, 447, 521
49   Ibid, 447
50   Ibid, 450, 452, 531; Scarborough Memorials, f.14r.
51   BL, TT, E6(29), *KWI,* 14-20 Aug 1644, 560; Jones, thesis, 311-12

52 Clarendon, *Rebellion,* ii, 468
53 BL, TT, E85(17)
54 Scarborough Memorials, ff.l0r.-v.; HMC, *Portland* I, 113-14; Ibid, *Var(ious) Coll(ections)* viii, 59; *CJ* iii, 86
55 HMC, *Portland* I, 121
56 HMC, *Var Coll* vii, 59
57 NYCRO, DC/SCB, B2, 10 Nov 1643
58 NYCRO, DC/SCB, G1l, Customs Book, 24 Dec - 24 Mar 1643; Account Book, 10 Oct-30 Dec 1643
59 Ashcroft, ii, 29-30
60 *CSPD 1644,* 157-8, 159, 160; Brooke, thesis, 131-2
61 Ibid, 274
62 *CSPV 1643-47,* 21, 115, 118
63 BL, TT, E669(9,8), Summer Guard 1644; *CSPD 1644,* 557: Brooke, thesis, 132
64 Wedgwood, *King's War,* 353; *CSPD 1644,* 356 fn.
65 *CJ* iii, 29
66 *MA,* 30 June 1643
67 Ashcroft, ii, 30-5
68 *ODNB;* J Binns, Captain Browne Bushell: North Sea Adventurer and Pirate, *NH* XXVII (1991), 90-105
69 HMC, *Portland* I, 167; Powell & Timings, *Docs,* 120-1
70 HMC, *Sixth Report,* 434(a); Ashcroft, ii, 31, 34, 35, 179
71 J U Nef, *The Rise of the British Coal Industry,* 2 vols (1932), ii, 287
72 BL, TT, E81(29), E90(17), E99(6), Ordinances of Parliament, 13 Jan, 13 Feb, 15 Apr 1643; *CJ* iii, 46, 68
73 *CSPV 1643-47,* 106, 116
74 BL, TT, E86(20), Sea coale, Char-coale, and Small-coale, 27 Jan 1643
75 *CJ* iii, 432
76 BL, TT, E40(27), Report from ... Sunderland, 6 Apr 1644
77 *MA,* 11 Oct 1644
78 *CSPD 1644-5,* 94
79 BL, TT, E269(8), *(The) L(ondon) P(ost),* 23, 3 Feb 1645
80 BL, TT, E269(14), *(A) Diary (or An Exact Journal),* 39, 7 Feb 1645
81 BL, TT, E270(23), *P(erfect) P(assages),* 19-25 Feb 1645; Ibid, E270(29), 20-27 Feb 1645
82 Scarborough Memorials, f.14v.
83 YML Add MS 343, f.28r.
84 Ashcroft ii, 23
85 BL, TT, E270(23), *PP,* 19-25 Feb 1645
86 J Schofield, *An Historical... Guide to Scarborough* (York, 1787), 88-9
87 Ashcroft ii, 27-8
88 Ibid, 28
89 NYCRO, DC/SCB, H1, Assessment Lists 1601-65
90 Ashcroft, ii, 36
91 Ibid,.
92 NYCRO, DC/SCB, C2, Chamberlains' Accounts 1644
93 YML, Add MS 343, f.27v.; Scarborough Memorials, f.12r.

94   Ashcroft ii, 28, 29, 40
95   Ibid, 41-2
96   NYCRO, DC/SCB, A20, Common Hall Memoranda, 23 Nov 1644
97   For a more detailed description of Scarborough in 1643-4, see J Binns, *"A Place of Great Importance"* (Preston, 1996), 113-130

Chapter 12

1   BL, TT, E271(5), *M(ercurius) B(ritanicus)*, 24 Feb - 3 Mar 1645. There were other reports in E258(27), *A Perfect Diurnal*, 17-24 Feb 1645 and E258(28), *Perfect Occurrences*, 22 Feb 1645. For a full list of news-sheet sources see Binns, *"Place of Great Importance"*, 279-80
2   Scarborough Memorials, ff.14v., 15r.
3   J Vicars, *England's Parliamentary Chronicle*, iv, (1646), 110
4   Scarborough Memorials, f.15r.
5   Ibid
6   BL, TT, E270(6), *(The) W(eekly) A(ccount)*, Tuesday, 18 Feb 1645
7   Ibid, E270(5), *PP*, 18 Feb 1645
8   *CSPD 1644-5*, 323; Ibid, *1645-7*, 95, 110
9   BL, TT, E270(15), *MB*, 17-24 Feb 1645
10   BL, TT, E270(33), *The Scottish Dove*, 21-28 Feb 1645
11   BL, TT, E258(27), *A Perfect Diurnal*, 17-24 Feb 1645
12   Hinderwell, 85
13   *CJ* iv, 59, 97, 149
14   *CSPD 1644-5*, 323; *MA*, 8 Mar 1645
15   BL, TT, E270(21), *LP*, 25
16   BL, TT, E270(23), *PP*, 19-25 Feb 1645
17   Hinderwell, 87
18   *CSPD 1644-5*, 304
19   Ibid
20   HMC, *Tenth Report*, appendix, pt.6, Lord Braye's MSS, 155-6
21   Ibid, 156-7
22   Brooke, thesis, 146
23   Vicars, *Parliamentary Chronicle*, iv, 110
24   T S Willan, The Parliamentary Surveys of the North Riding, *YAJ* xxxi (1934), 255, n.3
25   R B Turton (ed.), *A Survey of the Honour and Forest of Pickering 1651*, NRRS I (1894), 65
26   Ibid, 40
27   Hinderwell, iii, 87
28   Rushworth, *Collections*, v, 642; J Tucker & I Winstock, *The English Civil War: A Military Handbook* (1972), 57; Hinderwell, iii, 86; Scarborough Memorials, ff.15r.-v.; Schofield, *Guide*, 53
29   Whitelocke, *Memorials*, 142; Hinderwell, 87
30   Powell & Timings, *Docs*, 200-1
31   BL, TT, E258(27), *A P(erfect) D(iurnall)*, 17-24 Feb 1645
32   BL, TT, E285(5), *Exchange Intelligencer*, May 1645
33   BL, TT, E292(8), *M(ercurius) V(eridicus)*, 28 June-5 Jly 1645

34   Powell & Timings, *Docs,* 203-4
35   Suffolk County Record Office, Ipswich, HD 36, 2672/25, 69, 77. I am indebted to Mrs Rosalin Barker of Whitby for this revealing source.
36   *CSPD 1645-7,* 31
37   Ibid, 55
38   *CSPD 1644-5,* 446-7
39   Scarborough Memorials, ff.14v.-19r.
40   Schofield, *Guide,* 91; Hinderwell, ii, 69, 74; Baker, 76, 81; but not Hinderwell, iii, 79
41   *EHR* xxxii (1917), 568
42   *MA,* 8 Mar, 11 Apr 1645; Hinderwell, iii, 88
43   BL, TT, 260(36), *PP,* 13 May 1645; Ibid, E260(39), 19 May 1645; Ibid; E285(12), *MV,* 17-24 May 1645
44   BL, TT, E260(5), *APD,* 87, 24 Mar 1645
45   Scarborough Memorials, f.*15v.*
46   Ibid
47   Ibid
48   BL, TT, 260(32), *PP,* 6 May 1645
49   Hinderwell, iii, 109; Baker, 88; but not Rowntree, 237-8.
50   *CJ* iv, 528; Ibid, v, 325; Ibid, vii, 47; *LJ* x, 247-8; *CSPD 1649-50,* 230; Ibid, *1651,* 187, 249; Ibid, *1651-2,* 46-7
51   Hinderwell, iii, 86; Rowntree, 233; Scarborough Memorials, f.15r.
52   Scarborough Memorials, f.15r.
53   Ibid. 16r.
54   Ibid
55   Ibid, 16r.-v.
56   BL, TT, E260(36), *PP,* 13 May 1645; Ibid. E260(39), *PP,* 17 May 1645; E260(41), *APD,* 19 May; E284(5), *WA,* 13 May 1645; E284(7), *M(ercurius) C(ivicus),* 11 May 1645
57   Scarborough Memorials, f.16v.
58   BL, TT, E260(41), *APD,* 19 May 1645; Ibid, E285(2), *MC,* 17 May 1645; Ibid, E260(39), *PP,* 19 May 1645
59   BL, TT, E284(7), *MC,* 17 May 1645
60   Scarborough Memorials, f.16v.
61   BL, TT, E260(41), *APD,* 19 May 1645
62   Ibid, E285(3), *MC,* 17 May 1645
63   Ibid, E260(40), *P0,* 16-23 May 1645
64   Scarborough Memorials, f.16v.
65   BL, TT, E286(12), *The True Informer,* 30 May 1645
66   BL, TT, E285(7), *TMI,* 16 May 1645
67   Ibid, E260(39), *PP,* 19 May 1645; Ibid, E260(41), *APD,* 19 May *1645;* Ibid, E284(23), *TWI,* May 1645
68   Ibid, E285(12), *MV,* 17-24 May 1645
69   Scarborough Memorials, f.16v.
70   Ibid
71   BL, TT, E290(8), *MV,* 21-28 June 1645
72   Wedgwood, *King's War,* 414-40, 446-8, 459-61; Young & Holmes, 249

73   *VCH, Yorks,* iii, 427-8

74   BL, TT, E293(24), *MC,* 17-24 Jly 1645

75   Ibid, E293(29), *TSD,* 18-25 Jly 1645

76   Ibid, E294(5), *MB,* 21-28 Jly 1645; E294(8), *TWA,* 29 Jly 1645; E294(11), *Parliament's Post,* 23-29 Jly 1645

77   Scarborough Memorials, f.17r.

78   Ibid, ff.17r.-v.

79   Ibid, f.19r.

80   BL, TT E294(15), *An Exact Relation of the Surrender of Scarborough Castle,* 25 Jly 1645

81   Ibid, E294(11), *PP,* 23-29 Jly 1645

82   R Wittie, *Scarbrough Spaw* (1660), 204

83   Scarborough Memorials, f.17r.

84   BL, TT, E284(8), *A Diary, or An Exact Journal,* 14 May 1645

85   Scarborough Memorials, f.17v.

86   Ibid

87   Ibid, ff. 17r.-v.

88   Ibid, f.17v.

89   Ibid, ff.17r.-v.

90   BL, TT, E294(17), *The Coppie of a Letter from Major General Poines,* 31 Jly 1645

91   Ibid, E294(15), *An Exact Relation,* 26 Jly 1645; Ibid, E294(18), *MC,* 24-31 Jly 1645

92   BL, TT, E294(11), *PP,* 23-29 Jly 1645; Ibid, E294(8), *TWA,* 29 Jly 1645

93   Ibid, E294(5, 9), *MB,* 91, 92, 21-28 Jly, 28 Jly-4 Aug 1645

94   Ibid, E294(20), *TSD,* 25 Jly -1 Aug 1645

95   Scarborough Memorials, f.17v.

96   Rushworth, *Collections* v, 118; Scarborough Memorials, ff.18r.-v.

97   Scarborough Memorials, f.19r.

98   Ibid

99   BL, TT, E294(15), *An Exact Relation,* 26 Jly 1645

100   Ibid, E294(8), *TWA,* 29 Jly 1645

101   Ibid, E294(15), *AER,* 26 Jly 1645

102   NYCRO, DC/SCB, C2, Chamberlains' Accounts, 1648-9

103   Hinderwell, iii, 95-7; Ashcroft, ii, 52-3

104   Scarborough Memorials, f.19r.

105   YML, Add MS 343, f.28r.

106   Ibid, 28r., 28v.-29r.

107   Ibid. f.33v.

108   Scarborough Memorials, f.16r.

109   YML, Add MS 343, f.33v.

110   Ibid, f.33r.

111   Ibid, f.33v.

112   Scarborough Memorials, f.18r.

113   YML, Add MS 343, 33v.

114   Ibid

115   Scarborough Memorials, f. 19r.

Chapter 13

1   Scarborough Memorials, f.19r.
2   YML, Add MS 343, ff.28r.-v.
3   Ibid
4   Ibid, f.28v.
5   Ibid
6   *Cholmley Memoirs* (1787), iv
7   YML, Add MS 343, f.28v.
8   Ibid, ff.28v.-29r.
9   *Clarendon State Papers* ii (1773), 181-6
10   Observations, f.238r.
11   *CJ* ii, 371,372
12   Observations, f.238r.
13   Ibid, f.238v.
14   HMC, *Hastings* ii, 92; BL, TT, E95(9), *Letter from a Worthy Captain. . .* 7 Apr 1643; *MA,* 8, 15 Feb 1643
15   Observations, f.238v.
16   Binns, *Memoirs and Memorials,* 127, n.10
17   Observations, f.239r.
18   Ibid
19   Ibid, f.239v.; *CJ* iii, 734; Ibid, iv, 4
20   Observations, f.240r.
21   Ibid
22   Ibid, f.240v.; Clarendon, *Rebellion* ii, 259, 261-2, 263
23   E H Firth, Marston Moor, *TRHS,* 2nd series, xii (1898), 62
24   *MA,* 6, 13 JIy 1644
25   *CSPD 1644,* 311
26   P R Newman, *The Battle of Marston Moor 1644* (Chichester, 1981), 128-9
27   Margaret, Duchess of Newcastle, *The Life of the Duke of Newcastle* (1667), 49-50
28   Slingsby, *Diary,* 110-16
29   Firth, *TRHS,* 71-2
30   Ibid, 52-3; P R Newman, *Marston Moor, 2 July 1644: The Sources and the Site,* Borthwick paper 53 (University of York, 1978), 13-14
31   T Carte (ed.), *Ormonde Papers* I (1739), 55-8; Newman, *Sources,* 13-14
32   Firth, *TRHS,* 62-3
33   Clarendon, *Rebellion* iii, 375
34   Rushworth, *Collections* v, 637; YML, Add MS 343, f.27v.
35   *ODNB*
36   Memorials (Marston Moor), f.153v.
37   Newman, *Sources,* 44-5, n.22
38   Newman, *Battle,* 6
39   Memorials (Marston Moor), f.154v.
40   J Barratt, *The Battle for York. Marston Moor 1644* (Stroud, 2002), 70
41   Memorials (Marston Moor), f.153r.
42   Ibid

43 Ibid, f.153v.; Clarendon iii, 376, n.; Gardiner, *Civil War* i, 374; Young, *Marston Moor,* 102-3

44 Memorials (Marston Moor), f.153v.

45 Ibid, f.154r.

46 Ibid, f.154v.

47 Newman, *Battle,* 128; Warburton, *Rupert,* ii, 444; Clarendon, *Rebellion,* ii, 466

48 YML, Add MS 343, f.29r.

49 Ibid; Ashcroft, ii, 179; Binns, Browne Bushell, *NH* xxvii, 103-5

50 J W Clay (ed.), *YRCP* ii, YASRS xviii (1895), 221-2; M A E Green (ed.), *CPCC* iii, 2062

51 For the treatment of other Yorkshire Royalists, see J Binns, *Yorkshire in the Civil Wars* (Pickering, 2004), 173-86

52 YML, Add MS 343, f.28v.; *YRCP* ii, 221

53 YML, Add MS 343, f.29v.

54 P Pickles, A Brief History of the Alum Industry, *The Cleveland Industrial Archaeologist,* II (1975), 11; D Pybus & J Rushton, Alum and the Yorkshire Coast, *The Yorkshire Coast* ed. D B Lewis (Beverley, 1991), 46-59

55 J Rushton, *Yorkshire Coast,* 53

56 WLPS, PB 5941

57 Pickles, Brief History, 7

58 YML, Add MS 343, ff.29v.-30r.

59 Ibid, ff.30r.-v.

60 Ibid, f.30v. In Cholmley's memoirs, Lord Astley became Lord "Aston" and Sir John Culpepper became Sir "Thom" Culpepper. Sir Roger Twysden, Certain Considerations upon the Government of England, ed. J M Keble *Camden Society* xlv (1848-9), lxxx-lxxxi

61 Jessup, *Twysden,* 99; YML, Add MS 343, f.31r.

62 YML, Add MS 343, f.31r.

63 *Cholmley Memoirs* (1787), vii-xxi

64 YML, Add MS 343, ff.31v., 34v.

65 HUL, DCYI9/2; London Probate Act Book, Register Nobbs, 8 Nov 1660, f.206

66 WLPS, PB411

67 Ibid, PB 1360

68 YML, Add MS 343, f.11r.

69 WLPS, PB 1162, 1181

70 Ibid, PB 6035

71 NYCRO, ZPK 11; ZCG iv, 5/2

72 Ibid

73 WLPS, PB 1424; NYCRO, ZCG iv, 5/2

74 YML, Add MS 343, f.29v.

75 WLPS, PB 1194

76 Ibid, PB 1162/1181, 6374

77 Charlton, *Whitby,* 326

78 WLPS, PB 1424

79 Ibid, PB 1162/1181, 6374; NYCRO, ZCG iv, 5/2

80 Ibid, PB 650, 1552, 1162/1181; HUL, DCY 18/3

81 Ibid, PB 1162/1181, 6374, 989, 1783, 1756; HUL, DCY 18/3

82   Ibid, PB 1162/1 181, 6374; NYCRO, ZCG iv, 5/2
83   Ibid, PB 2017A, 6374, 1360
84   Ibid, PB 1762, 1764, 1765, 1761, 1767

Chapter 14

1   Charlton, *Whitby,* 318
2   Young, *Whitby,* ii, 831, 838
3   Gaskin, *Seaport,* 129, 144, 148
4   Shaw Jeffrey, *Lore & Legend,* 76-9; F R Pearson, *The Abbey House under the Cholmley Family* (Whitby, 1954), 15-16
5   L Clarke, *Family Chronicles* (Wellingborough, 1911), 42
6   Ibid
7   Ibid
8   L T Smith (ed.), *The Itinerary of John Leland,* i (1907), 51, 61
9   J C Atkinson (ed.), *NRQSR,* NRRS, 5 vols (1884-7), i, 124
10   B Hall, The Trade of Newcastle and the North East Coast, 1600-1640, unpub. PhD thesis, London Univ., 1933, 211, 225-6, 235, 237
11   Hinderwell, ii, 288
12   Shaw Jeffrey, *Lore & Legend,* 78
13   I am obliged to Mr Peter Townend of Ugglebarnby for this reference.
14   WLPS, PB 1560, 2016
15   Ibid, PB 4311
16   NA, AO 1, 2486/350; Hall, thesis, 210
17   Nef, *Coal Industry,* ii, 383-4
18   NYCRO, ZCG(W), Cholmley Lease Book; WLPS, PB 1784, 1381, 1067
19   YML, Add MS 343, ff.23r., 23v.; Turton, *Alum Farm,* 174, 193; BIHR, PW, V5OA, ff.115-119
20   Gaskin, *Seaport,* 223; WLPS, PB 5941
21   WLPS, PB 1566. These miles were 2,428 not 1760 yards long, a measure still then used in Yorkshire.
22   NYCRO, ZCG iv, 5/2, MIC 1336; WLPS, PB 6106
23   NYCRO, ZCG iv, 5/2, MIC 1336; WLPS, PB 5941
24   NA, AO 3, 1243/3A; S K Jones, A Maritime History of the Port of Whitby 1700-1914, unpub PhD thesis, London Univ., 1982, 82; T S Willan, *The English Coasting Trade 1600-1750* (Manchester, 1967), 118
25   *APC 1623-5,* 439-40
26   *CSPD 1625-6,* 532; Ibid, *1627-8,* 500; Gaskin, *Seaport,* 231
27   Hall, thesis, 235
28   Ibid, 211, 225-6, 237
29   Charlton, *Whitby,* 318; Young, *Whitby,* ii, 531; Gaskin, *Seaport,* 142, 330; Shaw Jeffrey, *Lore & Legend,* 76-7; Pearson, *Abbey House,* 20; G H J Daysh (ed.) *Survey of* Whitby (Windsor, 1958)58
30   Charlton, *Whitby,* 318; Atkinson, *Memorials,* 163-6; Gaskin, *Seaport,* 328-9; WLPS, PB 1546
31   *Test. Ebor.,* Surtees Society, 79 (1884), 300-02; BIHR, PW V2, f.197; Young, *Whitby,* ii, 530n.; Gaskin, *Seaport,* 60-1
32   Gaskin, *Seaport,* 329-30 quoting HMC, *Eighth Report,* Trinity House, 241b

33   NYCRO, DC/SCB, B1; Ashcroft i, 161-2
34   Hinderwell iii, 191-4; Chapman, *Records,* iii, 19; Ashcroft i, 80, 161-2
35   Ashcroft i, 160-1
36   YML, Add MS 343, f.21v.; WLPS, PB 4328, 48
37   SCL, WWM, SP 15(76)
38   Ibid, SP 10(214)
39   Charlton, *Whitby,* 314
40   Young, *Whitby,* ii, 530
41   Pearson, *Abbey House,* 20; *Survey of Whitby,* 58
42   *Cholmley Memoirs* (1787), ii, v, vi
43   Account of Tangier, 48-9
44   Ibid, 50
45   Charlton, *Whitby,* 314; Young, *Whitby* ii, 573, 589; Atkinson, *Memorials,* 263;
       Pearson, *Abbey House,* 20; H P Kendall, *The Streets of Whitby* (Whitby, 1938),
       21; P Burnett, *The Streets of Whitby* (Whitby, 1976), 21
46   Young, *Whitby* ii, 572-3; WLPS, PB 1784
47   Charlton, *Whitby,* 288-9, 313; Young, *Whitby* ii, 542-3; Shaw Jeffrey, *Lore &
       Legend,* 78; *Survey of Whitby,* 58
48   J R Boyle,The *Lost Towns of the Humber* (Hull, 1889), 55
49   Gaskin, *Seaport,* 344
50   Ibid, 343-6
51   BIHR, PW, V6, f.242; *Test. Ebor.*, Surtees Society, 6 (1902), 109, 149
52   *NRQSR,* i, 124, 133, 167
53   Ibid, ii, 298, 304, 319-20; iii, 3, 46, 48
54   WLPS, PB 1532/3; Gaskin, *Seaport,* 346-7; *NRQSR,* v, 219
55   *NRQSR,* iv, 217; Gaskin, *Seaport,* 348; WLPS, PB 1532/3
56   *NRQSR,* iv, 14-17, 177, 222
57   NYCRO, DC/SCB, B1, 17, 31 Jan, 1, 2, 26, Feb 1628
58   NA, SP 16/159/43, 30 Jan 1630
59   Ibid
60   Gaskin, *Seaport,* 311-15
61   Turton, *Alum Farm,* 93, 127, 159; NA, SP 16/160/9, 4 Feb 1630
62   NA, SP 16/162/84, 14 Mar 1630
63   Ibid, SP16/166/26, 6 May 1630
64   Turton, *Alum Farm,* 161; NA, Chancery, C66/2456/8; J Cooper, The Fortunes of
       Thomas Wentworth, *EcHR,* 2nd series, xi (1958), 237
65   Gaskin, *Seaport,* 315-16
66   Ibid
67   *NRQSR,* iii, 234-5; Ibid, iv, 177
68   WLPS, PB 2143, 1822; Young, *Whitby* ii, 585-7
69   *NRQSR,* i, 36
70   Ibid, i, 133; Ibid, iii, 134; Ibid, v, 219; WLPS, PB 1532
71   WLPS, PB 1464; *NRQSR,* ii, 120
72   *NRQSR,* iii, 235; Ibid, iv, 67; WLPS, Audrey's Book, NRQSR, Helmsley, 12 Jly
       1625
73   Charlton, *History,* 68; Gaskin, *Seaport,* 166; Pearson, *Abbey House,* 20-1
74   Young, *History* ii, 831; Pearson, *Abbey House,* 17-18

75   YML, Add MS 343, ff.23r., 31r.
76   Ibid, f.23r.
77   Ibid
78   Young, *Whitby* ii, 592-3, 624-5
79   *NRQSR* iv, 55
80   Ibid, 67, 75, 85
81   NYCRO, ZCG, MIC 1286, DN184; WLPS, PB 4199, 554
82   *NRQSR,* iv, 85
83   WLPS, PB 4199, 554
84   *NRQSR,* v, 55
85   *CSPD 1635,* 273, 294, 322-3, 326-7, 336, 339, 365, 572; YML, Add MS 343, ff.23r., 23v.; NYCRO, DC/SCB, v, i, ff. i-iv; Whitby parish register, 1600-1676, i, 102-11
86   *NRQSR,* iii, 324, 326
87   Ibid, iv, 16
88   Ibid, 31
89   Ibid, 88, 91
90   YML, Add MS 343, f.22v.
91   *NRQSR,* iv, 107, 116
92   WLPS, PB 3772-5
93   Charlton, *History,* 145; Young, *History* ii, 501, n.+
94   Atkinson, *Memorials,* 182-93
95   Gaskin, *Seaport,* 240
96   References to local ownership of Whitby ships can be found in wills: BIHR, PW, V45B, ff. 307, 308; Ibid, V46A, ff.239, 240; Ibid, V47, f.217; Ibid, 48A, f.281
97   J C Atkinson (ed.), Ministers' Accounts, Surtees Society, 72 (1879), ii, 721-4; NYCRO, ZPK 11
98   *Archaeologia Aeliana,* iii (1859), 22
99   NYCRO, ZCG, MIC 1286; Ibid, ZRY, i, 4/4; ZK 10821, 10822, 10824; WLPS, PB 6086, 4194, 1162, 1181, 985
100   WLPS, PB 995/x1705; NYCRO, ZRY, i, 5/2, 7/6/1, 7/6/2, 7/7; WLPS, PB 774, 776, 777, 780, 781, 784, 785, 294(1)
101   WLPS, PB 1381, 1449, 1769; Ibid, Bagdale MSS, vol.7, no.36; NYCRO, ZRY 1, 7/9, 15, 16
102   NYCRO, ZCG, MIC 1286; Ibid, ZK 10821, 10822, 10824
103   NYCRO, ZKH, 700, 704, 707; WLPS, PB 28
104   Young, *History* ii, 482-3; WLPS, PB 286, 4199, 1804
105   Dugdale's *Visitation,* iii, 508-9
106   WLPS, Jeffrey MSS, Box A; Ibid, PB 1461
107   D M Meads (ed.), *The Diary of Lady Margaret Hoby 1599-1605* (1930), 193
108   J Foster (ed.), *The Visitation of Yorkshire in 1584-5 and 1612* (1875), 220
109   WLPS, Jeffrey MSS, Box A; Ibid, Bagdale Old Hall papers, 3, 4, 5, 6; Ibid, PB 878; BL, TT. E626(14), *The speech and confession of Capt. Brown-Bushel, 1651*
110   BL, TT, E270(21), *The London Post,* 25, 18 Feb 1645
111   HMC, *Various Collections,* ii (1903), 174, 176; Shaw Jeffrey, *Lore & Legend,* 148
112   Young, *History* ii, 814; Pickles, *Cleveland Industrial Archaeologist,* II, 9

113 Atkinson, *Memorials,* 157, n.1, 180, n.1; *The Parish Registry of Whitby, 1600-1676,* i (Yorks Parish Register Society, 1928)

114 Aveling, *NR,* 426

115 For these valuable demographic statistics I am indebted to Mrs Rosalin Barker of Whitby.

116 NA, Hearth Tax 1673-4, E179/261/32; A Whiteman (ed.), *The Compton Census of 1676,* Records of Social & Economic History, NS, x (1986), 600; NYCRO, ZW (PC/WH), MIC 1231, Whitby Poor Rate Assessment List, 1713

117 NA, E179/261/32

118 NYCRO, ZW (PC/WH), MIC 1231

119 Binns, *Memoirs & Memorials,* Appendix D, 176-7

120 Ibid, Appendix E, 178-9

121 WLPS, PB 1244, 4199

122 Young, *History* ii, 814

Chapter 15

1   YML, Add MS 343, f lr.

2   Ibid, f.14r.

3   Ibid, f.34r.

4   Ibid, f.10r.

5   Ibid, 1r.

6   Cliffe, *Yorks Gentry,* 11

7   YML, Add MS 343, f.24v.

8   Ibid, f.4r.

9   Ibid, f.4v.

10 Ibid, f.6r.

11 Ibid, f.6v.

12 Ibid, f.llr.

13 Ibid, f.4r.

14 Ibid, f.llv.

15 Ibid, f.14v.

16 Ibid, f.4r.

17 Ibid, f.6r.

18 Ibid, f.10r.

19 Ibid, f.l0v.

20 Ibid, ff.9v.-l0r.

21 Ibid, f.5v.

22 Ibid, f.4r.

23 Ibid

24 Ibid, f.llv.

25 Ibid, f.15v.

26 Ibid, f.16r.

27 Ibid, f.lr.

28 *Gentleman's Magazine,* LVIII (1788), 618

29 J A Sharpe, *Early Modern England, A Social History 1550-1760* (1987), 171, 353

30 Charlton, *History,* 315-16; *Memoirs* (1787), 56-7; YML, Add MS 343, ff.23r.-v.

31 Atkinson, *Memorials,* viii

32 Schofield, *Guide,* 92
33 *Memoirs* (1787), 66; YML, Add MS 343, f.26v.
34 Charlton, *History,* 316
35 Schofield, *Guide,* 96
36 Hinderwell i, 54-9; Ibid, ii, 64-9; Ibid, iii, 54-9
37 YML, Add MS 343, f.27v.; *Memoirs* (1787), 69; Hinderwell i, 54; Ibid, ii, 67; Ibid, iii, 76
38 YML, Add MS 343, f.2v.
39 Ibid. f.20v.; WLPS, MS 292.2. For some time this latter manuscript was thought to be the original holograph of Sir Hugh, but clearly it was the work of the Revd George Young, minister at Whitby's West Cliff Lane Presbyterian chapel from 1806 until his death in 1848 and secretary of Whitby's Literary and Philosophical Society from its foundation in 1823.
40 Brooke, thesis, 1. WLPS has three copies of the 1870 edition but none of that of 1787. Scarborough Central Library has a fine copy of the 1787 print; Cambridge University Library has two of 1787, one of them annotated; and the Bodleian only one of 1870 used by Brooke. A rebound 1787 edition, annotated by a mid-nineteenth-century Cholmley descendant, was sold at auction in Whitby in 1990 for £300.
41 YML, Add MS 343, f.7v.
42 Ibid, ff.l0r., 21v.; *Memoirs* (1787), 27, 52, *Memoirs* (1870), 17, 32
43 YML, Add MS 343, f.16v.; *Memoirs* (1787), 40, (1870), 25
44 YML, Add MS 343, f.19v.; *Memoirs* (1787), 47, (1870), 29
45 YML, Add MS 343, f.29v.; WLPS, PB 4328/69; *Memoirs* (1787), 75, (1870), 45
46 YML, Add MS 343, f.5r.
47 Ibid, ff.4r., 5r.; *Memoirs* (1787), 12, (1870), 14
48 YML, Add MS 343, f.28r.; *Memoirs* (1787), 72, (1870) 43
49 YML, Add MS 343, f.18r.: *Memoirs*(1787), 44, (1870), 27
50 YML, Add MS 343, f.30v.; *Memoirs*(1787), 78, (1870), 47
51 Gaskin, *Seaport,* 103-89
52 YML, Add MS 343, f.6v.; Gaskin, *Seaport,* 120
53 Brooke, thesis, 1, 9
54 Ibid, 9-10, 162-309
55 Ibid. 10, 12
56 WLPS, PB 4328/1
57 YML, Add MS 343
58 At this point I should acknowledge my heavy debt to the former librarians of WLPS, particularly G N Benson and Harold Brown, who gave me every assistance and provided me with their personal recollections of Percy Burnett, who had died in 1972.
59 There is another manuscript copy in the Cholmley (Howsham) papers kept by the Archives Department of HUL, DCY 17/4, but it is a very incomplete, nineteenth-century copy of the printed edition of 1787, not of Sir Hugh's holograph.
60 J Binns (ed.), *The Memoirs and Memorials of Sir Hugh Cholmley of Whitby 1600-1657,* YASRS, cliii(2000)
61 Brooke, thesis, 10,12
62 YML, Add MS 343, f.16r.

63   Ibid, f.16v.

Postscript

1   WLPS *Annual Report* (2005), 40-4
2   NYCRO, ZCG, v/1/1-6
3   Ibid, iv/5/2/8
4   WLPS, PB 527, 1348, 2696-8, 2709, 2018
5   L Colley, *Captives: Britain, Empire and the World 1600-1850* (2002), 389, n. 1
6   Ibid, 33
7   The best, brief summary of his life and career is in Henning, ii, 62-3
8   *Memoirs* (1787), iv; L Butler, Whitby in North Africa, *YAJ* 76(2004), 171-5. Sir Hugh's dates were given there as "1627-1688"! (173, n.3)
9   For example, C Tomalin, *Samuel Pepys: The Unequalled Self* (New York, 2003), 327-8; R Ollard, *Pepys: A Biography* (1991), 125, 299, 300-05
10   *Memoirs* (1787), 236
11   S Jenkins, *England's Thousand Best Houses* (2004), 903
12   NA, Hearth Tax returns, E179/215/451; Ibid, El79/216/462; J Rushton, *The History of Ryedale* (Pickering, 2003), 235
13   *Memoirs* (1787), 295-6
14   *Calendar of Treasury Books 1667-8, 1669-72, 1681-5, 1685-9*
15   NA, Chancery, C33/229/ ff.292-3; Ibid, 269/ ff.663-6; Ibid, 273/f.153. I owe these valuable references to Dr J T Cliffe.
16   WLPS, PB 4311, Attorney General vesus Strickland, 1907
17   *Calendar of Treasury Books 1685-9,* 321, 332, 350, 353, 364, 378, 394, 402, 410
18   Henning ii, 63
19   HMC, *Various Collections,* ii (1903), 174, 176
20   Shaw Jeffrey, *Lore & Legend,* 129, 148
21   *NRQSR,* Thirsk, 6 Oct 1685; Ibid, Pickering, 12 Jan 1686
22   Ibid, Thirsk, 28 Apr 1685
23   Reference from Henning ii, 62. *Pepys' Diary* refers in complimentary terms to Cholmley on 6 Mar, 2l June, 12 Jly and 9 Aug 1667.
24   Colley, *Captives,* 389 n. 1

INDEX

MP 30-1, 50-2, 59-64, 75; Memoirs 168-78;
Memorials on the Hothams 130-2;
Memorials on Marston Moor 132-6;
Parliamentary colonel 76-87;
religious views 64-70; royal family 55-7,
63-4, 94, 103-4; Royalist colonel 88-111;
Strafford 19, 21, 39, 40, 42, 46, 48, 50, 51,
52, 53, 56, 57, 61-3; Whitby 146-67;
will 142-3
Cholmley, Sir Hugh, 3rd baronet *(1655-65)*
142
Cholmley, Sir Hugh, 4th baronet *(1632-89)*
35, 127, 129, 136, 138, 139, 143, 154,
179-83
Cholmley, Sir James 94, 95, 107, 137, 159
Cholmley, Joan(e) 8, 170
Cholmley, Katherine/Catherine (Scrope) 1,
4, 5, 6, 7, 9, 10, 169, 170
Cholmley, Lady Margaret 9, 10, 23
Cholmley, Mary 182
Cholmley, Nathaniel *(d. 1687)* 144, 182
Cholmley, Nathaniel *(1721-91)* 150, 155,
171, 172, 174, 179
Cholmley, Sir Richard (I) 1
Cholmley, Sir Richard (II) 1-7, 8, 16, 157,
169
Cholmley, Sir Richard (III) 11-22, 26, 27,
31, 32, 35, 67, 68, 69, 152, 156-9, 163, 169,
170
Cholmley, Sir Richard of Grosmont
(1617-44) 142, 143, 169
Cholmley, Richard *(1624-30)* 30, 34-5
Cholmley, Sir William, 2nd baronet
(1625-63) 30, 72-3, 127, 129, 138-40, 142,
143, 147, 148, 161, 167, 181, 182
Clarendon, Lord 63, 68, 76, 133, 135, 136
Cliffe, Dr 71
Clifford, Catherine 39
coal trade 149, 152
Cob, Margaret 20
Colley, Linda 180
Compton Census 166
Constable, Henry 1st Viscount Dunbar 65,
133

Constable, Sir William 81, 100
Conyers family 156, 164
Conyers, George 34, 37, 152
Court of Exchequer 16, 17
Coventry, Lord 41
Crispe, Sir Nicholas 137
Crompton, Maj T 101, 121, 127
Cromwell, Oliver 26, 89, 131, 132, 136
Croning, Capt Alexander 42
Crossland, Sir Jordan 112, 113 127

Daletown 35, 142, 145
Danby, Sir Thomas 61, 63
Darley, Henry 57, 59, 101, 103
Dawnay, William 12, 13
Denton, John 116, 122, 136
Dering, Sir Edward 67
D'Ewes, Simmonds 67
Dickinson, Henry 153, 155, 167
Digby, Lord 117
Dunkirk 106, 107, 116

East Peckham 141
Egton 13, 65
Egton Bridge 13
Egton players 15
Escrick, Lord Howard of 72
Eskdaleside 11
Essex conspiracy 14
Essex, earl of 72, 78
Eure, Ralph 12, 13
Eure, Sir William 12, 13
Eythin, baron 86, 133, 134, 135

Fairfax family 130, 131
Fairfax, Ferdinando Lord 56, 59, 72, 82, 83,
84, 98, 103, 104, 117, 136
Fairfax, Henry 34
Fairfax, Sir Thomas 21, 101
Fairfaxes of Denton 81
Falsgrave 95, 112, 126